Microsoft® Windows® Command-Line Administrator's Pocket Consultant

William R. Stanek

PUBLISHED BY
Microsoft Press
A Division of Microsoft Corporation
One Microsoft Way
Redmond, Washington 98052-6399

Library of Congress Cataloging-in-Publication Data
Stanek, William R.
   Microsoft Windows Command-Line Administrator's Pocket Consultant / William R. Stanek.
     p. cm.
   Includes bibliographical references and index.
   ISBN 0-7356-2038-5
   1. Microsoft Windows (Computer file)   2. Operating systems (Computers)   I. Title.

   QA76.76.O63S73449   2004
   005.4'4682--dc22   2004044882

Printed and bound in the United States of America.

1 2 3 4 5 6 7 8 9   QWE   9 8 7 6

Distributed in Canada by H.B. Fenn and Company Ltd.

A CIP catalogue record for this book is available from the British Library.

Microsoft Press books are available through booksellers and distributors worldwide. For further information about international editions, contact your local Microsoft Corporation office or contact Microsoft Press International directly at fax (425) 936-7329. Visit our Web site at www.microsoft.com/learning/. Send comments to *mspinput@microsoft.com*.

Acquisitions Editor: Martin DelRe
Project Editor: Valerie Woolley
Technical Editor: Jim Johnson

Body Part No. X10-42151

Contents at a Glance

Table of Contents

Part II
Windows Systems Administration

Tables

Acknowledgments

Wanting to do something fundamentally different than it's been done before turned out to be much harder than I ever thought and completely rewarding for you the reader, I hope. You see, there were plenty of books for Windows administrators and plenty of books for people who wanted to script Windows; but no one had really sat down before and written an entire book on Windows administration from the command line that was really focused on administration and not the commands themselves. So I hope the result of all the hard work is that the book you hold in your hands is something unique. This isn't the kind of command-line book that says "here's the Edit command; you use this command to do this and this; and here are its parameters." Sure there's some of that—as there is any book for administrators—but rather than that being the focus this is a book that uses the command line in the context of everyday administration. It teaches you how to perform the daily administrative procedures and details how those procedures are implemented from the command line. So whether you want to learn how to use the command line to manage daily operations, track Windows performance, view the event logs, partition disks, configure TCP/IP, or perform hundreds of other tasks, this book has the answers.

As I've stated in *Microsoft Windows Server 2003 Administrator's Pocket Consultant* and in *Microsoft IIS 6.0 Administrator's Pocket Consultant*, the team at Microsoft Press is top-notch. Valerie Woolley was instrumental throughout the writing process. She helped me stay on track and coordinated the materials after I submitted chapters. Martin DelRe was the acquisitions editor for the project. He believed in the book and my unique approach and was really great to work with. Completing and publishing the book wouldn't have been possible without their help! Susan McClung headed up the editorial process for nSight, Inc. As the project manager for this and many other pocket consultants I've written, she wears many hats and always helps out in many ways. Thank you!

Unfortunately for the writer (but fortunately for readers), writing is only one part of the publishing process. Next came editing and author review. I must say, Microsoft Press has the most thorough editorial and technical review process I've seen anywhere—and I've written a lot of books for many different publishers. Jim Johnson was the technical editor for the book. I believe this was the first time we worked together and it turned out to be a wonderful experience. He was very thorough and helped with testing to ensure things worked as expected on both Windows XP Professional and Windows Server 2003. I'd also like to thank Peter Tietjen for his careful copy editing of this book.

As ever I would also like to thank Michael Bolinger, Anne Hamilton, and Juliana Aldous Atkinson. They've helped out at many points of my writing career and been there when I needed them the most. Thank you also for shepherding my many projects through the publishing process!

Thanks also to Studio B literary agency and my agents, David Rogelberg and Neil Salkind. David and Neil are great to work with.

Hopefully, I haven't forgotten anyone but if I have, it was an oversight. *Honest.*;-)

Introduction

Microsoft Windows Command Line Administrator's Pocket Consultant is designed to be a concise and compulsively usable resource for Windows administrators. This is the readable resource guide that you'll want on your desk or in your pocket at all times. The book discusses everything you need to perform the core administrative tasks using the Windows command line. Because the focus is directed to providing you with the maximum value in a pocket-sized guide, you don't have to wade through hundreds of pages of extraneous information to find what you're looking for. Instead, you'll find exactly what you need to get the job done.

In short, the book is designed to be the one resource you consult whenever you have questions regarding Windows command-line administration. To this end, the book concentrates on daily administration procedures, frequently used tasks, documented examples, and options that are representative but not necessarily inclusive. One of the goals is to keep the content so concise that the book remains compact and easy to navigate while ensuring that the book is packed with as much information as possible—making it a valuable resource. Thus, instead of a hefty 1,000-page tome or a lightweight 100-page quick reference, you get a valuable resource guide that can help you quickly and easily perform common tasks, solve problems, and implement such advanced administration areas as automated monitoring, memory leak analysis, disk partitioning, Active Directory management, and network troubleshooting.

Who Is This Book For?

Microsoft Windows Command Line Administrator's Pocket Consultant covers Windows Server 2003 and Windows XP Professional. The book is designed for

- Current Windows Server 2003 administrators
- Support staff who maintain Windows XP Professional systems
- Accomplished users who have some administrator responsibilities
- Administrators upgrading to Windows Server from previous versions
- Administrators transferring from other platforms

To pack in as much information as possible, I had to assume that you have basic networking skills and a basic understanding of Windows and that Windows is already installed on your systems. With this in mind, I don't devote entire chapters to understanding Windows architecture, installing Windows, or Windows startup and shutdown. I do, however, cover scheduling tasks, monitoring Windows systems, managing accounts, administering network services, and much more.

I also assume that you are fairly familiar with Windows commands and procedures as well as the Windows user interface. If you need help learning Windows basics, you should read the Windows documentation.

How Is This Book Organized?

Microsoft Windows Command Line Administrator's Pocket Consultant is designed to be used in the daily administration of Windows systems, and as such, the book is organized by job-related tasks rather than by Windows features. If you are reading this book, you should be aware of the relationship between Pocket Consultants and Administrator's Companions. Both types of books are designed to be a part of an administrator's library. While Pocket Consultants are the down-and-dirty, in-the trenches books, Administrator's Companions are the comprehensive tutorials and references that cover every aspect of deploying a product or technology in the enterprise.

Speed and ease of reference are an essential part of this hands-on guide. The book has an expanded table of contents and an extensive index for finding answers to problems quickly. Many other quick reference features have been added as well. These features include quick step-by-step instructions, lists, tables with fast facts, and extensive cross-references. The book is organized into both parts and chapters. Each part contains an opening paragraph or two about the chapters contained in that part.

Part I, "Windows Command Line Fundamentals," reviews the fundamental tasks you need for command-line administration. Chapter 1 provides an overview of command-line administration tools, techniques, and concepts. Chapter 2 is designed to help you get the most out of the command shell. It details techniques for starting up the command shell using parameters, how to control command path settings, what redirection techniques are available, and how to use multiple commands in sequences. Chapter 3 discusses the essentials for creating command-line scripts. You'll learn how to set variables, work with conditional controls, and create procedures. Chapter 4 explains how to automate common administrative tasks using the command line.

Microsoft Windows provides many command-line tools to help in the management of daily operations. Part II, "Windows Systems Administration," discusses the core tools and techniques you'll use to manage Windows systems. Chapter 5 discusses many of the key administration tools, including those that help you gather system information, work with the Windows registry, configure Windows services, and shut down systems remotely. Chapter 6 examines tools that help you track information that is written to the Windows event logs, including warnings and errors. You'll also learn how to write events to the system and application logs. In Chapter 7, you'll learn about tools and techniques for monitoring applications, examining processes, and maintaining performance.

The book continues with Part III, "Windows File System and Disk Administration." Users depend on hard disk drives to store their word-processing documents, spreadsheets, and other types of data. If you've worked with Windows XP or Windows Server 2003 for any length of time, you've probably used the Disk Management tool. The command-line counterpart of Disk

Management is the disk partition utility (DiskPart). You can use DiskPart to handle most disk management tasks as well as to perform some additional tasks that cannot be performed in the GUI. Chapter 8 provides an introduction to DiskPart and also discusses FSUtil, CHKDSK, and CHKNTFS. Chapter 9 discusses partitioning basic disks. Chapter 10 examines dynamic disks and how they are used. The chapter also examines implementing, managing, and troubleshooting RAID.

In Part IV, "Windows Active Directory and Network Administration," concentrates on the core commands you'll use for configuring, managing, and troubleshooting Active Directory, print services, and TCP/IP networking. Chapter 11 discusses many of the key directory services administration tools, including tools that help you gather directory information. Chapter 12 examines tools that help you create and manage computer accounts in Active Directory. You'll also learn how to configure domain controllers as global catalogs and operations masters. Chapter 13 completes the directory services discussion with a look at creating and managing accounts for users and groups in Active Directory. Chapter 14 examines network printing and print services. Chapter 15 discusses configuring, maintaining, and troubleshooting TCP/IP networking from the command line.

Conventions Used in This Book

I've used a variety of elements to help keep the text clear and easy to follow. You'll find code terms and listings in monospace type, except when I tell you to actually type a command. In that case, the command appears in **bold** type. When I introduce and define a new term, I put it in *italics*.

Other conventions include

Notes To provide details on a point that needs emphasis

Best Practices To examine the best technique to use when working with advanced configuration and administration concepts

Cautions To warn you when there are potential problems you should look out for

More Info To provide more information on the subject

Real World To provide real-world advice when discussing advanced topics

Security Alerts To point out important security issues

Tips To offer helpful hints or additional information

I truly hope you find that *Microsoft Windows Command Line Administrator's Pocket Consultant* provides everything that you need to perform essential administrative tasks as quickly and efficiently as possible. You're welcome to send your thoughts to me at williamstanek@aol.com. Thank you.

Support

Every effort has been made to ensure the accuracy of this book and of the contents of the companion disc. Microsoft Press provides corrections for books through the World Wide Web at the following address:

http://www.microsoft.com/learning/support/

If you have comments, questions, or ideas about this book or the companion disc, please send them to Microsoft Press using either of the following methods:

Postal Mail:

> Microsoft Press
> Attn: Editor, *Microsoft Windows Command Line Administrator's Pocket Consultant*
> One Microsoft Way
> Redmond, WA 98052-6399

E-mail:

> mspinput@microsoft.com

Please note that product support isn't offered through these mail addresses. For support information about Windows Server 2003 or Windows XP Professional, you can call Windows Standard Support at (800) 936-4900 weekdays between 6 A.M. and 6 P.M. Pacific time.

Part I

Windows Command Line Fundamentals

Microsoft Windows Command-Line Administrator's Pocket Consultant is written for those using Microsoft Windows Server 2003 and Microsoft Windows XP Professional. In this part of the book, I'll explain command line fundamentals, starting in Chapter 1 with an overview of the command line and the command-line tools available. Chapter 2 follows this discussion with a look at batch scripting. You'll learn the technique necessary for creating and using command-line scripts. In Chapter 3, you'll learn how to schedule tasks to run automatically. The techniques discussed include those necessary for managing multiple systems across multiple domains. The final chapter in this part of the book discusses how to use the command line to monitor system health and status.

Chapter 1

Overview of the Windows Command Line

The command line is built into the Microsoft Windows operating system and is accessed through the command shell window. Every version of Windows has had a built-in command line, used to run built-in commands, utilities, and scripts. Although the command line is powerful and versatile, some Windows administrators never use it. If you are happy using the graphical administration tools, you may be able to use them forever without ever having to do anything more than point and click.

For proficient Windows administrators, skilled support staff and committed power users, however, the Windows command line is inescapable. Knowing how to use the command line properly, including which command-line tools to use when and how to put the tools to work effectively, can mean the difference between smooth-running operations and frequent problems. And if you're responsible for multiple domains or networks, learning the time-saving strategies that the command line offers is not only important, but essential, for sustaining day-to-day operations.

In this chapter, I'll explain command line essentials, how to use built-in commands, how to run command-line utilities, and how to work with support and resource kit tools.

Real World   As you read this chapter, and the rest of the book, keep in mind that this book is written for Windows Server 2003 and Windows XP Professional. Techniques that you learn in this book can be used on both operating systems, unless otherwise noted. In some cases, you might be able to use the techniques discussed with other Windows operating systems, though the options or functions may vary. In any case, you should always test commands, options, and scripts before using them. The best way to do this is in a development or test environment where the systems with which you are working are isolated from the rest of the network.

Command Line Essentials

Each new version of Windows has extended and enhanced the command line. The changes have been dramatic and they've not only improved the performance capabilities of the command line but its versatility as well. Today you can do things with the Windows command line that you simply could not do in previous versions of Windows. To help you put the available options to use in the fastest, most productive manner, the discussion that follows explores command shell options and configuration, as well as providing tips for using the command history.

Understanding the Windows Command Shell

The most commonly used command line is the Windows command shell. The Windows command shell is a 32-bit environment for working with the command line. You'll find the executable (Cmd.exe) in the *%SystemRoot%*\System32 directory. Other command lines are available, such as the MS-DOS command shell (Command.com) discussed in the next section.

 Note *%SystemRoot%* refers to the SystemRoot environment variable. The Windows operating system has many environment variables, which are used to refer to user-specific and system-specific values. Often, I'll refer to environment variables using the syntax *%VariableName%*.

You can start the command shell by using the RUN command. Click Start, select Run, and then enter **cmd** in the Open field. Or, you can click Start, point to Programs or All Programs (depending on whether you are using the Classic Start Menu or the system's default Start Menu), Accessories, and then choose Command Prompt.

The environment for the Windows command shell can be initialized in several ways, including passing startup parameters to Cmd.exe or using a custom startup file, which is placed in the *%SystemRoot%*\System32 directory. Figure 1-1 shows a command shell window. By default, the command line is 80 characters wide and, in Windows Server 2003, the command shell displays 25 lines of text. The default line-count for Windows XP Professional depends on the screen resolution, but always results in at least 25 lines being displayed. When additional text is to be displayed in the command shell window or you enter commands and the command shell's window is full, the current text is displayed in the window and prior text is scrolled up. If you want to pause the display temporarily when a command is writing output, press Ctrl+S. Afterward, press Ctrl+S to resume or Ctrl+C to terminate execution.

Figure 1-1. *The 32-bit command shell is the primary command-line window you'll use.*

Note   Custom startup files are used for MS-DOS programs that require special configurations. Prior to Windows XP, these files were named Autoexec.bat and Config.sys. Beginning with Windows XP and continuing with Windows Server 2003, these files are renamed Autoexec.nt and Config.nt. The files also get a new location, in *%SystemRoot%*\System32.

In this figure from Windows Server 2003, the display text is

```
Microsoft Windows [Version 5.2.3790]
(C) Copyright 1985-2003 Microsoft Corp.
C:\Documents and Settings\Administrator.MAILER1.001>
```

Here, the command prompt for the command line shows the current working directory, which by default is *%UserProfile%*, meaning the user profile directory for the current user. A blinking cursor following the command prompt indicates the command line is in interactive mode. In interactive mode, you can type commands directly after the prompt and press Enter to execute them. For example, type **dir** and then press Enter to get a listing of the current directory.

The command prompt also has a batch mode, which is used when executing a series of commands. In batch mode, the command prompt reads and executes commands one by one. Typically, batch commands are read from a script file, but batch commands can also be entered at the command prompt, such as when you use the FOR command to process each file in a set of files. (You'll learn more about batch scripts, loops, and command controls in Chapter 3, "Command Line Scripting Essentials.")

Whenever you work with the Windows command line, it is important to keep in mind where the commands you are using come from. Native commands (commands built into the operating system by Microsoft) include:

- Internal commands that exist internally within the command shell and do not have separate executable files
- External commands that have their own executable files and are normally found in the *%SystemRoot%*\System32 directory

Table 1-1 shows a list of internal commands for the command shell (Cmd.exe). Each internal command is followed by a brief description.

Table 1-1. Quick Reference to Internal Commands for the Command Shell (Cmd.exe)

Name	Description
assoc	Displays or modifies the current file extension associations.
break	Sets breaks for debugging.
call	Calls a procedure or another script from within a script.
cd (chdir)	Displays the current directory name or changes the location of the current directory.
cls	Clears the command window and erases the screen buffer.
color	Sets the text and background colors of the command shell window.
copy	Copies files from one location to another or concatenates files.
date	Displays or sets the system date.
del (erase)	Deletes the specified file, files, or directory.
dir	Displays a list of subdirectories and files in the current or specified directory.
echo	Displays text strings to the command line; sets command echoing state (on|off).
endlocal	Ends localization of variables.
exit	Exits the command shell.
for	Runs a specified command for each file in a set of files.
ftype	Displays current file types or modifies file types used in file extension associations.
goto	Directs the command interpreter to a labeled line in a batch script.
if	Performs conditional execution of commands.
md (mkdir)	Creates a subdirectory in the current or specified directory.

Table 1-1. Quick Reference to Internal Commands for the Command Shell (Cmd.exe)

Name	Description
move	Moves a file or files from the current or designated source directory to a designated target directory. Can also be used to rename a directory.
path	Displays or sets the command path the operating system uses when searching for executables and scripts.
pause	Suspends processing of a batch file and waits for keyboard input.
popd	Makes the directory saved by PUSHD the current directory.
prompt	Sets the text for the command prompt.
pushd	Saves the current directory location and then optionally changes to the specified directory.
rd (rmdir)	Removes a directory or a directory and its subdirectories.
rem	Sets a remark in batch scripts or Config.sys.
ren (rename)	Renames a file or files.
set	Displays current environment variables or sets temporary variables for the current command shell.
setlocal	Marks the start of variable localization in batch scripts.
shift	Shifts the position of replaceable parameters in batch scripts.
start	Starts a separate window to run a specified program or command.
time	Displays or sets the system time.
title	Sets the title for the command-shell window.
type	Displays the contents of a text file.
verify	Causes the operating system to verify files after writing files to disk.
vol	Displays the disk's volume label and serial number.

The syntax for using any internal (and most external commands) can be obtained by typing the command name followed by /? at the prompt, such as

`copy /?`

You'll find there are many more external commands than internal commands, including ones that are very similar to those built into the command line. Most of these similar commands are extended or enhanced in some way. For example, the external XCOPY command is more versatile than the COPY command because it allows you to copy directory trees as well as files and offers many more parameters. With the external SETX command, you can write environment variable changes directly to the Windows registry, which makes the changes permanent rather than temporary as the SET command does.

Tip   You can also use SETX to obtain current Registry key values and write them to a text file. While this command is included with Windows Server 2003, it is available on Windows XP Professional only when you install the Windows XP Professional version of the Windows Support Tools.

Beyond this, the difference between internal and external commands isn't that important. Many Windows utilities have command-line extensions that allow parameters to be passed to the utility from the command line, and thus are used like external commands. Later in this chapter, I discuss the two key sources for Windows utilities: the Microsoft Windows Support Tools and the Microsoft Windows Server 2003 Resource Kit. You can also find third-party utilities with command-line extensions.

Understanding the MS-DOS Command Shell

The MS-DOS command shell (Command.com) includes 16-bit commands for the MS-DOS subsystem and other subsystems. You can start the MS-DOS command shell using the RUN command. Click Start, select Run, and then enter **command** in the Open field. Or, within another command line, type **command** and then press Enter.

Tip   If you are using the MS-DOS command shell from within Cmd.exe, the command shell title should change to "Command Prompt – Command" to let you know this. When you finish working with Command.com, you can quit the MS-DOS command shell and return to the Windows command line by typing **exit**.

The environment for the MS-DOS command shell can be initialized in several ways, including passing startup parameters to Command.com and using a Config.nt startup file, which is placed in the *%SystemRoot%*\System32 folder. As with Cmd.exe, the MS-DOS command window is 80 characters wide and, depending on operating system and screen resolution, displays at least 25 lines of text by default. When you start an MS-DOS command shell, the standard display text is

```
Microsoft(R) Windows DOS
(C) Copyright Microsoft Corp 1990-2001.
C:\>
```

As with the Windows command shell, the MS-DOS command shell has interactive and batch processing modes. It also has native commands built in by Microsoft. These commands are divided into two categories:

- **Internal configuration commands**   Commands used to configure the MS-DOS subsystem, which should be placed in startup or program information files, such as Config.nt or Autoexec.nt. Configuration commands include

BUFFERS, COUNTRY, DEVICE, DEVICEHIGH, DOS, DOSONLY, DRIVE-PARM, ECHOCONFIG, FCBS, FILES, INSTALL, LOADHIGH, LASTDRIVE, NTCMDPROMPT, SHELL, STACKS, and SWITCHES.

- **Standard external commands** Commands that you can type at the command prompt, place in scripts, and in some cases use in startup files. Standard external commands include APPEND, DEBUG, EDIT, EDLIN, EXE2BIN, EXPAND, FASTOPEN, FORCEDOS, GRAPHICS, LOADFIX, MEM, NLSFUNC, SETVER, and SHARE. These MS-DOS commands can also be run in Cmd.exe.

When you execute other commands in the MS-DOS shell, these commands are passed through to the 32-bit command shell where they are executed. This, for example, is why you can use the internal command COPY from within the MS-DOS shell. One detail to note about the MS-DOS shell is that the standard external commands are not available on 64-bit versions of Windows Server 2003.

Configuring Command-Line Properties

If you use the command shell frequently, you'll definitely want to customize its properties. For example, you can add buffers so that text scrolled out of the viewing area is accessible. You can resize the command shell, change its fonts, and more.

To get started, click the command-prompt icon at the top of the command-shell window or right-click the console's display bar, and then select Properties. As Figure 1-2 shows, the Command Prompt Properties dialog box has four tabs:

- **Options** Allows you to configure cursor size, display options, edit options, and command history. Select QuickEdit Mode if you want to use the mouse to cut and paste text within the command window. Clear Insert Mode to use overwrite as the default editing mode. Use the command history to configure how previously used commands are buffered in memory. (You'll find more on the command history in the next section of this chapter titled, "Working with the Command History.")

Tip While working with text-only commands and tools, you may want to use Full Screen display mode to reduce the amount of memory used by the command prompt itself. Afterward, type **exit** to exit the command prompt and return to the Windows desktop.

- **Font** Allows you to set the font size and face used by the command prompt. Raster font sizes are set according to their pixel width and height. For example, the size 8 x 12 is 8 screen pixels wide and 12 screen pixels high. Other fonts are set by point size, such as 10-point Lucida Console. Interestingly, when you select a point size of n, the font will be n pixels high; therefore a 10-point font is 10 screen pixels high. These fonts can be designated as a bold font type as well, which increases their screen pixel width.

- **Layout** Allows you to set the screen buffer size, window size, and window position. Size the buffer height so that you can easily scroll back through previous listings and script output. A good setting is in the range of 1,000 to 2,000. Size the window height so that you can view more of the command-shell window at one time. A good setting is 45 lines on 800 x 600 screens with a 12-point font. If you want the command-prompt window to be in a specific screen position, clear Let System Position Window and then specify a position for the upper-left corner of the command window using Left and Top.

- **Colors** Allows you to set the text and background colors used by the command prompt. Screen Text and Screen Background control the respective color settings for the command-prompt window. Popup Text and Popup Background options control the respective color settings for any popup dialog boxes generated when running commands at the command prompt.

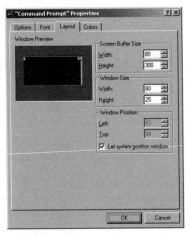

Figure 1-2. *Configure the command-line properties for your environment.*

When you are finished updating the command-shell properties, click OK. Windows displays a prompt that asks you to specify how the settings should be applied. Either apply the property changes to the current window only or save the property changes for future windows with the same title, which applies to all command lines you access later. You may also see an option to modify the shortcut that started the current window. In this case, any time you start a command line using the applicable shortcut, it will use these settings.

Working with the Command History

The command history buffer is a feature of the Windows command shell (Cmd.exe) that remembers commands you've used in the current command line and allows you to access them without having to retype the command text. The maximum number of commands to buffer is set through the command-line Properties dialog box discussed in the previous section. By default, up to 50 commands are stored.

You can change the history size by completing these steps:

1. Right-click the command shell's title bar, select Properties, and then click the Options tab.

2. Use the Buffer Size field to set the maximum number of commands to store in the history and then click OK.

3. To save the history setting to use with future command lines, select Save Property Changes For Future Windows or Modify Shortcut That Started This Window as appropriate, and then click OK. Otherwise, just click OK.

You can access commands stored in the history in the following ways:

- **Browsing with the arrow keys**   Use the up-arrow and down-arrow keys to move up and down through the list of buffered commands. When you find the command you want to use, press Enter to execute it as previously entered. Or you can modify the displayed command text by adding or changing parameters and then pressing Enter.

- **Browsing the command history pop-up window**   Press F7 to display a pop-up window that contains a listing of buffered commands. Next, select a command using the arrow keys. (Alternatively, press F9, then the corresponding number on the keyboard, and finally the Enter key.) Execute the selected command by pressing Enter, or press Esc to close the pop-up window without executing a command.

- **Searching the command history**   Enter the first few letters of the command you want to execute and then press F8. The command shell searches through the history for the first command that begins with the characters you've entered. Press Enter to execute it. Or, press F8 again to search the history buffer for the next match in the command history.

As you work with the command history, keep in mind that each instance of Cmd.exe has its own set of command buffers. Thus, buffers are only valid in the related command shell context.

Using Windows Support Tools

The Windows Support Tools are a collection of utilities for handling everything from system diagnostics to network monitoring. These tools can be installed on, and used with, all versions of Windows Server 2003 and Windows XP Professional. You can install the support tools by completing the following steps:

1. Insert the appropriate operating system CD-ROM (Windows Server 2003 or Windows XP Professional) into the CD-ROM drive.

Caution Because the Support Tools installation modifies the Help And Support Center, you should close any instances of this console that are running before you start the installation process. If you don't do this, the installation will fail.

2. When the Autorun screen appears, click Perform Additional Tasks, and then click Browse This CD. This starts Windows Explorer.

3. In Windows Explorer, double-click Support and then double-click Tools.

 Note Throughout this book, I refer to double-clicking, which is the most common technique used for accessing folders and for running programs. With a double click, the first click selects the item and the second click opens/runs the item. In both Windows Server 2003 and in Windows XP Professional, you can also configure single-click open/ run. Here, moving the mouse over the item selects it and a single click opens/runs the item. You can change the mouse click options with the Folder Options utility in the Control Panel. To do this, select the General tab, and then choose Single-Click To Open An Item or Double-Click To Open An Item, as desired.

4. Double-click Suptools.msi. This starts the Windows Support Tools Setup Wizard. Click Next.

5. Read the End User License Agreement and then, if you agree and want to continue, click I Agree and then click Next.

6. Enter your user information, and then click Next.

7. In Windows XP Professional, you then see the Select An Installation Type page. Select Complete and then click Next.

8. Select the destination directory for the support tools. The default location is *%ProgramFiles%*\Support Tools. If you don't want to use the default location, type a new directory path or click Browse to search for a location. In Windows Server 2003, the support tools use about 24 megabytes (MB) of disk space. Selecting the Complete option when installing the Windows XP Professional version of the support tools requires about 12 MB of disk space.

9. Click Install Now.

10. Click Finish on the Completing The Windows Support Tools Setup Wizard page.

After installation you can access the support tools through the Help And Support Center, as shown in Figure 1-3. (This figure shows the Windows Server 2003 window, though the Windows XP Professional window is very similar.) Click Start, click Programs or All Programs as appropriate, click Windows Support Tools, and then select Support Tools Help. As the figure shows, the tools are organized by file name, tool name, and category. Clicking a tool name accesses a help page that displays the online help documentation for the tool and that you can also use to run the tool.

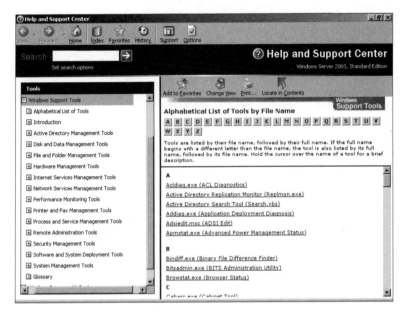

Figure 1-3. *Use support tools to perform such tasks as system diagnostics and network monitoring.*

Most of the support tools have extensions that allow you to run them from the command line. You will find the executables for the support tools in the installation directory, which by default is *%SystemDrive%*\Program Files\Support Tools.

Because the system path is updated to include the support tools installation directory, you do not need to be in this directory to execute the support tools. You can, in fact, run the tools at any command prompt regardless of the current directory. As with other Windows utilities and commands, you can display the syntax for a particular support tool by typing the command name following by a space and /?, such as **spcheck /?**.

Using Windows Server 2003 Resource Kit Tools

Another great resource for Windows utilities is the Microsoft Windows Server 2003 Resource Kit. As with the support tools, the resource kit tools are available for installation on Windows Server 2003 systems and can be used with all versions of Windows Server 2003 and Windows XP Professional.

The resource kit tools are distributed on CD-ROM as part of the boxed resource kit set and also available as a free download from the Microsoft Windows Download Center. You can install the resource kit tools by completing the following steps:

1. Insert the Windows Server 2003 Resource Kit CD-ROM into the CD-ROM drive or double-click the executable file, Rktools.exe, that you downloaded from Microsoft.

 Caution Because the resource kit modifies Windows consoles, including the Help And Support Center, you should close any programs you are running prior to installing the resource kit. If you don't do this, the installation may fail completely or it may simply fail to update the shared components of programs that are currently running (which may lead to unpredictable results).

2. When the Windows Resource Kit Tools Setup Wizard starts, click Next.

3. Read the End User License Agreement and then, if you agree and want to continue, click I Agree and then click Next.

4. Enter your user information, and then click Next.

5. Select the destination directory for the support tools. The default location is *%ProgramFiles%*\Windows Resource Kits\Tools. If you don't want to use the default location, type a new directory path or click Browse to search for a location. The resource kit uses about 37 MB of disk space.

6. Click Install Now.

7. Click Finish on the Completing The Windows Resource Kit Tools Setup Wizard page.

When the installation is complete, you can access the resource kit tools through the Windows Resource Kit Tools Help. Click Start, click Programs or All Programs as appropriate, click Windows Resource Kit Tools, and then select Windows Resource Kit Tools Help. As with support tools, resource kit tools are organized by file name, tool name, and category. Clicking a tool name accesses a help page that displays the online help documentation for the tool and that you can also use to run the tool.

You will find the executables for the resource kit tools in the installation directory, which by default is *%SystemDrive%*\Program Files\Windows Resource Kits\Tools, and once again, the system path is updated to include the resource kit installation directory. This allows you to run the tools at any command prompt regardless of the current directory. Type the command name followed by a space and /?, such as **creatfil /?**, to display the command syntax. Keep in mind, however, that not all commands have help documentation that can be accessed in this way.

Chapter 2

Getting the Most from the Command Line

The command shell provides a powerful environment for working with commands and scripts. As discussed in the previous chapter, you can run many types of commands at the command line, including built-in commands, Windows utilities, and applications with command-line extensions. Regardless of source, every command you'll use follows the same syntax rules. These rules state that a command consists of a command name followed by any required or optional arguments. Arguments can also use redirection to specify the sources for inputs, outputs, and errors.

When you execute a command in the command shell, you start a series of events that are similar to the following:

1. The command shell replaces any variables you've entered in the command text with their actual values.

2. Multiple commands that are chained or grouped, and passed on a single line, are broken into individual commands, separated into command-name and related arguments. The individual commands are then processed.

3. If the command name has a file path, the command shell uses this path to find the command. If the command cannot be found in the specified location, the command shell returns an error.

4. If the command name doesn't specify a file path, the command shell tries to resolve the command name internally. A match means that you've referenced a built-in command that can be executed immediately. If no match is found, the command shell looks in the current directory for the command executable, and then searches the command path for the command executable. If the command cannot be found in any of those locations, the command shell returns an error.

5. If the command is located, the command is executed using any specified arguments, including those that specify the inputs to use. Command output and any errors are written to the command window or to the specified destinations for output and error.

As you can see, many factors can affect command execution, including command path settings, redirection techniques used, and whether commands are chained or grouped. In this chapter, we'll use this breakdown of command execution to help you get the most out of the command shell. Before we dive into those discussions, however, let's look at special considerations for starting the command shell and introduce the concept of nesting command shells.

Managing Command Shell Startup

When you previously worked with the command line, you probably started it by clicking Start, pointing to Programs or All Programs, Accessories, and then choosing Command Prompt. Another way to start a command line is to use the Run dialog box or type **cmd** in an open command-shell window. These techniques enable you to pass arguments to the command line, including switches that control how the command line works as well as parameters that execute additional commands. For example, you can start the command shell in quiet mode (meaning command echo is turned off) by using the startup command **cmd /q** and if you wanted the command shell to execute a command and then terminate, you could type **cmd /c** followed by the command text enclosed in quotation marks. The following example starts a command shell, sends the output of ipconfig to a file, and then exits the command shell:

```
cmd /c "ipconfig > c:\ipconfig.txt"
```

Table 2-1 summarizes the key parameters for the Windows command shell (Cmd.exe). Note that several command-line parameters are set by default. Because of this, the command line normally uses standard ANSI character codes for command output, as opposed to Unicode character codes, and enables command extensions that add features to most built-in commands.

Table 2-1. Essential Parameters for the Command Line

Parameter	Description
/C	Executes the command specified and then exits the command shell.
/K	Executes the command specified and then remains in interactive mode.
/A	Command output to files (or pipes) is set to ANSI format (default).
/U	Command output to files (or pipes) is set to Unicode.
/U	Turns on quiet mode, meaning command echo is off. By default, command echo is on.
/T:FG	Sets the foreground and background colors for the console window.
/E:ON	Enables command extensions, which is the default.
/E:OFF	Disables command extensions.

Note   Some parameters cannot be used with other switches. For example, you can't enable both Unicode and ANSI character codes. If you use both */A* and */U*, or */E:ON* and */E:OFF*, the command line applies the last option you passed on the command line.

Sometimes you may want to use different environment settings or parameters for a command line and then go back to your original settings without exiting the console window. To do this, you can use a technique called *nesting*. With nesting, you start a command line within a command line and the nested command line inherits its environment settings from the current command line. You can then modify the environment as necessary and execute commands and scripts using those settings. When you type **exit** to end the nested command-line instance, you return to the previous command line and the previous environment settings are restored.

Tip   As you set out to work with the command shell, keep in mind that some characters have special meanings and that whenever the command shell encounters one of these characters, it attempts to carry out the special procedure associated with that character. Special characters include < > ( ) & | @ ^. If you want to use a special character as a regular character, you must escape the special character for the command shell to look at it literally, without invoking the special procedures with which it is associated. The escape character is the caret (^), which is the character above the 6 key on a standard keyboard, and is placed to immediately precede the special character.

Working with the Command Path

The Microsoft Windows operating system uses the command path to locate executables. The types of files that Windows considers to be executables are determined by the file extensions for executables. File extensions can also be mapped to specific applications using file associations. The two sections that follow discuss techniques for working with the command path, file extensions, and file associations.

Managing the Command Path

You can view the current command path for executables by using the PATH command. Start a command shell, type **path** on a line by itself, and press Enter. If you've installed the Windows Support Tools and the Windows Resource Kit, the results should look similar to the following:

```
PATH=C:\Program Files\Windows Resource Kits\Tools\;C:\Program
Files\Support Tools\;C:\WINDOWS\system32;C:\WINDOWS;C:\WINDOWS\
System32\Wbem
```

Note Observe the use of the semicolon (;) to separate individual paths. The command shell uses the semicolon to determine where one file path ends and another begins.

The command path is set during logon using system and user environment variables, namely the *%PATH%* variable. The order in which directories are listed in the path indicates the search order used by the command line when looking for executables. In the previous example, the command line searches in this order:

1. C:\Program Files\Windows Resource Kits\Tools\
2. C:\Program Files\Support Tools\
3. C:\Windows\System32
4. C:\Windows
5. C:\Windows\System32\Wbem

You can permanently change the command path in the system environment using the SETX command. (The SETX command is a native external command in Windows Server 2003, but is available in Windows XP Professional only after the Windows XP Professional version of the Windows Resource Kit has been installed from the operating system CD-ROM.) For example, if you use specific directories for scripts or applications, you may want to update the path information. You can do this by using the SETX command to add a specific path to the existing path, such as **setx PATH "%PATH%;C\Scripts"**.

 Note Observe the use of the quotation marks and the semicolon (;). The quotation marks are necessary to ensure that the value %PATH%;C:\Scripts is read as the second argument for the SETX command. And, as discussed previously, the semicolon is used to specify where one file path ends and another begins.

In this example, the directory C:\Scripts is appended to the existing command path and the sample path listed previously would be modified to read as follows:

```
PATH=C:\Program Files\Windows Resource Kits\Tools\;C:\Program
Files\SupportTools\;C:\WINDOWS\system32;C:\WINDOWS;C:\WINDOWS
\System32\Wbem;C:\Scripts
```

Don't forget about the search order that Windows uses. Because the paths are searched in order, the C:\Scripts directory will be the last one searched. This can sometimes slow the execution of your scripts. To help Windows find your scripts faster, you may want C:\Scripts to be the first directory searched. In this case, you could set the command path using the command

```
setx PATH "C:\Scripts;%PATH%"
```

Be careful when setting the command path. It is easy to overwrite all path information accidentally. For example, if you don't specify the *%PATH%* environment variable when setting the path, you will delete all other path information. One way to ensure that you can easily recreate the command path is to keep a copy of the command path in a file. To write the current command path to a file, type **path > orig_path.txt**. To write the command path to the command-shell window, type **path**.

Now you have a listing or a file that contains a listing of the original command path. Not only does the path command list the current command path, it also can be used to set the command path temporarily for the current command shell. For example, type **path %PATH%;C:\Scripts** to append the C:\Scripts directory to the command path in the current command shell.

Managing File Extensions and File Associations

File extensions are what allow you to execute commands by typing just their command name at the command line. Two types of file extensions are used:

- **File extensions for executables** Executable files are defined with the *%PATHEXT%* environment variable. You can view the current settings by typing **set pathext** at the command line. The default setting is PATHEXT=.COM;.EXE;.BAT;.CMD;.VBS;.VBE;.JS;.JSE;.WSF;.WSH. With this setting, the command line knows which files are executable and which files are not, so you don't have to specify the file extension at the command line.

- **File extensions for applications** File extensions for applications are referred to as file associations. File associations are what enable you to pass arguments to executables and to open documents, spreadsheets, or other application files by double-clicking their file icon. Each known extension on a system has a file association that can be viewed by typing **assoc** followed by the extension, such as **assoc.exe**. Each file association in turn specifies the file type for the file extension. This can be viewed by typing the FTYPE command followed by the file association, such as **ftype exefile**.

With executables, the order of file extensions sets the search order used by the command line on a per-directory basis. Thus, if a particular directory in the command path has multiple executables that match the command name provided, a .com file would be executed before a .exe file and so on.

Every known file extension on a system has a corresponding file association and file type—even extensions for executables. In most cases, the file type is the extension text without the period followed by the keyword *file*, such as cmdfile, exefile, or batfile, and the file association specifies that the first parameter passed is the command name and that other parameters should be passed on to the application.

You can look up the file type and file association for known extensions using the ASSOC and FTYPE commands. To find the association, type **assoc** followed by the file extension that includes the period. The output of the ASSOC command is the file type. So if you type **ftype *association*** (where *association* is the output of the ASSOC command), you'll see the file type mapping. For example, if you type the following command to see the file associations for .exe executables: **assoc .exe,** you then type **ftype exefile**.

You'll see the file association is set to

```
exefile="%1" %*
```

Thus, when you run an .exe file, Windows knows the first value is the command that you want to run and anything else provided are parameters to pass along.

 Tip File associations and types are maintained in the Windows Registry and can be set using the ASSOC and FTYPE commands respectively. To create the file association, type **assoc** followed by the extension setting, such as **assoc .pl=perlfile**. To create the file type, set the file type mapping, including how to use parameters supplied with the command name, such as **perlfile=C:\Perl\Bin\Perl.exe "%1" %***. To learn more about setting file associations and types, refer to the documentation for these two commands in Help And Support Center.

Redirecting Standard Input, Output, and Error

By default, commands take input from the parameters specified when they are called by the command shell and then send their output, including errors, to the standard console window. Sometimes, though, you'll want to take input from another source or send output to a file or other output device such as a printer. You may also want to redirect errors to a file rather than the console window. You can perform these and other redirection tasks using the techniques introduced in Table 2-2 and discussed in the sections that follow.

Table 2-2.   Redirection Techniques for Input, Output, and Errors

Redirection Technique	Description
command1 | command2	Sends the output of the first command to be the input of the second command.
command < [path]filename	Takes command input from the specified file path.
command > [path]filename	Sends output to the named file, creating the file if necessary or overwriting it if it already exists.
command >> [path]filename	Appends output to the named file if it exists or creates the file and then writes to it.
command < [path]filename > [path]filename	Gets command input from the specified file and then sends command output to the named file.
command < [path]filename >> [path]filename	Gets command input from the specified file and then appends command output to the named file.

Table 2-2.   Redirection Techniques for Input, Output, and Errors

Redirection Technique	Description
command 2> [path]filename	Creates the named file and sends any error output to it. If the file exists, it is overwritten.
command 2>&1 filename	Sends error output to the same destination as standard output.

Redirecting Standard Output to Other Commands

Most commands generate output that can be redirected to another command as input. To do this, you use a technique called *piping*, whereby the output of a command is sent as the input of the next command. Following this, you can see the general syntax for piping is

```
Command1 | Command2
```

where the pipe redirects the output of Command1 to the input of Command2. But you can also redirect output more than once, such as

```
Command1 | Command2 | Command3
```

The two most common commands that are piped include FIND and MORE. The FIND command searches for strings in files or in text passed to the command as input and then lists the text of matching lines as output. For example, you could obtain a list of all .txt files in the current directory by typing the command

```
dir | find ".txt "
```

The MORE command accepts output from other commands as input and then breaks this output into sections which can be viewed one console page at a time. For example, you could page through a log file called Dailylog.txt using the following command:

```
type c:\working\logs\dailylog.txt | more
```

Type **find /?** or **more /?** at the command line to get a complete list of the syntax for these commands.

Redirecting I/O to and from Files

Another command redirection technique is to get input from a file using the input redirection symbol (<). For example, the following command sorts the contents of the Usernames.txt file and displays the results to the command line:

```
sort < usernames.txt
```

Just as you can read input from a file, you can also send output to a file. To do this, you can use > to create or overwrite, or >> to create or append data to a named file. For example, if you want to write the current network status to a file, you could use the command

```
netstat -a > netstatus.txt
```

Unfortunately, if there is an existing file in the current directory with the same file name, this command overwrites the file and creates a new one. If you want to append this information to an existing file rather than overwrite an existing file, change the command text to read

```
netstat -a >> netstatus.txt
```

The input and output redirection techniques can be combined as well. You could, for example, obtain command-input from a file and then redirect command-output to another file. In this example, a list of user names is obtained from a file and sorted, and then the sorted name list is written to a new file:

```
sort < usernames.txt > usernames-alphasort.txt
```

Redirecting Standard Error

By default, errors from commands are written as output on the command line. If you are running unattended batch scripts or utilities, however, you may want to redirect standard error to a file so that errors are tracked. One way to redirect standard error is to tell the command line that errors should go to the same destination as standard output. To do this, type the **2>&1** redirection symbol as shown in this example:

```
chkdsk /r > diskerrors.txt 2>&1
```

Here, you send standard output and standard error to a file called Diskerrors.txt. If you want to see only errors, you can redirect only the standard error. In this example, standard output is displayed at the command line and standard error is sent to the file Diskerrors.txt:

```
chkdsk /r 2> diskerrors.txt
```

Chaining and Grouping Commands

In previous sections, I discussed redirection techniques that included piping commands. You may have wondered if there were other ways to execute a series of commands. There are. You can chain commands and execute them in sequence, and you can execute commands conditionally based on the success or failure of previous commands. You can also group sets of commands that you want to execute conditionally.

You'll learn more about these techniques in the sections that follow. Before you proceed however, take note of Table 2-3, which provides a quick reference for the basic syntax to use when chaining or grouping commands. Keep in mind that the syntax provided is not intended to be all-inclusive. The chaining syntax can be extended for additional commands to be conditionally executed. The syntax for grouping may vary, depending on the actual situation.

Table 2-3.   Quick Reference for Chaining and Grouping Commands

Symbol	Syntax	Description
&	Command1 & Command2	Execute Command1 and then execute Command2.
&&	Command1 && Command2	Execute Command2 if Command1 is completed successfully.
||	Command1 || Command2	Execute Command2 only when Command1 doesn't complete successfully.
( )	(Command1 & Command2) && (Command3)	Use parentheses to group sets of commands for conditional execution based on success.
	(Command1 & Command2) || (Command3)	Use parentheses to group sets of commands for conditional execution based on failure.

Using Chains of Commands

Sometimes, to be more efficient, you'll want to execute commands in a specific sequence. For example, you may want to change to a particular directory and then obtain a directory listing, sorted by date. Using chaining, you can perform both tasks by entering this one line of command text:

```
cd c:\working\docs & dir /O:d
```

In scripts, you'll often need to chain commands such as this to be certain the commands are carried out exactly as you expect. Still, it makes more sense to chain commands when the execution of later commands depends upon whether previous commands succeeded or failed. In this example, a log file is moved only if it exists:

```
dir c:\working\logs\current.log && move current.log d:\history\logs
```

Why would you want to do this? Well, one reason would be so that an error isn't generated as output of a script.

You may also want to perform a task only if a preceding command failed. For example, if you are using a script to distribute files to a group of workstations, some of which have a C:\Working\Data folder and some of which have a C:\Data folder, you could copy sets of files to either folder, regardless of the workstation configuration, using the following commands:

```
cd C:\working\data || cd C:\data
xcopy n:\docs\*.*
```

Grouping Command Sequences

When you combine multiple commands, you may need a way to group commands to prevent conflicts or to ensure that an exact order is followed. You group commands using a set of parentheses. To understand why grouping may be needed, consider the following example. Here, you want to write the host name, IP configuration, and network status to a file, so you use this statement:

```
hostname & ipconfig & netstat -a > current-config.log
```

When you examine the log file, however, you find that it contains only the network status. The reason for this is that the command line executes the commands in sequence as follows:

1. hostname
2. ipconfig
3. netstat - a > current_config.log

Because the commands are executed in sequence, the system host name and IP configuration are written to the command line, and only the network status is written to the log file. To write the output of all the commands to the file, you would need to group the commands as follows:

```
(hostname & ipconfig & netstat -a) > current_config.log
```

Here, the output of all three commands is collected and then redirected to the log file. You can also use grouping with conditional success and failure. In the following example, both Command1 and Command2 must succeed for Command3 to execute:

```
(cd C:\working\data & xcopy n:\docs\*.*) && (hostname >
n:\runninglog.txt)
```

In the next chapter, you'll see how command grouping is used with *if* and *if...else* constructs.

Chapter 3

Command Line Scripting Essentials

In a world dominated by whiz-bang graphical user interfaces, you may wonder what command-line scripting has to offer that Microsoft Windows and point-and-click dialog boxes don't. Well, to be honest, more than most people realize, especially considering that most people regard command-line scripts as glorified batch files—the kind you used on computers with 8088 processors and MS-DOS. Today's command-line scripting environment is an extensive programming environment, which includes

- Variables
- Arithmetic expressions
- Conditional statements
- Control flow statements
- Procedures

You can use these programming elements to automate repetitive tasks, perform complex operations while you're away from the computer, find resources that others may have misplaced, and perform many other time-saving activities that you would normally have to type in at the keyboard. Command-line scripts not only have complete access to the command line, they can also call any utilities that have command-line extensions, including the Windows Support Tools and the Windows Resource Kit tools.

Creating Command Line Scripts

Command line scripts are text files containing the commands you want to execute. These are the same commands you would normally type into the Windows command shell. However, rather than enter the commands each time you want to use them, you create a script to store the commands for easy execution.

Because scripts contain standard text characters, you can create and edit scripts using a standard text editor, such as Notepad. When you enter commands, be sure to place each command or group of commands that should be executed together on a new line. This ensures proper execution of the commands. When you have finished creating a command-line script, save the script file using the

.bat or .cmd extension. Both extensions work with command-line scripts in the same way. For example, if you wanted to create a script to display the system name, Windows version and IP configuration, you could enter these three commands into a file called SysInfo.bat or SysInfo.cmd:

```
hostname
ver
ipconfig -all
```

Once you save the script, you can execute it as if it were a Windows utility; simply type the name of the script in a command shell and press Enter. When you do this, the command shell reads the script file and executes its commands one by one. It stops executing the script when it reaches the end of the file or reads an EXIT command. For the example script, the command line would display output similar to Listing 3-1.

Listing 3-1 Output of Sample Script

```
C:\>hostname
mailer1

C:\>ver
Microsoft Windows [Version 5.2.3790]

C:\>ipconfig -all
Windows IP Configuration
        Host Name . . . . . . . . . . . . : mailer1
        Primary Dns Suffix  . . . . . . . : adatum.com
        Node Type . . . . . . . . . . . . : Unknown
        IP Routing Enabled. . . . . . . . : No
        WINS Proxy Enabled. . . . . . . . : No
        DNS Suffix Search List. . . . . . : adatum.com

Ethernet adapter Local Area Connection:

        Connection-specific DNS Suffix  . :
        Description . . . . . . . . . . . : Intel(R) PRO/100 VE Network
            Connection
        Physical Address. . . . . . . . . : X0-EF-D7-AB-E2-1E
        DHCP Enabled. . . . . . . . . . . : No
        IP Address. . . . . . . . . . . . : 192.168.10.50
        Subnet Mask . . . . . . . . . . . : 255.255.255.0
        Default Gateway . . . . . . . . . : 192.168.10.1
        DNS Servers . . . . . . . . . . . : 192.168.10.155
```

If you examine the listing, you'll see that the command prompt and the actual commands are displayed as well as the output of the commands themselves. The reason for this is that the command shell does some extra work behind the scenes while executing scripts in the default processing mode. First, the command shell displays the command prompt. Next, it reads a line from the script, displays it, and then interprets it. If the command shell reaches the end of the file or reads an EXIT command, execution stops. Otherwise, the command shell starts this process all over again by displaying the prompt and preparing to read the next line in the script.

Although the default processing mode with command echoing on can be useful for troubleshooting problems in scripts, you probably don't want to use this display mode with scripts you'll use regularly. Fortunately, you can change the default behavior by turning command echo off, as I'll show you later in the chapter in the section titled "Managing Text Display and Command Echoing."

Common Statements and Commands for Scripts

So far in this book, I've discussed commands but haven't really introduced what a statement is. While these terms are often used interchangeably, the term *statement* technically refers to the keyword for a command, such as the *rem* statement, but it can also refer to a line of code that includes all the command text on that line. In some programming languages, such as Java, each statement must be terminated with a specific character. With Java, the terminator is a semicolon. The command line doesn't look for a specific terminator, other than the end of the line, which is assumed when the command interpreter reads any of the following:

- Line break (such as when you press Shift+Enter)
- Carriage return and line break (such as when you press Enter)
- End-of-file marker

Now that we've discussed how to create scripts, let's look at common statements and commands you'll use in scripts, including

- **Cls** Clears the console window and resets the screen buffer
- **Rem** Creates comments in scripts
- **Echo** Displays messages at the command line and turns command echoing on or off
- **@** Controls command echo on a line-by-line basis
- **Title** Sets the title for the command shell window
- **Color** Sets the text and background colors used in the command shell window

Clearing the Command-Shell Window

Clearing the command-shell window before writing script output is usually a good idea. You clear the command-shell window using the CLS command. Why not try it? At the command line, type **cls** and press Enter. The console window clears and the cursor is positioned in the top left corner of the window. All the text in the screen buffer is cleared as well.

You could add the CLS command to the sample script listed previously, as shown in this example:

```
cls
hostname
ver
ipconfig -all
```

Adding Comments to Scripts

You use the *rem* statement to add comments to your scripts. Every script you create should have comments detailing

* When the script was created and last modified
* Who created the script
* What the script is used for
* How to contact the script creator
* Whether and where script output is stored

Not only are the answers to these Who, What, How, Where, and When questions important for ensuring that the scripts you create can be used by other administrators, they can also help you remember what a particular script does, especially if weeks or months have passed since you last worked with the script. An example of a script that uses comments to answer these questions is shown as Listing 3-2.

Listing 3-2 Updated Sample Script with Comments

```
rem ************************
rem Script: SystemInfo.bat
rem Creation Date: 2/2/2004
rem Last Modified: 3/15/2004
rem Author: William R. Stanek
rem E-mail: williamstanek@aol.com
rem ************************
rem Description: Displays system configuration information
rem              including system name, IP configuration
rem              and Windows version.
rem ************************
rem Files: Stores output in c:\current-sys.txt.
rem ************************

hostname > c:\current-sys.txt
ver >> c:\current-sys.txt
ipconfig -all >> c:\current-sys.txt
```

Later in this chapter, in the section titled "Passing Arguments to Scripts," I'll show you how to use your comments as automated help documentation. Before we get to that, however, keep in mind that *rem* statements can also be used to

- Insert explanatory text within scripts, such as documentation on how a procedure works.

- Prevent a command from executing. On the command line, add **rem** before the command to comment it out.

- Hide part of a line from interpretation. Add **rem** within a line to block interpretation of everything that follows the *rem* statement.

Managing Text Display and Command Echoing

The echo command has two purposes. You use the ECHO command to write text to the output, which can be the command shell or a text file. You also use the ECHO command to turn command echoing on or off. Normally, when you execute commands in a script, the commands as well as the resulting output of the command are displayed in the console window. This is called *command echoing*.

To use the ECHO command to display text, enter **echo** followed by the text to display, such as

```
echo The system host name is:
hostname
```

To use ECHO to control command echoing, type **echo off** or **echo on** as appropriate, such as

```
echo off
echo The system host name is:
hostname
```

Use output redirection to send output to a file rather than the command shell, as follows:

```
echo off
echo The system host name is: > current.txt
hostname >> current.txt
```

To experiment with suppressing command echoing, start a command shell, type **echo off**, and then enter other commands. You'll find that the command prompt is no longer displayed. Instead, you see only what you type into the console window and the resulting output from the commands you've entered. In scripts, the ECHO OFF command turns off command echoing as well as the command prompt. By adding the command ECHO OFF to your scripts, you keep the command-shell window or the output file from getting cluttered with commands when all you care about is the output from those commands.

Tip By the way, if you want to determine whether command echoing is enabled or disabled, type the ECHO command by itself. Give it a try. If command echoing is on, you'll see the message Echo Is On. Otherwise, you'll see the message Echo Is Off. Experiment with the ECHO OFF command in your scripts and you may detect a bit of a problem here. If the ECHO OFF command turns off command echoing, how do you prevent the ECHO OFF command itself from echoing? Don't worry; that's discussed in the next section.

Real World One question that other command-line programmers frequently ask me is, How do you get a blank line to echo in the command shell? You might think that putting the ECHO command on a line by itself would do the job, but it doesn't. Typing **echo** on a line by itself displays the status of command echoing as mentioned in the previous tip. Typing **echo** followed by a space doesn't work either, because the Windows command line treats spaces (in this situation) as meaningless and you get the same results as typing **echo** followed by nothing at all. To get ECHO to display a blank line, you must enter **echo.** (Note that there is no space between the period and the ECHO command.)

Fine-Tuning Command Echo with @

The @ command prevents commands from echoing to the output on a line-by-line basis and you can think of it as a line-specific *echo off* statement. You could use @ to turn off command echoing like this:

```
@echo The system host name is:
@hostname
```

Using @, the output that shows the command prompt and commands like this:

```
C:\>echo The system host name is:
The system host name is:

C:\>hostname
mailer1
```

becomes

```
The system host name is:
mailer1
```

But the real value of @ is that it allows you to tell the command shell not to display the command prompt or ECHO OFF command, and thereby ensures that the only output of your scripts is the output of the commands you enter. Here is an example of a script that uses @ to hide the ECHO OFF command so that it isn't displayed in the output:

```
@echo off
echo The system host name is:
hostname
```

The output from this script is

```
The system host name is:
mailer1
```

Tip I recommend using *@echo off* at the beginning of all your command-line scripts. By the way, if you start a command shell and type **@echo off**, you can turn off the display of the command prompt as well.

Setting the Console Window Title and Colors

If you're going to take the time to write a script, you might as well add a few special features to jazz it up. Some of the basic techniques that I've already discussed are using the ECHO OFF command and clearing the console window before you write output. You may also want to set a title for the window or change the colors the window uses.

The title bar for the command shell is located at the top of the console window. Normally, this title bar displays "Command Prompt" or the file path to the command shell. You can customize the title using the TITLE command. This command works much like the ECHO command in that it displays whatever text follows it on the console's title bar. For example, if you wanted to set the title of the current console to "System Information," you could do this by entering the following at the command line:

```
title System Information
```

You can not only use the TITLE command to show the name of the script that is running; you can also use TITLE to show the progress of the script as it executes, such as

```
rem add blocks of work commands
title Gathering Information

rem add blocks of logging commands
title Logging System Information
```

By default, the console window displays white text on a black background. As you learned in Chapter 1, "Overview of the Windows Command Line," you can modify this behavior using the Colors tab of the Command Prompt Properties dialog box. You can also set console colors by using the COLOR command. You do this by passing the command a 2-digit hexadecimal code. The first digit corresponds to the background color and the second digit corresponds to the text color, such as

```
color 21
```

which sets the text to blue and the background color to green.

The color codes you can use with the COLOR command are shown in Table 3-1. Keep in mind that you can't set the text and background colors to the same value. If you try to do this, the color doesn't change. Additionally, you can restore the default colors at any time by using the COLOR command without any arguments, such as

```
color
```

Table 3-1.   Color Codes for the Command Shell Window

Code	Color	Code	Color
0	Black	8	Gray
1	Blue	9	Bright Blue
2	Green	A	Bright Green
3	Aqua	B	Bright Aqua
4	Red	C	Bright Red
5	Purple	D	Bright Purple
6	Yellow	E	Bright Yellow
7	White	F	Bright White

Passing Arguments to Scripts

As with most command-line utilities, arguments can be passed to scripts when they are started. You use arguments to set special parameters in a script or to pass along information needed by the script. Each argument should follow the script name and be separated by a space (and enclosed in quotation marks if necessary). In the following example, a script named Check-sys is passed the parameters Mailer1 and Full:

```
check-sys mailer1 full
```

Each value passed along to a script can be examined using formal parameters. The script name itself is represented by the parameter %0. The parameter %1 represents the first argument passed in to the script, %2 the second, and so on until %9 for the ninth argument. For example, if you create a script called Check-sys and then use the following command to call the script:

```
check-sys mailer1 full actual
```

you would find that the related parameter values are

- *%0* — check-sys
- *%1* — mailer1
- *%2* — full
- *%3* — actual

You access arguments in scripts using the parameter name: *%0* for the script name, *%1* for the first script parameter, and so on. For example, if you wanted to display the script name and the first argument passed to the script, you could enter

```
echo %0
echo %1
```

If you pass in more than nine parameters, the additional parameters are not lost. Instead, they are stored in a special parameter: *%** (percent + asterisk). The *%** parameter represents all arguments passed to the script and you can use the SHIFT command to examine additional parameters. If you call SHIFT without arguments, the script parameters are shifted by 1. This means the related value for *%0* is discarded and replaced by the related value for *%1*, and the related value for *%2* becomes the related value for *%1*, and so on. You can also specify where shifting begins so you can retain previous parameters if necessary. For example, if you use

```
shift /3
```

%4 becomes *%3*, *%5* becomes *%4*, and so on. But *%0*, *%1*, and *%2* are unaffected.

Getting Acquainted with Variables

In command-line scripting, what we commonly call variables are more properly called *environment variables*. Environment variables can come from many sources. Some variables are built into the operating system or derived from the system hardware during startup. These variables, called *built-in system variables*, are available to all Windows processes regardless of whether anyone is logged on interactively. System variables can also come from the Windows Registry. Other variables are set during logon and are called *built-in user variables*. The built-in user variables available are the same, no matter who is logged on to the computer. As you might expect, they are valid only during an actual logon session, that is, when a user is logged on.

You can see a listing of all the variables known in the current instance of the command shell by typing **set** at the prompt. In addition to the normal system and user variables, you can create variables whenever Windows is running, which is exactly what you'll do when you program in the command shell. You define variables for the current instance of the command shell using the SET command and the following syntax:

```
set variable_name=variable_value
```

such as

```
set working=C:\Work\Data
set value=5
set string="Hello World"
```

Some variables, including system and user environment variables, have special meaning in the command shell. These variables include *path*, *computername*, *homedrive*, and many other important environment variables. One environment variable that you should learn more about is *errorlevel*, which tracks the exit code of the most recently used command. If the command executes normally, the error level is zero (0). If an error occurs while executing the command, the error level is set to an appropriate nonzero value. Error values include

- **1** Indicates a general error
- **2** Indicates an execution error, meaning the command failed to execute properly
- **–2** Indicates a math error, such as when you create a number that is too large for the command shell to handle

You can work with the *errorlevel* variable in several ways. You can check for a specific error condition, such as

```
if "%ERRORLEVEL%"=="2" echo "An error occurred!"
```

Or, you can use the following special syntax and check for a condition equal to or greater than the specified exit code:

```
if errorlevel 2 echo "An error occurred!"
```

 Note You'll see more on *errorlevel* and *if* statements later in the chapter in the section titled "Using Conditional Statements."

When you are finished working with variables, it's good form to dispose of them. You do this to free memory used by the variable and prevent problems or unexpected results if you accidentally refer to the variable in the future. To clear out a variable, you simply set the variable equal to nothing, such as

```
set working=
```

Now the variable is cleared out of memory and is no longer available.

Using Variables in Scripts

In scripts, you'll use variables to store values as you perform various types of operations. Unlike most programming languages, you cannot declare a variable in a command-line script without simultaneously assigning it a value. This makes a certain amount of sense because from a practical point of view, there's no reason to have a variable that contains nothing. The sections that follow discuss key concepts for working with variables, including

- Variable names
- Variable values
- Variable substitution
- Variable scope

Naming Variables

The command shell tracks variable names in the case you use but doesn't care about the case when you are working with the variable. This means variable names aren't case-sensitive but are case-aware. Beyond this, very few restrictions apply to variable names and you can use just about any combination of letters, numbers, and characters to form the variable name. In fact, all the following variable names are technically valid:

```
2six
85
!
?
```

But why in the world you'd want to use such horrendous variable names is beyond me. With that said, how should you name your variables? Well, the most important rule to keep in mind is that variable names should be descriptive. Use names such as

```
System-name
CurrentStats
mergetotal
Net_Address
```

These descriptive variable names are helpful when you or someone else needs to modify the script. And notice that there are many ways to create multiple-word variable names. Although you are free to use whatever style you like, most programmers format multiword variable names with a lowercase initial letter on the first word and uppercase initial letter on each subsequent word. Why? The reason is simple: this is a standard naming convention. Following this convention, the variable names used previously are created as

```
systemName
currentStats
mergeTotal
netAddress
```

 Note Keep in mind that the command shell doesn't care about the case. Variable names are case-aware but they're not case-sensitive. This means that you could refer to the *systemName* variable as *SYSTEMNAME*, *systemname*, or even *sYStemNAMe*.

Setting Variable Values

As discussed previously, you define new variables using the following syntax:

```
set variable_name=variable_value
```

where *variable_name* is the variable name and *variable_value* is its related value. Spaces are valid in both names and values. So only use spaces around the equal sign (=) if you want the name and/or the value to include these spaces.

Unlike many programming languages, the command shell doesn't differentiate between various data types. All variables are stored as character strings. This is true even when you set the variable value to a number. Thus, the following values are stored as strings:

```
Current status:
311
"Error!"
12.75
```

using commands such as:

```
set varA=Current status:
set varB=311
set varC="Error!"
set varD=12.75
```

Don't forget that some characters are reserved in the command line, including @ < > & | ^. Before you use these characters, you must escape them with the caret symbol (^) as discussed in Chapter 2, "Getting the Most from the Command Line"—no matter where they occur in the variable value. For example, to set these literal string values:

```
2 & 3 = 5
2^3
```

you must set the variable value as follows:

```
2 ^& 3 = 5
2^^3
```

using statements such as

```
set example1=2 ^& 3 = 5
set example3=2^^3
```

Note An odd thing happens if you try to echo the example values. Instead of the equations you expect, you get either an error or an odd value. What is happening here is that when you echo the value, the special characters are reparsed. If you want to set a variable to a value that includes a special character and also be able to display this value to users, you must use three escape codes, meaning that you would use `set example1=2 ^^^& 3 = 5` or `set example2=2^^^^3`. This is necessary because the value is double parsed (once when the value is set and once when the value is displayed).

Substituting Variable Values

Variables wouldn't be very useful if the only way you could access them was with the SET command. Fortunately, you can access variable values in other ways. One of these ways is to use variable substitution to compare a variable name with its actual value. You saw this type of substitution at work in the following line from a previous example in this chapter:

```
if "%ERRORLEVEL%"=="2" echo "An error occurred!"
```

Here, you are determining whether the value of the *errorlevel* environment variable is equal to 2 and, if it is, you display text stating that an error occurred. The percent signs surrounding the variable name tell the command shell you are referencing a variable. Without these percent signs, Windows would perform a literal comparison of "ERRORLEVEL" and "2". Note also the use of quotation marks in the example. The quotation marks ensure an exact comparison of string values.

Another way to use substitution is to replace a variable name with its actual value. For example, you might want to create a script that can be run on different computers, so rather than hard-coding the path to the system root directory as C:\Windows, you could use the environment variable *systemroot*, which references the system root of the particular computer being accessed. With this in mind, you use the following line of code in your script:

```
cd %SYSTEMROOT%\System32
```

instead of this line of code:

```
cd C:\Windows\System32
```

You can also use variable substitution when you are assigning variable values, such as

```
systemPath=%SystemRoot%\System32
```

Variable substitution can be quite powerful. Consider the code snippet shown as Listing 3-3.

Listing 3-3 Sample Script Header

```
@echo off
@if not "%OS%"=="Windows_NT" goto :EXIT
@if "%1"=="" (set INFO=echo && set SEXIT=1) else (set INFO=rem &&
set SEXIT=0)

%INFO% ************************
%INFO% Script: SystemInfo.bat
%INFO% Creation Date: 2/2/2004
%INFO% Last Modified: 3/15/2004
%INFO% Author: William R. Stanek
%INFO% E-mail: williamstanek@aol.com
%INFO% ************************
%INFO% Description: Displays system configuration information
%INFO%              Including system name, IP configuration
%INFO%              and Windows version.
%INFO% ************************
%INFO% Files: Stores output in c:\current-sys.txt.
%INFO% ************************

@if "%SEXIT%"=="1" goto :EXIT

@title "Configure Scheduling..."
cls
color 07
```

Listing 3-3 is a standard header that I use in some of my scripts. The first *if* statement checks to see what operating system is running. If it is Windows 2000 or later, meaning Windows 2000, Windows XP, or Windows Server 2003, the script continues execution. Otherwise a *goto* subroutine is called. The second *if* statement checks the value of the first argument passed in to the script. If the script is called with no arguments, instances of *%INFO%* are replaced with *echo*, which writes the script documentation to the output. If the script is called with one or more arguments, instances of *%INFO%* are replaced with *rem* to designate that the associated lines are comments.

 Note Don't worry if you don't understand the example completely. You'll learn all about conditional execution and subroutines later in the chapter in the sections titled, "Command-Line Selection Statements" and "Creating Subroutines and Procedures."

Localizing Variable Scope

Changes you make to variables in the command shell using *set* are localized, meaning that they apply only to the current command shell instance or to command shells started within the current command shell (nested command shells) and are not available to other system processes. Further, once you exit the command shell in which variables were created, the variables no longer exist.

Sometimes you may want to limit the scope of variables even further than their current command-shell process. To do this, you can create a local scope within a script that ensures any variable changes are localized to that specific area within the script. Later, you can end the local scope and restore the environment to its original settings.

You can mark the start of a local scope within a script using the SETLOCAL command and then end the local scope with an ENDLOCAL command. Several events take place when you use these commands. The call to SETLOCAL creates a snapshot of the environment. Any changes you make within the scope are then localized and discarded when you call ENDLOCAL. An example using SETLOCAL and ENDLOCAL follows:

```
@echo off
set sysCount=0
set deviceCount=0

rem Start localization
setlocal
set sysCount=5
set deviceCount=5
echo Local count: %sysCount% system edits ^& %deviceCount% device
checks
endlocal

echo Count: %sysCount% system edits ^& %deviceCount% device checks
```

The output of the script is

```
Local count: 5 system edits & 5 device checks
Count: 0 system edits & 0 device checks
```

As you can see, local scopes behave much like nested command shells. As with the nested command shells, you can nest several layers of localization. And though each layer inherits the environment settings of its parent, any changes in the nested layer are not reflected in the parent environment.

Using Mathematical Expressions

At times, you'll want to perform some kind of mathematical operation in your scripts and assign the results to a variable. As with most programming languages, the command shell allows you to write mathematical expressions using a variety of operators, including

- Arithmetic operators to perform standard mathematical operations (such as addition, subtraction, multiplication, and division)
- Assignment operators that combine an assignment operation (symbolized by the equal sign) with an arithmetic operation
- Comparison operators that compare values and are usually used with *if* statements
- Bitwise operators that allow you to manipulate the sequences of binary values

Math operations are performed using set with the /A (arithmetic) parameter, such as

```
set /a theTotal=18+2
set /a theTotal=18*2
set /a theTotal=18/2
```

All mathematical expressions are evaluated using 32-bit signed integer arithmetic. This allows for values -2^{32} to $2^{32}-1$. If you exceed this range, you'll get an arithmetic error (code -2) instead of the intended value.

The most commonly used operators are those for arithmetic, assignment, and comparison. Arithmetic and assignment operators are discussed in the sections that follow. Comparison operators are discussed in the section titled "Making Comparisons in If Statements," later in this chapter. Pay particular attention to the additional discussions on operator precedence and simulating exponents in scripts.

Working with Arithmetic and Assignment Operators

You use arithmetic operators to perform basic math operations on numerical values. These values can be expressed literally as a number, such as 5, or as a variable that contains the value you want to work with, such as *%TOTAL%*.

Table 3-2 summarizes the available arithmetic and assignment operators. Most of the arithmetic operators are fairly straightforward. You use * in multiplication, / in division, + in addition, and – in subtraction. You use the equal sign (=) to assign values to variables. You use % (modulus) to obtain the remainder from division. For example, if you divide 8 into 60, the answer is 7 Remainder 4; the value 4 is what the result would be if you use the modulus operator.

Examples of working with arithmetic operators follow:

set /a theCount=5+3

set /a theCount=%nServers% + %nWstations%

set /a theCount=%nServers% - 1

Tip Earlier, I stated that everything stored in a variable is a string, and that remains true. However, the command shell can detect when a string contains only numerals, and this is what allows you to use variables in expressions. The key detail to remember is to use the proper syntax for substitution, which is *%variableName%*.

Table 3-2. Arithmetic and Assignment Operators

Arithmetic Operators	Assignment Operators
+ (Addition)	+= (Increment, that is, add and assign)
- (Subtraction)	-= (Decrement, that is, subtract and assign)
* (Multiplication)	*= (Scale up, that is, multiply and assign)
/ (Division)	/= (Scale down, that is, divide and assign)
% (Modulus)	%= (Modulus and assign)

You use assignment operators to increment, decrement, scale up, or scale down. These operators combine arithmetic and assignment operation functions. For example, the += operator is used to increment a value and combines the effects of the + operator and the = operator. Thus, the following two expressions are equivalent and yield the identical results when entered at the command line:

```
set /a total=total+1
set /a total+=1
```

Understanding Operator Precedence

One thing you should understand when working with mathematic operations is operator precedence. Operator precedence determines what happens when the command shell must evaluate an expression that involves more than one operator. For example:

```
set /a total=8+3*4
```

If evaluated from left to right, this expression equals 44 (8+3=11, 11*4=44). But as in standard mathematics, that's not how the command line evaluates the expression. Instead, the command shell evaluates the expression as 20 (3*4=12, 8+12=20) because the precedence of operations is the following:

1. Modulus
2. Multiplication and division
3. Addition and subtraction

 Note When an expression contains multiple operations at the same precedence level, these operations are performed from left to right. Hence set /a total=10-4+2 equals 8 (10-4=6, 6+2=8).

However, as with standard mathematics, you can use parenthetical grouping to ensure numbers are processed in a certain way. This means you can use the expression

```
set /a total=(8+3)*4
```

to ensure that the command-line interprets the expression as (8+3=11, 11*4=44).

Simulating Exponents

Although you can perform many mathematical operations at the command line, there is no way to raise values to exponents. You can, however, perform these operations manually. For example, the easiest way to get a value for 2^3 is to enter

```
set /a total=2*2*2
```

The result is 8. Similarly, you can get a value for 10^5 by entering

```
set /a total=10*10*10*10*10
```

The result is 100,000.

Command-Line Selection Statements

Now that you know how to work with variables and form expressions, let's look at something more advanced: selection statements used with the command line. When you want to control the flow of execution based upon conditions known only at run time, you'll use

- *if* to execute a statement when a condition is true, such as if the operating system is Windows 2000 or later. Otherwise, the statement is bypassed.
- *if not* to execute a statement when a condition is false, such as if a system doesn't have a C:\Windows directory. Otherwise, the statement is bypassed.

- *if...else* to execute a statement if a condition is matched (true or false) and to otherwise execute the second statement.

Although some of the previous examples in this chapter have used conditional execution, we haven't discussed the syntax for these statements or the associated comparison operators. If your background doesn't include programming, you probably will be surprised by the power and flexibility of these statements.

Using If

The *if* statement is used for conditional branching. It can be used to route script execution through two different paths. Its basic syntax is

```
if condition (statement1) [else (statement2)]
```

Here each statement can be a single command or multiple commands chained, piped, or grouped within parentheses. The condition is any expression that returns a Boolean value of True or False when evaluated. The *else* clause is optional, meaning you can also use the syntax

```
if condition (statement)
```

Tip Technically, parentheses aren't required, but using them is a good idea, especially if the condition includes an *echo* statement or a command with parameters. If you don't use parentheses in these instances, everything that follows the statement on the current line will be interpreted as part of the statement, which usually results in an error.

The *if* statement works like this: If the *condition* is true, then *statement1* is executed. Otherwise *statement2* is executed (if it is provided). In no case will both the *if* and the *else* clauses be executed. Consider the following example:

```
if "%1"=="1" (echo is one) else (echo is not one)
```

Here if the first parameter passed to the script is 1, then "is one" is written to the output. Otherwise, "is not one" is written to the output.

The command shell expects only one statement after each condition. Typically, the statement is a single command to execute. If you want to execute multiple commands, you'll need to use one of the command piping, chaining, or group techniques, as in this example:

```
if "%1"=="1" (hostname & ver & ipconfig /all) else (netstat -a)
```

Here all three commands between parentheses will execute if the first parameter value is 1.

Using If Not

When you want to execute a statement only if a condition is false, you can use *if not*. The basic syntax is

```
if not condition (statement1) [else (statement2)]
```

Here the command shell evaluates the *condition*. If it is false, the command shell executes the statement. Otherwise, the command doesn't execute and the command shell proceeds to the next statement. The *else* clause is optional, meaning you can also use the syntax

```
if not condition (statement1)
```

Consider the following example:

```
if not errorlevel 0 (echo An error has occurred!) & (goto :EXIT)
```

Here you check for error conditions other than zero. If no error has occurred (meaning the error level is zero), the command shell continues to the next statement. Otherwise, the command shell writes "An error has occurred!" to the output and exits the script. (You'll learn all about *goto* and subroutines later in the chapter.)

Using If Defined and If Not Defined

The final types of *if* statements you can use are *if defined* and *if not defined*. These statements are designed to help you check for the existence of variables, and their respective syntaxes are

```
if defined variable statement
```

and

```
if not defined variable statement
```

Both statements are useful in your shell scripts. In the first case, you execute a command if the specified variable exists. In the second case, you execute a command if the specified variable does not exist. Consider the following example:

```
if defined numServers (echo Servers: %numServers%)
```

Here, if the *numServers* variable is defined, the script writes output. Otherwise, the script continues to the next statement.

Nesting Ifs

A nested *if* is an *if* statement within an *if* statement. Nested *if*s are very common in programming, and command-shell programming is no exception. When you nest *if* statements, pay attention to the following points:

1. Use parentheses to define blocks of code and the @ symbol to designate the start of the nested *if* statement.

2. Remember that an *else* statement always refers to the nearest *if* statement that is within the same block as the *else* statement and that is not already associated with another *else* statement.

Here is an example:

```
if "%1"=="1" (
@if "%2"=="2" (hostname & ver) else (ver)) else (hostname & ver &
netstat -a)
```

The first *else* statement is associated with `if "%2"=="2"`. The final *else* statement is associated with `if "%1"=="1"`.

Making Comparisons in If Statements

Frequently, the expression used to control *if* statements will involve comparison operators as shown in previous examples. The most basic type of string comparison is when you compare two strings using the equality operator (=), such as

`if stringA==stringB statement`

Here, you are performing a literal comparison of the strings and if they are exactly identical, the command statement is executed. This syntax works for literal strings but is not ideal for scripts. Parameters and arguments may contain spaces or there may be no value at all for a variable. In this case, you may get an error if you perform literal comparisons. Instead, use double quotation marks to perform a string comparison and prevent most errors, such as

`if "%varA%"=="%varB%" statement`

or

`if "%varA%"=="string" statement`

String comparisons are always case-sensitive unless you specify otherwise with the */i* switch. The */i* switch tells the command shell to ignore the case in the comparison, and you can use it as follows:

`if /I "%1"=="a" (echo A) else (echo is not A)`

To perform more advanced equality tests, you'll need to use the comparison operators shown in Table 3-3. These operators are used in place of the standard equality operator, such as

`if "%varA%" equ "%varB%" (echo The values match!)`

Table 3-3. Using Comparison Operators

Operator	Description
equ	Checks for equality and evaluates to true if the values are equal
neq	Checks for inequality and evaluates to true if the values are not equal
lss	Checks for less than condition and evaluates to true if *value1* is less than *value2*

Table 3-3. Using Comparison Operators

Operator	Description
leq	Checks for less than or equal to condition, and evaluates to true if *value1* is less than or equal to *value2*
gtr	Checks for greater than condition and evaluates to true if *value1* is greater than *value2*
geq	Checks for greater than or equal to condition, and evaluates to true if *value1* is greater than or equal to *value2*

Command Line Iteration Statements

When you want to execute a command or a series of commands repeatedly, you'll use the *for* statement. The *for* statement is a powerful construct, and before you skip this section because you think you know how the *for* statement works, think again. The *for* statement is designed specifically to work with the command-shell environment and is very different from any other *for* statement you may have worked with in other programming languages. Unlike most other *for* statements, the one in the command line is designed to help you iterate through groups of files and directories, and to parse text files, strings, and command output on a line-by-line basis.

Iteration Essentials

The command shell has several different forms of *for* statements. Still, the basic form of all *for* statements is

```
for iterator do (statement)
```

Here the iterator is used to control the execution of the *for* loop. For each step or element in the iterator, the specified *statement* is executed. The *statement* can be a single command or multiple commands chained, piped, or grouped within parentheses.

The iterator usually consists of an initialization variable and a set of elements to execute against, such as a group of files or a range of values to step through. Initialization variables are essentially placeholders for the values you want to work with. When you work with initialization variables, keep in mind the following:

- Iterator variables only exist within the context of a *for* loop.
- Iterator variable names must be in the range from a to z or A to Z, such as *%%A*, *%%B*, or *%%C*.
- Iterator variable names are case-sensitive, meaning *%%a* is different from *%%A*.

As Table 3-4 shows, the various structures used with *for* statements have specific purposes and forms. When the *for* statement is initialized, iterator variables, such as *%%B*, are replaced with their actual values. These values come from the element set specified in the *for* statement and could consist of a list of files, a list of directories, a range of values, and so on.

Table 3-4. Forms for Iteration

Iteration Purpose	Form Syntax
Sets of files	for *%%variable* in (fileSet) do *statement*
Sets of directories	for /D *%%variable* in (directorySet) do *statement*
Files in subdirectories	for /R [*path*] *%%variable* in (fileSet) do *statement*
Stepping through a series of values	for /L *%%variable* in (*stepRange*) do *statement*
Parsing text files, strings, and command output	for /F ["*options*"] *%%variable* in (*source*) do *statement*

Real World The forms provided are *for* scripts. You can also use for statements interactively at the command line. In this case, use *%variable* instead of *%%variable*. Beyond this, *for* statements within scripts or at the command line are handled in precisely the same way.

Stepping through a Series of Values

The "traditional" way to use *for* statements is to step through a range of values and perform tasks using these values. You can do this in the command shell and the basic syntax of this type of *for* loop is

```
for /l %%variable in (start,step,end) do (statement)
```

This type of *for* statement operates as follows. First, the command shell initializes internal *start*, *step*, and *end* variables to the values you've specified. Next, it compares the start value with the end value to determine if the statement should be executed, yielding a true condition if the start value can be incremented or decremented as specified in the step and a false condition otherwise. In the case of a true condition, the command shell executes the statement using the start value, then increments or decrements the start value by the step value specified and afterward, repeats this process. In the case of a false condition, the command shell exits the *for* statement, moving on to the next statement in the script.

Consider the following example that counts from 0 to 10 by 2's:

```
for /l %%B in (0,2,10) do echo %%B
```

The output is

```
0
2
4
6
8
10
```

You can also use a negative step value to move through a range in decreasing values. You could count from 10 to 0 by 2's as follows:

```
for /l %%B in (10,-2,0) do echo %%B
```

The output is

```
10
8
6
4
2
0
```

Iterating Through Groups of Files

A more powerful way to use *for* statements in the command shell is to use them to work with files and directories. The *for* statement syntax for working with groups of files is

```
for %%variable in (fileSet) do (statement)
```

Here you use *fileSet* to specify a set of files that you want to work with. A file set can be

- Individual files as specified by a filename, such as MyFile.txt
- Groups of files specified with wildcards, such as *.txt
- Multiple files or groups of files with spaces separating file names, such as *.txt *.rtf *.doc

Now that you know the basic rules, working with files is easy. For example, if you want to list all text files in an application directory, you can use the following command in a script:

```
for %%B in (C:\Working\*.txt) do (echo %%B)
```

Here B is the initialization variable, C:\Working*.txt specifies that you want to work with all text files in the C:\Working directory, and the statement to execute is *echo %%B*, which tells the command shell to display the current value of *%%B* each time it iterates through the *for* loop. The result is that a list of the text files in the directory is written to the output.

You could extend this example to examine all .txt, .rtf, and .doc files like this:

```
for %%B in (%AppDir%\*.txt %AppDir%\*.rtf %AppDir%\*.doc) do (echo
%%B)
```

You can also use multiple commands using piping, grouping, and chaining techniques, such as

```
for %%B in (%AppDir%\*.txt %AppDir%\*.rtf %AppDir%\*.doc) do (echo %%B
& move C:\Data)
```

Here you list the .txt, .rtf, and .doc files in the location specified by the *AppDir* variable and then move the files to the C:\Data directory.

Iterating Through Directories

If you want to work with directories rather than files, you can use the following *for* statement style:

```
for /d %%variable in (directorySet) do (statement)
```

Here you use *directorySet* to specify the group of directories you want to work with. Iterating directories works exactly like iterating files, except you specify directory paths rather than file paths. If you wanted to list all the base directories under *%SystemRoot%*, you would do this as follows:

```
for /d %%B in (%SystemRoot%\*) do echo %%B
```

On Windows Server 2003, a partial result list would be similar to

```
C:\Windows\AppPatch
C:\Windows\Cluster
C:\Windows\Config
C:\Windows\Cursors
C:\Windows\Debug
```

Note Note that the *for /d* loop iterates through the specified directory set but doesn't include subdirectories of those directories. To access subdirectories (and indeed the whole directory tree structure), you use *for /r* loops, which I'll discuss in a moment.

You can specify multiple base directories by separating the directory names with spaces, such as

```
for /d %%B in (%SystemRoot% %SystemRoot%\*) do echo %%B
```

Here you examine the *%SystemRoot%* directory itself and then the directories immediately below it. So now your list of directories would start with C:\Windows (if this is the system root) and continue with the other directories listed previously.

You can also combine file and directory iteration techniques to perform actions against all files in a directory set, such as

```
for /d %%B in (%APPDATA% %APPDATA%\*) do (
@for %%C in ("%%B\*.txt") do echo %%C)
```

The first *for* statement returns a list of top-level directories under *%APPDATA%*, which also includes *%APPDATA%* itself. The second *for* statement iterates all .txt files in each of these directories. Note the @ symbol before the second *for* statement. As with *if* statements, this indicated the second *for* statement is nested and is required to ensure proper execution. The double quotations with the file set ("%%B*.txt") ensure that directory and file names containing spaces are handled properly.

Because you'll often want to work with subdirectories as well as directories, the command shell provides *for /r* statements. Using *for /r* statements, you can examine an entire directory tree from a starting point specified as a path. The syntax is

```
for /r [path] %%variable in (fileSet) do (statement)
```

Here path sets the base of the directory tree you want to work with, such as C:\. The path is not required, however, and if the path is omitted, the current working directory is assumed.

Using a *for /r* statement, you could extend the previous example to list all .txt files on the C: drive without needing a double *for* loop, as shown here:

```
for /r C:\ %%B in (*.txt) do echo %%B
```

As you can see, *for /r* statements are simpler than double *for* loops and more powerful. You can even combine /r and /d without needing a double loop. In this example, you obtain a listing of all directories and subdirectories under *%SystemRoot%*:

```
for /r %SystemRoot% /d %%B in (*) do echo %%B
```

Parsing File Content and Output

Just as you can work with file and directory names, you can also work with the contents of files and the output of commands. To do this, you'll use the following *for* statement style:

```
for /f ["options"] %%variable in (source) do (statement)
```

Here, *options* sets the text matching options, *source* specifies where the text comes from, which could be a text file, a string, or command output, and *statement* specifies what commands should be performed on matching text. Each line of text in the source is handled like a record where fields in the record are delimited by a specific character, such as a tab or a space (which are the default delimiters). Using substitution, the command shell then replaces placeholder variables in the statement with actual values.

Consider the following line of text from a source file:

```
William Stanek Engineering Williams@adatum.com 3408
```

One way of thinking of this line of text is as a record with five fields:

- **First Name**   William
- **Last Name**   Stanek
- **Department**   Engineering
- **E-Mail Address**   Williams@adatum.com
- **Phone Extension**   3408

To parse this and other similar lines in the associated file, you could use the following *for* statement:

```
for /f "tokens=1-5" %%A in (current-users.txt) do (
@echo Name: %%A %%B Depart: %%C E-mail: %%D Ext: %%E)
```

Here you specify that you want to work with the first five fields (token fields separated by spaces or tabs by default) and identified by iterator variables, starting with *%%A*, which means the first field is *%%A*, the second *%%B*, and so on. The resulting output would look like this:

```
Name: William Stanek Depart: Engineering E-Mail: Williams@adatum.com
Ext: 3408
```

Table 3-5 shows a complete list of options that you can use. Examples and descriptions of the examples are included.

Table 3-5.   Options for File Content and Command Output Parsing

Option	Description	Example	Example Description
eol	Sets the end-of-line comment character. Everything after the end-of-line comment character is considered to be a comment.	"eol=#"	Sets # as the end-of-line comment character.
skip	Sets the number of lines to skip at the beginning of files.	"skip=5"	Tells the command shell to skip lines 1 through 5 in the source file.
delims	Sets delimiters to use for fields. The defaults are space and tab.	"delims=,.:"	Specifies that commas, periods, and colons are delimiters.

Table 3-5. Options for File Content and Command Output Parsing

Option	Description	Example	Example Description
tokens	Sets which token fields from each source line are to be used. You can specify up to 26 tokens provided you start with a or A as the first iterator variable. By default, only the first token is examined.	"tokens=1,3" "tokens=2-5"	First example sets fields to use as 1 and 3. Second example sets fields 2, 3, 4, and 5 as fields to use.
usebackq	Specifies that you can use quotation marks in the source designator: double quotation marks for file names, back quotation marks for command to execute, and single quotation marks for a literal string.	"usebackq"	—

To see how additional options can be used, consider the following example:

```
for /f "skip=3 eol=; tokens=3-5" %%C in (current-users.txt) do (
@echo Depart: %%C E-mail: %%D Ext: %%E)
```

Here, three options are used. The *skip* option is used to skip the first three lines of the file. The *eol* option is used to specify the end-of-line comment character as a semicolon (;). Finally, the *tokens* option specifies that tokens 3 to 5 should be placed in iterator variables, starting with %%C.

With tokens, you can specify which fields you want to work with in many different ways. Here are some examples:

- **tokens=2,3,7** Use fields 2, 3, and 7.
- **tokens=3-5** Use fields 3, 4, and 5.
- **tokens=*** Examine each line in its entirety and do not break into fields.

When you work with text files, you should note that all blank lines in text files are skipped and that multiple source files can be specified with wild cards or by entering the file names in a space-separated list, such as

```
for /f "skip=3 eol=; tokens=3-5" %%C in (data1.txt data2.txt) do (
@echo Depart: %%C E-mail: %%D Ext: %%E)
```

If a file name contains a space or you want to execute a command, specify the *usebackq* option and quotation marks, such as

```
for /f "tokens=3-5 usebackq" %%C in ("user data.txt") do (
@echo Depart: %%C E-mail: %%D Ext: %%E)
```

or

```
for /f "tokens=3-5 usebackq" %%C in (`type "user data.txt"`) do (
@echo Depart: %%C E-mail: %%D Ext: %%E)
```

Tip Remember the backquote (`) is used with commands and the single quotation mark (') is used with string literals. In print, these characters no doubt look very similar. However, on a standard keyboard, the backquote (`) is on the same key as the tilde (~) and the single quotation mark (') is on the same key as a double quotation mark (").

Note In the second example, I use the TYPE command to write the contents of the file to standard output. This is meant to be an example of using a command with the backquote.

Speaking of quotation marks, you use quotation marks when you want to process strings and variable values. Here, you enclose the string or variable name you want to work with in double quotation marks to ensure the string or variable can be evaluated properly. You do not, however, need to use the *usebackq* option.

Consider the following example:

```
set value=All,Some,None
for /f "delims=, tokens=1,3" %%A in ("%VALUE%") do (echo %%A %%B)
```

The output is

```
All None
```

Creating Subroutines and Procedures

Normally, the Windows command shell executes scripts line by line, starting at the beginning of the file and continuing until the end of the file. You can change the order of execution and to do this, you use either of the following:

- **Subroutines** With subroutines, you jump to a label within the current script, and execution proceeds to the end of the file.

- **Procedures** With procedures, you call another script and execution of the called script proceeds to the end of its file, and then control returns to the line following the call statement in the original script.

As you can see, the difference between a subroutine and a procedure is primarily in what you want to do. Additionally, while arguments passed in to the script are available in a *goto* subroutine directly, the list of arguments within a called procedure is changed to include the procedure name rather than the script name as argument 0 (*%0*).

Using Subroutines

Subroutines have two parts:

- A *goto* call that specifies the subroutine to which you want to jump
- A label that designates the start of the subroutine

Consider the following subroutine call:

```
if "%1"=="1" goto SUB1
```

Here if the first parameter passed into the script is a 1, the subroutine called *SUB1* is called and the command shell would jump to the corresponding subroutine label. To create a label, you enter a keyword on a line by itself, beginning with a colon, such as

```
:SUB1
```

Although labels can contain just about any valid type of character, you'll usually want to use alphanumeric characters as this makes the labels easy to read when you or someone else is going through the code.

When you use *goto*, execution of the script resumes at the line following the target label and continues to the end of the file, unless it's necessary to process any procedure calls or *goto* statements encountered along the way. If the label is before the current position in the script, the command shell can go back to an earlier part of the script. This can create an endless loop (unless there is a control to bypass the *goto* statement). Here's an example of an endless loop:

```
:START
.
.
.
goto START
```

If the label is after the *goto* statement, you can skip commands and jump ahead to a new section of the script, such as

```
goto MIDDLE
.
.
.
:MIDDLE
```

Here, execution of the script jumps to the :MIDDLE label and continues to the end of the file. You cannot go back to the unexecuted commands unless you use another *goto* statement.

Sometimes you may not want to execute the rest of the script and instead will want to exit the script after executing subroutine statements. To do this, create an exit label and then go to the exit at the end of the routine, such as

```
goto MIDDLE
.
.
.
:MIDDLE
.
.
.
goto EXIT
.
.
.
:EXIT
```

Listing 3-4 shows a detailed example of working with *goto* and labels. In this example, the value of the script's first parameter determines what subroutine is executed. The first *if* statement handles the case when no parameter is passed in by displaying an error message and exiting. The *goto EXIT* statement following the *if* statements handles the case when an invalid parameter is passed in. Here, the script simply goes to the :EXIT label.

Listing 3-4 Using goto
```
@echo off
if "%1"=="" (echo Error: No parameter passed with script!) & (goto
EXIT)
if "%1"=="1" goto SUBROUTINE1
if "%1"=="2" goto SUBROUTINE2
if "%1"=="3" goto SUBROUTINE3
goto EXIT

:SUBROUTINE1
echo In subroutine 1
goto EXIT

:SUBROUTINE2
echo In subroutine 2
goto EXIT

:SUBROUTINE3
echo In subroutine 3
goto EXIT

:EXIT
echo Exiting...
```

Tip Remember if the label you call doesn't exist, you'll get an error when the end of the file is reached during the search for the nonexistent label, and then the script exits without executing the other subsequent commands. Old-school command-shell programmers who have been at this for a long time, like me, like to use *goto EXIT* and then provide an actual :EXIT label, as shown in the previous example. However, the command interpreter for Windows Server 2003 and Windows XP supports a target label of :EOF, which transfers control to the end of the file. This makes :EOF an easy way to exit a batch script without defining a label.

Using Procedures

You use procedures to call other scripts without exiting the current script. When you do this, the command shell executes the named script, executing its commands, and then control returns to the original script, starting with the first line following the original call. Consider the following example:

```
if "%1"=="1" call system-checks
if "%1"=="2" call C:\scripts\log-checks
```

 Caution If you forget to use the *call* statement and reference a script name within a script, the second script executes, but control isn't returned to the caller.

Here the first call is made to a script expected to be in the current working directory or in the command path. The second call is made to a script with the file path c:\scripts\log-checks.

Any arguments passed to the original script are passed to the called script with one change: The list of arguments is updated to include the procedure name as argument 0 (%0). These procedure-specific arguments remain in effect until the end of the file is reached and control returns to the original script.

You can also pass arguments to the called script, such as

```
set Arg1=mailer1
set Arg2=dc2
set Arg3=web3
call system-checks Arg1 Arg2 Arg3
```

Now within the called script, the variables Arg1, Arg2, and Arg3 are available.

Chapter 4
Scheduling Tasks to Run Automatically

As an administrator, you probably find yourself repeatedly performing the same or similar tasks every day. You may also find that you have to come in to work early or stay late to perform tasks during non-business hours. These tasks might be routine maintenance activities, such as deleting temporary files so that disks don't run out of space or backing up important data. Tasks might be more involved processes, such as searching the event logs on all business servers for problems that need to be resolved. The good news is that if you can break down these tasks into a series of steps, chances are that you can also automate these tasks and Microsoft Windows provides several ways to do this, including

- **Schtasks** Advanced command-line utility for running commands, scripts, and programs on a scheduled basis. Tasks can be scheduled to run one time only, on a minute-by-minute basis, at a specific interval (such as hourly, daily, weekly, or monthly), at system startup, at logon, or whenever the system is idle.

- **Task Scheduler** Graphical utility for running commands, scripts, and programs on a scheduled basis. Task Scheduler performs the same operations as the Schtasks command-line utility, allowing you to use Task Scheduler and Schtasks together, and to manage tasks created in either utility by using one tool or the other.

Because Schtasks and Task Scheduler can be used interchangeably, this chapter discusses how both utilities can be used to automate the running of programs, command-line utilities, and scripts. In most cases, you'll find that it is useful to know both utilities and that even when you use Task Scheduler for point-and-click convenience, you'll still work with the command line.

Scheduling Tasks on Local and Remote Systems

Whatever you can execute at the command line can be configured as a scheduled task, including command-line utilities, scripts, applications, shortcuts, and documents. You can also specify command-line arguments. At times when you schedule tasks, you'll do so for the computer to which you are currently logged on (that is, a local system). More typically, however, when you schedule tasks you'll do so for remote systems throughout your network from your local computer (that is, a remote computer).

Introducing Task Scheduling

The following Windows features work together to enable local and remote task scheduling:

- **Task Scheduler** The Windows service that controls task scheduling. This service must be running for each system on which you want to schedule tasks. Task Scheduler logs on as the LocalSystem account by default and usually doesn't have adequate permissions to perform administrative tasks. Because of this, you should configure each task individually to use an account with adequate user privileges and access rights to run the tasks you want to schedule. You should also make sure that the Task Scheduler service is configured to start automatically on all the systems for which you want to schedule tasks. Be sure to set the Task Scheduler startup and logon account options appropriately.

- **File And Printer Sharing For Microsoft Networks** The Windows networking component that allows other computers to access resources on a system. This component must be installed and enabled on each system that you want to access and control remotely through the task scheduler. It also enables many other remote-management functions.

 Note Errors that you may see if the File And Printer Sharing For Microsoft Networks component isn't installed or enabled include "RPC Server unavailable" and "Network path not found." See the section in Chapter 16 titled "Configuring Additional Networking Components" in *Microsoft Windows Server 2003 Administrator's Pocket Consultant* (Microsoft Press, 2003), for details on installing and configuring networking components.

Each scheduled task runs only one program, utility, or script, and can be configured to run

- At a specific time and date, such as at 5:45 P.M. on October 25, 2004
- At a specified interval, such as every Monday, Wednesday, and Friday at 5:45 P.M.

- When a specific system event occurs, such as when someone logs on to the system

Event-based tasks deserve special attention because they don't always work as you might expect and include tasks triggered by

- **System Start** If you schedule a task to run when the system starts, Task Scheduler runs the task as a noninteractive process whenever the computer is started. The task will continue to run until it finishes, is terminated, or the system is shut down. Keep in mind that only the owner of the task or an administrator can terminate running tasks.

- **System Logon** If you schedule a task to run when a user logs on, Task Scheduler runs that task whenever anyone logs on (regardless of who configured the task to run), and continues to run until it finishes, is terminated, or the user logs off. Logon tasks can run interactively or noninteractively, depending on how they are configured.

Tip If a user configures an interactive task using his or her logon and someone else logs on, the task runs with the original user's permissions and may not terminate when the other user logs off (because it is owned by someone else and the current user may or may not have appropriate permissions to terminate the task). Further, with Fast User Switching on Windows XP, logon tasks do not run when you switch users. Logon tasks only run when someone logs on while all users are logged off.

- **System Idle** If you schedule a task to run when the system is idle, Task Scheduler runs the task whenever there is no user activity for a specified amount of time. For example, you might create a task that runs only when the system has been idle for five minutes. Keep in mind, however, that subsequent user activity will not terminate the task. The task will continue to run until it finishes or is terminated.

To run multiple commands, programs, and utilities, you can create a command-line script that performs the necessary tasks. Here, you'll want the script to run with specific user or administrator credentials to ensure that the script has the necessary permissions and access rights. The script should also configure whatever user settings are necessary to ensure that everything it does is under its control and that domain user settings, such as drive mappings, are available as necessary.

Real World When you configure tasks to run, you can specify the user account and logon password to use when the task runs. With recurring tasks, this tactic can lead to problems, especially if permissions or passwords change—and they inevitably do. If account permissions or passwords change, you'll need to edit the task's properties and supply the new logon credentials for the account.

Accessing and Scheduling Tasks

Any user can schedule a task on the local computer, and they can view and change the tasks that they've scheduled. Administrators can schedule, view, and change all tasks on the local computer. To schedule, view, or change tasks on remote computers, you must be a member of the Administrators group on the remote computer, or you must be able to provide the credentials of an Administrator of the remote computer when prompted.

Regardless of whether you use the Scheduled Task Wizard or Schtasks, you can access and manage a system's tasks using the Scheduled Tasks folder, which you can think of as your central interface for task scheduling. You can access the Scheduled Tasks folder on a local system with either of the following techniques:

- Start Control Panel and then click Scheduled Tasks.
- Start Windows Explorer, click My Computer, then Control Panel, and then Scheduled Tasks.

In a Windows domain, you can access the Scheduled Tasks folder on a remote system by completing the following steps:

1. Start Windows Explorer, then use the My Network Places node to navigate to the computer you want to work with.
2. Click the computer's icon, and then click Scheduled Tasks, as shown in Figure 4-1.

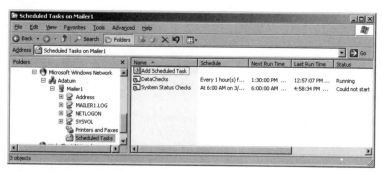

Figure 4-1. *The Scheduled Tasks folder shows any tasks currently configured on the system by name, run time, and status.*

Real World   In a workgroup, the easiest way to access the Scheduled Tasks folder on a remote system is to use a Remote Desktop connection. You also can use this technique for computers in a domain, of course, but it isn't necessary. In either case, you must first ensure that the Allow Users To Connect Remotely To This Computer check box is selected on the Remote tab of the System utility in Control Panel. Next, set up a remote desktop connection by performing the following steps:

1. Click Start, Programs or All Programs, Administrative Tools, and finally Remote Desktops. This starts the Remote Desktops console.

2. Right-click Remote Desktops below the Console Root in the left pane and then select Add New Connection.

3. Type the computer name or IP address of the workgroup or domain computer you wish to access and the user name and logon information, and then click OK.

For a workgroup computer, you use a user account that is on the computer you are accessing. Afterward, connect to the computer using the Remote Desktop connection by right-clicking the connection and selecting Connect. Now start Windows Explorer on the remote computer and navigate to the Scheduled Tasks folder.

Notice in Figure 4-1 that the Scheduled Tasks folder shows

- **Name**   The name of the task. Task names can be any string of characters and, like other task properties, are set when you create the task.

- **Schedule**   The run schedule of the task. "Disabled" means that task has been disabled and will not run.

- **Next Run Time**   The next date and time the task will run. "Never" indicates the task will not run again after the scheduled run time and is probably a one-time task.

- **Last Run Time**   The last date and time the task ran. "Never" indicates the task has not run for the first time.

- **Status**   The current status of the task. "Running" indicates the task has been started by the task scheduler and is running. "Could not start" indicates the task could not be started and that there is a problem with the task.

- **Last Result**   The exit error code. An error code of zero indicates no error occurred. Any other value indicates some type of error occurred.

- **Creator**   The user name of the person who created the scheduled task.

Monitoring Scheduled Tasks

The Task Scheduler service doesn't verify the information you provide or the availability of programs, commands, or utilities. If you don't specify the correct information, the task simply won't run or will generate errors when it does run. One way to check tasks is to view their status and last result in the Scheduled Tasks folder. This information pertains to the last time the scheduled task ran. It won't tell you, however, if there were problems running tasks prior to the last run time. To dig deep and get a better understanding of how tasks are running, you should periodically check the Task Scheduler log file, Schedlgu.txt, located in the *%SystemRoot%*/Tasks folder.

You can examine the log file by selecting View Log from the Advanced menu when the Scheduled Tasks folder is selected in Windows Explorer. If you examine the task scheduler log, you'll find

- Entries that record when the Task Scheduler Service was started and when the service exited (was stopped).

- Entries that record when tasks are started, when they finished running, and the exit error code. An exit error code of zero (0) means that the task executed normally. Any other exit code indicates an error may have occurred.

 Note *%SystemRoot%*\Tasks is a special folder with a view that allows you to work with scheduled tasks. If you access this folder in Windows Explorer, you won't see the SchedLgU.txt log. It is there, however, and if you access the related directory from the command prompt—by changing the directory to *%SystemRoot%*\Tasks—you'll see the log in the listing.

You may also want a more detailed understanding of what happens when scripts run. To do this, you may want to record the output of commands and utilities in a separate log file, thereby giving you the opportunity to determine that those commands and utilities produced the expected results. As discussed in the previous chapter, you can write command output to a named file by redirecting standard output and standard error. In the following examples, the output of the DEFRAG command is appended to Stat-log.txt and any DEFRAG errors are written to this file as well:

```
defrag c: >> c:\logs\stat-log.txt 2>&1
defrag d: >> c:\logs\stat-log.txt 2>&1
```

Caution   If you are working with a directory, as shown in these examples, the directory must already exist. It will not be created for you, and any errors resulting from the lack of a directory will not be written to the log file.

Real World   Writing command output to a log file won't help you resolve every problem that can occur, but it goes a long way toward ensuring that scheduled tasks run as expected. If you are trying to troubleshoot problems, keep in mind that tasks can fail to run for many reasons, some of which are beyond your control. For example, scheduled tasks won't run if the system is shut down when the task is scheduled to run. If you want to be notified when tasks are missed, select Notify Me Of Missed Tasks from the Advanced menu when the Scheduled Tasks folder is selected in Windows Explorer. With this feature enabled, a message is displayed when you log on that tells you if you missed a task because the system was shut down.

Scheduling Tasks with the Scheduled Task Wizard

You can use the Scheduled Task Wizard to schedule tasks on the local or remote system to which you're connected. Access the Scheduled Task Wizard and currently scheduled tasks through the Scheduled Tasks folder.

Entries in the Scheduled Tasks folder show currently scheduled tasks. You can access the Scheduled Tasks folder on a local system with either of the following techniques:

- Start Control Panel, and then click Scheduled Tasks.
- Start Windows Explorer, click My Computer, then click Control Panel, and then click Scheduled Tasks.

In a Windows domain, you can access the Scheduled Tasks folder on a remote system by completing the following steps:

1. Start Windows Explorer, and then use the My Network Places node to navigate to the computer you want to work with.
2. Click the computer's icon, and then click Scheduled Tasks.

In a workgroup, establish a Remote Desktop connection as discussed previously, then use Windows Explorer to access the Scheduled Tasks folder. You can also use this technique for computers in a domain, but the procedure described previously is more convenient.

Creating Tasks with the Scheduled Task Wizard

To schedule a task with the Scheduled Task Wizard, follow these steps:

1. Start the Scheduled Task Wizard by double-clicking Add Scheduled Task in the Scheduled Tasks folder. Read the Welcome page, and then click Next.

2. Using the page shown in Figure 4-2, select a program to schedule by clicking Browse to open the Select Program To Schedule dialog box and then use the dialog box to find the program, command-line utility, or script that you want to run. Afterward, click Open.

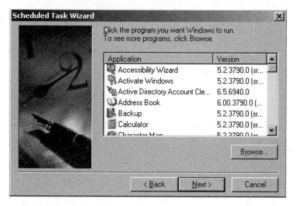

Figure 4-2. *Use the Scheduled Task Wizard to select a program to run, and then click Browse to find scripts and other applications.*

3. Type a name for the task, as shown in Figure 4-3. The name should be short but descriptive so you can quickly determine what the task does.

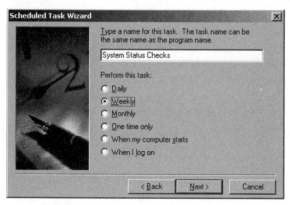

Figure 4-3. *Use the Scheduled Task Wizard to name a task, and then select how often you'd like to perform this task.*

4. Select a run schedule for the task. Tasks can be scheduled to run periodically (daily, weekly, or monthly), or when a specific event occurs, such as when the computer starts or when the task's user logs on.

5. Click Next. If a period is to be scheduled, select a date and time to run the scheduled task. The next page you see depends on when the task is scheduled to run.

6. If you've selected a daily running task, the date and time page appears as shown in Figure 4-4.

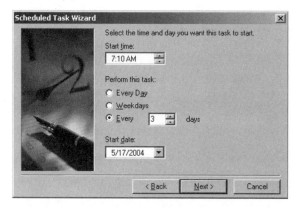

Figure 4-4. *Use this page to configure a daily scheduled task.*

Set a start time and date. Daily scheduled tasks can be configured to run

- *Every Day*—Seven days a week.
- *Weekdays*—Monday through Friday only.
- *Every ... Days*—Every 2, 3, ... *N* days.

7. If you've selected a weekly running task, the date and time page appears as shown in Figure 4-5.

Figure 4-5. *Use this page to configure a weekly scheduled task.*

Configure the task using these fields:

- *Start Time*—Sets the start time of the task.
- *Every … Weeks*—Allows you to run the task every week, every two weeks, or every *N* weeks.
- *Select The Day(s) Of The Week Below*—Sets the day(s) of the week when the task runs, such as on Monday or on Monday and Friday.

8. If you've selected a monthly running task, the date and time page appears as shown in Figure 4-6.

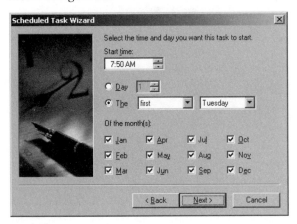

Figure 4-6. *Use this page to configure a monthly scheduled task.*

Configure the task using these fields:

- *Start Time*—Sets the start time of the task.
- *Day*—Sets the day of the month the task runs. For example, if you select 5, the task runs on the fifth day of the month.
- *The …*—Sets task to run on the *N*th occurrence of a day in a month, such as the second Monday or the third Tuesday of every month.
- *Of The Month(s)*—These check boxes let you select the months in which the task runs.

9. If you've selected One Time Only for running the task, the date and time page appears as shown in Figure 4-7. Set the start time and start date.

 Tip With tasks that run automatically when the computer starts or when the task's user logs on, you don't have to set the start date and time. If you want to configure a startup task for a specific user through the wizard, you'll need to log on as that user and then run the wizard.

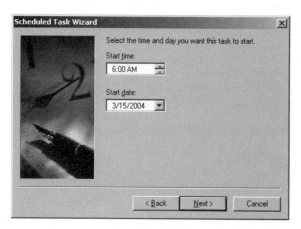

Figure 4-7. *Use this page to configure a one-time-only scheduled task.*

10. After you've configured a start date and time, click Next to continue.

11. In the next dialog box, type a user name and password that can be used when running the scheduled task. This user name must have appropriate permissions and privileges to run the scheduled task.

Note In Windows domains, be sure to enter the user name in the form: Domain\UserName, such as Adatum\wrstanek, where Adatum is the domain and wrstanek is the user account.

12. The final wizard page provides a summary of the task you're scheduling as follows:

- If you want to set command-line arguments, select Open Advanced Properties For This Task When I Click Finish, or double-click the task in Windows Explorer after clicking Finish. Then, in the Run field, type the parameters after the task path. If the task path includes spaces, be sure to enclose the path in double quotation marks ("). Likewise, if a command-line argument includes spaces, enclose the argument in double quotation marks (").

- If an error occurs when you create the task, you'll see an error prompt. Click OK. The task should still be created. You may, however, need to edit the task's properties. In Windows Explorer, double-click the task to correct the specified error. One of the more common errors you'll see is Access Denied. This error can occur if the user credentials provided are incorrect, such as occurs if you enter the wrong password or the user account doesn't exist in the domain.

Click Finish to complete the scheduling process.

Real World Many problems with getting tasks to run are fairly obvi-ous. For example, any task listed as "Could not start" should be exam-ined. Sometimes, however problems with tasks aren't so clear. A task that is listed as "Running" may not in fact be running and instead may be a hung process. To check for hung processes, use the Last Run Time; it tells you when the task was started. If the task has been run-ning for more than a day, there is usually a problem. A script may be waiting for input, it may have problems reading or writing files, or it may simply be a runaway task that needs to be stopped. To stop the task, right-click the task in the Scheduled Tasks folder, then select End Task. You can also wait for the system to stop the task. By default, all tasks time out after running for 72 hours. You can change the timeout using the Settings tab of the task's Properties dialog box.

Changing Task Properties

To change the settings for a task, access the Scheduled Tasks folder. On a local system, double-click Scheduled Tasks in the Control Panel. On a remote system, start Windows Explorer, use the My Network Places node to navigate to the computer you want to work with, click the computer's icon, and then click Scheduled Tasks. Next, double-click the task you want to work with and then use the Properties dialog box to make the necessary changes.

Note If you change the way a task runs, you may be prompted to set the account information. In this case, you will need to accept the cur-rent account the task is configured to run as, or enter a new account in Domain\UserName format. Either way, you will need to enter and confirm the password for the account you've used.

Copying and Moving Tasks from One System to Another

If you want to take tasks created on one system and use them on another sys-tem, you don't have to recreate them manually. Instead, in a domain, follow this procedure:

1. Use the My Network Places node to navigate to the computer where the tasks you want to use are currently stored. Click the computer's icon and then click Scheduled Tasks.

2. Right-click one of the tasks you want to use, and then select Copy.

3. Again, use the My Network Places node to navigate through the organiza-tion. This time, navigate to the computer on which you want to use the task.

4. With the destination computer's icon selected, right-click Scheduled Tasks and then select Paste.

5. The scheduled task should be copied to the new location. Be sure to check the properties of the task on the destination computer, making sure the settings are suitable.

You can also move tasks from one computer to another. To move tasks in a domain, follow these steps:

1. Use the My Network Places node to navigate to the computer where the tasks you want to use are currently stored. Click the computer's icon and then click Scheduled Tasks.

2. Right-click one of the tasks you want to use, and then select Cut.

3. Again, use the My Network Places node to navigate through the organization. This time, navigate to the computer to which you want to move the task.

4. With the destination computer's icon selected, right-click Scheduled Tasks and then select Paste.

5. The scheduled task should be moved to the new location. Be sure to check the properties of the task on the destination computer, making sure the settings are suitable.

Enabling and Disabling Tasks

Tasks can be enabled or disabled as needed, depending on your preference. If you temporarily don't want to use a task, you can disable it. When you are ready to use the task again, you can enable it. By enabling and disabling tasks rather than deleting them, you save the time involved in reconfiguring task settings.

You can enable or disable a task by following these steps:

1. Access the Scheduled Tasks folder. On a local system, select or double-click Scheduled Tasks in the Control Panel. On a remote system, start Windows Explorer, use the My Network Places node to navigate to the computer you want to work with, click the computer's icon, and then click Scheduled Tasks.

2. Select or double-click the task you want to modify. This displays a Properties dialog box that is named for the task in question. The Task tab should be selected by default.

3. Select Enabled to enable the task or clear Enabled to disable the task. Click OK.

Running Tasks Immediately

You don't have to wait for the scheduled time to run a task. To run a task at any time, access the Scheduled Tasks folder, right-click the task you want to run, and then select Run.

Removing Unwanted Tasks

If you no longer need a task, you can delete it permanently by accessing the Scheduled Tasks folder, right-clicking the task you want to delete, and then selecting Delete.

Scheduling Tasks with Schtasks

With Schtasks, you can perform the same task scheduling operations as with the Scheduled Task Wizard. Any tasks you create using Schtasks are displayed as scheduled tasks in the Scheduled Tasks folder and can be managed from the command line or from the graphical user interface (GUI).

Schtasks has several different sets of subcommands and is one of the more complex utilities available at the command line. The sections that follow discuss each of the following subcommands:

- **Schtasks /Create**   Used to create scheduled tasks
- **Schtasks /Change**   Used when you want to change the properties of existing tasks
- **Schtasks /Query**   Used to display scheduled tasks on the local or named computer
- **Schtasks /Run**   Used to start a scheduled task immediately
- **Schtasks /End**   Used to stop a running task
- **Schtasks /Delete**   Used to remove scheduled tasks that are no longer wanted

Creating Scheduled Tasks with Schtasks /Create

With Schtasks /Create, you can create one-time-only tasks, recurring tasks, and tasks that run based on specific system events, such as logon and startup. The basic syntax for defining these types of tasks is as follows:

```
schtasks /create /tn TaskName /tr TaskToRun /sc ScheduleType [/mo
Modifier]
```

where *TaskName* sets the task name string, *TaskToRun* specifies the file path to the command-line utility or script that you want to run, *ScheduleType* specifies the run schedule, and *Modifier* is an optional value that modifies the run schedule based on the schedule type. Any tasks you create using this syntax are created on the local computer and use your user permissions. Further, if you don't provide your account password, you are prompted for your user password when you create tasks.

Valid values for *ScheduleType* are shown in Table 4-1. Note the usage and modifiers that the various schedule types accept. We will discuss each schedule type and modifier in detail later in the chapter. Note the following as well:

- Days of the week can be entered in a comma-separated list, such as Mon, Wed, Fri, or with a hyphen to specify a sequence of days, such as Mon-Fri for Monday through Friday.

- Months of the year can be entered in a comma-separated list, such as Jan, Mar, Jun, or with a hyphen to specify a sequence of months, such as Jan-Jun for January through June.

- With week of the month, you can only enter one value, such as FIRST or LAST.

Table 4-1. Schedule Types for Schtasks /Create

Schedule Type	Description	Modifier Values
MINUTE	Task runs at a specified interval in minutes. By default, tasks run once a minute.	/mo 1-1439; the number of minutes between each run of the task. The default modifier is 1.
HOURLY	Task runs at a specified interval in hours. By default, tasks run once an hour.	/mo 1-23; the number of hours between each run of the task. The default modifier is 1.
DAILY	Task runs every day or every *N* days. By default, tasks run once a day.	/mo 1-365; the number of days between each run of the task. The default modifier is 1.
WEEKLY	Task runs every week or every *N* weeks, on designated days. By default, tasks run once a week on Mondays.	/mo 1-52; the number of weeks between each run of the task. Optionally, use /d to specify the days of the week to run. Use MON, TUE, WED, THU, FRI, SAT, and SUN to specify days. * for every day of the week.
MONTHLY	Task runs every month or every *N* months on designated days. By default, tasks run the first day of every month.	/mo 1-12; the number of months between each run of the task. Optionally, use /d MON-SUN; sets day of the week to run during the month. Use * to have the task run every day.
	2nd monthly variant for specific day of month. Use /mo and /m, or /m and /d.	/mo LASTDAY; last day of month /m JAN, FEB, ..., DEC; sets the month(s). /d 1-31; day of month

Table 4-1. Schedule Types for Schtasks /Create

Schedule Type	Description	Modifier Values
	3rd monthly variant for specific week of the month.	/mo FIRST | SECOND | THIRD | FOURTH | LAST; sets week of month. /d MON-SUN; sets day of week. /m JAN, FEB, …, DEC; sets month(s).
ONCE	Task runs once at a specified date and time.	—
ONSTART	Task runs whenever the system starts.	—
ONLOGON	Task runs whenever a user logs on.	—
ONIDLE	Task runs whenever the system is idle for a specified period of time.	/i 1-999; the number of minutes the system has to be idle before the task starts.

To see how Schtasks /Create can be used, consider the following examples:

Task runs once immediately and then doesn't run again:

```
schtasks /create /tn "SysChecks" /tr c:\scripts\sch.bat /sc once
```

Task runs when the system starts:

```
schtasks /create /tn "SysChecks" /tr c:\scripts\sch.bat /sc onstart
```

Task runs whenever the system is idle for more than 10 minutes:

```
schtasks /create /tn "SysChecks" /tr c:\scripts\sch.bat /sc onidle
/i 10
```

Task runs every 15 minutes on the local computer:

```
schtasks /create /tn "SysChecks" /tr c:\scripts\sch.bat /sc minute
/mo 15
```

Task runs every five hours on the local computer:

```
schtasks /create /tn "SysChecks" /tr c:\scripts\sch.bat /sc hourly
/mo 5
```

Task runs every two days on the local computer:

```
schtasks /create /tn "SysChecks" /tr c:\scripts\sch.bat /sc daily
/mo 2
```

Task runs every two weeks on Monday (the default run day):

```
schtasks /create /tn "SysChecks" /tr c:\scripts\sch.bat /sc weekly
/mo 2
```

Task runs every week on Monday and Friday:

```
schtasks /create /tn "SysChecks" /tr c:\scripts\sch.bat /sc weekly
/d mon,fri
```

Task runs on the first day of every month:

```
schtasks /create /tn "SysChecks" /tr c:\scripts\sch.bat /sc monthly
```

Task runs on the fifth day of every other month:

```
schtasks /create /tn "SysChecks" /tr c:\scripts\sch.bat /sc monthly
/mo 2 /d 5
```

Task runs the last day of every month:

```
schtasks /create /tn "SysChecks" /tr c:\scripts\sysch.bat /sc
monthly/mo lastday
```

Task runs the first Monday of April, August, and December:

```
schtasks /create /tn "SysChecks" /tr c:\scripts\sysch.bat /sc
monthly /mo first /d mon /m apr,aug,dec
```

When the path of the specified task includes a space, enclose the file path in double quotation marks as shown in the following example:

```
schtasks /create /tn "SysChecks" /tr "c:\My Scripts\sch.bat" /sc
onstart
```

If you do not enclose the file path in quotation marks, an error will occur when Schtasks attempts to run the task. Further, if you want to pass arguments to a program, utility or script, simply follow the Task To Run file path with the arguments you want to use. Any argument that contains spaces should be enclosed in quotation marks so that it is properly interpreted as a single argument rather than multiple arguments. Here are examples:

```
schtasks /create /tn "SysChecks" /tr c:\scripts\sch.bat 1 Y LAST /sc
onstart

schtasks /create /tn "SysChecks" /tr "c:\My Scripts\sch.bat" Y N /sc
onstart

schtasks /create /tn "SysChecks" /tr "c:\My Scripts\sch.bat" "Full
Checks"
```

You can also schedule tasks for remote computers as well as tasks that should run with different user permissions. The key detail to remember when scheduling tasks on remote computers is that the computer you are using should be in the same domain as the remote computer or in a domain that the remote computer trusts. To do this, you must use the expanded syntax which includes the following parameters:

```
/s Computer /u [Domain\]User [/p Password]
```

where *Computer* is the remote computer name or IP address, *Domain* is the optional domain name in which the user account is located, *User* is the name of the user account whose permissions you want to use, and *Password* is the optional password for the user account. If you don't specify the domain, the current domain is assumed. If you don't provide the account password, you are prompted for the password.

 Tip If you want a task to run only when a specific user is logged on, use the optional /It parameter, which specifies that the task should run only when the user who owns the task is logged on. The /It parameter is only valid for Windows Server 2003. It cannot be used with Windows XP.

To see how the computer and user information can be added to the syntax, consider the following examples:

Use the account adatum\wrstanek when setting permissions for the task on the local computer:

```
schtasks /create /tn "SysChecks" /tr c:\scripts\sch.bat /sc onstart
/s mailer01 /u adatum\wrstanek
```

Set the remote computer as mailer01 and the account to use as adatum\wrstanek:

```
schtasks /create /tn "SysChecks" /tr c:\scripts\sch.bat /sc onstart
/s mailer01 /u adatum\wrstanek
```

Finally, if desired, you can add specific start times and dates, as well as end times and dates, using

- /st StartTime, where *StartTime* is in 24-hour clock format (*HH:MM*), such as 15:00 for 3 P.M.

- /et EndTime, where *EndTime* is in 24-hour clock format (*HH:MM*), such as 15:00 for 3 P.M. Used only with /sc minute and /sc hourly. Applies to Windows Server 2003 only.

- /du Duration, where *Duration* is the number of hours and minutes to run, in the form *HHHH:MM*. Used only with /sc minute and /sc hourly. Applies to Windows Server 2003 only.

- /sd StartDate, where *StartDate* is the start date using the default system format for dates, such as *MM/DD/YYYY*.

- /ed EndDate where *EndDate* is the end date using the default system format for dates, such as MM/DD/YYYY.

Tip   If you specify an end date or time, you can also specify the /Z parameter, which tells the Task Scheduler to delete the task upon completion of its schedule. This applies only to Windows Server 2003.

To see how specific start times and dates, as well as end times and dates, can be used, consider the following examples:

Start the hourly task at midnight:

```
schtasks /create /tn "SysChecks" /tr c:\scripts\sch.bat /sc hourly
/st 00:00
```

Start the hourly task at 3 A.M. and stop it at 7 A.M.:

```
schtasks /create /tn "SysChecks" /tr c:\scripts\sch.bat /sc hourly
/st 03:00 /et 07:00
```

Start the weekly task at 3 A.M. on February 20, 2004:

```
schtasks /create /tn "SysChecks" /tr c:\scripts\sch.bat /sc weekly
/st 03:00 /sd 02/20/2004
```

Start the weekly task at 3 A.M. on February 20, 2004 and end at 2:59 A.M. on March 15, 2004:

```
schtasks /create /tn "SysChecks" /tr c:\scripts\sch.bat /sc weekly
/st 03:00 /sd 02/20/2004 /et 02:59 /ed 03/15/2004
```

Note   Date and time formats are determined by the Regional And Language options settings used by the computer. In these examples, the date format preference is English (United States).

Changing Scheduled Tasks with Schtasks /Change

You use Schtasks /Change to change key parameters associated with scheduled tasks. The basic syntax of Schtasks /Change is

```
schtasks /change /tn TaskName ParametersToChange
```

where *TaskName* is the name of the task you want to change and *Parameters-ToChange* are the parameters you want to change. Parameters you can work with include

- /ru *Domain\User* changes the user to run the task as, such as /ru adatum/ wrstanek.
- /rp *Password* sets the password for the previously specified or newly designated run as user account.
- /tr *TaskToRun* changes the command-line utility or script that is run for the named task.
- /st *StartTime* sets the start time for minute or hourly tasks. This applies to Windows Server 2003 only.
- /ri *Interval* sets the run interval in minutes. This applies to Windows Server 2003 only.
- /et *EndTime* sets the end time for minute or hourly tasks. This applies to Windows Server 2003 only.
- /du *Duration* sets the number of hours and minutes to run the task. Minute and hourly tasks only. This applies to Windows Server 2003 only.
- /sd *StartDate* sets the start date for the task. This applies to Windows Server 2003 only.
- /ed *EndDate* sets the end date for the task. This applies to Windows Server 2003 only.
- /k specifies that the task should not be started again when the end time or duration interval is reached, but it doesn't stop the task if it is already running (the current run will be the last one). This applies to Windows Server 2003 only.
- /it specifies that the task should run only when the user who owns the task is logged on. This applies to Windows Server 2003 only.

To see how you can change tasks, consider the following examples:

Change the script that is run:

```
schtasks /change /tn "SysChecks" /tr c:\scripts\systemchecks.bat
```

Change the run as user and password:

```
schtasks /change /tn "SysChecks" /ru adatum\hthomas /rp gophers
```

Change task to start weekly at 7 A.M. on March 1, 2004 and end at 6:59 A.M. on March 30, 2004:

```
schtasks /change /tn "SysChecks" /st 07:00 /sd 03/01/2004 /et 06:59
/ed 03/30/2004
```

Note As mentioned previously, date and time formats are determined by the Regional And Language options settings used by the
computer. Here, the date format is English (United States).

When you change a task, Schtasks displays a message that states whether the
changes succeeded or failed, such as

```
SUCCESS: The parameters of the scheduled task "SysChecks" have been
changed.
```

If you are working with a remote computer or aren't logged in with a user
account that has permission to change the task, you can specify the computer
and account information as necessary. The syntax is

```
schtasks /change /tn TaskName /s Computer /u [Domain\]User [/p
Password]
```

where *Computer* is the remote computer name or IP address, *Domain* is the
optional domain name in which the user account is located, *User* is the name of
the user account whose permissions you want to use, and *Password* is the
optional password for the user account. If you don't specify the domain, the current domain is assumed. If you don't provide the account password, you are
prompted for the password.

In the following example, the remote computer is mailer1 and the user account
that has authority to change the SysChecks task is wrstanek's Adatum domain
account:

```
schtasks /change /tn "SysChecks" /tr c:\scripts\systemchecks.bat
/s mailer01 /u adatum\wrstanek
```

Because a password isn't specified, Schtasks will prompt for one. In Windows
Server 2003 only, you can also quickly enable or disable tasks by name. Use the
following syntax to enable tasks:

```
schtasks /change /tn TaskName /enable
```

Use this syntax to disable tasks:

```
schtasks /change /tn TaskName /disable
```

where *TaskName* is the name of the task you want to enable or disable, such as

```
schtasks /change /tn "SysChecks" /disable
```

Querying for Configured Tasks with Schtasks /Query

You can quickly determine what tasks are configured on a computer by typing **schtasks query** at the command prompt and, as necessary for a remote computer, you can specify the computer and the account information needed to access the computer using the form:

```
schtasks /query /s Computer /u [Domain\]User [/p Password]
```

where *Computer* is the remote computer name or IP address, *Domain* is the optional domain name in which the user account is located, *User* is the name of the user account with appropriate access permissions on the remote computer, and *Password* is the optional password for the designated user account.

In the following example, the remote computer is mailer1 and the user account is wrstanek's Adatum domain account:

```
schtasks /query /s mailer01 /u adatum\wrstanek
```

Because a password isn't specified, Schtasks will prompt for one.

The basic output of Schtasks /Query is in table format and provides TaskName, Next Run Time, and Status columns. You can also format the output as a list or lines of comma-separated values using /Fo List or /Fo Csv, respectively. The list output works best with the /V (verbose) parameter, which provides complete details on all task properties and which can be used as shown in the following example:

```
schtasks /query /s mailer01 /u adatum\wrstanek /fo list /v
```

Another parameter that is useful is /Nh, which specifies that table- or CSV-formatted output should not have headings.

 Tip You may wonder why you'd want to use the various formats. It's a good question. I recommend using the verbose list format (/Fo List /V) when you want to see all details about tasks configured on a system and when you are troubleshooting, and I recommend using comma-separated values when you want to store the output in a file that may later be exported to a spreadsheet or flat-file database. Remember you can redirect the output of Schtasks to a file using output redirection (> or >>).

Running Tasks Immediately with Schtasks /Run

You can run a task at any time using

```
schtasks /run /tn TaskName
```

where *TaskName* is the name of the task you want to run, such as

```
schtasks /run /tn "SysChecks"
```

Running a task does not affect its schedule and does not change the next run time for the task. If the task can be successfully started, you should see a message stating so. Additionally, you can specify the name of the remote computer on which the task is configured and as necessary the account to run the task as, including an optional password. Here are examples:

```
schtasks /run /tn "SysChecks"/s 192.168.1.100
schtasks /run /tn "SysChecks"/s 192.168.1.100 /u adatum/wrstanek
```

Note If you specify a user and don't provide a password, you will be prompted immediately to enter the password.

Stopping Running Tasks with Schtasks /End

You can stop a task at any time using

```
schtasks /end /tn TaskName
```

where *TaskName* is the name of a task that is currently running and should be stopped, such as

```
schtasks /end /tn "SysChecks"
```

The task is only stopped if it is running and if successful, the output message should be similar to the following:

```
SUCCESS: The scheduled task "SysChecks" has been terminated
successfully.
```

You can also specify the name of the remote computer on which the task is configured and as necessary the account with authority to stop the task, including an optional password, such as:

```
schtasks /end /tn "SysChecks"/s 192.168.1.100
```

Or

```
schtasks /end /tn "SysChecks"/s 192.168.1.100 /u adatum/wrstanek
```

Because a password isn't specified, Schtasks will prompt for one.

Deleting Tasks with Schtasks /Delete

You can delete tasks by name on local and remote computers using the syntax

```
schtasks /delete /tn TaskName [/s Computer /u [Domain/]User [/p
Password]]
```

where *TaskName* is the name of a task that should be deleted and the rest of the parameters optionally identify the remote computer, the user account to use when deleting the task and the password for the account, such as

```
schtasks /delete /tn "SysChecks"
```

or

```
schtasks /delete /tn "SysChecks"/s 192.168.1.100 /u adatum/wrstanek
/p frut5
```

 Note If you specify a user name and don't provide a password, you will be prompted immediately to enter the password.

After entering the Schtasks /Delete command, you should see a warning asking you to confirm that you want to remove the task. Press the appropriate letter on your keyboard. If you don't want to see a warning prompt use the /f parameter, such as

```
schtasks /delete /tn "SysChecks" /f
```

Here, you force Schtasks to delete the task without a warning.

In addition, if you want to delete all scheduled tasks on the local computer or the specified remote computer, enter asterisk (*) as the task name, such as

```
schtasks /delete /tn *
```

Confirm the action when prompted.

Part II

Windows Systems Administration

Microsoft Windows provides many command-line tools to help in the management of daily operations. The chapters in this part of the book discuss the core tools and techniques you'll use to manage Windows systems. Chapter 5 discusses many of the key administration tools, including tools that help you gather system information, work with the Windows registry, configure Windows services, and shut down systems remotely. Chapter 6 examines tools that help you track information that is written to the Windows event logs, including warnings and errors. You'll also learn how to write events to the system and application logs. Finally, in Chapter 7 you'll learn about tools and techniques for monitoring applications, examining processes, and maintaining performance.

Chapter 5
Managing Windows Systems

As an administrator, it's your job to plan, organize, and track the details that keep the network running. If you're to survive without just muddling through, you need to learn how to do those jobs quickly and efficiently. Fortunately, Windows supplies plenty of command-line tools to help you with these tasks and this chapter discusses some of the more important tools for daily systems management.

Examining System Information

Often when you are working with a user's computer or a remote server, you'll want to examine some basic system information, such as who is logged on, the current system time, or the location of a certain file. Commands that help you gather basic system information include

- **NOW**   Displays the current system time and date using a 24-hour clock, such as Sat May 9 12:30:45 2003. Available in the Windows Server 2003 Resource Kit only.

- **WHOAMI**   Displays the name of the user currently logged on the system, such as adatum\administrator.

- **WHERE**   Searches for files using a search pattern and returns a list of matching results.

To use NOW or WHOAMI, simply type the command in a command shell window and press Enter. With WHERE, the most common syntax you'll use is

```
where /r baseDir filename
```

Here, */r* is for a recursive search starting from the specified directory (*BaseDir*) and including all subdirectories, and *filename* is the name or partial name of the file to search for, which can include wildcards. Use *?* as a wildcard to match a single character and * as a wildcard to match multiple characters, such as data???.txt or data*.*. In the following example, you search the C:\ directory and all subdirectories for text files that begin with *data*, as follows:

```
where /r C:\ data*.txt
```

You can also search for files of all types that begin with *data*, as in this example:

```
where /r C:\ data*.*
```

Sometimes when you are working with a computer, you'll want to obtain information on the system configuration or the system environment. With mission-critical systems, you may want to save or print this information for easy reference. Commands that help you gather system information include

- **DRIVERQUERY** Displays a list of all installed device drivers and their properties, including module name, display name, driver type, and driver link date. With verbose output, the command also lists the driver status, state, start mode, memory usage, and file system path. Use the /V parameter to get verbose output of all unsigned drivers.

- **SYSTEMINFO** Displays detailed system configuration information, including operating system version, system type, system manufacturer, processor, BIOS version, memory size, local setting, time zone setting, and network card configuration.

- **NLSINFO** Displays detailed locale information, including default language, system locale, windows code page, time and number formats, time zone, and installed code pages. Available in the Windows Server 2003 Resource Kit only.

To use these commands on a local computer, simply type the command name in a command shell window and press Enter. With DRIVERQUERY, use the /V parameter to get verbose output and the /Si parameter to display properties of signed drivers, such as

```
driverquery /v /si
```

With the DRIVERQUERY and SYSTEMINFO commands, you can also specify the remote computer to query and the Run As permissions. To do this, you must use the expanded syntax, which includes the following parameters:

```
/S Computer /U [Domain\]User [/P Password]
```

where *Computer* is the remote computer name or IP address, *Domain* is the optional domain name in which the user account is located, *User* is the name of the user account whose permissions you want to use, and *Password* is the optional password for the user account. If you don't specify the domain, the current domain is assumed. If you don't provide the account password, you are prompted for the password.

To see how the computer and user information can be added to the syntax, consider the following examples:

Use the account adatum\wrstanek when querying MAILER1 for driver settings:

```
driverquery /s mailer1 /u adatum\wrstanek
```

Use the account adatum\administrator when querying CORPSERVER01 for system information:

```
systeminfo /s corpserver01 /u adatum\administrator
```

Tip The basic output of these commands is in table format. You can also format the output as a list or lines of comma-separated values using /Fo List or /Fo Csv, respectively. You may wonder why you should use the various formats. That's a good question. I recommend using the verbose list format (/Fo List /V) when you want to see all details about tasks configured on a system and when you are troubleshooting. I recommend using comma-separated values when you want to store the output in a file that may later be exported to a spreadsheet or flat-file database. Remember you can redirect the output of the DRIVERQUERY and SYSTEMINFO commands to a file using output redirection (> or >>).

Working with the Registry

The Windows registry stores configuration settings. Using the Reg command-line utility, you can view, add, delete, compare, and copy registry entries. Because the Windows registry is essential to the proper operation of the operating system, make changes to the registry only when you know how these changes will affect the system. Before you edit the registry in any way, perform a complete system backup and create a system recovery data snapshot. This way, if you make a mistake, you can recover the registry and the system.

Caution Improperly modifying the Windows registry can cause serious problems. If the registry becomes corrupted, you might have to reinstall the operating system. Double-check the commands you use before executing them. Make sure that they do exactly what you intend.

Understanding Registry Keys and Values

The Windows registry stores configuration settings for the operating system, applications, users, and hardware. Registry settings are stored as keys and values, which are placed under a specific root key controlling when and how the keys and values are used.

Table 5-1 lists the registry root keys as well as a description and the reference name you will use to refer to the root key when working with the REG command. Under the root keys, you'll find the main keys that control system, user, application, and hardware settings. These keys are organized into a tree structure, with folders representing keys. For example, under

HKEY_LOCAL_MACHINE\SYSTEM\CurrentControlSet\Services, you'll find folders for all services installed on the system. Within these folders are the registry keys that store important service configuration settings and their subkeys.

Table 5-1. Keys in the Windows Registry

Root Key	Reference Name	Description
HKEY_CURRENT_USER	HKCU	Stores configuration settings for the current user.
HKEY_LOCAL_MACHINE	HKLM	Stores system-level configuration settings.
HKEY_CLASSES_ROOT	HKCR	Stores configuration settings for applications and files. Also ensures the correct application is opened when a file is accessed.
HKEY_USERS	HKU	Stores default-user and other-user settings by profile.
HKEY_CURRENT_CONFIG	HKCC	Stores information about the hardware profile being used.

Keys that you want to work with must be designated by their folder path. For example, the path to the DNS key is HKEY_LOCAL_MACHINE\SYSTEM\CurrentControlSet\Services\DNS and, using the abbreviated path HKLM\SYSTEM\CurrentControlSet\Services\DNS, you can view and manipulate this key.

Key values are stored as a specific data type. Table 5-2 provides a summary of the main data types used with keys.

Table 5-2. Registry Key Values and Data Types

Data Type	Description	Example
REG_BINARY	Identifies a binary value. Binary values are stored using base-2 (0 or 1 only) but are displayed and entered in hexadecimal (base-16) format.	01 00 14 80 90 00 00 9c 00
REG_SZ	Identifies a string value containing a sequence of characters.	DNS Server
REG_DWORD	Identifies a DWORD value, which is composed of hexadecimal data with a maximum length of four bytes.	0x00000002
REG_MULTI_SZ	Identifies a multiple string value.	Tcpip Afd RpcSc
REG_EXPAND_SZ	Identifies an expandable string value, which is usually used with directory paths.	*%SystemRoot%*\dns.exe

So long as you know the key path and understand the available key data types, you can use the REG command to view and manipulate keys in a variety of ways. REG has several different subcommands, and we'll explore several. The sections that follow discuss each of the following REG subcommands:

- **REG add**   Adds a new subkey or entry to the registry
- **REG delete**   Deletes a subkey or entries from the registry
- **REG query**   Lists the entries under a key and the names of subkeys (if any)
- **REG compare**   Compares registry subkeys or entries
- **REG copy**   Copies a registry entry to a specified key path on a local or remote system
- **REG restore**   Writes saved subkeys, entries, and values back to the registry
- **REG save**   Saves a copy of specified subkeys, entries, and values to a file

Note   The REG command is run using the permissions of the current user. If you want to use a different set of permissions, the easiest way is to log on as that user.

Querying Registry Values

Using REG query, you can read registry values by referencing the full path and name of a key or key value that you want to examine. The basic syntax is

```
reg query KeyName [/v ValueName]
```

where *KeyName* is the name of the key you want to examine and *ValueName* is an optional parameter that specifies a specific key value. In the following example, you query the DNS key under the current control set:

```
reg query HKLM\SYSTEM\CurrentControlSet\Services\DNS
```

Alternatively, if you know the specific key value you want to examine, you can limit the query results using the /V parameter. In this example, you list the value of the ImagePath entry for the DNS key:

```
reg query HKLM\SYSTEM\CurrentControlSet\Services\DNS /v ImagePath
```

The key path can also include the UNC name or IP address of a remote computer that you want to examine, such as \\Mailer1 or \\192.168.1.100. However, keep in mind that on a remote computer, you can only work with the HKLM and HKU root keys. In this example, you examine the DNS key on MAILER1:

```
reg query \\Mailer1\HKLM\SYSTEM\CurrentControlSet\Services\DNS
```

Note   If you specify a nonexistent key or value, an error message is displayed. Typically, it reads: ERROR: The system was unable to find the specified registry key or value.

Comparing Registry Keys

With REG compare, you can compare registry entries and values between two systems or between two different keys on the same system. Performing registry comparisons is useful in the following situations:

- **When you are trying to troubleshoot service and application configuration issues** At such times, it is useful to compare the registry configurations between two different systems. Ideally, these systems include one that appears to be configured properly and one that you suspect is misconfigured. You can then perform a comparison of the configuration areas that you suspect are causing problems.

- **When you want to ensure an application or service is configured the same way on multiple systems** Here you would use one system as the basis for testing the other system configurations. Ideally, the basis system is configured exactly as expected before you start comparing its configuration to other systems.

The basic syntax for REG compare is

```
reg compare KeyName1 KeyName2 [/v ValueName]
```

where *KeyName1* and *KeyName2* are the names of the subkeys that you want to compare and *ValueName* is an optional parameter that specifies a specific key value to compare. The key name can include the UNC name or IP address of a remote computer that you want to examine. In the following example, you compare the DNS key under the current control set on MAILER1 and MAILER2:

```
reg compare \\Mailer1\HKLM\SYSTEM\CurrentControlSet\Services\DNS
\\Mailer2\HKLM\SYSTEM\CurrentControlSet\Services\DNS
```

If the keys are configured the same, the output is

```
Results Compared: Identical
The operation completed successfully.
```

If the keys are configured differently, the output shows the differences. Any differences that begin with the < character pertain to the first key specified and differences that begin with the > character pertain to the second key specified. The output will also state

```
Results Compared: Different
The operation completed successfully.
```

Tip Differences are displayed because the /Od parameter is assumed by default. Using additional parameters, you can also specify that you want to see all differences and matches (/Oa), only matches (/Os), or only the results (/On).

Additionally, if you want to compare all subkeys and entries recursively, you can add the /S parameter, as shown in the following example:

```
reg compare \\Mailer1\HKLM\SYSTEM\CurrentControlSet\Services\DNS
\\Mailer2\HKLM\SYSTEM\CurrentControlSet\Services\DNS /s
```

Now the key, all subkeys, and all related entries for the DNS key on MAILER1 and MAILER2 are compared.

Saving and Restoring Registry Keys

Before modifying registry entries, it is a good idea to save the keys you will use. If anything goes wrong, you can restore those keys to their original settings. To save a copy of a registry subkey and all its related subkeys and values, use REG save, as shown here:

```
reg save KeyName "FileName"
```

where *KeyName* is the path to the subkey you want to save and *FileName* is the text name of the registry hive file you want to create. The subkey path can include the UNC name or IP address of a remote computer. However, on a remote computer, you can only work with the HKLM and HKU root keys. Additionally, the file name must be enclosed in double quotation marks and should end in the .hiv extension to indicate it is a registry hive file, as shown in the following example:

```
reg save HKLM\SYSTEM\CurrentControlSet\Services\DNS "DNSKey.hiv"
```

Here, you are saving the DNS subkey and its related subkeys and values to the file named Dnskey.hiv. The file name can also include a directory path, as shown in this example:

```
reg save \\Mailer1\HKLM\SYSTEM\CurrentControlSet\Services\DNS
"\\Mailer1\SavedData\DNSKey.hiv"
```

If the registry hive file exists, you will be prompted to overwrite the file. Press Y to overwrite. If you want to force overwrite without prompting, use the /Y parameter.

To restore a registry key that you saved previously, use Reg restore. The syntax for REG restore is

```
reg restore KeyName "FileName"
```

where *KeyName* is the path to the subkey you want to save and *FileName* is the text name of the registry hive file you want to use as the restore source. Unlike REG copy, REG restore can be used only on a local computer, meaning you cannot restore registry keys on a remote computer using the command. You can, however, start a remote desktop session on the remote computer and then use the remote desktop logon to restore the registry key on the local computer.

An example using REG restore is shown here:

```
reg restore HKLM\SYSTEM\CurrentControlSet\Services\DNS "DNSKey.hiv"
```

Here, you are restoring the DNS key saved previously to the DNSKey.hiv file.

Adding Registry Keys

To add subkeys and values to the Windows registry, use REG add. The basic syntax for creating a key or value is

```
reg add KeyName /v ValueName /t DataType /d Data
```

where *KeyName* is the name of the key you want to examine, *ValueName* is the subkey or key value to create, *DataType* is the type of data, and *Data* is the actual value you are inserting. That seems like a lot of values, but it is fairly straightforward. Consider the following example:

```
reg add HKLM\SYSTEM\CurrentControlSet\Services\DNS /v DisplayName
/t REG_SZ /d "DNS Server"
```

Here, you add a key value called DisplayName to the DNS key in the registry. The key entry is a string with the "DNS Server" value. Note the double-quotation marks. The quotation marks are necessary in this example because the string contains a space.

When you set expandable string values (REG_EXPAND_SZ), you must use the caret (^) to escape the percent symbols (%) that designate the environment variable you use. Consider the following example:

```
reg add HKLM\SYSTEM\CurrentControlSet\Services\DNS /v ImagePath
/t REG_EXPAND_SZ /d ^%SystemRoot^%\System32\dns.exe
```

Here, you enter **^%SystemRoot^%** so that the *SystemRoot* environment variable is properly entered and interpreted.

When you set non-string values, you don't need to use quotation marks, as shown in this example:

```
reg add HKLM\SYSTEM\CurrentControlSet\Services\DNS /v ErrorControl
/t REG_DWORD /d 0x00000001
```

Copying Registry Keys

Using REG copy, you can copy a registry entry to a new location on a local or remote system. The basic syntax for REG copy is

```
reg copy KeyName1 KeyName2
```

where *KeyName1* is the path to the subkey you want to copy and *KeyName2* is the path to the subkey destination. Although the subkey paths can include the UNC name or IP address of a remote computer, REG copy is limited in scope with regard to which root keys you can use when working with remote source or destination keys, as follows:

- A remote source subkey can use only the HKLM or HKU root keys.
- A remote destination subkey can use only the HKLM or HKU root keys.

In the following example, you copy the DNS subkey on the local system to the DNS subkey on MAILER2:

```
reg copy HKLM\SYSTEM\CurrentControlSet\Services\DNS
    \\Mailer2\HKLM\SYSTEM\CurrentControlSet\Services\DNS
```

By adding the /S parameter, you can copy the specified subkey as well as all subkeys and key entries under the specified subkey. In this example, the DNS subkey and all related subkey and values are copied:

```
reg copy HKLM\SYSTEM\CurrentControlSet\Services\DNS
    \\Mailer2\HKLM\SYSTEM\CurrentControlSet\Services\DNS /s
```

If values exist at the destination path, REG copy will prompt you to confirm that you want to overwrite each existing value. Press Y or N as appropriate. You can also press A to overwrite all existing values without further prompting.

Note If you don't want prompts to be displayed, you can use the /F parameter to force overwrite without prompting. However, before you copy over existing registry keys, you may want to save the key so that it can be restored if problems occur. To do this, use REG save and REG restore as discussed earlier in the section of this chapter titled "Saving and Restoring Registry Keys."

Deleting Registry Keys

To delete subkeys and values from the Windows registry, use REG delete. REG delete has several different syntaxes. If you want to delete a subkey and all subkeys and entries under the subkey, use the following syntax:

```
reg delete KeyName
```

where *KeyName* is the name of the subkey you want to delete. Although the subkey path can include the UNC name or IP address of a remote computer, a remote source subkey can use only the HKLM or HKU root keys. Consider the following example:

```
reg delete \\Mailer1\HKLM\SYSTEM\CurrentControlSet\Services\DNS2
```

Here you delete the DNS2 subkey and all subkeys and entries under the subkey on MAILER1.

If you want to limit the scope of the deletion, specify that only a specific entry under the subkey should be deleted using the following syntax:

```
reg delete KeyName /v ValueName
```

where *KeyName* is the name of the subkey you want to work with and *Value-Name* is the name of the specific entry to delete. As before, the subkey path can include the UNC name or IP address of a remote computer. However, a remote source subkey can use only the HKLM or HKU root keys. In this example, you delete the Description entry for the DNS2 subkey on MAILER2:

```
reg delete \\Mailer2\HKLM\SYSTEM\CurrentControlSet\Services\DNS2 /v
Description
```

 Tip In both cases, you will be prompted to confirm that you want to delete the specified entry permanently. Press Y to confirm the deletion. You can force deletion without prompting using the /F parameter. Another useful parameter is /Va. Using the /Va parameter, you can specify that only entries under the subkey should be deleted. In this way, subkeys under the designated subkey are not deleted.

Managing System Services

Services provide key functions to workstations and servers. To manage system services on local and remote systems, you'll use the service controller command SC, which has several subcommands, only some of which are explored here. The sections that follow discuss each of these subcommands:

- **SC config**   Configures service startup and logon accounts
- **SC query**   Displays the list of all services configured on the computer
- **SC qc**   Displays the configuration of a specific service
- **SC start**   Starts services
- **SC stop**   Stops services
- **SC pause**   Pauses services
- **SC continue**   Resumes services
- **SC failure**   Sets the actions to take upon failure of a service
- **SC qfailure**   Views the actions to take upon failure of a service

With all commands, you can specify the name of the remote computer whose services you want to work with. To do this, insert the UNC name or IP address of the computer before the subcommand you want to use. This makes the syntax

```
sc ServerName Subcommand
```

Viewing Configured Services

To get a list of all services configured on a system, type the following command at the command prompt:

```
sc query type= service state= all
```

or

```
sc ServerName query type= service state= all
```

where *ServerName* is the UNC name or IP address of the remote computer, such as \\Mailer1 or \\192.168.1.100, as shown in the following examples:

```
sc \\Mailer1 query type= service state= all
sc \\192.168.1.100 query type= service state= all
```

Note There must be a space after the equal sign (=) as used with *type= service* and *state= all*. If you don't use a space, the command will fail.

With the *state* flag, you can also use the value *active* (to show running services only) or *inactive* (to show all paused or stopped services). Consider the following examples:

```
sc \\Mailer1 query type= service state= active
sc \\Mailer1 query type= service state= inactive
```

In the first example, you query MAILER1 for a list of all services that are running. In the second example, you query MAILER1 for a list of all services that are stopped.

The output of SC query shows the services and their configurations. Each service entry is formatted as follows:

```
SERVICE_NAME: W3SVC
DISPLAY_NAME: World Wide Web Publishing Service
        TYPE               : 20  WIN32_SHARE_PROCESS
        STATE              : 4   RUNNING
                             (STOPPABLE, PAUSABLE, ACCEPTS_SHUTDOWN)
        WIN32_EXIT_CODE    : 0   (0x0)
        SERVICE_EXIT_CODE  : 0   (0x0)
        CHECKPOINT         : 0x0
        WAIT_HINT          : 0x0
```

As an administrator, the fields you will work with the most are

- **Service Name** The abbreviated name of the service. Only services installed on the system are listed here. If a service you need isn't listed, you'll need to install it.
- **Display Name** The descriptive name of the service.
- **State** The state of the service as Running, Paused, or Stopped.

As you'll see if you run the SC query command, the output is very long and is best used with a filter to get only the information you want to see. For example, if you use the following command, you clean up the output to show only the most important fields:

```
sc query type= service | find /v "x0"
```

Here you pipe the output of SC query through the FIND command and clean up the output so the service entries appear, as shown in this example:

```
SERVICE_NAME: W3SVC
DISPLAY_NAME: World Wide Web Publishing Service
        TYPE              : 20  WIN32_SHARE_PROCESS
        STATE             : 4   RUNNING
                            (STOPPABLE, PAUSABLE, ACCEPTS_SHUTDOWN)
```

 Note The parameter /V "x0" tells the FIND command to display only lines of output that do not contain the text *x0*, which is the common text on WIN32_Exit_Code, Service_Exit_Code, Checkpoint, and Wait_Hint fields. By specifying that you don't want to see lines of output that contain this value, you therefore remove these unwanted fields from the display.

If you know the name of a service you want to work with, you can use SC qc to display its configuration information. The syntax is

```
sc qc ServiceName
```

where *ServiceName* is the name of the service you want to examine. The output for individual services looks like this:

```
SERVICE_NAME: w3svc
        TYPE              : 20  WIN32_SHARE_PROCESS
        START_TYPE        : 2   AUTO_START
        ERROR_CONTROL     : 1   NORMAL
        BINARY_PATH_NAME  : C:\WINDOWS\System32\svchost.exe -k
         iissvcs
        LOAD_ORDER_GROUP  :
        TAG               : 0
        DISPLAY_NAME      : World Wide Web Publishing Service
        DEPENDENCIES      : RPCSS
                          : HTTPFilter
                          : IISADMIN
        SERVICE_START_NAME : LocalSystem
```

Note that the output doesn't tell you the current status of the service. It does, however, tell you the following:

- **Binary Path Name**   The file path to the executable for the service
- **Dependencies**   Services that cannot run unless the specified service is running
- **Display Name**   The descriptive name of the service
- **Service Start Name**   The name of the user account the service logs on as
- **Start Type**   The startup configuration of the service

Note Services that are configured to start automatically are listed as AUTO_START. Services that are configured to start manually are listed as DEMAND_START. Services that are disabled are listed as DISABLED.

• **Type** The type of service and whether it is a shared process

Note When you are configuring a service logon, it is sometimes important to know whether a process runs in its own context or is shared. Shared processes are listed as WIN32_SHARE_PROCESS. Processes that run in their own context are listed as WIN32_OWN_PROCESS.

Starting, Stopping, and Pausing Services

As an administrator, you'll often have to start, stop, or pause Windows services. The related SC commands and their syntaxes are

Start a service:

```
sc start ServiceName
```

Pause a service:

```
sc pause ServiceName
```

Resume a paused service:

```
sc continue ServiceName
```

Stop a service:

```
sc stop ServiceName
```

where *ServiceName* in each case is the abbreviated name of the service you want to work with, such as

```
sc start w3svc
```

As with all SC commands, you can also specify the name of the remote computer whose services you want to work with. For example, to start the w3svc on MAILER1, you would use the following command:

```
sc \\Mailer1 start w3svc
```

The state listed in the results should show START_PENDING. With stop, pause, and continue you'll see STOP_PENDING, PAUSE_PENDING, and CONTINUE_PENDING respectively as well. If an error results, the output states

FAILED and error text is provided to describe the reason for the failure in more detail. If you are trying to start a service that is already started, you'll see the error

```
An instance of the service is already running.
```

If you are trying to stop a service that is already stopped, you'll see the error

```
The service has not been started.
```

Configuring Service Startup

You can set Windows services to start manually or automatically. You can also turn them off permanently by disabling them. You configure service startup using

```
sc config ServiceName start= flag
```

where *ServiceName* is the abbreviated name of the service you want to work with and *flag* is the startup type to use. For services, valid flag values are

- **Auto** Start service at system startup
- **Demand** Allow the services to be started manually
- **Disabled** Turns off the service

Following this, you can configure a service to start automatically by using:

```
sc config w3svc start= auto
```

or

```
sc \\Mailer1 config w3svc start= auto
```

 Note There must be a space after the equal sign (=) as used with *start= auto*. If you don't use a space, the command will fail. Note also the command only reports SUCCESS or FAILURE. It won't tell you that the service was already configured in the startup mode you've specified.

 Security Alert Disabling a service doesn't stop a running service. It only prevents it from being started the next time the computer is booted. To ensure the service is disabled and stopped, run SC stop and then SC config.

Configuring Service Logon

You can configure Windows services to log on as a system account or as a specific user. To ensure a service log on as the LocalSystem account, use

```
sc config ServiceName obj= LocalSystem
```

where *ServiceName* is the name of the service you are configuring to use the LocalSystem account. If the service provides a user interface that can be manipulated, add the flags **type= interact type= own**, as shown in the following example:

```
sc config w3svc obj= LocalSystem type= interact type= own
```

The *type= interact* flag specifies that the service is allowed to interact with the Windows desktop. The *type= own* flag specifies that the service runs in its own process. In the case of a service that shares its executable files with other services, you would use the *type= share* flag, as shown in this example:

```
sc config w3svc obj= LocalSystem type= interact type= share
```

Tip If you don't know whether a service runs as a shared process or in its own context, use SC qc to determine the service's start type. This command is discussed in the section of this chapter titled "Viewing Configured Services."

Services can also log on using named accounts. To do this, use

```
sc config ServiceName obj= [Domain\]User password= Password
```

where *Domain* is the optional domain name in which the user account is located, *User* is the name of the user account whose permissions you want to use, and *Password* is the password of that account. Consider the following example:

```
sc config w3svc obj= adatum\webbies password= blue5!CraZy
```

Here, you configure W3svc to use the Webbies account in the Adatum domain. The output of the command should state SUCCESS or FAILED. The change will fail if the account name is invalid or doesn't exist, or if the password for the account is invalid.

Note If a service has been previously configured to interact with the desktop under the LocalSystem account, you cannot change the service to run under a domain account without using the *type= own* flag. The syntax therefore becomes sc config ServiceName obj= [Domain\]User password= Password type= own.

Security Alert As an administrator, you should keep track of any accounts that are used with services. These accounts can be the source of huge security problems if they're not configured properly. Service accounts should have the strictest security settings and as few permissions as possible while allowing the service to perform necessary functions. Typically, accounts used with services don't need many of the permissions you would assign to a normal user account. For example, most service accounts don't need the right to log on locally. Every administrator should know what service accounts are used (so they can better track use of these accounts), and the accounts should be treated as if they were administrator accounts. This means secure passwords, careful monitoring of account usage, careful application of account permissions and privileges, and so on.

Configuring Service Recovery

Using the SC failure command, you can configure Windows services to take specific actions when a service fails. For example, you can attempt to restart the service or run an application.

You can configure recovery options for the first, second, and subsequent recovery attempts. The current failure count is incremented each time a failure occurs. You can also set a parameter that specifies the time that must elapse before the failure counter is reset. For example, you could specify that if 24 hours have passed since the last failure, the failure counter should be reset.

Before you try to configure service recovery, check the current recovery settings using SC qfailure. The syntax is

```
sc qfailure ServiceName
```

where *ServiceName* is the name of the service you want to work with, such as

```
sc qfailure w3svc
```

You can of course specify a remote computer as well, such as

```
sc \\Mailer1 qfailure w3svc
```

or

```
sc \\192.168.1.100 qfailure w3svc
```

In the output, the failure actions are listed in the order they are performed. In the following example output, W3svc is configured to attempt to restart the service the first and second time the service fails and to restart the computer if the service fails a third time:

```
[SC] QueryServiceConfig2 SUCCESS

SERVICE_NAME: w3svc
        RESET_PERIOD (in seconds)    : 86400
        REBOOT_MESSAGE               :
        COMMAND_LINE                 :
        FAILURE_ACTIONS              : RESTART -- Delay = 1 milliseconds.
                                       RESTART -- Delay = 1 milliseconds.
                                       REBOOT -- Delay = 1000 milliseconds.
```

 Note Windows automatically configures recovery for some critical system services during installation. Typically, these services are configured so that they attempt to restart the service. A few services are configured so that they run programs. For example, the IIS Admin service is configured to run a program called Iisreset.exe if the service fails. This program is an application that corrects service problems and safely manages dependent IIS services while working to restart the IIS Admin service.

The command you use to configure service recovery is SC failure and its basic syntax is

```
sc failure ServiceName reset= FailureResetPeriod actions=
RecoveryActions
```

where *ServiceName* is the name of the service you are configuring, *FailureReset-Period* specifies the time, in seconds, that must elapse without failure in order to reset the failure counter, and *RecoveryActions* are the actions to take when failure occurs plus the delay time (in milliseconds) before that action is initiated. The available recovery actions are

- **Take No Action** The operating system won't attempt recovery for this failure but might still attempt recovery of previous or subsequent failures.

- **Restart The Service** Stops and then starts the service after a brief pause.

- **Run A Program** Allows you to run a program or a script in case of failure. The script can be a batch program or a Windows script. If you select this option, set the full file path to the program you want to run and then set any necessary command-line parameters to pass in to the program when it starts.

- **Reboot The Computer** Shuts down and then restarts the computer after the specified delay time is elapsed.

Best Practices When you configure recovery options for critical services, you might want to try to restart the service on the first and second attempts and then reboot the server on the third attempt.

When you work with SC failure, keep the following in mind:

- **The reset period is set in seconds.** Reset periods are commonly set in multiples of hours or days. An hour is 3,600 seconds and a day is 86,400 seconds. For a two-hour reset period, for example, you'd use the value 7,200.

- **Each recovery action must be followed by the time to wait (in milliseconds) before performing the action.** For a service restart you'll probably want to use a short delay, such as 1 millisecond (no delay), 1 second (1,000 milliseconds), or 5 seconds (5,000 milliseconds). For a restart of the computer, you'll probably want to use a longer delay, such as 15 seconds (15,000 milliseconds) or 30 seconds (30,000 milliseconds).

- **Enter the actions and their delay times as a single text entry with each value separated by a forward slash (/).** For example, you could use the value: restart/1000/restart/1000/reboot/15000. Here, on the first and second attempts the service is restarted after a 1-second delay, and on the third attempt the computer is rebooted after a 15-second delay.

Consider the following examples:

```
sc failure w3svc reset= 86400 actions= restart/1/restart/1/reboot/30000
```

Here, on the first and second attempts the service is restarted almost immediately, and on the third attempt the computer is rebooted after a 30-second delay.

In addition, the failure counter is reset if no failures occur in a 24-hour period (86,400 seconds). You can also specify a remote computer by inserting the UNC name or IP address as shown in previous examples.

If you use the Run action, you specify the command or program to run using the *Command=* parameter. Follow the *Command=* parameter with the full file path to the command to run and any arguments to pass to the command. Be sure to enclose the command path and text in double quotation marks, as in the following example:

```
sc failure w3svc reset= 86400 actions= restart/1/restart/1/run/30000
command= "c:\restart_w3svc.exe 15"
```

Restarting and Shutting Down Systems from the Command Line

You'll often find that you need to shut down or restart systems. One way to do this is to use the Shutdown utility, which can be used to work with both local and remote systems. Another way to manage system shutdown or restart is to schedule a shutdown. Here, you can use Schtasks to specify when shutdown should be run or you can create a script with a list of shutdown commands for individual systems.

 Real World Although Windows systems usually start up and shut down without problems, they can occasionally stop responding during these processes. If this happens, try to determine the cause. Some of the reasons systems might stop responding include the following:

1. The system is attempting to execute or is running a startup or shut-down script that has not completed or is itself not responding (and in this case, the system might be waiting for the script to time out).

2. A startup initialization file or service may be the cause of the problem and if so, you might need to troubleshoot startup items using the System Configuration Utility (Msconfig). Disabling a service, startup item, or entry in a startup initialization file might also solve the problem.

3. The system may have an antivirus program that is causing the problem. In some cases, the antivirus program may try to scan the floppy disk drive when you try to shut down the system. To resolve this, configure the antivirus software so that it doesn't scan the floppy drive or other drives with removable media on shutdown. You could also try temporarily disabling or turning off the antivirus program.

4. Improperly configured sound devices can cause startup and shut-down problems. To determine what the possible source is, examine each of these devices in turn. Turn off sound devices and then restart the computer. If the problem clears up, you have to install new drivers for the sound devices you are using or you may have a corrupted Start Windows or Exit Windows sound file.

5. Improperly configured network cards can cause startup and shutdown problems. Try turning off the network adapter and restarting. If that works, you might need to remove and then reinstall the adapter's driver or obtain a new driver from the manufacturer.

6. Improperly configured video adapter drivers can cause startup and shutdown problems. From another computer, remotely log in and try to roll back the current video drivers to a previous version. If that's not possible, try uninstalling and then reinstalling the video drivers.

Managing Restart and Shutdown of Local Systems

On a local system, you can manage shutdown and restart using the following commands:

Shutdown local system:

```
shutdown /s /t ShutdownDelay /l /f
```

Restart local system:

```
shutdown /r /t ShutdownDelay /l /f
```

Cancel delayed shutdown of local computer:

```
shutdown /a
```

where /T *ShutdownDelay* is used to set the optional number of seconds to wait before shutdown or restart, /L optionally logs off the current user immediately, and /F optionally forces running applications to close without warning users in advance. In this example, the local system is restarted after a 60-second delay:

```
shutdown /r /t 60
```

Best Practices In most network environments, system uptime is of the utmost importance. Systems that are restarting or shutting down aren't available to users, which might mean someone won't be able to finish her work and might get upset as a result. Rather than shut down systems in the middle of business hours, consider performing shutdowns before or after normal business hours. But if you need to shut down a system during business hours, warn users beforehand if possible, allowing them to save current work and log off the system as necessary.

Managing Restart and Shutdown of Remote Systems

With remote systems, you need to specify the UNC name or IP address of the system you want to shut down or restart using the /M parameter. Thus, the basic syntax for shutdown, restart, and cancel delayed shutdown become

Shutdown remote system:

```
shutdown /s /t ShutdownDelay /l /f /m \\System
```

Restart remote system:

```
shutdown /r /t ShutdownDelay /l /f /m \\System
```

Cancel delayed shutdown of remote computer:

```
shutdown /a /m \\System
```

In this example, MAILER1 is restarted after a 30-second delay:

```
shutdown /r /t 30 /m \\Mailer1
```

In this example, the system with the IP address 192.168.1.105 is restarted immediately and running applications are forced to stop running:

```
shutdown /r /f /m \\192.168.1.105
```

Adding Shutdown or Restart Reasons and Comments

In most network environments, it's a good idea to document the reasons for shutting down or restarting computers. With unplanned shutdowns, you can document the shutdown in the computer's system log by expanding the syntax to include the following parameters:

```
/e /c "UnplannedReason" /d MajorCode:MinorCode
```

where /C *"UnplannedReason"* sets the detailed reason (which can be up to 127 characters in length) for the shutdown or restart, and /D *MajorCode:MinorCode* sets the reason code for the shutdown. Reason codes are arbitrary, with valid major codes ranging from 0 to 255 and valid minor reason codes ranging from 0 to 65,535. Consider the following example:

```
shutdown /r /e /m \\Mailer1 /c "System Reset" /d 5:15
```

In this example, you are restarting MAILER1 and documenting the reason for the unplanned restart as a "System Reset" using the reason code 5:15.

With planned shutdowns and restarts, prefix the reason codes with **p:** to indicate a planned shutdown, as shown here:

```
/e /c "PlannedReason" /d p:MajorCode:MinorCode
```

For instance, consider the following code:

```
shutdown /r /e /m \\Mailer1 /c "Planned Application Upgrade" /d p:4:2
```

In this example, you are restarting MAILER1 and documenting the reason for the planned restart as a "Planned Application Upgrade" using the reason code 4:2.

Chapter 6

Event Logging, Tracking, and Automated Monitoring

Up to this point, we have focused on tools and techniques used to manage local and remote systems from the command line. Now let's look at how the event logs can be used for monitoring and optimization. Monitoring is the process by which systems are regularly checked for problems. Optimization is the process of fine-tuning system performance to maintain or achieve its optimal capacity.

This chapter examines logging tools available for Windows systems that can help you to identify and track system problems, monitor applications and services, and maintain system security. When systems slow down, behave erratically, or experience other problems, you may want to look to the event logs to identify the potential source of the problem. Once problem sources or issues are identified, you can perform maintenance or preventative tasks to resolve or eliminate them. Using event triggers, which watch for events to occur and take appropriate action to resolve them, you can even automate the monitoring and maintenance processes.

Windows Event Logging

In Microsoft Windows, an *event* is any significant occurrence in the operating system that requires users or administrators to be notified. Events are recorded in the Windows event logs and provide important historical information to help you monitor systems, maintain system security, solve problems, and perform diagnostics. It is important to sift regularly through the information collected in these logs, it is essential. Administrators should closely monitor the event logs of every business server and ensure that workstations are configured to track important system events. On servers, you want to ensure that systems are secure, that applications and services are operating normally, and that the server isn't experiencing errors that could hamper performance. On workstations, you want to ensure that the events you need to maintain systems and resolve problems are being logged, and that the logs are accessible to you as necessary.

The Windows service that manages event logging is called the Event Log service. When this service is started, Windows logs important information. The logs available on a system depend on the system's role and the services installed. Logs you may see include the following:

- **Application** This log records significant incidents associated with specific applications. For example, Exchange Server logs events related to mail exchange, including events for the information store, mailboxes, and service states. By default, this log is stored in *%SystemRoot%*\System32\Config\Appevent.evt.

- **Directory Service** On domain controllers, this log records incidents from Active Directory, including events related to directory startup, global catalogs, and integrity checking. By default, this log is stored in *%SystemRoot%*\System32\Config\Ntds.evt.

- **DNS Server** On DNS servers, this log records DNS queries, responses, and other DNS activities. By default, this log is stored in *%SystemRoot%*\System32\Config\Dnsevent.evt.

- **File Replication Service** On domain controllers and other servers using replication, this log records file replication activities on the system, including events for service status and control, scanning data in system volumes, and managing replication sets. By default, this log is stored in *%SystemRoot%*\System32\Config\Ntfrs.evt.

- **Security** This logs records events related to security such as logon/logoff, privilege use and resource access. By default, this log is stored in *%SystemRoot%*\System32\Config\Secevent.evt.

Security Alert To gain access to security logs, users must be granted the user right Manage Auditing And Security Log. By default, members of the administrators group have this user right. You will learn more about assigning user rights in the section titled, "Configuring User Rights Policies" of Chapter 9 in the *Microsoft Windows Server 2003 Administrator's Pocket Consultant*.

- **System** This log records events from the operating system or its components, such as the failure of a service to start, driver initialization, system-wide messages, and other messages that relate to the system in general. By default, this log is stored in *%SystemRoot%*\System32\Config\Sysevent.evt.

Events range in severity from informational messages to general warnings to serious incidents such as critical errors and failures. The category of an event is indicated by its event type. Event types include

- **Information** Indicates an informational event has occurred, which is generally related to a successful action.

- **Warning** Indicates a general warning. Warnings are often useful in preventing future system problems.

- **Error** Indicates a critical error, such as the failure of a service to start.

- **Success Audit** Indicates the successful execution of an action that you are tracking through auditing, such as privilege use.

- **Failure Audit** Indicates the failed execution of an action that you are tracking through auditing, such as failure to log on.

Note Of the many event types, the two you'll want to monitor closely are warnings and errors. Whenever these types of events occur and you're unsure of the reason, you should take a closer look to determine if you need to take further action.

In addition to type, each event has the following common properties associated with it:

- **Date Time** Specifies the date and time the event occurred.

- **Event** Details the specific event that occurred with a numeric identifier called an event ID. Event IDs are generated by the event source and used to uniquely identify the event.

- **Source** Identifies the source of the event, such as an application, service, or system component. The event source is useful for pinpointing the cause of an event.

- **Computer** Identifies the computer that caused the event to occur.

- **Category** Specifies the category of the event, which is sometimes used to further describe the related action. Each event source has its own event categories. For example, with the security source, categories include logon/logoff, privilege use, policy change, and account management.

- **User** Identifies the user account that caused the event to be generated. Users can include special identities, such as Local Service, Network Service, and Anonymous Logon, as well as actual user accounts. The user account can also be listed as N/A to indicate that a user account is not applicable in this situation.

- **Description** Provides a detailed description of the event and may also include details about where to find more information to resolve or handle an issue. This field is available when you double-click a log entry in Event Viewer.

The GUI tool you use to manage events is Event Viewer. You can start this tool by typing **eventvwr** at the command –line for the local computer, or **eventvwr /computer=*ComputerName***, where *ComputerName* is the name of the remote computer whose events you wish to examine. As with most GUI tools, Event Viewer is easy to use and you will want to continue to use it for certain management tasks. For example, you must use Event Viewer to control the size of the event logs, to specify how logging is handled and to archive event logs. These tasks cannot be performed at the command line.

Event Viewer falls short, however, in its ability to filter events and work with event logs on remote computers. Sure, you can use Event Viewer to handle these tasks, but there are other utilities better suited to these tasks, including the following:

- **Eventquery** Searches event logs and collects event entries that match specific criteria. In a script, you could use Eventquery to examine events on multiple systems and then store the results in a file, making it easier to track information as well as warnings and errors on the network as a whole.

- **Eventcreate** Creates custom events in the event logs. Whenever you run custom scripts on a schedule or as part of routine maintenance, you may want to record the action in the event logs and Eventcreate provides a way to do this.

- **Eventtriggers** Monitors event logs for specific events and then acts on those events by running tasks or commands. Using triggered events, you can configure systems to be self-monitoring. Triggered events are similar to scheduled tasks, except they run based on the occurrence of system events rather than on a recurring or one-time basis.

 Real World Monitoring system events isn't something you should do haphazardly. Rather, it is something you should do routinely and thoroughly. With servers, you will want to examine event logs at least once a day and configure event triggers that alert you of any critical issues immediately. With workstations, you will want to examine logs on specific workstations as necessary, such as when a user reports a problem.

Viewing and Filtering Event Logs

You can view events recorded in the Windows event logs using the Eventquery utility. Eventquery flags set the format of the output, control the level of detail, and allow you to use filters to include or exclude events from the result set. When working with Eventquery, don't overlook the power of automation. You don't have to run the command manually each time. Instead, you can create a script to query the event logs on multiple systems and then save the results to a file. If you copy that file to a published folder on an intranet server, you can use your Web browser to examine event listings. Not only will that save you time, it will give you a single location for examining event logs and determining if there are issues that require further study.

Viewing Events and Formatting the Output

The basic syntax for Eventquery is

```
eventquery /l "LogName"
```

where *LogName* is the name of the log you want to work with, such as "Application," "System," or "Directory Service." In this example, you examine the Application log:

```
eventquery /l "Application"
```

The output of this query would look similar to the following:

```
-----------------------------------------------------------------------------
Listing the events in 'application' log of host 'MAILER1'
-----------------------------------------------------------------------------
Type          Event   Date        Time          Source               ComputerName
-----------   ------  ----------  -----------    ------------------   ------------
Warning       9220    5/19/2004   4:38:01 PM     MSExchangeMTA        MAILER1
Information    1001    5/19/2004   4:28:50 PM     MSExchangeIS         MAILER1
Information    9600    5/19/2004   4:28:50 PM     MSExchangeIS         MAILER1
Information    9523    5/19/2004   4:28:50 PM     MSExchangeIS Publ    MAILER1
Information    9523    5/19/2004   4:28:49 PM     MSExchangeIS Mail    MAILER1
Information    9523    5/19/2004   4:28:48 PM     MSExchangeIS Publ    MAILER1
Information    9523    5/19/2004   4:28:47 PM     MSExchangeIS Mail    MAILER1
Information    9523    5/19/2004   4:28:46 PM     MSExchangeIS Mail    MAILER1
Information    3000    5/19/2004   4:28:45 PM     MSExchangeIS Publ    MAILER1
Information    1133    5/19/2004   4:28:41 PM     MSExchangeIS Publ    MAILER1
```

As you can see, the output shows the Type, Event, Date Time, Source, and ComputerName properties of events. Using the /V (verbose) option, you can add category, user, and description properties to the output. Thus, if you wanted a verbose view of the application log, you'd use the command:

```
eventquery /l "Application" /v
```

Note Technically, the quotation marks are necessary only when the log name contains a space, as is the case with the DNS Server, Directory Service, and File Replication Service logs. However, I recommend using the quotation marks all the time; that way, you won't forget them when they are needed and they won't cause your scripts or scheduled tasks to fail.

Tip Unlike previous command-line utilities that we've worked with, Eventquery is configured as a Windows script. If this is your first time working with Windows scripts from the system's command line or you've configured WScript as the primary script host, you will need to set CScript as the default script host. You do this by typing **cscript //h:cscript //s** at the command prompt. This is necessary because you want to work with the command line rather than with the GUI.

Real World The script host is set on a per-user basis and if you are running a script as a specific user, that use might not have CScript configured as the default script host. An effective workaround for this is to enter **cscript //h:cscript //s** as a line of the script and then enter your event queries.

Eventquery runs by default on the local computer with the permissions of the user who is currently logged on. As necessary, you can also specify the remote computer whose tasks you want to query and the Run As permissions by using the expanded syntax which includes the following parameters:

```
/s Computer /u [Domain\]User [/p Password]
```

where *Computer* is the remote computer name or IP address, *Domain* is the optional domain name in which the user account is located, *User* is the name of the user account whose permissions you want to use, and *Password* is the optional password for the user account. For example, if you wanted to examine directory service events on MAILER1 using the Adatam\WRStanek account, you could use the following command:

```
eventquery /l "Directory Service" /s Mailer1 /u Adatam\WRStanek
```

 Note If you don't specify the domain, the current domain is assumed. If you don't provide the account password, you are prompted for the password.

The syntax can be extended to include the following format options as well:

- **/Nh** Removes the heading row from the output of Table- or CSV-formatted data.

- **/Fo *Format*** Changes the output format, which by default is table (/Fo Table). Use /Fo Csv to format the output as comma-separated values. Use /Fo List to format the output as a list.

Where Eventquery gets interesting is in the range and filter facilities. With ranges, you can view

- **The *N* most recent events** Type **/r *N*** where *N* is the number of recent events to view, such as **/r 50** for the 50 most recent events.

- **The *N* oldest events** Type **/r -*N*** where -*N* is the number of the oldest events to view, such as **/r -50** for the 50 oldest events.

- **Events from *N1* to *N2*** Type **/r *N1-N2*** where *N1* is the first event and *N2* is the last event to view, with 1 being the most recent event recorded, 2 being the next previous event recorded, and so on. For example, to see events 10 to 20 you'd use **/r 10-20**.

Techniques for filtering events are discussed in the next section.

Filtering Events

One of the key reasons for using Eventquery is its ability to use filters to include or exclude events from the result set. Typically, you won't want to see every event generated on a system. More often, you will want to see only warnings or critical errors, and that is precisely what filters are for. Using filters, you can include only events that match the criteria you specify.

Any of the information fields available can be filtered, even if the information field is only listed with the verbose flag (/V) and you haven't specified the verbose flag for the current command. This means you can filter events by type, date time, source, computer name, event ID, category, and user.

You designate how a filter should be applied to a particular Eventquery information field using filter operators. The filter operators available are

- **Eq** Equals. If the field contains the specified value, the event is included in the output.

- **Ne** Not equals. If the field contains the specified value, the event is excluded from the output.

- **Gt** Greater than. If the field contains a numeric value and that value is greater than the value specified, the event is included in the output.

- **Lt** Less than. If the field contains a numeric value and that value is less than the value specified, the event is included in the output.

- **Ge** Greater than or equal to. If the field contains a numeric value and that value is greater than or equal to the value specified, the event is included in the output.

- **Le** Less than or equal to. If the field contains a numeric value and that value is less than or equal to the value specified, the event is included in the output.

As Table 6-1 shows, the values that can be used with filter operators depend on the event information field you are using. Again remember that all fields are available even if they aren't normally displayed with the parameters you've specified. For example, you can match the status field without using the /V (verbose) flag.

Table 6-1. Filter Operators and Valid Values for Eventquery

Filter Field Name	Valid Operators	Valid Values
Category	eq, ne	Any valid string of characters.
Computer	eq, ne	Any valid string of characters.
Datetime	eq, ne, gt, lt, ge, le	Any valid time in the format $mm/dd/yy$, $hh:mm:ss$AM or $mm/dd/yy$, $hh:mm:ss$PM.
ID	eq, ne, gt, lt, ge, le	Any valid positive integer, up to 65,535.
Source	eq, ne	Any valid string of characters.
Type	eq, ne	Information, Warning, Error, SuccessAudit, FailureAudit.
User	eq, ne	Any valid user name, with user name only or in $domain\backslash user$ format.

Quotation marks must be used to enclose the filter string. Consider the following examples to see how filters can be used:

Look for error events in the application log:

```
eventquery /l "application" /fi "type eq error"
```

Look for system log events on MAILER1 that occurred after midnight on 05/06/04:

```
eventquery /s Mailer1 /l "system" /fi "date gt 05/06/04,00:00:00AM"
```

Look for DNS server log errors on MAILER1 with event ID 4004:

```
eventquery /s Mailer1 /l "dns server" /fi "id eq 4004"
```

Enter multiple /Fi parameters to specify that output must match against multiple filters:

```
eventquery /l "system" /fi "date gt 05/06/04,00:00:00AM" /fi "type
eq error"
```

Here, Eventquery would examine the system logs for error events that were created after midnight on 05/06/04. Keep in mind that filters are mutually exclusive. You can't specify that you want to see both error and warning events using a single command line. You would need to enter two different commands. One with /Fi "type eq error" and the other with /Fi "type eq warning."

However, if you are working with a log other than security (in which only success audit and failure audit events are logged), you can simply specify that you don't want to see informational events. That way, you will only see warning and error events as shown in the following example:

```
eventquery /l "system" /fi "type ne information"
```

You can automate the event querying process by creating a script that obtains the event information you want to see and then writes it to a text file. Consider the following example:

```
@echo off
eventquery /s Mailer1 /l "system" /r 100 /fi "type ne information" >
\\CorpIntranet01\www\currentlog.txt

eventquery /s Mailer1 /l "application" /r 100 /fi "type ne
information" >> \\CorpIntranet01\www\currentlog.txt

eventquery /s Mailer1 /l "directory service" /r 100 /fi "type ne
information" >> \\CorpIntranet01\www\currentlog.txt
```

Here, you are examining the system, application and directory service event logs on MAILER1 and writing any resulting output to a network share on CorpIntranet01. If any of the named logs have warning or error events among the 100 most recent events in the logs, the warnings or errors are written to the Currentlog.txt file. Because the first redirection is overwrite (>) and the remaining entries are append (>>), any existing Currentlog.txt file is overwritten each time the script runs. This ensures only current events are listed. To take the automation process a step further, you can create a scheduled task that runs the script each day or at specific intervals during the day.

Writing Custom Events to the Event Logs

Whenever you work with automated scripts, scheduled tasks, or custom applications, you might want those scripts, tasks, or applications to write custom events to the event logs. For example, if a script runs normally, you might want to write an informational event in the application log that specifies this so it is easier to determine that the script ran and completed normally. Similarly, if a script doesn't run normally and generates errors, you might want to log an error or warning event in the application log so that you'll know to examine the script and determine what happened.

Tip You can track errors that occur in scripts using *%ErrorLevel%*. This environment variable tracks the exit code of the most recently used command. If the command executes normally, the error level is zero (0). If an error occurs while executing the command, the error level is set to a nonzero value. To learn more about working with error levels, see the section of Chapter 3 titled, "Getting Acquainted with Variables."

To create custom events, you'll use the Eventcreate utility. Custom events can be logged in any available log except the security log, and can include the event source, ID and description you want to use. The syntax for Eventcreate is

```
eventcreate /l LogName /so EventSource /t EventType /id EventID /d
EventDescr
```

where

- **LogName** Sets the name of the log to which the event should be written. Use quotation marks if the log name contains spaces, as in "DNS Server."

Tip You cannot write custom events to the security logs. You can, however, write custom events to the DNS Server, Directory Service, File Replication Service, or other service-related logs. Start by writing a dummy event using the event source you want to register for use with that log. The initial event for that source will be written to the application log. You can then use the source with the specified log and your custom events.

- **EventSource** Specifies the source to use for the event and can be any string of characters. If the string contains spaces, use quotation marks, as in "Event Tracker." In most cases, you'll want the event source to identify the application, task, or script that is generating the error.

Caution Carefully plan the event source you want to use before you write events to the logs using those sources. Each event source you use must be unique and cannot be the same name as an existing source used by an installed service or application. For example, you cannot use DNS, W32Time or Ntfrs as sources because these sources are already used by installed services or applications. Additionally, once you use an event source with a particular log, the event source is registered for use with that log on the specified system. For example, you cannot use "EventChecker" as a source in the application log and in the system log on MAILER1. If you try to write an event using "EventChecker" to the system log after writing a previous event with that source to the application log, you will see the following error message: "ERROR: Source already exists in 'Application' log. Source cannot be duplicated."

- **EventType** Sets the event type as Information, Warning, or Error. "Success Audit" and "Failure Audit" event types are not valid; these events are used with the security logs and you cannot write custom events to the security logs.

- **EventID** Specifies the numeric ID for the event and can be any value from 1 to 1000. Before you assign event IDs haphazardly, you may want to write a list of the general events that can occur and then break these down into categories. You could then assign a range of event IDs to each category. For example, events in the 100s could be general events, events in the 200s could be status events, events in the 500s could be warning events, and events in the 900s could be error events.

- **EventDescr** Sets the description for the event and can be any string of characters. Be sure to enclose the description in quotation marks.

Note Eventcreate runs by default on the local computer with the permissions of the user who is currently logged on. As necessary, you can also specify the remote computer whose tasks you want to query and the Run As permissions using /S *Computer* /u [*Domain*]*User* [/P *Password*], where *Computer* is the remote computer name or IP address, *Domain* is the optional domain name in which the user account is located, *User* is the name of the user account whose permissions you want to use, and *Password* is the optional password for the user account.

To see how Eventcreate can be used, consider the following examples:

Create an information event in the application log with the source Event Tracker and event ID 209:

```
eventcreate /l "application" /t information /so "Event Tracker" /id
209 /d "evs.bat script ran without errors."
```

Create a warning event in the system log with the source CustApp and event ID 511:

```
eventcreate /l "system" /t warning /so "CustApp" /id 511 /d
"sysck.exe didn't complete successfully."
```

Create an error event in the system log on MAILER1 with the source "SysMon" and event ID 918:

```
eventcreate /s Mailer1 /l "system" /t error /so "SysMon" /id 918 /d
"sysmon.exe was unable to verify write operation."
```

Monitoring Systems Using Event Triggers

Now that you know how to view, filter, and create events, let's look at a technique using event triggers that you can use to automate the event monitoring process. With event triggers, you can configure system tasks that monitor the event logs and then take a specific action if an event occurs. For example, you can create a trigger that monitors the event logs for low disk space events and if such events occur, you can run a script that removes any temporary or unnecessary files to resolve the low disk space condition. Thus, not only can event triggers help you automate the monitoring process, the actions triggers take can also help you resolve issues as they arise to maintain system performance, ensure system integrity, and more.

Creating event triggers isn't something you should do casually, without careful forethought. You need to have a clear plan of action—a set of goals that you hope to achieve by using event triggers. Let's take a look at the reasons you might want to use event triggers and then look at the tools you can use to manage them.

Why Use Event Triggers?

Maintaining application and system performance is a key reason for using event triggers. For example, if an application running on a server has known issues that you usually have to resolve manually, you may be able to configure event triggers that monitor the event logs for related errors and then run scripts that take the appropriate actions to resolve the problem. Here, you would want to track down the known issues for the application by searching the event logs, asking other administrators about issues, or searching for knowledge-base articles that describe the issues. Afterward, match issues to specific events or types of events for which you can configure event triggers to monitor, and then write a script that notifies administrators of the issue or takes appropriate actions to resolve the issue. This script is then used as the task that the event trigger runs.

Another common reason for using event triggers is to help you identify application and service outages quickly, and to possibly restore normal operations. When an application or service stops, users can no longer use the resource and this can cost the organization dearly in time, money, and wasted resources. Here, you would want to search for documentation on the types of errors that can occur if the application or service isn't responding normally. Then, searching the event logs to see if you find similar or matching events in the logs, you would note sources, event IDs, and descriptions used so that you can create event triggers to watch for the related events. Finally, you could write a script that restarts the application or takes other appropriate actions to resolve the outage.

You may also want to use event triggers to help you maintain system security and integrity. When a system is under attack, events may be written to the log files that indicate the application, component or service that is under attack. With a brute force attack, a hacker may be trying various user name and password combinations in an attempt to gain access. If you are monitoring the system under attack, you would see failed logon attempts in the security logs as the hacker attempts to gain access. A hacker may also try to bring down the system, application, or service using a denial-of-service attack. Typically hackers deny service by sending continuous streams of malformed service requests. These attempts should show up in the related application, system, or service-specific logs as errors. To combat such attacks, you could configure event triggers that watch for related events, such as account lockouts due to a series of failed logon attempts.

Getting Ready to Use Event Triggers

Before you start creating event triggers, you should consider what you hope to achieve through automated monitoring, as well as any impact the monitoring might have on the affected systems and the network as a whole. You should

1. Identify the events you want to monitor and define the reasons for monitoring each event. Use the event logs on multiple systems and documentation of known issues and errors, such as knowledge-base articles, to help you pinpoint places to start.

2. Specify the actions you want to take when an event occurs. Initially, write this as a list. Be sure to consider the impact any corrective actions might have on the system or the network as a whole.

3. Write scripts or applications to handle the necessary corrective actions or user notifications. Don't implement them as triggers yet. You should test the scripts first on an isolated network or development system to uncover any flaws in the planning.

4. Define the event triggers and the tasks to execute, and then implement the triggers. Make sure you monitor the affected systems closely for the next several days or weeks to ensure there are no adverse affects.

5. Maintain and remove triggers as necessary to ensure continuing operations.

Steps 1, 2, and 3 can be accomplished using the earlier discussions in this and other chapters of this book. Steps 4 and 5, however, involve the processes of defining, maintaining, and removing event triggers. These processes are handled with the following subcommands of the Eventtriggers utility:

- **Eventtriggers /create**   Creates a new event trigger and sets the action to take

- **Eventtriggers /query**   Displays the event triggers currently configured on a specified system

- **Eventtriggers /delete**   Removes an event trigger when it is no longer needed

Note   Unlike most other commands with subcommands, Eventtriggers subcommands use a forward slash (/).

The sections that follow discuss each of these subcommands and their usage.

Creating Event Triggers

Event triggers can be configured to run executable programs with the .exe extension and scripts with the .bat or .cmd extension when an event occurs. You create event triggers using

```
eventtriggers /create /tr Name /l LogName [Constraints] /d Description
/tk Task
```

where

- **Name**   Sets the name of the trigger as a string of characters enclosed in quotation marks, such as "Connection Failure".

- **LogName**   Sets the name of the log to monitor. Use quotation marks if the log name contains spaces, as in "DNS Server." The default value is asterisk (*), which specifies that all logs should be monitored.

- **Constraints**   Sets the constraints that determine whether an event matches the trigger. Constraints limit the trigger's scope according to event ID, event source, or event type, using the /Eid *EventID*, /So *EventSource*, or /T *Event-Type* parameters respectively.

Tip You can use multiple constraints as well. If you do, the event must match each constraint in order to be triggered. Thus, additional constraints narrow the scope of the trigger.

- **Task** Sets the program or script to execute. Be sure to type the full path to the program or scripts you want to run.

 Note Eventtriggers does not verify file paths and if you enter an invalid file path, you will not see a warning. To pass arguments to an executable or script, enclose the file path and the command arguments in a set of double quotation marks, such as "c:\scripts\trackerror.bat system y".

- **Description** Sets the description for the trigger and can be any string of characters. Be sure to enclose the description in double quotation marks.

Don't be intimidated by the parade of parameters here. It's a lot easier than it looks once you get started. Consider the following examples:

Create an event trigger that monitors all the event logs for events with the ID 9220 and then runs Record-prob.bat:

```
Eventtriggers /create /tr "Monitor 9220 Errors" /eid 9220 /tk
\\Mailer1\scripts\record-prob.bat
```

Create an event trigger that monitors the DNS Server log for events with the source as DNS and the event ID 4004 and then runs Dns-adfix.bat:

```
Eventtriggers /create /tr "DNS AD Fix" /l "DNS Server" /so "DNS"
/eid 4004 /tk c:\admin\scripts\dns-adfix.bat
```

Create an event trigger that monitors the security log for failure audit events with the source as Security:

```
Eventtriggers /create /tr "Failure Audit Checks" /l "Security" /so
"Security" /t Failureaudit
```

Event triggers are created and their associated tasks are run by default on the local computer with the permissions of the user who is currently logged on. Because this command is used primarily for administration, you will be prompted for a password before the event trigger is added. If the triggered task needs to run with different or specific user permissions, provide the Run As permissions using /u [*Domain*\]*User* [/p *Password*], where *Domain* is the optional domain name in which the user account is located, *User* is the name of the user account whose permissions you want to use, and *Password* is the optional password for the user account, such as

```
Eventtriggers /create /u adatam\wrstanek /p R4Runner! /tr "Exchange
Monitor" /l "Application" /so "MSExchangeMTA" /t warning /tk c:\ admin
\scripts\exe-errlog.bat
```

As necessary, you can also specify the remote computer on which you want to create the event trigger using /S *Computer*, where *Computer* is the remote computer name or IP address, such as

```
Eventtriggers /create /s 192.168.1.150 /tr "Exchange Monitor" /l
"Application" /so "MSExchangeMTA" /t warning /tk c:\admin\scripts
\exe-errlog.bat
```

Displaying Currently Configured Event Triggers

You can obtain information about currently configured event triggers using Eventtriggers /query. Simply type the command at the prompt, such as

```
eventtriggers /query
```

The basic output of the query shows you the event trigger ID, event trigger name, and the task that is run, as shown in the following example:

```
Trigger ID       Event Trigger Name        Task
==========       ====================      ===================================
         4       Failure Audit Checks      c:\admin\scripts\auditing.bat
         2       Monitor 9220 Errors       \\Mailer1\scripts\record-prob.bat
         3       DNS AD Fix                c:\admin\scripts\dns-adfix.bat
         1       Disk Cleanup              d:\windows\system32\cleanmgr.exe
```

Note You will use the trigger ID to delete the trigger. The output format, by default, is table (/Fo Table). You can use /Fo Csv to format the output as comma-separated values or /Fo List to format the output as a list. You can also use the /Nh parameter to turn off the display of headers, if either the Table or the Csv format option is specified.

To get more detailed information, use the /V (verbose) flag. With verbose output the additional columns of information are

- **Hostname** The computer name or IP address of the computer on which the event trigger is configured.
- **Query** The complete command text used to create the event trigger.
- **Description** The description of the trigger, if provided when the trigger was created.
- **Run As (User name)** The Run As user used to create the task and run the associated task for the event trigger.

As necessary, you can specify the remote computer whose triggers you want to query using /s *Computer*, where *Computer* is the remote computer name or IP address, such as

```
eventtriggers /query /s Mailer1
```

You can also specify the Run As user permissions using /U [*Domain*]*User* [/P *Password*], where *Domain* is the optional domain name in which the user account is located, *User* is the name of the user account whose permissions you want to use, and *Password* is the optional password for the user account, such as

```
eventtriggers /query /s Mailer1 /u adatam\administrator /p dataset5
```

Deleting Event Triggers

When event triggers are no longer needed, you can delete them using the event-triggers /delete command. The syntax is

eventtriggers /delete /tid *ID*

where *ID* is the trigger ID you want to delete. You can also use asterisk (*) as the trigger ID to delete all event triggers. Consider the following examples:

Delete event trigger 5:

```
eventtriggers /delete /tid 5
```

Delete all event triggers:

```
eventtriggers /delete /tid *
```

As necessary, you can specify the remote computer whose triggers you want to delete using /S *Computer*, where *Computer* is the remote computer name or IP address, and the Run As permission using /U [*Domain*]*User* [/P *Password*], where *Domain* is the optional domain name in which the user account is located, *User* is the name of the user account whose permissions you want to use, and *Password* is the optional password for the user account, such as

```
eventtriggers /delete /tid 3 /s Mailer1 /u adatam\wrstanek /p outreef7
```

Caution You can't restore event triggers once you've deleted them. If you think you may use an event trigger again, write the output produced from Eventtriggers /query /v to a file and then save the file for future reference. With the /V parameter, the file will contain the complete command text used to create the trigger.

Chapter 7

Monitoring Processes and Performance

An important part of every administrator's job is to monitor network systems and ensure that everything is running smoothly—or as smoothly as can be expected, anyway. As you learned in the previous chapter, watching the event logs closely can help you detect and track problems with applications, security, and essential services. Often when you detect or suspect a problem, you'll need to dig deeper to search out the cause of the problem and correct it. Hopefully, by pinpointing the cause of a problem, you can prevent it from happening again.

Managing Applications, Processes, and Performance

Whenever the operating system or a user starts a service, runs an application, or executes a command, Microsoft Windows starts one or more processes to handle the related program. Several command-line utilities are available to help you manage and monitor programs. These utilities include

- **Process Resource Manager (Pmon)** Displays performance statistics, including memory and CPU usage, as well as a list of all processes running on the local system. Used to get a detailed snapshot of resource usage and running processes. Pmon is included in the Windows Resource Kit.

- **Task List (Tasklist)** Lists all running processes by name and process ID. Includes information on the user session and memory usage.

- **Task Kill (Taskkill)** Stops running processes by name or process ID. Using filters, you can also halt processes by process status, session number, CPU time, memory usage, user name, and more.

In the sections that follow, you'll find detailed discussions on how these command-line tools are used. First, however, let's look at the ways processes are run and the common problems you may encounter when working with them.

Understanding System and User Processes

Generally, processes that the operating system starts are referred to as *system processes*; processes that users start are referred to as *user processes*. Most user processes are run in interactive mode. That is, a user starts the processes interactively with the keyboard or mouse. If the application or program is active and selected, the related interactive process has control over the keyboard and mouse until you switch control by terminating the program or selecting a different one. When a process has control, it's said to be running "in the foreground."

Processes can also run in the background, independently of user logon sessions. Background processes do not have control over the keyboard, mouse, or other input devices and are usually run by the operating system. Using the Task Scheduler, users can run processes in the background as well, however, and these processes can operate regardless of whether the user is logged on. For example, if Task Scheduler starts a scheduled task while the user is logged on, the process can continue even when the user logs off.

Windows tracks every process running on a system by image name, process ID, priority, and other parameters that record resource usage. The image name is the name of the executable that started the process, such as Msdtc.exe or Svchost.exe. The process ID is a numeric identifier for the process, such as 2588. The process priority is an indicator of how much of the system's resources the process should get relative to other running processes. With priority processing, a process with a higher priority gets preference over processes with lower priority and may not have to wait to get processing time, access memory, or work with the file system. A process with lower priority, on the other hand, usually must wait for a higher-priority process to complete its current task before gaining access to the CPU, memory, or the file system.

In a perfect world, processes would run perfectly and would never have problems. The reality is, however, that problems occur and they often appear when you'd least want them to. Common problems include the following:

- Processes become nonresponsive, such as when an application stops processing requests. When this happens, users may tell you that they can't access a particular application, that their requests aren't being handled, or that they were kicked out of the application.

- Processes fail to release the CPU, such as when you have a runaway process that is using up CPU time. When this happens, the system may appear to be slow or nonresponsive because the runaway process is hogging processor time and is not allowing other processes to complete their tasks.

- Processes use more memory than they should, such as when an application has a memory leak. When this happens, processes aren't releasing memory that they're using properly. As a result, the system's available memory may gradually decrease over time and as the available memory gets low, the system may be slow to respond to requests or it may become nonresponsive. Memory leaks can also make other programs running on the same system behave erratically.

In most cases, when you detect these or other problems with system processes, you'll want to stop the process and start it again. You would also want to examine the event logs to see if the cause of the problem can be determined. With memory leaks, you would want to report the memory leak to the developers and see if an update that resolves the problem is available.

Tip   A periodic restart of an application with a known memory leak is often useful. Restarting the application should allow the operating system to recover any lost memory.

Examining Running Processes

When you want to examine processes that are running on a local or remote system, you can use the Tasklist command-line utility. With Tasklist, you can:

- Obtain the process ID, status, and other important information about processes running on a system.
- View the relationship between running processes and services configured on a system.
- View lists of DLLs used by processes running on a system.
- Use filters to include or exclude processes from Tasklist queries.

Each of these tasks is discussed in the sections that follow.

Obtaining Detailed Information on Processes

On a local system, you can view a list of running tasks, simply by typing **tasklist** at the command prompt. As with many other command-line utilities, Tasklist runs by default with the permissions of the currently logged on user and you can also specify the remote computer whose tasks you want to query, and the Run As permissions. To do this, use the expanded syntax, which includes the following parameters:

`/s Computer /u [Domain\]User [/p Password]`

where *Computer* is the remote computer name or IP address, *Domain* is the optional domain name in which the user account is located, *User* is the name of the user account whose permissions you want to use, and *Password* is the optional password for the user account. If you don't specify the domain, the current domain is assumed. If you don't provide the account password, you are prompted for the password.

To see how the computer and user information can be added to the syntax, consider the following examples:

Query Mailer1 for running tasks:

```
tasklist /s mailer1
```

Query 192.168.1.5 for running tasks using the account adatum \wrstanek:

```
tasklist /s 192.168.1.5 /u adatum\wrstanek
```

 Tip The basic output of these commands is in table format. You can also format the output as a list or lines of comma-separated values using /Fo List or /Fo Csv, respectively. Remember you can redirect the output to a file using output redirection (> or >>), such as `tasklist /s mailer1 >> current-tasks.log`.

Regardless of whether you are working with a local or remote computer, the output should be similar to the following:

Image Name	PID	Session Name	Session#	Mem Usage
System Idle Process	0	Console	0	16 K
System	4	Console	0	216 K
smss.exe	420	Console	0	480 K
csrss.exe	472	Console	0	4,420 K
sqlgea.exe	496	Console	0	3,352 K
services.exe	540	Console	0	3,288 K
sqlmon.exe	552	Console	0	32,508 K
sdman.exe	728	Console	0	2,856 K
sdman.exe	788	Console	0	3,840 K
sdman.exe	988	Console	0	4,016 K
sdman.exe	1036	Console	0	2,032 K
sdman.exe	1048	Console	0	15,624 K
spoolsv.exe	1348	Console	0	4,728 K
msdtc.exe	1380	Console	0	3,808 K

The Tasklist fields provide the following information:

- **Image Name** The name of the process or executable running the process.

 Note The first process is named System Idle Process. This special system process is used to track the amount of system resources that aren't being used. For more information on this process, see the "Monitoring Processes and System Resource Usage" section of this chapter.

- **PID** The process identification number.
- **Session Name** The name of the session from which the process is being run. An entry of *console* means the process was started locally.
- **Session #** A numerical identifier for the session.
- **Memory Usage** The total amount of memory being used by the process at the specific moment that Tasklist was run.

If you want more detailed information you can specify that verbose mode should be used by including the /V parameter. Verbose mode adds the following columns of data:

- **Status** Current status of the process as Running, Not Responding, or Unknown. A process can be in an Unknown state and still be running and responding normally. A process that is Not Responding, however, more than likely must be stopped or restarted.
- **User Name** User account under which the process is running, listed in *domain\user* format. For processes started by Windows, you will see the name of the system account used, such as SYSTEM, LOCAL SERVICE, or NETWORK SERVICE, with the domain listed as NT AUTHORITY.
- **CPU Time** The total amount of CPU cycle time used by the process since its start.
- **Window Title** Windows display name of the process if available. Otherwise, the display name is listed as *N/A* for not available. For example, the Helpctr.exe process is listed with the Windows title Help And Support Center

Viewing the Relationship Between Running Processes and Services

When you use Tasklist with the /Svc parameter, you can examine the relationship between running processes and services configured on the system. In the output, you'll see the process image name, process ID, and a list of all services that are using the process, similar to that shown in the following example:

```
Image Name                    PID    Services
===========================   =====  ==============================================
System Idle Process             0    N/A
System                          4    N/A
smss.exe                      408    N/A
csrss.exe                     456    N/A
winlogon.exe                  484    N/A
services.exe                  528    Eventlog, PlugPlay
lsass.exe                     540    HTTPFilter, kdc, Netlogon, NtLmSsp,
                                     PolicyAgent, ProtectedStorage, SamSs
svchost.exe                   800    RpcSs
svchost.exe                   956    Dnscache
svchost.exe                   984    LmHosts
```

```
svchost.exe                    996    AudioSrv, Browser, CryptSvc, dmserver,
                                      EventSystem, helpsvc, lanmanserver,
                                      lanmanworkstation, Netman, Nla, Schedule,
                                      seclogon, SENS, ShellHWDetection, W32Time,
                                      winmgmt, wuauserv, WZCSVC
spoolsv.exe                   1300    Spooler
msdtc.exe                     1332    MSDTC
dfssvc.exe                    1400    Dfs
dns.exe                       1436    DNS
svchost.exe                   1492    ERSvc
inetinfo.exe                  1552    IISADMIN, IMAP4Svc, POP3Svc, RESvc, SMTPSVC
ismserv.exe                   1568    IsmServ
ntfrs.exe                     1584    NtFrs
svchost.exe                   1688    RemoteRegistry
mad.exe                       1724    MSExchangeSA
mssearch.exe                  1784    MSSEARCH
exmgmt.exe                    1824    MSExchangeMGMT
svchost.exe                   2000    W3SVC
store.exe                     2108    MSExchangeIS
```

By default, the output is formatted as a table, and you cannot use the *list* or *CSV* format. Beyond formatting, the important thing to note here is that services are listed by their abbreviated name, which is the naming style used by Sc, the service controller command-line utility, to manage services.

You can use the correlation between processes and services to help you manage systems. For example, if you think you are having problems with the World Wide Web Publishing Service (W3svc), one step in your troubleshooting process is to begin monitoring the service's related process or processes. You would want to examine

- Process status
- Memory usage
- CPU time

By tracking these statistics over time, you can watch for changes that could indicate the process has stopped responding, is a runaway process hogging CPU time, or that there is a memory leak.

Viewing Lists of DLLs Being Used by Processes

When you use Tasklist with the /M parameter, you can examine the relationship between running processes and DLLs configured on the system. In the output, you'll see the process image name, process ID, and a list of all DLLs that the process is using, as shown in the following example:

```
Image Name                  PID   Modules
========================   ======  =============================================
System Idle Process           0   N/A
System                        4   N/A
smss.exe                    408   ntdll.dll
csrss.exe                   456   ntdll.dll, CSRSRV.dll, basesrv.dll,
                                  winsrv.dll, KERNEL32.dll, USER32.dll,
                                  GDI32.dll, sxs.dll, ADVAPI32.dll, RPCRT4.dll,
                                  Apphelp.dll, VERSION.dll
```

Knowing which DLL modules a process has loaded can further help you pinpoint what may be causing a process to become nonresponsive, to fail to release the CPU, or to use more memory than it should. In some cases, you might want to check DLL versions to ensure they are the correct DLLs that the system should be running. Here, you would need to consult the Microsoft Knowledge Base or manufacturer documentation to verify DLL versions and other information.

If you are looking for processes using a specified DLL, you can also specify the name of the DLL you are looking for. For example, if you suspect that the printer spooler driver Winspool.drv is causing processes to hang up, you can search for processes that use Winspool.drv instead of Winspool32.drv and check their status and resource usage.

The syntax that you use to specify the DLL to find is

tasklist /m **DLLName**

where *DLLName* is the name of the DLL to search for. Tasklist matches the DLL name without regard to the letter case, and you can enter the DLL name in any letter case. Consider the following example:

tasklist /m winspool.drv

In this example, you are looking for processes using Winspool.drv. The output of the command would show the processes using the DLL, with their process IDs, as shown in the following example:

```
Image Name                  PID   Modules
========================   ======  =============================================
winlogon.exe                484   WINSPOOL.DRV
spoolsv.exe                1300   winspool.drv
explorer.exe               3516   WINSPOOL.DRV
mshta.exe                  3704   WINSPOOL.DRV
```

Filtering Task List Output

Using the /Fi parameter of the Tasklist utility, task lists can be filtered using any of the information fields available, even if the information field isn't normally included in the output due to the parameters you've specified. This means you can specify that you want to see only processes listed with a status of Not Responding, only information for Svchost.exe processes, or only processes that use a large amount of CPU Time.

You designate how a filter should be applied to a particular Tasklist information field using filter operators. The filter operators available are

- **Eq**   Equals. If the field contains the specified value, the process is included in the output.

- **Ne**   Not equals. If the field contains the specified value, the process is excluded from the output.

- **Gt**   Greater than. If the field contains a numeric value and that value is greater than the value specified, the process is included in the output.

- **Lt**   Less than. If the field contains a numeric value and that value is less than the value specified, the process is included in the output.

- **Ge**   Greater than or equal to. If the field contains a numeric value and that value is greater than or equal to the value specified, the process is included in the output.

- **Le**   Less than or equal to. If the field contains a numeric value and that value is less than or equal to the value specified, the process is included in the output.

As Table 7-1 shows, the values that can be used with filter operators depend on the task list information field you use. Remember that all fields are available even if they aren't normally displayed with the parameters you've specified. For example, you can match the status field without using the /V (verbose) flag.

Table 7-1.   Filter Operators and Valid Values for Tasklist

Filter Field Name	Valid Operators	Valid Values
CPUTime	eq, ne, gt, lt, ge, le	Any valid time in the format *hh:mm:ss*
Services	eq, ne	Any valid string of characters
ImageName	eq, ne	Any valid string of characters
MemUsage	eq, ne, gt, lt, ge, le	Any valid integer, expressed in kilobytes (KB)
PID	eq, ne, gt, lt, ge, le	Any valid positive integer
Session	eq, ne, gt, lt, ge, le	Any valid session number
SessionName	eq, ne	Any valid string of characters
Status	eq, ne	Running, Not Responding, Unknown
Username	eq, ne	Any valid user name, with user name only or in *domain\user* format
WindowTitle	eq, ne	Any valid string of characters

Double quotation marks must be used to enclose the filter string. Consider the following examples to see how filters can be used:

Look for processes that are not responding:

```
tasklist /fi "status eq not responding"
```

Note When working with remote systems, you can't filter processes by status or Window title. A work around for this in some cases is to pipe the output through the FIND command, such as **tasklist /v /s Mailer1 /u adatum\wrstanek | find /i "not responding"**. Note that, in this case, the field you are filtering must be in the output, which is why the /V parameter was added to the example. Further, you should specify that the find command should ignore the letter case of characters by using the /I parameter.

Look for processes on Mailer1 with a CPU time of more than 30 minutes:

```
tasklist /s Mailer1 /fi "cputime gt 00:30:00"
```

Look for processes on Mailer1 that use more than 20,000 KB of memory:

```
tasklist /s Mailer1 /u adatum\wrstanek /fi "memusage gt 20000"
```

Enter multiple /Fi "Filter" parameters to specify that output must match against multiple filters:

```
tasklist /s Mailer1 /fi "cputime gt 00:30:00" /fi "memusage gt 20000"
```

Monitoring Processes and System Resource Usage

Process Resource Monitor (Pmon) displays a snapshot of system resource usage and running processes. When you run this utility by typing **pmon** at the command prompt, the Process Resource Monitor collects information on the current system resource usage and running processes and displays it in the console window. The statistics are collected again every five seconds and redisplayed automatically. Pmon continues to run until you press the Q key to quit, and any other key you press tells Pmon to update the statistics.

Note Pmon output cannot be redirected, and you can only run Pmon on a local computer. To examine the resources of a remote computer, remotely access the computer using Remote Desktop. Further, you cannot use Pmon with the REMOTE command. Pmon redirects command output and is incompatible with the REMOTE command.

Pmon output is in table format with columns and rows of data, as follows:

```
Memory:  523248K Avail: 300516K PageFlts:    905 InRam Kernel: 2444K P:11496K

Commit: 337868K/ 214648K Limit:1280320K Peak: 345720K  Pool N: 8372K P:11648K
```

CPU	CpuTime	Mem Usage	Mem Diff	Page Faults	Flts Diff	Commit Charge	Usage NonP	Page	Pri	Hnd Cnt	Thd Cnt	Image Name
		39448	64	59570	282							File Cache
96	0:38:42	16	0	0	0	0	0	0	0	0	1	IdleProcess
0	0:00:03	216	0	4080	0	28	0	0	8	1810	59	System
0	0:00:00	480	0	197	0	164	0	5	11	17	3	smss.exe
2	0:00:09	5236	56	2803	24	3216	5	48	13	756	10	csrss.exe
0	0:00:01	4624	0	12878	0	7620	8	50	13	537	21	sqlgea.exe
0	0:00:05	4740	0	2181	0	3932	12	52	9	388	19	services.exe
0	0:00:04	30676	0	19113	0	28856	83	80	9	1040	61	sqlmon.exe
0	0:00:00	2860	0	780	2	1040	23	21	8	242	11	sdman.exe
0	0:00:00	3788	0	1076	0	1272	4	28	8	127	14	sdman.exe
0	0:00:00	944	0	232	0	340	1	7	13	7	1	pmon.exe
0	0:00:00	1776	0	464	0	536	1	25	8	15	1	notepad.exe

As shown, the first two rows of data provide a summary of memory usage. The values are in kilobytes (KB) and provide the following information:

- **Memory, Avail** Provides information on the total RAM on the system. *Memory* shows the amount of physical RAM. *Avail* shows the RAM not currently being used and available for use.

- **InRam Kernel** Provides information on the memory used by the operating system kernel. Critical portions of kernel memory must operate in RAM and can't be paged to virtual memory. This type of kernel memory is listed as InRam Kernel. The rest of kernel memory can be paged to virtual memory and is listed after the InRam Kernel.

- **Commit, Limit, Peak** Provides information on committed physical and virtual memory. *Commit* lists physical memory which has space reserved on the disk page file, followed by the current amount of committed virtual memory. *Limit* lists the amount of virtual memory that can be committed without having to extend the paging file(s). *Peak* lists the maximum memory used by the system since the system was started. If the difference between the total memory available and the committed memory used is consistently small, you might want to add physical memory to the system to improve performance. If the peak memory usage is within 10 percent of the *Limit* value, you might want to add physical memory or increase the amount of virtual memory or both.

- **Pool N and P** Pooled memory values provide information on the paged pool, which is physical memory used by the operating system that can be written to disk when they are not being used, and the nonpaged pool, which is physical memory used by the operating system that cannot be written to disk and must remain in memory so long as they are allocated. *Pool N* is the size of the nonpaged pool and the value that follows it (*Pool P*) is the size of the paged pool.

Following the two rows of memory usage statistics, you'll find columns of information detailing resource usage for individual processes. These data points provide lots of information about running processes and you can use this information to determine which processes are hogging system resources, such as CPU time and memory. The fields displayed are the following:

- **CPU**   The percentage of CPU utilization for the process.

- **CpuTime**   The total amount of CPU cycle time used by the process since it was started.

- **Mem Usage**   The amount of memory the process is using.

- **Mem Diff**   Displays the change in memory usage for the process recorded since the last update.

- **Page Faults**   A page fault occurs when a process requests a page in memory and the system can't find it at the requested location. If the requested page is elsewhere in memory, the fault is called a soft page fault. If the requested page must be retrieved from disk, the fault is called a hard page fault. Most processors can handle large numbers of soft faults. Hard faults, however, can cause significant delays, and if there are a lot of hard faults, you may need to increase the amount of memory or reduce the system cache size. To learn how to determine the volume of hard faults, see the section of this chapter titled "Monitoring Memory Paging for Individual Processes."

- **Flts Diff**   Displays the change in the number of page faults for the process recorded since the last update.

- **Commit Charge**   Displays the amount of virtual memory allocated to and reserved for the process.

- **Usage NonP/Page**   Shows nonpaged pool and paged pool usage. The non paged pool is an area of system memory for objects that can't be written to disk. The paged pool is an area of system memory for objects that can be written to disk when they aren't used. You should note processes that require a high amount of nonpaged pool memory. If there isn't enough free memory on the server, these processes might be the reason for a high level of page faults.

- **Pri**   Shows the priority of the process. Priority determines how much of the system resources are allocated to a process. Standard priorities are Low (4), Below Normal (6), Normal (8), Above Normal (10), High (13), and Real-Time (24). Most processes have a normal priority by default. The highest priority is given to real-time processes. You may also see other priorities. For example, the Idle Process thread has a priority of 0, as this thread doesn't use CPU time but rather tracks when the CPU is idle. Some system service processes have priority 9 or 11, to give either a slightly higher than normal priority or a slightly above normal priority to an important process.

- **Hnd Cnt** The total number of file handles maintained by the process. Use the handle count to gauge how dependent the process is on the file system. Some processes, such as those used by Microsoft Internet Information Services (IIS), have thousands of open file handles. System memory is required to maintain each file handle.

- **Thd Cnt** The current number of threads that the process is using. Most server applications are multithreaded. Multithreading allows concurrent execution of process requests. Some applications can dynamically control the number of concurrently executing threads to improve application performance. Too many threads, however, can cause the operating system to switch thread contexts too frequently, actually reducing performance.

- **Image Name** The name of the process or executable running the process.

As you examine processes, keep in mind that a single application might start multiple processes. Generally, these processes are dependent on a central process, and from this main process a process tree containing dependent processes is formed. When you terminate processes, you'll usually want to target the main application process or the application itself rather than dependent processes. This ensures that the application is stopped cleanly.

If you use Pmon to examine running processes, you'll note three unique processes:

- **File Cache** The file system cache is an area of physical memory that stores recently used pages of data for applications. When you see changes in the file cache, you are seeing I/O activity for applications. Memory usage shows the total physical memory used by the file cache. Page faults shows the number of pages sought but not found in the file system cache and had to be retrieved elsewhere in memory (soft fault) or from disk (hard fault). If you monitor the Flts Diff for the File Cache, you can determine the cache fault rate. A consistently high cache fault rate may indicate the need to increase the amount of physical memory on the system.

- **Idle Process** Unlike other processes that track resource usage, Idle Process tracks the amount of CPU processing time that isn't being used. Thus, a 99 in the CPU column for the Idle Process means 99 percent of the system resources currently aren't being used. If you believe that a system is overloaded, you should monitor the idle process. Watch the CPU usage and the total CPU time. If the system consistently has low idle time (meaning high CPU usage), you may want to consider upgrading the processor or even adding processors.

- **System** System shows the resource usage for the local system process.

Stopping Processes

When you want to stop processes that are running on a local or remote system, you can use the Taskkill command-line utility. With Taskkill, you can stop processes by process ID using the /Pid parameter or image name using the /Im parameter. If you want to stop multiple processes by process ID or image name, you can enter multiple /Pid or /Im parameters as well. With image names, however, watch out, because Taskkill will stop all processes that have that image name. Thus if there are three instances of Helpctr.exe running, all three processes would be stopped if you use Taskkill with that image name.

As with Tasklist, Taskkill runs by default with the permissions of the user who is currently logged on and you can also specify the remote computer whose tasks you want to query, and the Run As permissions. To do this, you use the expanded syntax, which includes the following parameters:

/s `Computer` /u `[Domain\]User` `[/p Password]`

where *Computer* is the remote computer name or IP address, *Domain* is the optional domain name in which the user account is located, *User* is the name of the user account whose permissions you want to use, and *Password* is the optional password for the user account. If you don't specify the domain, the current domain is assumed. If you don't provide the account password, you are prompted for the password.

Note Sometimes it is necessary to force a process to stop running. Typically, this is necessary when a process stops responding while opening a file, reading or writing data, or performing other read/write operations. To force a process to stop, you use the /F parameter. This parameter is only used with processes running on local systems. Processes stopped on remote systems are always forcefully stopped.

Tip As you examine processes, keep in mind that a single application might start multiple processes. Generally, these processes depend on a central process, and from this main process a process tree containing dependent processes is formed. Occasionally, you may want to stop the entire process tree, starting with the parent application process and including any dependent processes, and to do this, you can use the /T parameter.

Consider the following examples to see how Taskkill can be used:

Stop process ID 208:

```
taskkill /pid 208
```

Stop all processes with the image name Cmd.exe:

```
taskkill /im cmd.exe
```

Stop processes 208, 1346, and 2048 on MAILER1:

```
taskkill /s Mailer1 /pid 208 /pid 1346 /pid 2048
```

Force local process 1346 to stop:

```
taskkill /f /pid 1346
```

Stop a process tree, starting with process ID 1248 and including all child processes:

```
taskkill /t /pid 1248
```

To ensure that only processes matching specific criteria are stopped, you can use all the filters listed in Table 7-1 except Sessionname. For example, you can use a filter to specify that only instances of Cmd.exe that are not responding should be stopped rather than all instances of Cmd.exe (which is the default when you use the /Im parameter).

Taskkill adds a Modules filter with operators EQ and NE to allow you to specify DLL modules that should be excluded or included. As you may recall, you use the Tasklist /m parameter to examine the relationship between running processes and DLLs configured on the system. Using the Taskkill Modules filter with the EQ operator, you could stop all processes using a specific DLL. Using the Taskkill Modules filter with the NE operator, you ensure that processes using a specific DLL are not stopped.

 Tip When you use filters, you don't have to specify a specific image name or process ID to work with. This means you can stop processes based solely on whether they match filter criteria. For example, you can specify that you want to stop all processes that aren't responding.

As with Tasklist, multiple filters can be used as well. Again, double quotation marks must be used to enclose the filter string. Consider the following examples to see how filters can be used with Taskkill:

Stop instances of Cmd.exe that are not responding:

```
taskkill /im cmd.exe /fi "status eq not responding"
```

Stop all processes with a process ID greater than 4 if they aren't responding:

```
taskkill /fi "pid gt 4" /fi "status eq not responding"
```

Stop all processes using the Winspool.drv DLL:

```
taskkill /fi "modules eq winspool.drv"
```

Caution   Although the */lm* and */Pid* flags are not used in the previous example, the process IDs are filtered so that only certain processes are affected. You don't want to stop the system or system idle process accidentally. Typically, these processes run with a process IDs of 4 and 0 respectively, and if you stop them, the system will stop responding or shut down.

Detecting and Resolving Performance Issues Through Monitoring

Although Pmon provides an excellent starting point for detecting and resolving performance issues, you'll often need to dig deeper to determine whether a problem exists and if so, what is the possible cause. Several process management and monitoring tools can help you perform detailed analysis, including

- **Memory Monitor (Memmonitor)**   Displays detailed information regarding the memory a process is using.

- **Page Fault Monitor (Pfmon)**   Displays detailed information regarding page faults that are occurring on the system.

- **Resource Leak Triage Tool (Memtriage)**   Logs memory usage, including detailed information regarding memory allocated and freed by individual processes. Used to detect memory leaks and get memory pool details.

Note   Memmonitor, Pfmon, and Memtriage are intended for use by administrators. They are available in the Windows Server 2003 Resource Kit. If they wish, administrators can install the Windows Server 2003 Resource Kit on Windows XP Professional systems, and then the tools would be available on those systems.

These tools are discussed in the sections that follow.

Monitoring Memory Paging for Individual Processes

You can use the Page Fault Monitor (Pfmon) to get detailed data related to hard and soft page faults.

To see soft page faults, type

```
pfmon /c /p ProcessID
```

where *ProcessID* is the identification number of the process you want to monitor as determined by Tasklist, such as

```
pfmon /c /p 1348
```

To see hard page faults, type

```
pfmon /h /p ProcessID
```

where *ProcessID* is the identification number of the process you want to monitor as determined by Tasklist, such as

```
pfmon /h /p 1348
```

The output of Pfmon shows the page faults as they occur in real time. To stop Pfmon, press Ctrl+C. Page faults are shown according to the source that generated them and are similar to the following example:

```
HARD: HttpSendRequestExA+0xab1 : 00878000
HARD: URLQualifyW+0x356e : URLQualifyW+0x0000356D
HARD: CreateDataCache+0x3608 :
WdtpInterfacePointer_UserFree+0x00007165
HARD: OleSetClipboard+0x8df : OleSetClipboard+0x000008DE
HARD: DoFileDownloadEx+0xba2 : DoFileDownloadEx+0x00000BA1
HARD: RtlImageNtHeaderEx+0x3d : 03730000
HARD: RtlSetThreadErrorMode+0x2a1 : 60c0100c
HARD: GetSysColorBrush+0xa4 : 60c0e5f8
```

Although developers will be interested in the source of page faults, administrators are more interested in how many page faults are occurring. As discussed earlier, most processors can handle large numbers of soft faults. A soft fault simply means the system had to look elsewhere in memory for the requested memory page. With a hard fault, on the other hand, the requested memory page must be retrieved from disk and if there are a lot of hard faults, you may need to increase the amount of memory or reduce the system cache size.

Monitoring Memory Usage and the Working Memory Set for Individual Processes

You use the Memory Monitor (Memmonitor) to track detailed memory usage for individual processes. The syntax is

```
memmonitor /p ProcessID /nodbg [/int IntervalSeconds]
```

where *ProcessID* is the identification number of the process you want to monitor as determined by Tasklist, /nodbg tells the utility not to break to the debugger when finished, and *IntervalSeconds* sets the optional number of seconds to wait between each memory usage check. The default wait interval is 60 seconds.

Memmonitor output looks like this:

```
Monitor Process 1284 (Name: SQLAgent.exe)MemMon - 0:00:00
     PageFaults        : 13182
     PeakWSSize        : 22704K      WorkingSetSize: 22252K
     PeakPagedPool     :    58K      PagedPool     :    54K
     PeakNonPagedPool  :     8K      NonPagedPool  :     7K
     PeakPagefile      : 13632K      Pagefile      : 13176K
```

```
MemMon - 0:00:30
   PageFaults        : 16259
   PeakWSSize        : 24800K     WorkingSetSize: 24352K
   PeakPagedPool     :    58K     PagedPool     :    54K
   PeakNonPagedPool  :     8K     NonPagedPool  :     8K
   PeakPagefile      : 16256K     Pagefile      : 15804K
```

As you can see from the example, Memmonitor shows the elapsed running time, following by the current memory usage details. As with Pfmon, Memmonitor runs continuously. However, it displays output at the given interval only when there are memory usage changes for the specified process. You can stop Memmonitor at any time by pressing Ctrl+C.

The Memmonitor fields provide the following information:

- **PageFaults**   Shows the number of hard and soft page faults that have occurred for the process

- **PeakWSSize**   Shows the peak amount of memory used by the process

- **PeakPagedPool**   Shows the peak amount of paged memory used by the process

- **PeakNonPagedPool**   Shows the peak amount of nonpaged memory used by the process

- **PeakPagefile**   Shows the peak amount of page file memory used by the process

- **WorkingSetSize**   Shows the amount of memory allocated to the process by the operating system

- **PagedPool**   Shows the amount of allocated memory that is allowed to be paged to the hard disk

- **NonPagedPool**   Shows the amount of allocated memory that can't be written to disk

- **Pagefile**   Shows the size of the file on the hard disk to which memory may be paged

When you work with Memmonitor, you are zeroing in on the memory usage of a specific process. The key things to monitor are memory paging and the working memory set. Ideally, if the memory cache for the process (and its related application) is allocated properly, the relative frequency of memory paging won't be excessive. If paging does become excessive, you may need to allocate more memory-resident file cache for the application or add physical memory to the system.

Real World   Remember, this is all relative to the application being considered. Some applications will always have a lot of paging. Just keep in mind that accessing the page file is much slower than accessing physical memory.

The working set of memory shows how much memory is allocated to the process by the operating system. If the working set increases over time and doesn't eventually go back to baseline usage, the process may have a memory leak. With a memory leak, the process isn't properly releasing memory that it's using and this can lead to reduced performance of the entire system.

 Tip If you suspect a memory leak, you'll find several tools that can help you further analyze the problem, including the Resource Leak Triage Tool (Memtriage), Memory Snapshot (Memsnap) and Pool Monitor (Poolmon). In most cases, the best tool to use is Memtriage, which is discussed in the next section. Memtriage is available in the Windows Server 2003 Resource Kit, and Memsnap and Poolman are included in the Support Tools for both Windows XP Professional and Windows Server 2003.

Performing Detailed Memory Usage Analysis and Determining the Source of Memory Leaks

You use Memtriage to help you pinpoint the source of suspected memory leaks. With Memtriage, you use the following syntax:

```
memtriage /mp logName /t numSnapshots /w snapshotWindow
```

where /Mp tells Windows to take a snapshot of current system, process, and kernel pool information, *logName* is the name of the log file to use, *numSnapshots* is the number of times to write memory usage to the log, and *snapshotWindow* is the time interval between snapshots.

 Tip You don't have to log system, process, and kernel pool information at the same time. Instead of using /Mp, you can use /M to log system and process information only, or /P to log only kernel pool information.

In most cases, you'll want to create multiple snapshots and gather information over several hours. To see how this would work, consider the following example:

```
memtriage /mp C:\logs\memlog.log /t 8 /w 20
```

Here, eight memory snapshots are taken with 20 minutes between each snapshot and the logs are written to C:\logs\memlog.log: A partial output for Memtriage would be similar to the following:

```
Taking snapshot 1 @ 2003/10/24 19:32:32(Pacific Standard Time)
Creating local pool tag file: c:\localtag.txt ...
Poolsnap: Scan local pool tag file: c:\localtag.txt
Poolsnap: Scan pool tag file: C:\Program Files\Windows Resource
Kits\Tools\pooltag.txt
Sleeping 20 minutes
Taking snapshot 2 @ 2003/10/24 19:52:32(Pacific Standard Time)
```

```
Creating local pool tag file: c:\localtag.txt ...
Poolsnap: Scan local pool tag file: c:\localtag.txt
Poolsnap: Scan pool tag file: C:\Program Files\Windows Resource
Kits\Tools\pooltag.txt
```

As you can see, Memtriage creates a working file called Localtag.txt and examines a resource kit file called Pooltag.txt. Using the /Mp option with a log name of Mem.log, it also writes three log files:

- **Mem.log.system**   Contains the snapshot(s) of system information
- **Mem.log.process**   Contains the snapshot(s) of process information
- **Mem.log.pool**   Contains the snapshot(s) of kernel pool information

Note   Don't worry—you don't have to dig through all these log files. You should remember, however, that the log files are there, and use Memtriage to clean up those with which you have finished working.

When Memtriage finishes, you'll want to analyze the logs you've made, looking for potential memory leaks. To do this, use the following syntax:

```
memtriage /a logName
```

where *logName* is the log specified in the /Mp option, such as

```
memtriage /a c:\logs\memlog.log
```

The output of the memory triage analysis is very detailed. Not only does the analysis reveal changes in memory usage; it also points out usage trends and the rate of change on an hourly basis. An example of the analysis output follows:

```
================================ System ================================
Name          Inc-Trend Object         Change Start    End Percent  Rate/hour
System        Always    AvailableKByte  -1204 261928 260724       0     -21572
System        Sometime  NpagedPoolKByte    16   8276   8292       0        286

================================ Per Process ================================
Name          Inc-Trend Object         Change  Start    End Percent Rate/hour
sqlgea.exe    Sometime  CommitKByte        32   7536   7568      0       573
sqlgea.exe    Sometime  VirtualKByte      256  47956  48212      0      4586
sqlgea.exe    Sometime  Handles             7    533    540      1       125
sqlgea.exe    Sometime  Threads             1     20     21      5        17
sqlmon.exe    Sometime  PagedPoolKByte      1     77     78      1        17
sqlmon.exe    Sometime  NpagedPoolKByte     1     85     86      1        17
sqlmon.exe    Sometime  CommitKByte        52  29604  29656      0       931
sqlmon.exe    Sometime  VirtualKByte     1040  94280  95320      1     18634
sqlmon.exe    Sometime  Handles            10    994   1004      1       179
sdman.exe     Sometime  Handles             1    141    142      0        17
sdman.exe     Always    Handles             4    868    872      0        71
rrsrvc.exe    Sometime  Handles             2     83     85      2        35
sqldbms.exe   Sometime  Handles             2   2050   2052      0        35
mret.exe      Sometime  CommitKByte        12  13320  13332      0       215
mret.exe      Sometime  VirtualKByte      512 353088 353600      0      9173
mret.exe      Sometime  Threads             1     45     46      2        17
wmiprvse.exe  Sometime  CommitKByte       216   2944   3160      7      3870
wmiprvse.exe  Sometime  VirtualKByte      768  29484  30252      2     13760
```

In this data, you would look at the following items:

- **Inc-Trend** Indicates whether and the degree to which memory usage increases. Pay particular attention to processes whose memory usage always tends to increase.

- **Change, Start, End** Denotes the initial memory usage logged, the final memory usage logged, and the change or difference between the two values. A negative change indicates that the process freed memory. A positive change indicates the process used additional memory.

- **Percent** Specifies the percentage of change between the Start and End memory usage values. Watch for large percentage changes, but also note which processes show nominal increases. A nominal increase in successive analysis sets could point to a slow memory leak.

- **Rate/Hour** Specifies the estimated rate at which memory usage would change on an hourly basis given the current change and the trend for change. Large changes can be indicators of a memory leak. However, the Rate/Hour values are only meaningful if you've based the analysis on multiple snapshots taken over a period of several hours.

Part III

Windows File System and Disk Administration

Users depend on hard disk drives to store their word-processing documents, spreadsheets, and other types of data. If you've worked with Microsoft Windows XP or Windows Server 2003 for any length of time, you've probably used the Disk Management tool.

The command-line counterpart of Disk Management is the disk partition utility (DiskPart). You can use DiskPart to handle most disk management tasks as well as to perform some additional tasks that cannot be performed in the GUI. Chapter 8 provides an introduction to DiskPart and also discusses the FSUtil, CHKDSK, and CHKNTFS tools. Chapter 9 discusses partitioning basic disks, and Chapter 10 examines dynamic disks and how they are used, as well as examining the implementation, management, and troubleshooting of RAID.

Chapter 8
Configuring and Maintaining Hard Disk Drives

In this chapter, you'll learn techniques for configuring and maintaining hard disk drives—and there's a lot more to this than most people realize. With Microsoft Windows Server 2003 and Windows XP Professional, hard disk drives can be configured with two disk types, basic and dynamic, and two disk partition types, Master Boot Record (MBR) and GUID Partition Table (GPT). The disk type and partition type you choose primarily depends on the system architecture. If you are working with x86-based systems, you can use either basic or dynamic disk types with the MBR partition style. If you are working with IA64-based systems, you can use the basic disk type with the GPT partition style.

Getting Started with DiskPart

DiskPart is the tool of choice for working with disks, partitions, and volumes. Key tasks you'll use DiskPart for are to convert disk types, create partitions and volumes, and to configure RAID. Beyond this, you can also use DiskPart to configure automounting of new disks as well as to assign drive letters and drive paths. DiskPart isn't used for formatting disks, however. For this, you'll use the FORMAT command, as discussed in the section of Chapter 9, "Partitioning Basic Disks," titled "Formatting Partitions."

DiskPart Basics

Unlike all the other commands we've worked with so far in this book, DiskPart isn't a simple command-line utility that you invoke using a command line and parameters. Rather, it is a text-mode command interpreter that you invoke so that you can manage disks, partitions, and volumes using a separate command prompt and commands that are internal to DiskPart. You invoke the DiskPart interpreter by typing **diskpart** in a command window and pressing Enter.

DiskPart is designed to work with physical hard disks installed on a computer. No CD/DVD drives, removable media, or USB-connected flash RAM devices are supported. Before you can use DiskPart commands, you must first list, and then select, the disk, partition, or volume you want to work with to give it focus. When a disk, partition, or volume has focus, any DiskPart commands that you type will act on that disk, partition, or volume.

List the available disks, partitions, and volumes by using the following list commands:

- **list disk** Lists all physical hard disks on the computer
- **list volume** Lists all volumes on the computer (including hard disk partitions and logical drives)
- **list partition** Lists partitions, but only on the disk that has focus

 Note CD/DVD drives, removable media, and USB-connected flash RAM devices are included when you list volumes. However, as stated previously, you cannot use DiskPart to manage these devices.

When you use the list commands, an asterisk (*) appears next to the disk, volume, or partition with focus. You select a disk, volume, or partition by its number or drive letter, such as disk 0, partition 1, volume 2, or volume D.

When you are finished working with DiskPart, type **exit** at the DiskPart prompt to return to the standard command line.

DiskPart: An Example

To see how you can work with DiskPart, consider the following example that invokes DiskPart, lists the available disks, and then gives focus to disk 2:

1. To invoke DiskPart, type **diskpart** at the command prompt.
2. The command prompt changes to

   ```
   DISKPART>
   ```

3. This tells you that you are in the text-mode interpreter for DiskPart. To list available disks, type **list disk** after the command prompt.

4. The output of list disk shows you the available disks, their status, size, and free space:

   ```
   Disk ###      Status        Size      Free      Dyn     Gpt
   --------      ----------    -------   -------    ---     ---
   Disk 0        Online         56 GB       0 B
   Disk 1        Online         29 GB       0 B
   Disk 2        Online         37 GB      33 GB     *
   ```

5. Because disk 2 is the one we want to work with, we give it focus by typing **select disk 2** after the command prompt.

6. DiskPart reports:

   ```
   Disk 2 is now the selected disk.
   ```

7. Work with the disk, and when you are finished, exit the DiskPart prompt by typing **exit** after the command prompt.

Understanding Focus and What It Means

When you select a disk, partition, or volume, the focus remains on that object until you select a different object. In the previous example, the focus is set on disk 2, but if you were to select volume 2 on disk 0, the focus would shift from disk 2 to disk 0, volume 2. In some cases, the focus changes automatically, based on the command you use. For example, when you create a partition or volume, the focus automatically switches to the new partition or volume.

You can only give focus to a partition on the currently selected disk. When a partition has focus, the related volume, if any, also has focus. When a volume has focus, the related disk and partition also have focus if the volume maps to a single specific partition. If the volume doesn't map to a single specific partition, only the volume has focus.

DiskPart Commands and Scripts

LIST and SELECT are only two of the many commands that DiskPart has to offer. A complete list of DiskPart commands is shown in Table 8-1. Many of the commands listed accept Noerr as an additional parameter. The Noerr parameter is used with DiskPart scripts to indicate that, when an error is encountered, DiskPart should continue to process commands in the script. Without Noerr, an error causes DiskPart to exit with an error code, which halts execution of the script.

- Commands that use Noerr and exit with error codes are ADD, ASSIGN, AUTOMOUNT, BREAK, CONVERT, CREATE, DELETE, EXTEND, IMPORT, ONLINE, REMOVE, and REPAIR.

- Commands that don't use Noerr or exit with error codes are ACTIVE, CLEAN, DETAIL, EXIT, GPT, HELP, INACTIVE, LIST, REM, RESCAN, RETAIN, and SELECT.

Table 8-1. DiskPart Command Summary

Command	Description	Syntax
ACTIVE	On MBR disks, marks the partition with current focus as the active system partition, meaning it is the partition containing the operating system startup files.	active
ADD	Creates a mirrored volume on the selected dynamic disk.	add disk=n where n is the disk number that will contain the mirror
ASSIGN	Assign a drive letter or mount point to the selected partition, logical drive, or volume.	assign letter=x assign mount=*path*
AUTOMOUNT	Controls whether Windows automatically mounts new basic volumes that are added to the system and assigns them drive letters (Windows Server 2003 only).	automount enable | disable | scrub
BREAK	Break a mirror set. Add Nokeep to specify that only one volume should be retained, which means the other volume is deleted.	break disk=n break disk=n nokeep
CLEAN	Removes all partition or volume formatting on the disk that has focus. With CLEAN ALL, all disk sectors are set to zero.	clean clean all
CONVERT	Converts between different disk formats.	convert basic | dynamic convert gpt | mbr
CREATE	Creates a partition or volume of a specific type.	create partition efi | extended | logical | msr | primary create volume simple | raid | stripe
DELETE	Delete the disk, partition, or volume that has focus.	delete disk | partition | volume
DETAIL	Provide details about the disk, partition, or volume that has focus.	detail disk | partition | volume
EXIT	Exits the DiskPart interpreter.	exit
EXTEND	Extend the simple volume on the selected disk or spans the simple volume across multiple disks.	extend size=n disk=n

Table 8-1.   DiskPart Command Summary

Command	Description	Syntax
GPT	Changes GPT attributes on the partition with focus (Windows Server 2003 only).	gpt attributes=n
HELP	Displays a list of commands.	help
IMPORT	Imports a foreign disk.	import
INACTIVE	On MBR disks, marks the partition with focus as inactive, meaning the computer won't boot from the system partition and will instead look for the next boot option in BIOS (Windows Server 2003 only).	inactive
LIST	Displays a list of disks or volumes and information about them, or a list of partitions on the disk that has focus.	list disk | partition | volume
ONLINE	Brings the selected disk or volume online. Resychronizes the mirrored or RAID-5 volume that has focus.	online
REM	Marks the start of a comment in a DiskPart script.	rem *comment*
REMOVE	Removes a drive letter or mount point from the currently selected volume. Optionally, you can add the All and the Dismount parameters.	remove letter=x remove mount=*path*
REPAIR	Repairs the RAID-5 volume with focus by replacing the failed volume with the designated dynamic disk (Windows Server 2003 only).	repair disk=n
RESCAN	Looks for new disks that may have been added to the computer.	rescan
RETAIN	Prepares the selected simple volume to be used as the boot or system volume.	retain
SELECT	Selects a disk, partition, or volume, giving it focus.	select disk | partition | volume

Speaking of DiskPart scripts, the way you use scripts with DiskPart is a bit different from their use with other commands. The reason is that DiskPart is a text-mode interpreter, not a standard utility. When you invoke DiskPart (by typing **diskpart** at the command prompt), you tell the interpreter about the script you want to use by adding the /S parameter as shown here:

```
diskpart /s ScriptName.txt
```

where *ScriptName*.txt is the name of the text file that contains the script you want to use. By default, the output from DiskPart is written to the current command prompt. You can redirect the output to a file as shown here:

```
diskpart /s ScriptName.txt > LogFile.log
```

or

```
diskpart /s ScriptName.txt >> LogFile.log
```

where *LogFile*.log is the name of the text file to which DiskPart output should be written.

Note Remember that > is used to create or overwrite a file using output redirection and that >> is used to create or append to an existing file.

Tip The advantage of using scripts over directly inputting commands is that you can automate disk-related tasks so that they can be performed repeatedly and in exactly the same way each time. Scripting disk management tasks is useful if you are deploying Windows using unattended Setup, RIS or Sysprep, which do not support creating volumes other than the boot volume.

The error codes to look for when working with DiskPart scripts are as follows:

- **0** Indicates no errors occurred, execution proceeded without failure
- **1** Indicates a fatal exception occurred and there may be a serious problem
- **2** Indicates the parameters you specified for a command were incorrect
- **3** Indicates DiskPart was unable to open the specified script or output file
- **4** Indicates a service that DiskPart uses returned an error code or reported failure
- **5** Indicates that a command syntax error occurred; typically because a disk, partition, or volume was improperly selected or was invalid for use with the command

DiskPart: A Script Example

When you use DiskPart scripts, you should complete all the operations you want to perform as part of a single session. The script should contain all of the DiskPart commands you want to execute. It is not necessary to include the EXIT command because the text-mode interpreter exits automatically at the end of the script. Consider the following example script:

Listing 8-1 Sample DiskPart Script

```
rem Select disk 2
select disk 2

rem Create the primary partition on the disk and assign the drive
letter
create partition primary size=4096assign letter=s

rem Create extended partition with 2 logical drives
create partition extended size=4096
create partition logical size=2048
assign letter=u
create partition logical size=2047
assign letter=v
```

Here, you create a primary and an extended partition on disk 2. The primary partition is set to 4096 megabytes (MB) in size and is assigned the drive letter S. The extended partition is created, set to 4096 MB in size, and two logical partitions are added. The first logical partition is 2048 MB in size and is assigned drive letter U. The second logical partition is 2047 MB in size and is assigned drive letter V. The sizes are set this way on the logical partitions because you lose some space due to the partitioning. You could have also created a single logical partition that was 4096 MB in size.

Note   Creating partitions and assigning drive letters as shown in this example doesn't make the partitions available for use. They must still be formatted using the FORMAT command. For more information on formatting partitions and volumes, see the section of Chapter 9 titled "Formatting Partitions."

Tip   Because DiskPart must make and then apply changes, you shouldn't run multiple DiskPart scripts back to back. Instead, you should wait for 10 to 15 seconds in between running scripts or handle all tasks in a single DiskPart session. Not only does this help ensure that the last command issued by the previous DiskPart session is completed; it also ensures the previous DiskPart session is shut down before the next session begins.

You can run the example script by typing **diskpart /s *ScriptName***, such as **diskpart /s disk2config.txt**. When you run the script, the output you should expect is as follows:

```
Disk 2 is now the selected disk.
DiskPart succeeded in creating the specified partition.
DiskPart successfully assigned the drive letter or mount point.
```

```
DiskPart succeeded in creating the specified partition.
DiskPart succeeded in creating the specified partition.
DiskPart successfully assigned the drive letter or mount point.
DiskPart succeeded in creating the specified partition.
DiskPart successfully assigned the drive letter or mount point.
```

As you can see, DiskPart reports step-by-step success or failure. Keep in mind that the script doesn't have to be on the local computer. If the DiskPart script was saved to the network share \\corpserver01\scripts, you can invoke it by typing

diskpart /s \\corpserver01\scripts\disk2config.txt

This assumes that the network share is available to the local system. You can also map network drives at the command line with the NET USE command. The format is

```
net use DriveLetter \\ComputerName\ShareName
```

such as in this example:

```
net use X: \\corpserver01\scripts
```

 Note The NET USE command also accepts user name and password information provided in the form /USER:*Domain\User*. You can also specify whether the mapped drive is persistent (that is, whether the network share mapping should remain when the computer is restarted). Use the parameter /Persistent:Yes. Persistent network share mappings can be deleted by typing **net use *Computer-Name\ShareName* /DELETE**.

By default, if DiskPart encounters an error while executing a command, it stops processing the script and displays an error code. If you specify the Noerr parameter, however, DiskPart will report the error and continue execution of the script. Additionally, you don't have to type the command line that invokes DiskPart directly at the command prompt. The command could be part of a larger script, which I'll refer to as a master script. A sample master script is shown as Listing 8-2.

Listing 8-2 Sample Master Script
```
@echo off
@if not "%OS%"=="Windows_NT" goto :EXIT
@if "%1"=="" (set INFO=echo && set SEXIT=1) else (set INFO=rem &&
set SEXIT=0)

%INFO% *************************
%INFO% Script: Disk2Setup.bat
%INFO% Creation Date: 6/8/2004
%INFO% Last Modified: 9/23/2004
%INFO% Author: William R. Stanek
%INFO% Email: williamstanek@aol.com
%INFO% *************************
```

```
%INFO% Description: Configures the standard partitions on workstations
%INFO%with a third hard drive. The script is configured so
%INFO%that it will only run if you pass in a parameter, which
%INFO%can be any value. This is meant as a safeguard to help
%INFO%prevent accidental formatting of disks.
%INFO% ************************
@if "%SEXIT%"=="1" goto :EXIT

@title "Configuring Disk 2..."
cls
color 07

net use x: \\corpserver01\scripts
diskpart /s x:\disk2config.txt

format s: /fs:ntfs
format u: /fs:ntfs
format v: /fs:ntfs

:EXIT
echo Exiting...
```

That's it for the introduction to DiskPart, the remainder of this chapter discusses the specifics of using DiskPart and related commands such as CHKDSK and DEFRAG to create, manage, and maintain disks, partitions, and volumes.

Installing and Managing Hard Disk Drives

A key reason for using DiskPart is to help you to configure and maintain hard disk drives. Key management tasks include checking for new drives, determining drive status, and managing partition table styles.

Installing and Checking for a New Drive

Windows operating systems support both hot swappable and non-hot swappable drives. *Hot swapping* is a feature that allows you to remove devices without shutting off the computer. In most cases, hot swappable drives are installed and removed from the front of the computer, and if a computer supports hot swapping, you can install drives to the computer without having to shut down. After you hot-swap drives, start DiskPart, then type **rescan** to find the new drives. New drives that are found are added as basic disks. If a drive that you've added isn't found, reboot the computer.

If the computer doesn't support the hot swapping of drives, you must turn the computer off and then install the new drives. Afterward you can scan for new drives as previously described, if necessary.

Checking Drive Status and Configuration

You can use DiskPart to check the status of drives by typing **list disk** from the DiskPart prompt. Typical output from list disk looks like this:

```
Disk ###    Status         Size      Free       Dyn    Gpt
--------    ---------      -------   -------     ---    ---
Disk 0      Online          56 GB       0 B
Disk 1      Online          29 GB       0 B
Disk 2      Offline         37 GB      31 GB
```

As you can see, list disk shows each configured disk on the system by

- **Disk ###**   The number of the disk.

- **Status**   The current status of the disk.

- **Size**   The total capacity of the disk.

- **Free**   The available space for partitioning, not the amount of actual free space on the disk.

- **Dyn**   Indicates the disk type is dynamic if there is an asterisk in this column. Otherwise, the disk is the basic disk type.

- **Gpt**   Indicates the disk partition table type is GUID Partition Table (GPT) if there is an asterisk in this column. Otherwise, the partition type is Master Boot Record (MBR).

In the previous example, the computer had three basic disks that used the MBR partition type. Although disks 0 and 1 were online, disk 2 was offline and could be brought online by changing the focus to disk 2 (by typing **select disk 2**) and then typing **online**.

As you can see, knowing the drive status is useful when you install new drives but also when you want to troubleshoot drive problems. Table 8-2 summarizes the most common status values.

Table 8-2.   Common Drive Status Values and Their Meaning

Status	Description	Resolution
Audio CD	An audio CD is in the CD/DVD drive.	The drive doesn't have any known problems.
Foreign	The dynamic disk has been moved to your computer but hasn't been imported for use. A failed drive brought back online might sometimes be listed as Foreign.	Use the IMPORT command to add the disk to the system.
Initializing	A temporary status that occurs when you convert a basic disk to a dynamic disk.	When initialization is complete, the status should change to Online automatically.

Table 8-2.   Common Drive Status Values and Their Meaning

Status	Description	Resolution
Missing	The dynamic disk is corrupted, turned off, or disconnected. This value appears as the disk name instead of in the Status column.	Reconnect or turn on the missing disk, and then use RESCAN to locate the volume. If the disk won't be used again, use DELETE DISK to delete the disk from the disk list.
No Media	No media have been inserted into the CD-ROM or removable drive. Only CD-ROM and removable disk types display this status.	Insert a CD-ROM, floppy disk, or removable disk to bring the disk online.
Not Initialized	The disk does not contain a valid signature. Windows writes the MBR or GPT for the disk the first time you start Disk Management using a wizard that shows the new disks detected. If you cancel the wizard before the disk signature is written, this status occurs.	If you haven't started Disk Management yet, do so, and then use the Initialize Disk Wizard to write the disk signature. Otherwise, right-click the disk in Disk Management and then select Initialize Disk.
Offline	The dynamic disk isn't accessible and might be corrupted or temporarily unavailable. If the disk name changes to Missing, the disk can no longer be located or identified on the system.	Check for problems with the drive, its controller, and cables. Make sure that the drive has power and is connected properly. Use the ONLINE command to bring the disk back online (if possible).
Online	The normal disk status. It means the disk is accessible and doesn't have problems. Both dynamic disks and basic disks display this status.	The drive doesn't have any known problems.
Online (Errors)	Input/output (I/O) errors have been detected on a dynamic disk.	You can try to correct temporary errors using the ONLINE command. This command will also resynchronize mirrored and RAID-5 volumes.

Table 8-2.   Common Drive Status Values and Their Meaning

Status	Description	Resolution
Unreadable	The disk isn't currently accessible, which can occur when rescanning disks. Both dynamic and basic disks display this status.	If the drives aren't being scanned, the drive might be corrupt or have I/O errors. Use the RESCAN command to correct the problem (if possible). You might also want to reboot the system.
Unrecognized	The disk is of an unknown type and can't be used on the system. A drive from a non-Windows system might display this status.	You can't use the drive on the computer. Try a different drive.

Changing Drive Partition Styles

After you install a drive on a computer, you'll need to configure it for use. You configure the drive by partitioning it and creating file systems in the partitions, as needed. Two partition styles are used for disks: Master Boot Record (MBR) and GUID Partition Table (GPT).

MBR and GPT Partition Styles

X86-based computers use the MBR partition style. MBR contains a partition table that describes where the partitions are located on the disk. With this partition style, the first sector on a hard disk contains the master boot record and a binary code file called the master boot code that's used to boot the system. This sector is unpartitioned and hidden from view to protect the system.

With the MBR partitioning style, disks support volumes of up to 4 terabytes (TB) and use one of two types of partitions:

- Primary
- Extended

Each MBR drive can have up to four primary partitions or three primary partitions and one extended partition. Primary partitions are drive sections that you can access directly for file storage. You make a primary partition accessible to users by creating a file system on it. Unlike primary partitions, you can't access extended partitions directly. Instead, you can configure extended partitions with one or more logical drives that are used to store files. Being able to apportion extended partitions into logical drives allows you to apportion a physical drive into more than four sections.

Itanium-based computers running 64-bit versions of Windows use the GPT partition style. A GPT-based disk has two required partitions and one or more optional (OEM or data) partitions:

- EFI system partition (ESP)

- Microsoft Reserved partition (MSR)
- At least one data partition

Additionally, GPT disks support volumes of up to 18 exabytes (EB) and as many as 128 partitions. Although there are underlying differences between the GPT and MBR partitioning styles, most disk-related tasks are performed in the same way.

Converting Partition Table Styles

Using the CONVERT command, DiskPart can help you change partition table styles from MSR to GPT or from GPT to MSR. Changing partition table styles is useful when you

- Move disks between X86-based computers and IA64-based computers
- Receive new disks that are formatted for the wrong partition table style

You can only convert partition table styles on empty disks, however. This means the disks must either be new or newly formatted. You can, of course, empty the disk by removing any existing partitions or volumes on the disk that you want to convert.

Note   DiskPart provides the CLEAN command for wiping out all the volume or partition information on a disk. When you give a disk focus and then use the CLEAN command, all partition or volume information on the disk is removed. On MBR disks, this means that the MBR partition and hidden sector information are overwritten. On GPT disks, the GPT partition information, including the protected MBR, is overwritten. You can also use CLEAN ALL to specify that each and every sector on the disk should be set to zero.

Caution   If you haven't backed up the data on the drives you want to convert, don't delete any partitions or volumes. Doing so will clear all data on the disk.

The procedure you use to convert the partition table style is as follows:

1. Invoke DiskPart by typing **diskpart** at the command prompt.
2. Select the disk to work with to give it focus, such as

    DISKPART> **select disk 2**

3. Convert the disk, as follows:

    - To convert a disk from MBR to GPT, type **convert gpt** at the command prompt.
    - To convert a disk from GPT to MBR, type **convert mbr** at the command prompt.

Working with Basic and Dynamic Disks

Windows Server 2003 and Windows XP support two types of disk configurations:

- **Basic** The standard disk type used in previous versions of Windows. Basic disks are partitioned and can be used with current and previous versions of Windows.

- **Dynamic** An enhanced disk type that can be updated without having to restart the system (in most cases). Dynamic disks are apportioned into one or more volumes and can be configured with software RAID.

 Note You can't use dynamic disks on portable computers or with removable media. Dynamic disks are only supported on Windows 2000, Windows XP, and Windows Server 2003.

Understanding Basic and Dynamic Disks

When you upgrade to Windows XP or Windows Server 2003, disks with partitions are initialized as basic disks. When you install Windows XP or Windows Server 2003 on a new system with unpartitioned drives, you have the option of initializing the drives as either basic or dynamic.

Basic drives support all the fault-tolerant features found in Microsoft Windows NT 4; however, you can't create fault-tolerant drive sets using the basic disk type. Because of this, if you want to set up software RAID, you must convert to dynamic disks and then create volumes that use mirroring or striping. The fault-tolerant features and the ability to modify disks without having to restart the computer are the key capabilities that distinguish basic disks from dynamic disks.

Although you can use both basic and dynamic disks on the same computer, disk configuration tasks that you can perform with basic and dynamic disks are different. With basic disks, you work with partitions. This means you can

- Format partitions and mark them as active
- Create and delete primary and extended partitions
- Create and delete logical drives within extended partitions
- Convert from a basic disk to a dynamic disk

With dynamic disks, you work with volumes. This means you can

- Create standard and fault-tolerant volumes
- Remove a mirror from a mirrored volume
- Extend simple or spanned volumes
- Split a volume into two volumes

- Repair mirrored or RAID-5 volumes
- Reactivate a missing or offline disk
- Revert to a basic disk from a dynamic disk (which requires deleting all existing volumes prior to doing so)

With either disk type, you can

- View properties of disks, partitions, and volumes
- Make drive letter assignments
- Configure security and drive sharing

Whether you're working with basic or dynamic disks, you need to keep in mind three special types of drive sections:

- **System**   The system partition or volume contains the hardware-specific files needed to load the operating system.
- **Boot**   The boot partition or volume contains the operating system and its support files. The system and boot partition or volume can be the same.
- **Active**   The active partition or volume is the drive section from which the computer starts.

Note   You can't mark an existing dynamic volume as the active volume, but you can convert a basic disk containing the active partition to a dynamic disk. Once the update is complete, the partition becomes a simple volume that's active.

Setting the Active Partition

On an x86-based computer with the MBR partition style, you can mark a partition as active, which means the partition is the drive section from which the computer starts. You can't mark dynamic disk volumes as active. When you convert a basic disk containing the active partition to a dynamic disk, this partition becomes a simple volume that's active automatically.

Note   Before you mark a partition as active, make sure that the necessary startup files are on the primary partition that you want to make the active partition. For Windows Server 2003, these files are Boot.ini, Ntdetect.com, Ntldr, and Bootsect.dos. You might also need Ntbootdd.sys.

Follow these steps to designate the active partition:

1. Invoke DiskPart by typing **diskpart** at the command prompt.
2. Select the disk that contains the partition you want to make active, such as
   DISKPART> **select disk 0**

3. List the partitions on the disk by typing **list partition** at the command prompt.

4. Select the partition you want to work with, such as

   DISKPART> **select partition 0**

5. Make the selected partition the active partition by typing **active** at the command prompt.

 Caution The disk and partition numbers used in the steps are arbitrary and meant only to demonstrate the procedure. Make sure you've selected the right disk and partition in steps 2 and 4. If you incorrectly mark a partition as active and it does not contain the operating system startup files, your computer might not start.

Changing the Disk Type: Basic to Dynamic or Vice Versa

Windows XP and Windows Server 2003 support both basic and dynamic disk types. At times, you'll need to convert one disk type to the other and Windows provides the tools you'll need to do this. When you convert a basic disk to a dynamic disk, partitions are changed to volumes of the appropriate type automatically. You can't change these volumes back to partitions on a basic disk, however. Instead, you must delete the volumes on the dynamic disk and then change the disk back to a basic disk. Deleting the volumes destroys all the information on the disk.

Converting a Basic Disk

Converting a basic disk to a dynamic disk is a straightforward process, but there are lots of stipulations. To start with, consider the following:

- Only computers running Windows 2000, Windows XP, or Windows Server 2003 can use dynamic disks. Thus, if the disk you are converting contains earlier versions of the Windows operating system, you won't be able to boot the computer to those versions of Windows after the conversion.

- With MBR disks, you should ensure that the disk has 1 MB of free space at the end of the disk. Without the free space at the end of the disk, the conversion will fail. Both Disk Management and DiskPart reserve this space automatically; it is primarily when you use third-party disk-management utilities that you need to be concerned about whether this space is available.

- With GPT disks, you must have contiguous, recognized data partitions. If the GPT disk contains partitions that Windows doesn't recognize, such as those created by another operating system, you won't be able to convert to a dynamic disk.

In addition, with either type of disk, the following is true:

- You can't convert drives that use sector sizes larger than 512 bytes. If the drive has large sector sizes, you'll need to reformat before converting.

- You can't use dynamic disks on portable computers or with removable media. You can only configure these drives as basic drives with primary partitions.

- You can't convert a disk if the system or boot partition is part of a spanned, striped, mirrored, or RAID-5 volume. You'll need to stop the spanning, mirroring, or striping before you convert.

- You can, however, convert disks with other types of partitions that are part of spanned, striped, mirrored, or RAID-5 volumes. These volumes become dynamic volumes of the same type and you must convert all drives in the set together.

You can convert a basic disk to a dynamic disk by completing the following steps:

1. Invoke DiskPart by typing **diskpart** at the command prompt.
2. Select the disk that you want to convert to a dynamic disk, such as
   DISKPART> **select disk 0**
3. Convert the disk by typing **convert dynamic** at the command prompt.

Converting a Dynamic Disk

Once you convert a basic disk to a dynamic disk, the only way to revert to a basic disk is to remove all the volumes on the disk. This ensures the disk is empty and that all data it contains is removed. DiskPart does provide a command for wiping out all the volume or partition information on a disk. The command is CLEAN. When you give a disk focus and then type the CLEAN command, all partition or volume information on the disk is removed.

On MBR disks, this means that the MBR partition and hidden sector information are overwritten. On GPT disks, the GPT partition information, including the protected MBR, is overwritten. You can also use CLEAN ALL to specify that every sector on the disk should be set to zero, which completely deletes all data contained on the disk.

You can convert an empty dynamic disk to a basic disk by following these steps:

1. Invoke DiskPart by typing **diskpart** at the command prompt.
2. Select the disk that you want to convert to a basic disk, such as
   DISKPART> **select disk 0**
3. Convert the disk by typing **convert basic** at the command prompt.

This changes the dynamic disk to a basic disk and you can then create new partitions and logical drives on the disk.

Maintaining Hard Disk Drives

Many command-line utilities are available to help you maintain hard disk drives. Some of these utilities include FSUtil, ChkDsk, and Defrag.

Obtaining Disk Information and Managing File Systems with FSUtil

One tool we haven't examined until now is the File System Utility (FSUtil).

FSUtil: An Overview

FSUtil has a fairly complex command structure, but it all basically boils down to the fact that you need to type a command string containing a command and a subcommand to get FSUtil to do what you want it to do. The available FSUtil commands are summarized in Table 8-3.

Table 8-3. FSUtil Commands and Their Usage

BEHAVIOR	Use the related subcommands to view and control how short (MS-DOS) file names are generated, whether the last access timestamp on NTFS volumes is updated, how frequently quota events are written to the system log, the internal cache levels of NTFS paged pool and NTFS non-paged pool memory, and the amount of disk space reserved for the Master File Table (MFT).
DIRTY	Use the related subcommands to query or set a volume's dirty bit. If a volume is dirty, that means it is suspected to have errors and the next time the computer is restarted, a program called AUTOCHK will check the disk and run Check Disk if necessary to repair any errors.
FILE	Use the related subcommands to find a file by user name (only if disk quotas are enabled), check a file for sparse regions, sets a file's valid data length, and zero out portions of sparse files.
FSINFO	Use the related subcommands to list a computer's drives, to query drive type, and to obtain volume information.
HARDLINK	Use the related subcommands to create hard links so a single file can appear in multiple directories (or even in the same directory with multiple names). Programs can open any of the links to modify the file and the file is deleted from the file system only after all links to it have been deleted.
OBJECTID	Use the related subcommands to manage object identifiers for files and directories.
QUOTA	Use the related subcommands to manage disk quotas on NTFS volumes.
REPARSEPOINT	Use the related subcommands to view or delete reparse points. Primarily, reparse points are used for directory junction points and volume mount points.

Table 8-3.   FSUtil Commands and Their Usage

SPARSE	Use the related subcommands to manage sparse files. A sparse file is a file with one or more regions of unallocated data in it.
USN	Use the related subcommands to manage the update sequence number (USN) change journal. The USN change journal provides a persistent log of all changes made to files on the volume.
VOLUME	Use the related subcommands to dismount a volume or query to see how much free space is available.

Using FSUtil

Although FSUtil has many very advanced applications, such as allowing you to remove reparse points on disks, manage disk quotas, and designate sparse files, it also has some basic applications that you'll find useful if you want to obtain disk information.

Obtaining Drive Lists for a Computer   To obtain a list of drives on a computer by drive letter, type

fsutil fsinfo drives

The output shows you the drives available in alphabetical order, as follows:

```
Drives: A:\ C:\ D:\ F:\ G:\ T:\ U:\
```

Obtaining Drive Type   Once you know about the drives, you can obtain the drive type for a particular drive by typing **fsutil fsinfo drivetype** followed by the drive designator, such as

```
C:\>fsutil fsinfo drivetype g:
g: - CD-ROM Drive
```

Here, the G: drive is a CD-ROM drive. Of course, you could obtain similar information for all disks on the computer using DiskPart's list volume command. Still, this is another way to obtain information that you might find useful.

Obtaining Detailed Drive Information   To obtain detailed information about a drive, type **fsutil fsinfo volumeinfo** followed by the drive designator. You have to specify the drive in different ways based on whether you are using Windows Server 2003 or Windows XP. In Windows Server 2003, provide the drive letter followed by a colon, such as

```
C:\>fsutil fsinfo volumeinfo c:
```

For Windows XP, provide the drive letter followed by a colon and a backslash, such as

```
C:\>fsutil fsinfo volumeinfo c:\
```

FSUtil then lists the volume name, serial number, file system type, and the features supported, such as

```
Volume Name : Primary
Volume Serial Number : 0x23b36g45
Max Component Length : 255
File System Name : NTFS
Supports Case-sensitive filenames
Preserves Case of filenames
Supports Unicode in filenames
Preserves & Enforces ACL's
Supports file-based Compression
Supports Disk Quotas
Supports Sparse files
Supports Reparse Points
Supports Object Identifiers
Supports Encrypted File System
Supports Named Streams
```

Obtaining Sector and Cluster Information for Drives   If you want to determine an NTFS disk's sector or cluster information, type **fsutil fsinfo ntfsinfo** followed by the drive designator, such as

```
C:\>fsutil fsinfo ntfsinfo c:
```

FSUtil then lists detailed information on the number of sectors and clusters, including the total clusters used, free clusters and reserved clusters, such as

```
NTFS Volume Serial Number :              0x23b36g45
Version :       3.1
Number Sectors :        0x0000000008fcf7c3
Total Clusters :        0x0000000000eb9f38
Free Clusters   :       0x0000000000d12400
Total Reserved :        0x0000000000000000
Bytes Per Sector  :     512
Bytes Per Cluster :     4096
Bytes Per FileRecord Segment            :    1024
Clusters Per FileRecord Segment         :    0
```

Obtaining Free Space Information for a Drive   You can also use FSUtil to determine the amount of free space on a disk. Type **fsutil volume diskfree** followed by the drive designator, such as

```
C:\>fsutil volume diskfree c:
```

FSUtil will then report the total bytes on the disk as well as the total number of bytes free and available, such as

```
Total # of free bytes        :       52231667712
Total # of bytes             :       60028059648
Total # of avail free bytes :        52231667712
```

Checking Disks for Errors and Bad Sectors

When you want to check disks for errors and bad sectors, you can use the Check Disk (Chkdsk.exe) command-line utility. This utility checks the integrity of both basic and dynamic disks. You can use it to check for and optionally repair problems found on FAT, FAT32, and NTFS volumes.

Check Disk can check for and correct many kinds of errors. The utility primarily looks for inconsistencies in the file system and its related metadata. One of the ways Check Disk locates errors is by comparing the volume bitmap to the disk sectors assigned to files in the file system. Check Disk can't repair corrupted data within files that appear to be structurally intact, however.

Analyzing a Disk Without Repairing It

You can test the integrity of a drive by typing the command name followed by the drive letter and a colon. For instance, to check the integrity of the C drive, type

```
chkdsk c:
```

Check Disk reports its progress during each phase, as follows:

```
The type of the file system is NTFS.
Volume label is Primary.

WARNING!  F parameter not specified.
Running CHKDSK in read-only mode.

CHKDSK is verifying files (stage 1 of 3)...
File verification completed.
CHKDSK is verifying indexes (stage 2 of 3)...
Index verification completed.
CHKDSK is recovering lost files.
CHKDSK is verifying security descriptors (stage 3 of 3)...
Security descriptor verification completed.
CHKDSK discovered free space marked as allocated in the
master file table (MFT) bitmap.
CHKDSK discovered free space marked as allocated in the volume bitmap.
Windows found problems with the file system.
Run CHKDSK with the /F (fix) option to correct these.

  58621153 KB total disk space.
   7484424 KB in 42596 files.
     13188 KB in 2115 indexes.
        20 KB in bad sectors.
    113933 KB in use by the system.
     65536 KB occupied by the log file.
  51009588 KB available on disk.

      4096 bytes in each allocation unit.
  14655288 total allocation units on disk.
  12752397 allocation units available on disk.
```

As you can see, the Check Disk operation is performed in three stages. During the first stage, Check Disk verifies file structures:

```
CHKDSK is verifying files (stage 1 of 3)...
File verification completed.
```

During the second stage, Check Disk verifies disk index entries:

```
CHKDSK is verifying indexes (stage 2 of 3)...
Index verification completed.
CHKDSK is recovering lost files.
```

If there are lost files as a result of verifying the disk index entries, Check Disk will recover the lost files as it states. Typically, the recovered files are stored as .chk files in the root folder of the associated disk drive.

During the third stage, Check Disk verifies security descriptors:

```
CHKDSK is verifying security descriptors (stage 3 of 3)...
Security descriptor verification completed.
```

Finally, Check Disk completes the process by reporting whether there was any free space incorrectly marked as allocated and, if so, it recommends that you correct this by running Check Disk with the /F switch:

```
CHKDSK discovered free space marked as allocated in the
master file table (MFT) bitmap.
CHKDSK discovered free space marked as allocated in the volume bitmap.
Windows found problems with the file system.
Run CHKDSK with the /F (fix) option to correct these.
```

Fixing Disk Errors

When you analyze a disk, you are checking it but aren't really fixing anything. To check the disk and repair any problems found, you'll use the /F switch, which tells Check Disk to check for and fix errors:

```
chkdsk /f C:
```

Check Disk can't repair volumes that are in use. If the volume is in use, Check Disk displays a prompt that asks if you want to schedule the volume to be checked the next time you restart the system. The /F switch implies the /R and /X switches (note that the /X switch applies only to NTFS volumes). The /R switch is used to locate bad disk sectors and recover readable information, and the /X switch is used to force the NTFS volume to dismount if necessary.

You can tell Check Disk to display more information about what it is doing using the verbose switch (/V). On NTFS, you can tell Check Disk to perform limited checks of disk index entries using the /I switch and to skip checking of cycles within folder structures using /C.

To see how Check Disk can be used, consider the following examples:

Find and repair errors that are found on the C drive:

```
chkdsk /f C:
```

Note Remember that when you use /F, both /R and /X are implied.

Locate bad sectors and repair them on the C drive:

```
chkdsk /r C:
```

Perform minimum checks on the C drive, an NTFS volume:

```
chkdsk /i /c C:
```

Controlling Auto Check On Startup

By default, Windows Server 2003 and Windows XP check all disks on startup and if necessary start Check Disk to repair any errors. Two different programs control automatic disk checking on startup: AUTOCHK and CHKNTFS. Auto Check is used by the operating system to initiate automatic checking of drives on startup. You can't invoke Auto Check directly, but you can control how it works using Check NTFS. With Check NTFS, you can determine if a disk will be checked next time the computer starts and change options for automatic checking.

Determining Auto Check Status

To determine if a disk will be checked next time the computer starts, type

chkntfs *Volume*:

where *Volume:* is the drive letter to check followed by a colon, such as

```
chkntfs c:
```

You can specify multiple drive designators as well. Separate each drive designator with a space. In this example, you determine the Check Disk status of drive C, D, and E:

```
chkntfs c: d: e:
```

Check NTFS reports the file system type and whether the disk is dirty or not dirty, as shown in this example:

```
The type of the file system is NTFS.
C: is not dirty.
The type of the file system is NTFS.
D: is dirty.
```

Here, the C drive is not dirty and Auto Check won't trigger Check Disk to run on the drive. The D drive is dirty, on the other hand, which indicates the drive may have errors and Auto Check will trigger Check Disk to run when the computer is started.

Configuring Auto Check Parameters

Using Check NTFS, you can configure Auto Check to work in several key ways. When the computer reboots, the operating system displays a countdown timer that allows the user to cancel the Auto Check operation before it begins. Using the /T parameter, you can set the length of the countdown timer in the form

```
chkntfs /t:NumSeconds
```

where *NumSeconds* is the number of seconds for the timer, such as

```
chkntfs /t:15
```

To exclude a volume or volumes from being checked when the computer starts, even if the volume is marked as requiring Check Disk, you can use the /X parameter. Follow the /X parameter with the drive designators as shown in this example:

```
chkntfs /x d: e:
```

Here, the computer will skip checking of the D and E drives even if they were marked as dirty.

To include a volume for checking when the computer starts (which is the normal configuration for Auto Check), use the /C parameter. Follow the /C parameter with the drive designators, as shown in this example:

```
chkntfs /c c: d:
```

Here, the computer will Auto Check the C and D drives when it starts to determine their status as dirty or not dirty.

The final parameter you can use is /D, which restores the default Auto Check settings, except for the countdown timer. The default behavior is to Auto Check all drives when the computer starts.

Defragmenting Disks

Whenever you add files, move files, or remove files, the data on a computer's drives can become fragmented. When a drive is fragmented, large files can't be written to a single contiguous area on the disk. As a result, large files must be written to several smaller areas of the disk and more time is spent reading the file from the disk whenever it is accessed. To reduce fragmentation, you should periodically analyze and defragment disks using the Defrag command-line utility.

Understanding and Using Defrag

Typically, defragmentation is performed in two steps. First, the disk is analyzed to determine the level of fragmentation and whether the disk should be defragmented. You can perform both steps simply by typing defrag followed by the drive letter and a colon, such as

```
defrag c:
```

Defrag will analyze the disk and, if the disk needs to be defragmented, then begin defragmenting it. If the disk doesn't need to be defragmented, Defrag will stop after the analysis phase and report that the disk doesn't need to be defragmented.

Defrag requires at least 15 percent free space to defragment a disk completely. Defrag uses this space as a sorting area for file fragments. If a volume has less than 15 percent free space, Defrag will only partially defragment it. Additionally, you cannot defragment disks that the file system has marked as dirty, which indicates that the disk has errors. In this case, you must run Check Disk and repair the errors before you can defragment the disk.

Defrag accepts several parameters, including –a, which tells Defrag to analyze the disk but not to defragment it. Two additional switches you can use with Defrag are –v for verbose output and –f to force defragmentation a disk even if free space is low. Forcing defragmentation on such a disk, however, could mean that defragmentation will take a very long time or won't be completely finished.

Marking a Disk as Dirty

One way to tell if a disk has been marked as dirty is to use the File System Utility (FSUtil). Type **fsutil dirty query** followed by the drive letter and a colon, such as

```
fsutil dirty query c:
```

If the disk has errors that should be fixed (or has been marked as dirty), FSUtil reports:

```
Volume - c: is Dirty
```

If the disk doesn't have any known errors, FSUtil reports:

```
Volume - c: is NOT Dirty
```

Performing Defrag Analysis Only

Sometimes you'll only want to analyze a disk to determine if you should defragment it later. To analyze a disk without defragmenting it, type the **defrag –a** command followed by the disk letter and a colon. Defrag will then report whether the disk should be defragmented. The following is an analysis of a disk that doesn't need to be defragmented:

```
C:\>defrag -a c:
Windows Disk Defragmenter
Copyright (c) 2001 Microsoft Corp. and Executive Software
International, Inc.
```

```
Analysis Report
     28.62 GB Total,  4.78 GB (16%) Free,  2% Fragmented (5% file
fragmentation)

You do not need to defragment this volume.
```

As you can see, the disk is only 2 percent fragmented with a 5 percent file fragmentation rate. Because fragmentation is so low, the disk doesn't need to be defragmented. On the other hand, the following disk analysis shows a disk that is heavily fragmented:

```
C:\>defrag -a d:
Windows Disk Defragmenter
Copyright (c) 2001 Microsoft Corp. and Executive Software
International, Inc.

Analysis Report
     55.91 GB Total,  48.65 GB (87%) Free,  27% Fragmented (55% file
fragmentation)
You should defragment this volume.
```

Here, Defrag recommends that you defragment the disk and you could schedule this as necessary maintenance.

Chapter 9
Partitioning Basic Disks

When you install a new computer or update an existing computer, you'll often need to partition the drives on the computer. DiskPart can use the Master Boot Record (MBR) or GUID Partition Table (GPT) partition style. When you use the MBR partition style, a drive can have up to four primary partitions or three primary partitions and one extended partition. When you use the GPT partition style on Windows XP Professional or Windows Server 2003, there are two required partitions (the EFI system partition and the Microsoft Reserved partition) and one or more optional OEM or data partitions for a total of as many as 128 partitions.

Obtaining Partition Information

When you work with DiskPart, you can obtain partition information on the selected disk using the LIST PARTITION command. As shown in the following example, LIST PARTITION lists information on all partitions of the selected disk. For example, if you typed **select disk 2** and then type **list partition**, you would see a list of partitions on disk 2, such as

```
Partition ###     Type          Size        Offset
-------------     ----------    ---------   -------
Partition 1       Primary         706 MB      32 KB
Partition 2       Primary         706 MB     706 MB
Partition 3       Primary         706 MB    1412 MB
Partition 4       Extended       1004 MB    2118 MB
Partition 5       Logical         502 MB    2118 MB
Partition 6       Logical         502 MB    2620 MB
```

Note In the example, note the asterisk at the beginning of the entry for partition 6. This means the partition is currently selected and has focus.

As you can see, LIST PARTITION shows

- **Partition ###**   The number of the partition. You can use **select partition** *N* to work with the partition.

- **Type**   The layout type. Partition layouts include primary, extended, and logical.
- **Size**   The total storage size of the partition.
- **Offset**   The byte offset of the partition, which is always rounded to the nearest cylinder boundary.

 Note   A cylinder is a section of a drive within a partition. A cylinder is in turn apportioned into tracks; the tracks are apportioned into sectors; and finally the sectors are made up of individual data bytes. For example, a 4 GB drive could have 525 cylinders with 255 tracks per cylinder. Each track in turn could have 63 sectors and the sectors could have 512 bytes. Here, a cylinder is about 8 MB in size, so the byte offset of the partition would always be rounded to the nearest 8 MB.

Creating Partitions

How you create partitions on basic disks depends on the partition style of the disk. Because you create different types of partitions with MBR disks than you do with GPT disks, there are separate discussions about creating partitions for MBR and GPT disks.

Creating Partitions for MBR Disks

With MBR disks, you can use DiskPart to create primary and extended partitions. A primary partition can fill an entire disk, or you can size it as appropriate for the computer you're configuring. Each physical drive can have one extended partition. This extended partition can contain one or more logical drives, which are simply sections of the partition with their own file system. Although you can size the logical drive any way you want, you might want to consider how you'll use logical drives on the current workstation or server. Generally, you use logical drives to divide a large physical drive into manageable sections. With this in mind, you might want to apportion a 60-gigabyte (GB) extended partition into three logical drives of 20 GB each.

Creating Primary Partitions

Before you add a primary partition to a disk, you should assess the amount of free space on the disk and also check the current partition configuration. Follow these steps to perform these tasks:

1. Invoke DiskPart by typing **diskpart** at the command prompt.
2. List the disks on the computer by typing **list disk** and check the free space:

Disk ###	Status	Size	Free	Dyn	Gpt
Disk 0	Online	56 GB	0 B		
Disk 1	Online	29 GB	0 B		
Disk 2	Online	37 GB	37 GB		

3. In this example, disk 2 has 37 GB of free space for partitioning and no currently assigned partitions because the size of the disk is also 37 GB. If the disk size and free space aren't the same, however, some space has been assigned to partitions. If you wanted to work with disk 2, you would select the disk and then check the partitions on the disk by typing **select disk 2**, and then typing **list partition**.

Once you select a disk to work with and give the disk focus, you can create the primary partition using the command

```
create partition primary size=N
```

where N is the size of the space to allocate in megabytes. If no size is given, the partition is created to fill the unallocated space on the disk.

Note Here, the partition is created at the beginning of the first free space on the disk. DiskPart accomplishes this by automatically setting the offset parameter to the appropriate value. An important note is that the offset is rounded to the closest cylinder boundary. The value is therefore rounded up or down as appropriate to coincide with the closest cylinder boundary, which can change the final size of the partition or logical drive.

After you create the partition, it will automatically have focus, meaning it will be selected. The partition will not yet have a drive letter or mount point. You must use the ASSIGN command to do this. To finalize the partition, you must also format it using FORMAT, which is a standard Windows external command, not a DiskPart subcommand. For more information, see the sections titled "Assigning Drive Letters and Mount Points" and "Formatting Partitions," later in this chapter.

Creating Extended Partitions with Logical Drives

Each disk drive can have one extended partition. As with primary partitions, you should assess the amount of free space on the disk and also check the current partition configuration before creating an extended partition. After you do this, you can create the extended partition in the unallocated space on the disk you've selected (meaning that you have given that disk focus).

You create an extended partition using the command

```
create partition extended size=N
```

where N is the size of the space to allocate in megabytes. If no size is given, the partition is created to fill the unallocated space on the disk.

After you create the extended partition, it will automatically have focus, meaning that it will be selected. Unlike primary partitions, you don't assign drive letters or format extended partitions directly. Instead, you create one or more logical drives within the extended partition space and these drives are the ones to which you assign drive letters and then format.

You can create a logical drive within an extended partition using the command

```
create partition logical size=N
```

where N is the size of the space to allocate in megabytes. If no size is given, the logical drive will use all the available space in the extended partition. When you specify the size of logical drives, remember the size of all logical drives within the partition must be less than the size of the extended partition. That's why, in Chapter 8, "Configuring and Maintaining Hard Disk Drives," we created an extended partition of 4096 megabytes (MB) and logical drives within the partition of 2048 MB and 2047 MB, respectively.

After you create a logical drive, it will automatically have focus, but will not yet have a drive letter or mount point. You must use the ASSIGN command to assign the drive letter or mount point you want to use and then finalize the logical drive by formatting it using the FORMAT command.

Creating Partitions for GPT Disks

With GPT disks, you can use DiskPart to create the EFI system partition as well as MSR and data partitions. You can't arbitrarily create EFI and MSR partitions. On GPT disks that are used to start 64-bit Microsoft Windows XP or 64-bit Windows Server 2003 systems, the EFI system partition must be the first partition on the disk and the MSR partition must be the second partition on the disk. Because GPT disks that are not used for startup don't contain EFI system partitions, the MSR partition must be the first partition on the disk. Further, keep in mind that Windows doesn't mount MSR partitions and you cannot store data on them or delete them.

As with MBR disks, before you add partitions to GPT disks, you should assess the amount of free space on the disk and also check the current partition configuration. Once you select a disk to work with and give the disk focus, you can create the partition as follows:

Create an EFI system partition using the command:

```
create partition efi size=N
```

Create an MSR partition using the command:

```
create partition msr size=N
```

Create a basic data partition using the command:

```
create partition primary size=N
```

where N is the size of the space to allocate in megabytes. As with MBR disks, DiskPart automatically sets the offset parameter as appropriate; you shouldn't set the byte offset manually in most cases.

As discussed previously, the partition you create will automatically have focus, meaning that it will be selected. The partition will not yet have a drive letter or mount point, which is needed for EFI and data partitions. To finalize an EFI or data partition, you must also format it using the FORMAT command, which is a standard Windows external command, not a subcommand of DiskPart.

Managing Drive Letters and Mount Points

After partitioning a drive, you can assign each partition a drive letter or mount point and then format the partition so that it is ready to store data. Generally, the drive letters E through Z are available for use, with drive letters A to D reserved or already in use in most cases. On many systems, drive letter A is for the system's floppy, drive letter B is reserved for a removable disk drive, drive letter C is the primary disk drive, and drive letter D is for the CD-ROM or DVD drive.

If you need additional partitions, you can create them using mount points, which allow you to mount disks to a file system path, such as C:\Data. The only restriction for drive paths is that you must mount them to empty folders on NT File System (NTFS) drives.

Assigning Drive Letters or Mount Points

To assign a drive letter or mount point, follow these steps:

1. Invoke DiskPart by typing **diskpart** at the command prompt.
2. List the volumes on the computer and check the current assignments by typing **list volume**.

Note Only the LIST VOLUME command shows drive letter and mount point assignments, and it does so for all partitions, logical drives, and volumes on the computer. That's why you use this command instead of the LIST PARTITION command. Seems illogical, but that's how it works. The good news is that you use this same technique when assigning drive letters and mount points to volumes on dynamic disks.

3. Assign the drive letter or mount point as follows:

   • To assign a drive letter, type **assign letter=x** where *x* is the drive letter to use, such as

   DISKPART> `assign letter=f`

   • To assign a mount point, type **assign mount=Path** where *Path* is the path to the empty NTFS folder to use as the mount point, such as

   DISKPART> `assign mount=c:\data`

Changing Drive Letters or Mount Points

The ASSIGN command can also be used to change an existing drive letter or mount point assignment. Simply select the partition to work with and use ASSIGN to set the new drive letter or mount point. DiskPart will change the drive letter and report that you must reboot the computer before the changes take effect:

```
DiskPart assigned the drive letter, but your computer needs to be
rebooted before the changes take effect.
```

With a mount point, DiskPart will report that it made the requested change without requiring a reboot:

```
DiskPart successfully assigned the drive letter or mount point.
```

Removing Drive Letters or Mount Points

You can remove a drive letter or mount point from a partition that has focus by using the REMOVE command. Follow these steps:

1. Invoke DiskPart by typing **diskpart** at the command prompt.
2. List the volumes on the computer by typing **list volume**, and check the current assignments. Remember, only the LIST VOLUME command shows drive letter and mount point assignments, and it does so for all partitions, logical drives, and volumes on the computer.
3. Select the partition you want to work with by typing **select volume** followed by the number of the volume representing the desired partition. Again, it seems illogical to do this with partitions, but this is the easiest way.
4. Remove the current drive letter or mount point assignment from the select partition by typing **remove**.

When entered without any parameters, this command removes the first drive letter or mount point it encounters and reports:

```
DiskPart successfully removed the drive letter or mount point.
```

This technique is fine when the partition only has a single drive letter or mount point. If a partition has multiple drive letters or mount points, you'll want to specify the drive letter to remove by typing the parameter **letter=x** or the mount point to remove by typing the parameter **mount=$Path$**, such as

```
DISKPART> remove letter=d
```

or

```
DISKPART> remove mount=D:\Data
```

You can also specify that all drive letters and mount points should be removed and that DiskPart should close all open handles to the volume and then dismount it after removing the drive letter or mount point. To do this, you use the All and Dismount parameters, as shown in these examples:

Remove all drive letters and mount points:

```
DISKPART> remove all
```

Remove all drive letters and mount points and then dismount the related volumes:

```
DISKPART> remove all
```

Remove the volume mounted as d: and dismount it:

```
DISKPART> remove letter=d dismount
```

Note   On MBR disks, you cannot remove the drive letter from the system or boot partition, or any partition that contains the active paging file or crash dump (memory dump). On GPT disks, you cannot remove the drive letter for any EFI, OEM, unrecognized, or non-data partition. You can, however, use this command to remove the drive letter from a removable drive.

Formatting Partitions

Formatting creates a file system in a partition and permanently deletes any existing data. Windows XP and Windows Server 2003 support FAT, FAT32, and NTFS file systems. FAT is the file system type supported by MS-DOS and Windows 3.1, Windows 95, Windows 98, and Windows Millennium Edition (Windows Me). FAT32 is a 32-bit version of FAT. NTFS is the native file system type for Windows NT, Windows 2000, Windows XP, and Windows Server 2003.

More Info   To learn about the features of each file system, see Chapter 13 in *Microsoft Windows Server 2003 Administrator's Pocket Consultant* (Microsoft Press, 2003).

Using Format

To format a partition, you use the FORMAT command. If you are currently using DiskPart, type **exit** to leave its text-mode interpreter and return to the command prompt. When formatting hard disk drives, the basic syntax of the FORMAT command is

```
format Volume /fs:FileSystem /v:Label /a:UnitSize
```

where *Volume* specifies the drive letter or mount point to format, *FileSystem* sets the file system type, *Label* sets the descriptive text name, and *UnitSize* sets the allocation unit size for bytes per disk cluster. A disk cluster is a small section of a disk made up of individual sectors. The volume label can be a maximum of 11 characters (including spaces) and is used with drive letters, not mount points. If you don't set the allocation unit size, FORMAT chooses one for you based on the size of the volume. Valid allocation unit sizes include

- **512** Sets 512 bytes per cluster
- **1024** Sets 1024 bytes per cluster
- **2048** Sets 2048 bytes per cluster
- **4096** Sets 4096 bytes per cluster
- **8192** Sets 8192 bytes per cluster
- **16K** Sets 16 kilobytes per cluster
- **32K** Sets 32 kilobytes per cluster
- **64K** Sets 64 kilobytes per cluster

To see how the Format utility is used, consider the following examples:

Format the F drive to use the FAT32 file system and label it AppData:

```
format f: /fs:fat32 /v:AppData
```

Format the mount point C:\Data to use the NTFS file system and 512 bytes per disk cluster:

```
format c:\data /fs:ntfs /a:512
```

Format the S drive to use the NTFS file system and label it AppData:

```
format s: /fs:fat32 /v:AppData
```

 Note If there's an existing file system, FORMAT prompts you to enter the current volume label as a precaution. After you type the current volume label, you will also need to confirm that you want to proceed with the formatting, which will wipe out any existing data on the volume. You can't avoid these prompts.

Tip In some cases, you might need to dismount the volume before you can format it. You can do this with the /X parameter. In addition, if you are working with a previously formatted drive that doesn't have any known problems, you could perform a quick format instead of a thorough format using the /Q parameter. With a quick format, FORMAT prepares the file system for use without checking for errors. With large partitions, this option can save you a few minutes. However, it doesn't allow FORMAT to mark bad sectors on the disk and lock them out.

Formatting: An Example

When FORMAT starts, it will display the current file system type and tell you what the new file system type will be, as follows:

```
C:\>format e: /fs:ntfs
The type of the file system is RAW.
The new file system is NTFS.
```

Note In this example, an unallocated space is being formatted, which is why the type of file system is listed as RAW. Some applications also write RAW data to disks, and when they do, the data is written directly to the disk without the benefits of partitioning or an actual file system.

FORMAT will then warn you that any existing data will be lost and asks you to confirm that you want to continue:

```
WARNING, ALL DATA ON NON-REMOVABLE DISK
DRIVE E: WILL BE LOST!
Proceed with Format (Y/N)?
```

If you continue, FORMAT will verify the partition and then begin formatting it, showing the percentage of formatting complete:

```
Verifying 500M
25 percent completed.
```

FORMAT then creates the file system structures and reports that formatting is complete:

```
Creating file system structures.
Format complete.
```

FORMAT also reports the total disk space and the available disk space on the new partition:

```
    511999 KB total disk space.
    507066 KB are available.
```

Tip Use the /C parameter to turn on compression for the disk. Built-in compression is available only for NTFS. Under NTFS, compression is transparent to users and compressed files can be accessed just like regular files. If you select this option, files and directories on this drive are compressed automatically.

Managing Partitions

Common management tasks for partitions include converting FAT and FAT32 partitions to NTFS, changing volume labels, extending partitions, and deleting partitions. These tasks are discussed in this section.

Converting a Partition or Volume to NTFS

If you created a partition or volume using FAT or FAT32, you can convert it to NTFS without having to reformat using the FORMAT command. The advantage of this is that the file and directory structure is preserved and no data is lost. To convert from FAT or FAT32 to NTFS, use the CONVERT command.

Conversion: Preliminary Checks

Before you use CONVERT, you should do the following:

- **Check to see if the partition is being used as the active boot partition or a system partition containing the operating system.** With Intel x86 systems, you can convert the active boot partition to NTFS. If you do this, however, CONVERT must have exclusive access to the partition, which can only be obtained during startup. So if you attempt to convert the active boot or system partition to NTFS, you will see a prompt asking if you want to schedule the drive to be converted the next time the system starts. If you click Yes, you can restart the system to begin the conversion process. Just keep in mind that it usually takes several restarts to completely convert the active boot partition.

- **Check to see if the drive has enough free space to perform the conversion.** You'll need a block of free space that's roughly equal to 25 percent of the total space used by the partition or volume. For example, if the partition stores 20 GB of data, CONVERT will need about 5 GB of free space. CONVERT checks for this free space before running and aborts if there isn't enough.

Caution There isn't a utility for converting NTFS to FAT. The only way to go from NTFS to FAT or NTFS to FAT32 is to delete the partition or volume and then to recreate the partition as a FAT or FAT32 volume.

Handling Basic Conversions

CONVERT is run at the command prompt. If you want to convert a drive, use the following syntax:

```
convert volume /FS:NTFS
```

where *volume* is the drive letter followed by a colon, drive path, or volume name. For example, if you wanted to convert the D drive to NTFS, you'd use the following command:

```
convert D: /FS:NTFS
```

Tip For volumes converted from FAT or FAT32 to NTFS, the Master File Table (MFT) is created in a different location than on a volume originally formatted with NTFS, which can result in a slowdown in performance. For optimal performance, you might want to use a designated conversion area as discussed in Using the CvtArea Parameter.

On converted boot and system volumes, CONVERT applies the same default security that is applied during Windows Setup. On other volumes, CONVERT sets security so the Users group has access but doesn't give access to the special group Everyone. To give Everyone access to the data on the disk, you can remove the security settings using the /NoSecurity parameter, such as

```
convert D: /FS:NTFS /nosecurity
```

Caution The /NoSecurity parameter removes all security attributes and makes all files and directories on the disk accessible to the group Everyone.

CONVERT has several additional parameters. You can use the verbose switch (/V) to get more detailed information during the conversion and the force dismount switch (/X) to force the partition or volume to dismount before the conversation if necessary. The main reason for dismounting a drive prior to conversion is to ensure that no application or process tries to use the drive while it is being converted. You can't, however, dismount a boot or system drive. These drives will be converted when the system is restarted.

The basic conversion procedure works well with most types of disks. Sometimes, however, you may find that this procedure doesn't yield ideal results. For example, a converted drive could actually slow instead of accelerate. To work around this problem, you can use the /Cvtarea parameter, which sets the name of a contiguous file in the root directory to be a placeholder for NTFS system files.

Using the CvtArea Parameter

Ideally, the more often a file is accessed, the closer it should be placed to the beginning of the drive to decrease the amount of time required to find and read the file. When a drive is formatted, certain NTFS system files should be placed at the beginning of the drive precisely for this reason. However, when you use the basic conversion process, Windows is unable to place the new NTFS system files at the beginning of the disk because that space is already used by other files that need to be retained. As a result, a converted drive could perform somewhat slower than it did when formatted as FAT or FAT32.

Windows Server 2003 and Windows XP resolve this problem by allowing you to designate a conversion area using the CvtArea parameter followed by the name of a temporary file to use. The syntax is

```
convert volume /FS:NTFS /CVTAREA:FileName
```

where *FileName* is a file created in advance for use as a temporary location, such as

```
convert C: /FS:NTFS /CVTAREA:temp.txt
```

This specifies that the Master File Table (MFT) and other NTFS metadata files are written to an existing, contiguous placeholder file called temp.txt. When you use CONVERT without the CvtArea parameter, the FAT system files at the beginning of the disk aren't moved. They are deleted and subsequent regular files are placed in the location of the old system files. When you use CONVERT with the CvtArea parameter, CONVERT looks for the listed file name and puts a placeholder at the beginning of the disk instead of placing regular files in that location. When the drive is converted to NTFS, CONVERT deletes the CvtArea file and replaces it with the newly completed NTFS system files. Thus, using the /CvtArea parameter can result in a less fragmented file system after conversion.

You create the placeholder file by using the FSUTIL command prior to running CONVERT. CONVERT does not create this file for you. For optimal results, the size of this file should be 1 KB multiplied by the number of files and directories in the file system. The easiest way to determine the number of files and directories in the file system is to check the properties of each of the top-level folders on the drive, record the total number of files and folders, and then compute the totals for all top-level folders. To do this, follow these steps:

1. Start Windows Explorer, right-click a top-level folder on the drive, and then select Properties.

2. Note the total number of files and folders for the Contains: entry and then click OK.

3. Repeat this procedure for each top-level folder, and then add the totals.

Once you have the total number of file and folders, multiply this by 1 KB to determine the size of the placeholder file. For example, if there were 1,000 files and folders, the placeholder file's size would need to be 1,000 KB. To create the placeholder file, type

```
fsutil file createnew FileName ByteSize
```

where *FileName* is the name of the file to create and *ByteSize* is the size of the file in bytes. To create a 1,000 KB file named Temp.txt, we would create a file with 1024000 bytes (each KB is 1024 bytes), such as

```
fsutil file createnew temp.txt 1024000
```

Note Keep in mind, convert overwrites this file with NTFS metadata. After conversion, any unused space in this file is freed.

Changing or Deleting the Volume Label

The volume label is a text descriptor for a volume that has a drive letter. It can be a maximum of 11 characters (including spaces) and is displayed when the drive is accessed in various utilities, such as Windows Explorer. You can change or delete a volume label using the LABEL command.

You can change the volume's label by using the syntax

```
label drive: label
```

where *drive:* is the drive letter followed by a colon and *label* is the text description to assign, such as

```
label f: AppData
```

Note A useful command when working with volume labels is VOL. VOL lists the current volume name (if any).

Extending Partitions

If you create a partition that's too small, you'll sometimes want to be able to extend it. Previously, you could only extend partitions using third-party utilities. Now DiskPart provides a solution for extending partitions in one specific scenario: when you want to extend the last partition on the disk, you can do so using the EXTEND command. The last partition is the only one that DiskPart will extend and it does so regardless of whether you are working with a primary partition, extended partition, or logical drive. Keep in mind, however, that you can't extend boot or system partitions and that you can only extend partitions formatted as NTFS.

The steps you follow to extend the last partition on a disk are as follows:

1. Invoke DiskPart by typing **diskpart** at the command prompt.
2. List the disks on the computer by typing **list disk** and check the free space.
3. Select the disk you want to work, such as disk 2, by typing **select disk 2**.

4. List the partitions on the selected disk by typing **list partition**.

5. Select the last partition in the list. For instance, type **select partition 6**.

6. Extend the partition by typing **extend size=N**

where N is the amount of space to add in megabytes, such as

DISKPART> extend size=1000

 Note The size is rounded to the nearest cylinder boundary, which typically results in a slightly larger or smaller disk space being added. Here, the space added is 1004 MB. If no size is given, the partition is extended to fill the unallocated space on the disk.

 Tip You can extend logical drives within extended partitions as well. Here, you extend the logical drive, not the extended partition itself. When you do this, DiskPart will automatically add space to the extended partition and then add it to the selected logical drive.

Deleting Partitions

To change the configuration of a drive that's fully allocated, you might need to delete existing partitions. Deleting a partition removes the associated file system, and all data in the file system is lost. Before you delete a partition, therefore, you should back up any files and directories that the partition contains.

On a basic disk, you can delete the partition with focus using DELETE PARTITION. You cannot, however, use this command to delete the system or boot partition, or any partition that contains the active paging file or crash dump (memory dump). To see how DELETE PARTITION is used, consider the following example:

1. Invoke DiskPart by typing **diskpart** at the command prompt.

2. List the disks on the computer by typing **list disk** and hitting Enter and select the basic disk you want to work with by typing **select disk** followed by the disk number.

3. List the partitions on the selected disk by typing **list partition**.

4. Select the partition to delete by typing **select partition** followed by the partition number and then delete it by typing **delete partition**.

 More Info DiskPart allows you to delete only known data partitions. You can override this behavior if you are certain you know what you are doing. To do this, add the Override parameter to the DELETE PARTITION command.

Chapter 10

Managing Volumes and RAID on Dynamic Disks

When you work with dynamic disks, you create volumes instead of partitions. A *volume* is simply a disk section that you can use for storing data directly. Although you create volumes in much the same way as you do in creating partitions, volumes have many additional capabilities. You can

- Create a volume on a single drive, called a *simple* volume.
- Extend volumes to fill empty space on a disk, which creates an *extended* volume.
- Create a single volume that spans multiple drives, called a *spanned* volume.
- Configure RAID (a redundant array of independent disks). Microsoft Windows Server 2003 and Windows XP Professional support RAID-0, RAID-1, and RAID-5.

Because volumes and RAID arrays are created on dynamic drives, they are accessible only by Windows 2000, Windows XP, and Windows Server 2003. So if you dual-boot a computer to a previous version of Windows, the dynamic drives are unavailable. Over a network, however, dynamic drives can be accessed as you would access any other drive. This means that computers running previous versions of Windows can access the drives over the network.

Obtaining Volume Information and Status

When you are working with DiskPart and want to check the status of partitions and volumes, you can use the LIST VOLUME command. As shown in the following example, LIST VOLUME lists the current statistics of all volumes, partitions, and logical drives on the computer:

```
DISKPART> list volume

Volume ###  Ltr   Label      Fs     Type      Size     Status      Info
----------  ---   --------   -----  --------  -------  ---------  -------
Volume 0    T     Data       NTFS   Simple    502 MB   Healthy
Volume 1    U     Data2      NTFS   Simple    500 MB   Healthy
Volume 2    F                       DVD-ROM     0 B
Volume 3    G                       CD-ROM      0 B
Volume 4    C     Primary    NTFS   Partition  56 GB   Healthy    System
Volume 5    D     Secondary  NTFS   Partition  29 GB   Healthy
```

As you can see, LIST VOLUME shows the following:

- **Volume ###** The number of the volume. You can type **select volume *N*** to work with the volume.
- **Ltr** The drive letter of the volume.
- **Label** The volume label.
- **Fs** The file system type: FAT, FAT32, or NTFS.
- **Type** The layout type. With dynamic disks, volume layout type tells you the configuration of the volume as simple, spanned, mirrored, striped, or RAID-5.
- **Size** The total storage size of the volume.
- **Status** The state of the volume, shown as Healthy, Failed Redundancy, and so on.
- **Info** Provides additional information related to the volume.

One of the more important statistics provided is the volume status. Understanding the volume status is useful when you install new volumes or try to troubleshoot problems. Table 10-1 summarizes status values, which are primarily associated with dynamic volumes.

Table 10-1. Understanding and Resolving Volume Status Issues

Status	Description	Resolution
Data Incomplete	Spanned volumes on a foreign disk are incomplete. You must have forgotten to add the other disks from the spanned volume.	Move over the disks that contain the rest of the spanned volume and then import all the disks at one time.
Data Not Redundant	Fault-tolerant volumes on a foreign disk are incomplete (not redundant). You must have forgotten to add the other disks from a mirror or RAID-5 set.	Add the remaining disk(s) and then import all the disks at one time.

Table 10-1.   Understanding and Resolving Volume Status Issues

Status	Description	Resolution
Failed	A disk-error status. The disk is inaccessible or damaged.	Ensure that the related dynamic disk is online. If necessary, rescan for volumes or use the ONLINE command to bring the volume online.
Failed Redundancy	A disk-error status. One of the disks in a mirror or RAID-5 set is offline.	Ensure that the related dynamic disk is online. If necessary, try to bring the volume online. If the volume cannot be brought online, you might need to replace a failed mirror or repair a failed RAID-5 volume.
Formatting	A temporary status that indicates that the volume is being formatted.	The progress of the formatting is indicated as the percentage completed. On successful completion, the volume will be set to Healthy status.
Healthy	The normal volume status.	The volume doesn't have any known problems.
Regenerating	A temporary status that indicates that a mirrored volume is being added or imported, or data and parity for a RAID-5 volume are being regenerated.	Progress is indicated as the percentage completed. The volume should return to Healthy status.
Resynching	A temporary status that indicates that a mirror set is being resynchronized.	Progress is indicated as the percentage completed. The volume should return to Healthy status.
Stale Data	Data on foreign disks that are fault tolerant are out of sync.	Rescan or restart the computer, and then check the status. A new status should be displayed, such as Failed Redundancy.
Unknown	The volume's boot sector appears to be corrupted and you can no longer access data on the volume.	The disk may not have been initialized. Start Disk Management, then if the Initialize Disk Wizard doesn't start automatically, right-click the disk and select Initialize Disk.

Creating and Managing Simple Volumes

With dynamic disks, you can use DiskPart to create simple volumes, which is the most basic type of dynamic volume. Unlike partitions, a simple volume can fill an entire disk, or you can size a simple volume as appropriate for the computer you're configuring.

Creating Simple Volumes

Before you add a simple volume to a disk, you should assess the amount of free space on the disk and also check the current volume configuration. Follow these steps to perform these tasks:

1. Invoke DiskPart by typing **diskpart** at the command prompt.
2. List the disks on the computer and check the free space, as follows:

```
DISKPART> list disk

  Disk ###     Status       Size       Free      Dyn    Gpt
  --------   -----------   -------    -------    ---    ---
  Disk 0      Online        72 GB        0 B
  Disk 1      Online        29 GB       20 GB      *
  Disk 2      Online        37 GB       37 GB      *
```

In this example, Disk 1 and Disk 2 are formatted as dynamic disks (denoted by the asterisk in the Dyn column) using MBR partitioning (denoted by a blank entry in the Gpt column). Disk 1 has 20 gigabytes (GB) of free space and Disk 2 has 37 GB of free space available.

Once you identify the disk you want to work with, you can create the simple volume using the command

```
create volume simple size=N disk=N
```

where *size=N* sets the size of the volume in megabytes (MB) and *disk=N* specifies the disk you want to work with.

After you create the volume, the volume will automatically have focus, meaning it will be selected. The volume will not yet have a drive letter or mount point. You must use the ASSIGN command to do this. Then to finalize the partition, you must also format it using the FORMAT command, which is a standard Windows external command, not a DiskPart subcommand. These tasks are performed in the same way for volumes and partitions. See the sections of Chapter 9, "Partitioning Basic Disks," titled "Assigning Drive Letters or Mount Points" and "Formatting Partitions," respectively.

Extending Simple Volumes

If you find that you need more space on a simple volume, you can extend it in two ways: First, you can extend a simple volume within the same disk, creating what is called an extended volume. Or you can extend a simple volume onto other disks, creating what is called a spanned volume. In either case, the volume must be formatted as NTFS.

The steps you follow to extend a simple volume are as follows:

1. Invoke DiskPart by typing **diskpart** at the command prompt.
2. List the disks on the computer and check the free space, as follows:

   DISKPART> list disk
3. Lists the volumes on the computer, as follows:

   DISKPART> list volume
4. Select the volume you want to extend, such as volume 5:

   DISKPART> select volume 5
5. Extend the volume.

   - To extend the volume on the current disk, use the following command:

   DISKPART> extend size=N disk=N

   where *size=N* is the amount of space to add in megabytes and *disk=N* is the disk on which the volume is currently located. For example, if the volume were on disk 2, you could extend it by 1004 MB using the command

   DISKPART> extend size=1004 disk=2

Note   The size is rounded to the nearest cylinder boundary, which typically results in a slightly larger or smaller disk space being added.

   - To extend the volume onto another dynamic disk, use the following command:\

   DISKPART> extend size=N disk=N

   where *size=N* is the amount of space to add in megabytes and *disk=N* sets the disk onto which the volume should be extended. For example, if the volume were on disk 0 and you wanted to extend it onto disk 1, you could use the command

   DISKPART> extend size=2008 disk=1

   Here, you extend disk 0 onto disk 1. The size of the extended area on disk 1 is 2008 MB.

Caution   When extending volume sets, there are many things you cannot do. You can't extend boot or system volumes. You can't extend volumes that use mirroring or striping. You can't extend a volume onto more than 32 disks, either. Additionally, you can't extend FAT or FAT32 volumes; you must first convert them to NTFS.

Bringing Dynamic Disks Online

Dynamic disks are much more versatile than basic disks. You can easily resolve errors and return drives that have gone offline to service. You can also check for drive configuration changes and import disks moved from one computer to another.

As discussed in Chapter 8, "Configuring and Maintaining Hard Disk Drives," the LIST DISK command shows the status of each disk available on a system. If the status of a dynamic disk displays as Online (Errors) or Offline, you can often use the ONLINE command to correct the problem. Using DiskPart, simply designate the disk you want to work with, such as by typing **select disk 0**, and then by typing **online**. If the drive status doesn't change, you might need to reboot the computer. If a reboot still doesn't resolve the problem, check the drive, its controller, cables, and power supply to make sure everything is connected properly. ONLINE also resynchronizes mirrored or RAID-5 volumes.

If the drive configuration has changed or a disk has been added to the computer, you can use the RESCAN command to rescan all drives on the computer and to check for updates to the drive configuration. A rescan can sometimes resolve a problem with drives that show a status of Unreadable.

If you moved a dynamic disk from one computer to another, the disk might be marked as Foreign. A disk can also be marked as Foreign if it failed and you brought it back online. To bring the disk online using DiskPart, select the disk you want to work with, by typing **select disk 0** for example, and then typing **import**.

Deleting Volumes

You should not use the DELETE PARTITION command on a dynamic disk, because this could delete all the dynamic volumes on the disk. If you want to delete a volume with focus on a dynamic disk, use the DELETE VOLUME command. As with DELETE PARTITION, you cannot use this command to delete the system or boot volume, or any volume that contains the active paging file or crash dump (memory dump).

To see how DELETE VOLUME is used, consider the following example:

1. Invoke DiskPart by typing **diskpart** at the command prompt.
2. List the volumes on the computer, as follows:
   ```
   DISKPART> list volume
   ```
3. Select the volume to delete and then delete it as follows:
   ```
   DISKPART> select volume 5
   DISKPART> delete volume
   ```

More Info   By default, DiskPart allows you to delete only known data volumes. As with partitions, you can override this behavior by adding the Override parameter to the DELETE VOLUME command.

Providing Fault Tolerance with RAID on Dynamic Disks

With RAID, you can give important data increased protection from drive failures. RAID can be implemented at the hardware or software level. Hardware RAID is implemented and managed using the tools provided by the hardware vendor. Software RAID is implemented and managed by the operating system.

On dynamic disks, Windows XP Professional and Windows Server 2003 support three software RAID levels:

- **RAID-0**   Disk striping. Here, two or more volumes, each on a separate drive, are configured as a stripe set. Data is broken into blocks, called stripes, and then blocks of data are sequentially written to all drives in the stripe set. RAID-0 gives a speed and performance enhancement but is not fault-tolerant.

- **RAID-1**   Disk mirroring or duplexing. Here, two volumes on two drives are configured identically. Data is written to both drives. If one drive fails, there's no data loss because the other drive also contains the data. RAID-1 gives redundancy and better write performance than disk striping with parity (RAID-5).

- **RAID-5**   Disk striping with parity. Here, you use three or more volumes, each on a separate drive, to create a stripe set with parity error checking. In the case of failure, data can be recovered. RAID-5 gives fault tolerance with less overhead than mirroring and better read performance than disk mirroring.

Note   You can't implement software RAID on basic disks. Windows XP Professional and Windows Server 2003 only support a minimum set of management features for working with basic disks that use RAID on systems that have been upgraded. This discussion, however, focuses entirely on dynamic disks.

Implementing RAID-0: Disk Striping

With RAID-0, also known as disk striping, two or more volumes—each on a separate drive—are configured as a striped set. Data written to the striped set is separated into blocks that are called *stripes*. These stripes are written sequentially to all drives in the striped set. Although you can place volumes for a striped set on up to 32 drives, in most circumstances sets with two to five volumes offer the best performance improvements and beyond this the performance improvement decreases significantly.

Using RAID-0

One of the key reasons for using RAID-0 is the speed improvement. Because data can be accessed on multiple disks using multiple drive heads, read performance improves considerably. However, it also increases the chances of catastrophic failure. If any hard disk drive in the striped set fails, the striped set can no longer be used and all data in the striped set is lost. To recover, you would need to recreate the striped set and restore the data from backups. Data backup and recovery is discussed in Chapter 15 of the *Microsoft Windows Server 2003 Administrator's Pocket Consultant* (Microsoft Press, 2003).

When you create striped sets, you'll want to keep the following in mind:

- The boot and system volumes can't be part of a striped set. Don't use disk striping with these volumes.

- The overall size of the stripe set is based on the smallest volume size. Because of this, you should use volumes that are approximately the same size.

- You can maximize performance by using disks that are on separate disk controllers. This allows the system to simultaneously access the drives.

Running the LIST DISK or DETAIL DISK command on a disk with RAID-0 shows a volume type of STRIPED. If you run the DETAIL VOLUME command on the striped volume, DiskPart shows you all the simple volumes that are part of the striped set.

A disk status of "Missing" appears any time a striped volume is broken. You can use the DETAIL DISK command on one of the remaining drives, which should show a status of "Failed," indicating that the redundancy has failed. If you see a status of "Failed" but don't know which other disk was part of the striped set, you can track down the problem disk by running DETAIL DISK on all other disks on the computer. The status of the problem disk should appear as "Missing."

Fixing the striped set typically involves removing the failed disk, replacing it with a new one and then configuring the new disk to be a part of a new striped set. To do this, you would run DiskPart, select the new disk, and then run CONVERT DYNAMIC to convert the disk type. Afterward, you would need to format the new disk and assign a drive letter. Then you would need to use DiskPart to remove the volumes on the drives that were part of the broken striped set and then create a striped set using the command CREATE VOLUME STRIPE. When the process completes, you should be able to select the striped volume and use LIST VOLUME to view its status. The status should show as "Healthy."

 Caution All data is removed from the drives when you remove the volumes. You will need to recreate the data from backup. If you don't have a backup of the disks, don't overwrite the drives. You might be able to salvage some of the data using third-party recovery utilities.

Configuring the Stripe Set

To implement RAID-0, follow these steps:

1. Invoke DiskPart by typing **diskpart** at the command prompt.

2. List the disks on the computer, check the free space, and ensure that the disks you want to work with are all configured as dynamic disks, as follows:

   ```
   DISKPART> list disk
   ```

3. Create the stripe set as follows:

   ```
   DISKPART> create volume stripe size=N disk=N,N,N,...
   ```

   where *size=N* is the amount of space in megabytes that the volume will use on each disk. If no size is given, DiskPart uses all the remaining free space on the smallest disk and then uses the same amount of space on the remaining disks. *disk=N,N,N,...* sets the disks onto which the volume should be striped. You need to use at least two dynamic disks.

Consider the following examples:

Create a striped volume on disks 0, 1, and 2 using all available space on the smallest disk and then using the same amount of space on the remaining disks:

```
create volume stripe disk=0,1,2
```

Create a striped volume on disks 0, 1, and 2 using 4 GB (4096 MB) of space on each disk:

```
create volume stripe size=4096 disk=0,1,2
```

Implementing RAID-1: Disk Mirroring and Duplexing

With RAID-1, also known as disk mirroring, you use identically sized volumes on two different drives to create a redundant data set. Here, the mirrored drives contain identical sets of information, which means you read data from the primary mirror only, but write data to both drives. Because it is necessary to write the data twice, each mirrored drive often is given its own disk controller, which allows the data to be written simultaneously to both drives. When you use two disk controllers, the drives are said to be "duplexed." Thus, the difference between disk mirroring and disk duplexing lies in whether there is one disk controller or two (and for the remainder of this section, I won't distinguish between the two).

Using RAID-1

One of the key reasons to use disk mirroring is that, if one of the disks fails, the other disk can be used automatically for reading and writing data. The working drive can also be used to regenerate the failed drive onto the same or another disk. You'll need to break the mirror before you can fix it. To learn how, see the section of this chapter titled "Managing RAID and Recovering from Failure."

As you probably guessed, there is a trade-off to be made with disk mirroring: Disk mirroring effectively cuts the amount of storage space in half. For example, to mirror an 80 GB drive, you need another 80 GB drive. That means you use 160 GB of space to store 80 GB of information.

 Note Unlike disk striping, with disk mirroring you can mirror any type of simple volume. This means that you can mirror the boot and system volumes if you choose.

Running the LIST DISK or DETAIL DISK commands on a disk with RAID-1 shows a volume type of "Mirrored." If you run the DETAIL VOLUME command on the mirrored volume, DiskPart shows details on both volumes in the mirrored set.

A disk status of "Missing" appears any time a mirrored volume is broken. You can use the DETAIL DISK command on one of the remaining disks, which should show a status of "Failed Redundancy," indicating that the redundancy has failed. If you see a status of "Failed Redundancy" but don't know which other disk was part of the mirrored set, you can track down the problem drive by running DETAIL DISK on all other disks on the computer. The status of the problem disk should appear as "Missing."

Fixing the mirrored set typically involves removing the failed disk, replacing it with a new one, and then configuring the new disk to be a part of the mirrored set. To do this, you would run DiskPart, select the new disk, and then run CONVERT DYNAMIC to convert the disk type. Afterward, you would need to break the existing mirror using the BREAK DISK command and then use the ADD DISK command, designating the new disk as the disk to add to the new mirrored set. When the process completes, you should be able to select the mirrored volume and use the LIST VOLUME command to view its status, which should appear as "Healthy."

Configuring Mirroring or Duplexing

To create a mirrored set, you select the simple volume that you want to mirror and then add a disk to use as the second drive in the mirrored set. The secondary drive must have unallocated space at least as large as the size of the selected volume. Follow these steps:

1. Invoke DiskPart by typing **diskpart** at the command prompt.

2. List the disks on the computer, check the free space, and ensure that the disks you want to work with are all configured as dynamic disks, as follows:
   ```
   DISKPART> list disk
   ```

3. Select the disk you want to mirror. In this example, you select disk 0:
   ```
   DISKPART> select disk 0
   ```

4. Add a disk to use as the second drive in the mirrored set. In this example, you add disk 1:

```
DISKPART> add disk=1
```

When you do this, the operating system begins the mirror creation process and you'll see a status of "Resynching" on both volumes.

Implementing RAID-5: Disk Striping with Parity

With RAID-5, known as disk striping with parity, you use a minimum of three hard disk drives to set up fault tolerance using identically sized volumes. One of the key reasons to use RAID-5 is that it protects a computer from a single disk failure. If two disks fail, the parity information isn't sufficient to recover the data, and you'll need to rebuild the striped set from backup.

Using RAID-5

You can think of RAID-5 as an enhanced version of RAID-0, in which you gain the performance benefits of striping and add fault tolerance. Thus, unlike RAID-0, the failure of a single drive won't bring down the entire drive set. Instead, the set continues to function with disk operations directed at the remaining volumes in the set. These remaining volumes can also be used to regenerate the striped set onto a new disk or the restored disk that you've recovered as discussed in the section of this chapter titled "Managing RAID and Recovering from Failure."

Caution The boot and system volumes cannot be part of a striped set. Don't use disk striping with parity on these volumes.

Running the LIST DISK or DETAIL DISK command on a disk with RAID-5 shows a volume type of "RAID-5." If you run the DETAIL VOLUME command on the RAID-5 volume, DiskPart shows you all the volumes that are part of the set.

A disk status of "Missing" appears whenever a RAID-5 volume is broken. You can use the DETAIL DISK command on one of the remaining drives, which should show a status of "Failed Redundancy," indicating that the redundancy has failed. If you see a status of "Failed Redudancy, but don't know which other disk was part of the RAID-5 set, you can track down the problem disk by running DETAIL DISK on all applicable disks in the RAID-5 set. The status on the problem disk should appear as "Missing."

Fixing the RAID-5 set typically involves removing the failed disk, replacing it with a new one and then configuring the new disk to be a part of the RAID-5 set. To do this, you would run DiskPart, select the new disk, and then run CONVERT DYNAMIC to convert the disk type. Afterward, you would select the RAID-5 volume using SELECT DISK and then run REPAIR DISK, designating the new disk as the disk to use. This recreates the RAID-5 set and makes the new disk a member of the set. When the process completes, you should be able to select the RAID-5 volume and use LIST VOLUME to view its status. The status should appear as "Healthy."

Configuring Disk Striping with Parity

To implement RAID-5, select three dynamic disks with enough unallocated space to create the RAID set of the desired size. Follow these steps:

1. Invoke DiskPart by typing **diskpart** at the command prompt.

2. List the disks on the computer, check the free space, and ensure that the disks you want to work with are all configured as dynamic disks, as follows:

   DISKPART> list disk

3. Create the RAID-5 set as follows:

   DISKPART> create volume raid size=N disk=N,N,N,...

   where *size=N* is the amount of space in megabytes that the volume set will use on each disk. If no size is given, DiskPart uses all the remaining free space on the smallest disk and then uses the same amount of space on the remaining disks. *disk=N,N,N,...* sets the disks for the RAID-5 set. You need to use at least three dynamic disks.

Consider the following examples:

Create a RAID-5 set on disks 2, 3, and 4 using all available space on the smallest disk and then using the same amount of space on the remaining disks:

```
create volume raid disk=2,3,4
```

Create a RAID-5 volume on disks 2, 3, and 4 using 8 GB (8192 MB) of space on each disk:

```
create volume raid size=8192 disk=2,3,4
```

 Note You can't expand a RAID-5 set once it's created. Because of this, you should consider the setup carefully before you implement it.

Managing RAID and Recovering from Failure

You don't manage mirrored drives and stripe sets in the same way as you manage other types of volumes. If a mirrored drive or stripe set fails, it must be recovered in a specific way. If you want to stop using disk mirroring, you must break the mirrored set. If you want to stop using RAID-5, you must delete the entire volume set.

Breaking a Mirrored Set

Breaking a mirrored set is a standard procedure that you'll use when you want to stop using drive mirroring or when you need to rebuild the mirrored set. If you no longer want to mirror your drives, you can break the mirror and use the data on only one drive. This allows you to use the space on the other drive for a different purpose. If one of the mirrored drives in a set fails, disk operations continue using the remaining disk drive. To fix the mirror, you must first break the mirror set and then re-establish it.

Tip Although breaking a mirror doesn't delete the data in the set, you should always back up the data before breaking a mirrored set. This ensures that if you have problems, you can recover your data.

You can break a mirrored set by following these steps:

1. Invoke DiskPart by typing **diskpart** at the command prompt.
2. List the disks on the computer to determine which disks are part of the mirrored set, as follows:

   ```
   DISKPART> list disk
   ```
3. Break the mirror on the designated disk. The disk that you specify when breaking the mirror does not retain the drive letter or mount point. For example, if disks 0 and 1 are mirrored and you want users to continue using disk 0, you can break the mirror by typing

   ```
   DISKPART> break disk=1
   ```

   Once you break the mirror, you have two drives containing the same information. Only disk 0, however, has a usable drive letter or mount point. If you want to break the mirror and discard the duplicate information on the second disk, you can do this by adding the nokeep parameter, such as

   ```
   DISKPART> break disk=1 nokeep
   ```

Resynchronizing and Repairing a Mirrored Set

When one of the drives in a mirrored set fails, the mirrored set will need to be repaired before mirroring can be restored. You do this by breaking the mirrored set and then re-establishing mirroring on a new drive, or the newly recovered drive if you've recovered the failed drive. Sometimes, however, you won't have an outright failure; rather, you'll have a case in which data is out of sync. In such a situation, one of the drives in the set has probably gone offline for some reason and as a result, data was written to only one of the drives.

To recover the mirrored set, you need to get both drives in the mirrored set online and the corrective action you take depends on the failed volume's status, as follows:

- If the status is "Missing" or "Offline," make sure that the drive has power and is connected properly. Afterward, start DiskPart and use the RESCAN command to attempt to detect the volume. Then use ONLINE to resynchronize the mirrored volume. The drive status should change to "Regenerating" and then to "Healthy." If the volume doesn't return to "Healthy" status, try breaking the mirror and then adding the recovered disk to reestablish the mirror.

- If the status is "Online" (Errors), use ONLINE to resynchronize the mirrored volume. The drive status should change to "Regenerating" and then to "Healthy." If the volume doesn't return to "Healthy" status, use BREAK to stop mirroring and then use ADD to re-establish the mirror on the recovered disk or a new disk.

- If one of the drives shows as "Unreadable," use RESCAN to rescan the drives on the system. If the drive status doesn't change, you might need to reboot the computer.

- If one of the drives still won't come back online, break the mirror, designating the failed disk as the one to remove. Replace or repair the disk, and then use ADD to reestablish the mirror.

 Real World The failure of a mirrored drive might prevent your system from booting. This usually happens when you're mirroring the system or boot volume, and the primary mirror drive has failed. In this case, you need to edit the boot.ini file so that the secondary drive in the mirror set is used for startup. See Chapter 12 of the *Microsoft Windows Server 2003 Administrator's Pocket Consultant*.

Repairing a RAID-0 Striped Set Without Parity

As discussed previously, there is no fault tolerance when you use RAID-0. If a drive that's part of a RAID-0 set fails, the entire striped set is unusable. Before you try to restore the striped set, you should repair or replace the failed drive. Once you do this, you will need to recreate the RAID-0 set and then recover the data it contained from backup.

Regenerating a RAID-5 Striped Set with Parity

RAID-5 allows you to recover the striped set if a single drive fails. You'll know that a drive has failed because the set's status will change to "Failed Redundancy" and the corrective action you take depends on the failed volume's status:

- If the status is "Missing" or "Offline," make sure that the drive has power and is connected properly. Afterward, start DiskPart and then use ONLINE to resynchronize the volume set. The drive's status should change to

"Regenerating" and then to "Healthy." If the drive's status doesn't return to "Healthy," you'll need to use the REPAIR command.

- If the status is "Online" (Errors), use ONLINE to resynchronize the RAID-5 volume. The drive's status should change to "Regenerating" and then to "Healthy." If the drive's status doesn't return to "Healthy," you'll need to use the REPAIR command.

- If one of the drives shows as "Unreadable," use RESCAN to rescan the drives on the system. If the drive status doesn't change, you might need to reboot the computer.

- If one of the drives still won't come back online, you need to use the REPAIR command.

You can repair RAID-5 using the REPAIR command. If possible, you should back up the data before you perform this procedure. This ensures that if you have problems, you can recover your data. Follow these steps to resolve problems with the RAID-5 set:

1. Invoke DiskPart by typing **diskpart** at the command prompt.

2. List the disks on the computer to confirm that the RAID-5 set failed, as follows:

   `DISKPART> list disk`

3. Remove and replace the failed drive if necessary and possible. Then specify the new drive that should be part of the RAID set using the REPAIR command as follows:

   `DISKPART> repair disk=N`

   where N specifies the dynamic disk that will replace the failed RAID-5 drive. Keep in mind the specified disk must have free space equal to or larger than the total size used on the failed RAID disk.

Part IV

Windows Active Directory and Network Administration

This part of the book focuses on the core commands you'll use for configuring, managing, and troubleshooting Active Directory, print services, and TCP/IP networking. Chapter 11 discusses many of the key directory services administration tools, including tools that help you gather directory information. Chapter 12 examines tools that help you create and manage computer accounts in Active Directory. You'll also learn how to configure domain controllers as global catalogs and operations masters. Chapter 13 completes the directory services discussion with a look at creating and managing accounts for users and groups in Active Directory. Chapter 14 examines network printing and print services. Chapter 15 discusses configuring, maintaining, and troubleshooting TCP/IP networking from the command line.

Chapter 11

Core Active Directory
Services Administration

One of the more important areas of Windows networking has to do with Active Directory. Active Directory is an extensible and scalable directory service that provides a networkwide database for storing account and resource information. Using Active Directory, you have a consistent way to name, describe, locate, manage, and secure information for resources. This means that you can use Active Directory to work with user, group, and computer accounts as easily as you can use it to work with applications, files, printers, and other types of resources. You can use Active Directory to help you manage the network infrastructure, perform system administration, and control the user environment.

Active Directory is only available in Windows domains running Windows 2000 or later domain controllers. A *domain controller* is a server running a server version of the Windows operating system. One way to think of Active Directory is as an improvement to the domain-based architecture of Windows NT, in which the Security Accounts Manager (SAM) database is replaced by a more flexible, extensible, and scalable database. As with the SAM, Active Directory acts as the central authority for security; unlike the SAM, however, Active Directory also acts as the integration point for bringing together diverse systems. Active Directory consolidates management tasks into a single set of Windows-based management tools, and their counterparts are the directory service command-line tools discussed in this chapter.

Controlling Active Directory
from the Command Line

A basic understanding of Active Directory and its structures is all that it is needed to take advantage of the many command-line tools that are available to manage Active Directory. Microsoft designed Active Directory to use Domain Name System (DNS) as a naming system. With DNS, you organize network resources using a hierarchical structure that matches how you manage the resources. This hierarchy of domains, or domain tree, is the backbone of the Active Directory environment and looks much like a directory structure used with files. Another name for such a hierarchy or tree is a *namespace*. Every organization that uses Active Directory domains has an Active Directory hierarchy or namespace.

Understanding Domains, Containers, and Objects

The first Active Directory domain that you create is the *root* of the tree and the *parent* of all domains below it. Domains below the root are called *child domains*. Suppose, for example, that the root domain is cpandl.com. You can then decide to break down your organization geographically or functionally into child domains. Grouping geographically, you might have seattle.cpandl.com, ny.cpandl.com, and la.cpandl.com child domains. Grouping functionally, you might have sales.cpandl.com, support.cpandl.com, and tech.cpandl.com child domains. The key here is that child domains must have a name that extends from the parent domain. If the name doesn't extend from the parent domain, the domain is in a separate namespace. For example, microsoft.com, msn.com, and hotmail.com are all in different namespaces from cpandl.com.

You can create additional levels within the namespace if you choose. Under the la.cpandl.com child domain, you might have sales.la.cpandl.com, tech.la.cpandl.com, and support.la.cpandl.com. If this isn't enough, you can add another level, and then another and another to the namespace. Keep in mind that Active Directory manages the relationships within the tree and creates the appropriate trust relationships between domains.

In Active Directory, trusts are automatically two-way and transitive. Simply creating a child domain, such as tech.la.cpandl.com, creates a two-way trust relationship between tech.la.cpandl.com and la.cpandl.com. The trust continues up and down the tree as well, meaning that because la.cpandl.com trusts cpandl.com, tech.la.cpandl.com has an automatic trust relationship with cpandl.com, as well as with all the other domains in the same namespace.

Active Directory uses *objects* to represent network resources, such as users, groups, and computers. It also uses specialized objects called *containers* to organize network resources according to geographic, business, or functional needs. Typically, containers are used to group objects that have similar attributes. For example, you might want to apply a specific set of permissions to all engineers, and putting these users together in the same container will make this easier.

Each container represents a grouping of objects and each individual resource is represented by a unique Active Directory object. The most common type of Active Directory container is an organizational unit, or OU. Objects placed in an OU can only come from the related domain. For example, OUs associated with tech.la.cpandl.com contain objects for this domain only. This means you can't add objects from support.la.cpandl.com, la.cpandl.com, or tech.ny.cpandl.com to these containers.

Each Active Directory object class, such as container, user, group, or printer, is assigned a set of attributes that describes the individual resource. For example, user objects have attributes that describe user accounts including contact information along with their permissions and privileges. This means that user object attributes are related to first names, last names, display names, telephone numbers, e-mail addresses, passwords, and so on.

Because each object within Active Directory is really a record in a database, it is possible to expand the attribute set to meet the needs of individual organizations. This allows you to add custom attributes to help describe objects. For example, you can add an attribute to include an employee's identification code.

Understanding Logical and Physical Structures in Active Directory

So far we've talked about Active Directory structures that are used to organize directory data logically, including domains, subdomains, and OUs. You use these structures to organize Active Directory according to business or functional needs. You can also use them to specify geographic breakdowns, such as occurs if you had ny.cpandl.com, la.cpandl.com, and seattle.cpandl.com domains.

Insofar as Active Directory is concerned however, domains, subdomains, and OUs have no mapping to the real world—even if you create geographic breakdowns for domains or OUs. They are simply locations within the directory where related data is stored and, as far as Active Directory is concerned, they could all have one physical location, which is how Active Directory sees things until you tell the directory about the physical structures associated with your logical breakdowns of domains, subdomains, and OUs.

In the real world, any of these logical structures could span more than one physical location. It doesn't matter whether we are talking about different floors in a single building, different buildings entirely, or different cities; these are all different physical locations. To tell Active Directory about these multiple locations, you must define subnets and sites. A *subnet* is a network group with a specific IP address range and network mask. A *site* is a group of one or more subnets that maps your network's physical structure. Because site mappings are independent from logical domain structures, there's no necessary relationship between a network's physical structure and its logical domain structure.

You can create multiple sites within a single domain and you can create a single site that serves multiple domains. For example, if you group subdomains geographically, you might have seattle.cpandl.com, ny.cpandl.com, and la.cpandl.com child domains and corresponding sites named Seattle-Site, NY-Site, and LA-Site. But if your organization has only one office and you group subdomains functionally, you might have sales.cpandl.com, support.cpandl.com, and tech.cpandl.com child domains and a single site called Main-Site.

Understanding Distinguished Names

Every object in Active Directory has an associated distinguished name, or DN. The DN uniquely identifies the object by its common name and its location within the namespace. An object's common name is the plain-English name given to the object when you created it. You identify an object's common name using CN=*Name*, where *Name* is the common name of the object, such as:

CN=William Stanek

The common name is also referred to as an object's relative DN (RDN). What this refers to is the fact that this portion of the object's full name relates to its location in Active Directory. An object's location is determined by the names of the container objects and domains that contain the object. You identify OU containers using OU= and domain components using DC=. Each level within the domain tree is broken out as a separate domain component. Consider the following example:

OU=Engineering, DC=ny, DC=tech, DC=cpandl, DC=com

Here, you specify the DN for the Engineering OU in the ny.tech.cpandl.com domain. You use commas to separate each name component and the name components go from the lowest level of the tree to the highest level (that is, from the OU that contains the actual object you want to work with) to the child domain to the parent domain and finally to the root domain.

What makes the DN so important is that it specifies the exact location of an object; and the DN is what Active Directory uses to search for, retrieve, and manage objects within the database. Knowing the DN for an object allows you to perform these same tasks.

All objects have associated containers and domain components. Although the container for users, computers, groups, and other types of objects typically is an OU, this isn't always the case, because Active Directory includes several default containers where objects can be stored. These default containers are identified by their common name using CN= and include

- **Builtin**   A container for built-in security groups
- **Computers**   The default container for member servers and workstations in a domain
- **ForeignSecurityPrincipals**   A container for objects from a trusted external domain
- **Users**   The default container for users

 Note   The Domain Controllers container is created as an OU. This means you would use OU=Domain Controllers as the name identifier.

Knowing this, you can identify an object in any of these containers. For example, if you wanted to identify an object in the Users container for the tech.cpandl.com domain, you would use

CN=Users,DC=tech,DC=cpandl,DC=com

If the object is the user account for William Stanek, the complete DN would be

CN=William Stanek,CN=Users,DC=tech,DC=cpandl,DC=com

If the user account is later moved to the Engineering OU, its DN would become

CN=William Stanek,OU=Engineering,DC=tech,DC=cpandl,DC=com

Getting Started with the Active Directory Command-Line Tools

Once you know the basic structures of Active Directory and can identify the DN for the objects you want to use, you are ready to control Active Directory from the command line. You'll find that the key advantage of doing so is in the additional flexibility you gain. You can in fact perform many tasks easily from the command line that are either much more difficult to perform in the graphical tools or simply cannot be performed. For example, you might search for all computer accounts that have been inactive for more than a week and then disable them. Or you might modify the properties of multiple user accounts at the same time using a single command.

When you are working with Windows domains, both Windows Server 2003 and Windows XP Professional include a set of command-line tools that you can use to manage Active Directory. These tools include

- **DSADD** Adds objects to Active Directory
- **DSGET** Displays properties of objects registered in Active Directory
- **DSMOD** Modifies properties of objects that already exist in Active Directory
- **DSMOVE** Moves a single object to a new location within a single domain or renames the object without moving it
- **DSQUERY** Finds objects in Active Directory using search criteria
- **DSRM** Removes objects from Active Directory

Each of the various command-line utilities is designed to work with a specific set of objects in Active Directory. Table 11-1 provides an overview of the utilities and the objects they are designed to work with.

Table 11-1. AD Command Line Utilities and the Objects They Work With

Object	Dsquery	Dsget	Dsadd	Dsmod
Computer	Yes	Yes	Yes	Yes
Contact	Yes	Yes	Yes	Yes
Group	Yes	Yes	Yes	Yes
Partition	Yes	Yes	No	Yes
Quota	Yes	Yes	Yes	Yes
Server	Yes	Yes	No	Yes
Site	Yes	Yes	No	No
Subnet	Yes	Yes	No	No
User	Yes	Yes	Yes	Yes
OU	Yes	Yes	Yes	Yes

In most cases, AD objects are manipulated with a set of parameters specific to the type of object you are working with and the subcommand name used to access these parameters is the same as the object name. For example, if you wanted to add a computer to the domain, you would use DSADD COMPUTER and its related parameters. If you wanted to add a user account to the domain, you would use DSADD USER and its related parameters.

 Note DSMOVE and DSRM aren't listed in the table because they are designed to work with any object in the directory. You move or remove objects based on their DNs. In addition, using an asterisk (*) as the object name for DSQUERY, you can find any objects in the directory with criteria that match your query.

Making Directory Queries Using the DSQUERY Command

You use the DSQUERY command to search Active Directory for objects matching a specific set of criteria. For instance, you could search for all computer accounts that start with "D" or all user accounts that are disabled and DSQUERY would return a list of objects that match the criteria.

DSQUERY Subcommands and Syntax

You make directory queries using the following subcommands and command-line syntaxes:

- **DSQUERY COMPUTER** Searches for computer accounts matching criteria

  ```
  dsquery computer [{StartNode | forestroot | domainroot}] [-o {dn |
  rdn | samid}] [-scope {subtree | onelevel | base}] [-name Name]
  ```

```
[-desc Description] [-samid SAMName] [-inactive NumberOfWeeks]
[-stalepwd NumberOfDays] [-disabled] [{-s Server | -d Domain}]
[-u UserName] [-p {Password | *}] [-q] [-r] [-gc] [-limit
NumberOfObjects] [{-uc | -uco | -uci}]
```

- **DSQUERY CONTACT**   Searches for contacts matching criteria

  ```
  dsquery contact [{StartNode | forestroot | domainroot}] [-o {dn |
  rdn}] [-scope {subtree | onelevel | base}] [-name Name] [-desc
  Description] [{-s Server | -d Domain}] [-u UserName] [-p {Password
  | *}] [-q] [-r] [-gc] [-limit NumberOfObjects] [{-uc | -uco |
  -uci}]
  ```

- **DSQUERY GROUP**   Searches for group accounts matching criteria

  ```
  dsquery group [{StartNode | forestroot | domainroot}] [-o {dn | rdn
  | samid}] [-scope {subtree | onelevel | base}] [-name Name] [-desc
  Description] [-samid SAMName] [{-s Server | -d Domain}] [-u User
  Name] [-p {Password | *}] [-q] [-r] [-gc] [-limit NumberOfObjects]
  [{-uc | -uco | -uci}]
  ```

- **DSQUERY OU**   Searches for organizational units matching criteria

  ```
  dsquery ou [{StartNode | forestroot | domainroot}] [-o {dn | rdn }]
  [-scope {subtree | onelevel | base}] [-name Name] [-desc Description]
  [{-s Server | -d Domain}] [-u UserName] [-p {Password | *}] [-q]
  [-r] [-gc] [-limit NumberOfObjects] [{-uc | -uco | -uci}]
  ```

- **DSQUERY PARTITION**   Searches for Active Directory partitions matching criteria

  ```
  dsquery partition [-o {dn | rdn}] [-part Filter] [{-s Server | -d
  Domain}] [-u UserName] [-p {Password | *}] [-q] [-r] [-limit
  NumberOfObjects] [{-uc | -uco | -uci}]
  ```

- **DSQUERY QUOTA**   Searches for object quotas matching criteria

  ```
  dsquery quota {domainroot | ObjectDN} [-o {dn | rdn}] [-acct
  Name] [-qlimit Filter] [-desc Description] [{-s Server | -d
  Domain}] [-u UserName] [-p {Password | *}] [-q] [-r] [-limit
  NumberOfObjects] [{-uc | -uco | -uci}]
  ```

- **DSQUERY SERVER**   Searches for domain controllers matching criteria

  ```
  dsquery server [-o {dn | rdn}] [-forest] [-domain DomainName]
  [-site SiteName] [-name Name] [-desc Description] [-hasfsmo
  {schema | name | infr | pdc | rid}] [-isgc] [{-s Server | -d
  Domain}] [-u UserName] [-p {Password | *}] [-q] [-r] [-gc] [-limit
  NumberOfObjects] [{-uc | -uco | -uci}]
  ```

- **DSQUERY SITE**   Searches for Active Directory sites matching criteria

  ```
  dsquery site [-o {dn | rdn}] [-name Name] [-desc Description] [{-s
  Server | -d Domain}] [-u UserName] [-p {Password | *}] [-q] [-r]
  [-gc] [-limit NumberOfObjects] [{-uc | -uco | -uci}]
  ```

- **DSQUERY SUBNET** Searches for subnet objects matching criteria

```
dsquery subnet [-o {dn | rdn}] [-name Name] [-desc Description]
[-loc Location] [-site SiteName] [{-s Server | -d Domain}] [-u
UserName] [-p {Password | *}] [-q] [-r] [-gc] [-limit
NumberOfObjects] [{-uc | -uco | -uci}]
```

- **DSQUERY USER** Searches for user accounts matching criteria

```
dsquery user [{StartNode | forestroot | domainroot}] [-o {dn |
rdn | upn | samid}] [-scope {subtree | onelevel | base}] [-name
Name] [-desc Description] [-upn UPN] [-samid SAMName] [-inactive
NumberOfWeeks] [-stalepwd NumberOfDays] [-disabled] [{-s Server |
-d Domain}] [-u UserName] [-p {Password | *}] [-q] [-r] [-gc]
[-limit NumberOfObjects] [{-uc | -uco | -uci}]
```

- **DSQUERY *** Searches for any Active Directory objects matching criteria

```
dsquery * [{StartNode | forestroot | domainroot}] [-scope {subtree
| onelevel | base}] [-filter LDAPFilter] [-attr {AttributeList |
*}] [-attrsonly] [-l] [{-s Server | -d Domain}] [-u UserName] [-p
{Password | *}] [-q] [-r] [-gc] [-limit NumberOfObjects] [{-uc |
-uco | -uci}]
```

At first glance, the syntax is almost overwhelming. Don't let this put you off of using DSQUERY. Most DSQUERY subcommands share a standard syntax and include only a few extensions to the standard syntax that are specific to the type of object with which you are working. The best way to learn the DSQUERY subcommands is to dive right in. So here goes.

Searching Using Names, Descriptions, and SAM Account Names

Regardless of the other parameters you use, the search parameters should include the name, description, or SAM account name on which you want to search. When you type the **–name** parameter, you search for the specified type of object whose name matches the given value. You can use an asterisk as a wildcard to make matches using partial names, typing, for example, **–name Will*** to match *William Stanek*. A simple search on a name looks like this:

```
dsquery user -name Will*
```

The resulting output from this query is the DN of any matching user account or accounts, such as

```
"CN=William R. Stanek,CN=Users,DC=cpandl,DC=com"
```

That's all there is to a basic search. And you only had to use one parameter to get the results you needed.

Note   Keep in mind that with users, the –Name parameter searches on the Display Name as listed in the user's properties dialog box. In this example, the account display name is William R. Stanek. With other types of objects, this would be the value in the Name field on the General tab in the object's associated Properties dialog box.

The asterisk can appear in any part of the search criteria. If you know a user's last name but not the user's first name, you can search on the last name, such as

```
dsquery user -name *Stanek
```

You can also search using a partial beginning and ending of a name, such as

```
dsquery user -name W*Stanek
```

When you type the **–desc** parameter, you search for the specific type of object whose description matches the given value. Use an asterisk as a wildcard to make matches using partial descriptions, such as typing **–desc Eng*** to match Engineering Workstation. Consider the following example:

```
dsquery computer -desc Server*
```

The resulting output from this query is the DN of any matching computer account or accounts, such as

```
"CN=CORPSVR02,OU=Domain Controllers,DC=cpandl,DC=com"
```

Note   The –Desc parameter searches on the Description field as listed in the object's associated properties dialog box. In the previous example, the computer account description began with the word "Server."

When you use the –Samid parameter, you search for the specific type of object whose SAM account name matches the given value. Use an asterisk as a wild-card to make matches using partial SAM account names, such as typing **–samid wr*** to match *wrstanek*.

Note   In the user's properties dialog box, the SAM account name is listed on the Account tab as the User Logon Name. For computers and groups, the SAM account name is the same as the related account name.

Setting Logon and Run As Permissions for Searches

By default when you use DSQUERY you are connected to a domain controller in your logon domain. You can connect to a specific domain controller in any domain in the forest by using the –S parameter. Follow the –S parameter with the DNS name of the server, such as

```
-s corpdc01.cpandl.com
```

Here, you are connecting to the corpdc01 domain controller in the cpandl.com domain.

 Note Technically, you don't have to use the fully qualified domain name (DNS name) of the server. You can use only the server name if you want. However, this slows the search because Active Directory must perform a DNS lookup to obtain the full name and then make the query.

Rather than connect to a specific domain controller in a domain, you can connect to any available domain controller. To do this, you can use the –D parameter. Follow the parameter with the DNS name of the domain, such as

```
-d tech.cpandl.com
```

Here, you connect to any available domain controller in the tech.cpandl.com domain. Keep in mind that you can't use the –S and the –D parameters together. This means you either connect to a specific domain controller or any available domain controller in a given domain.

As with many other types of commands, you can authenticate yourself if necessary by specifying a user name and password. To do this, you use the following parameters:

```
-u [Domain\]User [-p Password]
```

where *Domain* is the optional domain name in which the user account is located, *User* is the name of the user account whose permissions you want to use, and *Password* is the optional password for the user account. If you don't specify the domain, the current domain is assumed. If you don't provide the account password, you are prompted for the password.

To see how these parameters can all be used together, consider the following examples:

Connect to the corpsvr02 domain controller in the tech.cpandl.com domain using the WRSTANEK user account in the CPANDL logon domain and search for a user account whose display name ends with Stanek:

```
dsquery user -name *Stanek -s corpsvr02.tech.cpandl.com -u
cpandl\wrstanek
```

Connect to any domain controller in the tech.cpandl.com domain using the Wrstanek user account in the cpandl logon domain and search for a user account whose display name begins with Will:

```
dsquery user -name Will* -d tech.cpandl.com -u cpandl\wrstanek
```

Setting the Start Node, Search Scope, and Object Limit

In the command syntax, the start node is denoted by {*StartNode* | **forestroot** | **domainroot**} or it may include *ObjectDN*. This specifies the node where the search will start. You can specify the forest root (type **forestroot**), domain root (type **domainroot**), or a node's DN (*StartNode*), such as: **"CN=Users,DC=cpandl, DC=com"**. If you specify by typing **forestroot**, the search is done using the global catalog. The default value is **domainroot**. This means that the search begins in the top container for the logon domain for the user account you are using. Some subcommands can be passed the actual DN of the object you want to work with (*ObjectDN*), such as: **"CN=William Stanek,CN=Users,DC=cpandl, DC=com"**.

Note You may have noticed that I'm using double-quotes to enclose both object DNs. This is a good technique because it is required if the DN contains a space, as is the case for the second object DN used.

When you want to perform exhaustive searches, you will want to specify a node's DN and the real value of doing so becomes apparent when you want to return complete object sets. You can, for example, return a list of all objects of a specific type in a specific container simply by specifying the start node to use and not specifying –Name, –Desc, or –Samid parameters.

To see how start nodes can be used, consider the following examples:

Return a list of all computer accounts in the domain:

```
dsquery computer "DC=cpandl,DC=com"
```

Return a list of all computer accounts in the Computers container:

```
dsquery computer "CN=Computers,DC=cpandl,DC=com"
```

Return a list of all computers in the Domain Controllers OU:

```
dsquery computer "OU=Domain Controllers,DC=cpandl,DC=com"
```

Return a list of all users in the domain:

```
dsquery user "DC=cpandl,DC=com"
```

Return a list of all users in the Users container:

```
dsquery user "CN=Users,DC=cpandl,DC=com"
```

Return a list of all users in the Tech OU:

```
dsquery user "OU=Tech,DC=cpand1,DC=com"
```

In addition to being able to specify the start node, you can specify the scope for the search. The search scope is denoted by {–scope **subtree** | **onelevel** | **base**} in the command syntax. By default, the **subtree** search scope is used, which means the scope is the **subtree** rooted at the start node. For **domainroot**, this means the search scope is the entire domain. For **forestroot**, this means the search scope is the entire forest. For a specific container, this means the search scope is the specified container and any child containers. For example if the start node is set as "OU=Tech,DC=cpandl,DC=com", Active Directory would search the Tech OU and any OUs within it.

You use a value of **onelevel** to set the scope for the specified start node and its immediate children. With **domainroot**, for example, this would mean that the domain and its top-level containers and OUs would be included. However, if any of the OUs contained additional (child) OUs these would not be searched.

If you use a value of **base**, this sets the scope to the single object represented by the start node. For example, you would only search the specified OU and not its child OUs.

 Note   **subtree** is the only valid value for the scope when **forestroot** is set as the start node.

To see how search scopes can be used, consider the following examples:

Search the Tech OU and any OUs below it for computer accounts:

```
dsquery computer "OU=Tech,DC=cpand1,DC=com"
```

 Note   The default scope is for a subtree, which means **–scope subtree** is implied automatically.

Search only the Tech OU for computer accounts:

```
dsquery computer "OU=Tech,DC=cpand1,DC=com" -scope base
```

Search the Tech OU as well as OUs immediately below it for computer accounts:

```
dsquery computer "OU=Tech,DC=cpand1,DC=com" -scope onelevel
```

Another optional parameter you can use is –Limit. This parameter sets the maximum number of objects to return in the search results. By default, if this parameter is not specified, the first 100 results are displayed. If you want to set a different limit, follow the parameter with the number of objects to return. For example, if you wanted only the first 10 results to be displayed, you can type **–limit 10**. To remove the limit and have all matching results displayed, you use a value of 0, typing **–limit 0**, for example.

Tip In a large organization where there are potentially thousands of objects, you shouldn't remove the limit. Instead, set a specific limit on the number of objects that can be returned or simply accept the default. This will ensure that your queries don't unnecessarily burden the domain controller you are working with.

Setting the Output Format for Names

With DSQUERY, you can set the output format for the name values returned as well as the format for individual characters. In the command syntax, the output format for names is denoted by **–o** followed by one of these elements: {dn | rdn | upn | samid}. By default, the output format is as a DN (designated as **–o dn**), such as **"CN=William R. Stanek,CN=Users,DC=cpandl,DC=com"**. You may also be able to specify the output format as a relative DN (by typing **–o rdn**), user principal name (by typing **–o upn**), or SAM account name (by typing **–o samid**).

The RDN is the common name of the object, taken from the lowest level name part of the DN. With users, the RDN is the same as the Display Name as listed in the associated properties dialog box. With other types of objects, this would be the value in the Name field on the General tab in the object's associated properties dialog box. Some examples of RDNs include

- "William R. Stanek"
- "CORPSVR01"
- "Administrators"

UPNs are applicable only to user accounts. In Active Directory, there is an actual field with this name, which is used for logon and authentication. In the user's properties dialog box, you'll find the user logon name and logon domain on the Account tab. An example of a UPN is wrstanek@cpandl.com. Here, wrstanek is the logon name and @cpandl.com is the logon domain information.

The SAM account name applies to users, computers, and groups. Again, there is an actual field with this name in Active Directory but you can navigate the properties dialog to find it as well. For users, the SAM account name is the pre–Windows 2000 account name as designated on the Account tab of the related properties dialog box. For groups, the SAM account name is the same as the value listed in the name field on the General tab. For computers, the SAM account name is the same as the value listed in the name field on the General tab with a dollar sign ($) as a suffix.

Note The dollar sign ($) is part of the actual computer account name but is normally hidden and isn't referenced. Active Directory uses $ to allow you to have a user account and a computer account with the same name. This allows, for example, the user JAMESW to have a computer named JAMESW, which wasn't possible with pre–Windows 2000 computers.

To learn more about name formats, consider the following examples:

Return the RDN for computers matching the search criteria:

```
dsquery computer -name corp* -o rdn
```

Return the SAM account name for the users matching the search criteria:

```
dsquery user -name Wi* -o samid
```

Return the UPN for the users matching the search criteria:

```
dsquery user "OU=Tech,DC=cpandl,DC=com" -o upn
```

Return the DN for the users matching the search criteria:

```
dsquery user "CN=Users,DC=cpandl,DC=com"
```

 Note The default format is as a DN, which means **-o dn** is implied automatically.

Using DSQUERY with Other AD Command-Line Tools

Because DSQUERY returns the DN of matching objects, the result set it returns is useful for piping as input to other Active Directory command-line utilities. Consider the following example where you search for all user accounts whose names begin with *Willia*:

```
dsquery user -name Willia*
```

The resulting output from this query is the DN of any matching account or accounts, such as

```
"CN=William R. Stanek,CN=Users,DC=cpandl,DC=com"
```

You could then pipe the result set as input for DSGET USER to display a list of groups of which this user is a member, such as

```
dsquery user -name Willia* | dsget user -memberof -expand
```

The resulting output would show the group memberships according to their DNs, such as

```
"CN=Domain Admins,CN=Users,DC=cpand1,DC=com"
"CN=Enterprise Admins,CN=Users,DC=cpand1,DC=com"
"CN=Administrators,CN=Builtin,DC=cpand1,DC=com"
"CN=Domain Users,CN=Users,DC=cpand1,DC=com"
"CN=Users,CN=Builtin,DC=cpand1,DC=com"
```

Searching for Problem User and Computer Accounts

DSQUERY USER and DSQUERY COMPUTER include several syntax extensions designed to help you search for problem accounts. You can use the –Disabled parameter to find accounts that have been disabled. To search the entire domain for disabled user accounts, type **dsquery user –disabled**.

The resulting output shows any computer accounts that have been disabled according to their DN, such as

```
"CN=Guest,CN=Users,DC=cpand1,DC=com"
"CN=SUPPORT_456945a0,CN=Users,DC=cpand1,DC=com"
"CN=krbtgt,CN=Users,DC=cpand1,DC=com"
```

Another very useful command option is –Stalepwd. This option lets you search for accounts that have not changed their password for at least the number of days specified. So for instance, you could search for all user accounts whose passwords haven't been changed for at least 15 days by typing **dsquery user –stalepwd 15**.

The resulting output is a list of users by DNs:

```
"CN=Administrator,CN=Users,DC=cpand1,DC=com"
"CN=Guest,CN=Users,DC=cpand1,DC=com"
"CN=SUPPORT_456945a0,CN=Users,DC=cpand1,DC=com"
"CN=krbtgt,CN=Users,DC=cpand1,DC=com"
"CN=William R. Stanek,CN=Users,DC=cpand1,DC=com"
"CN=Howard Smith,CN=Users,DC=cpand1,DC=com"
```

Real World   You can set password policies that require users to change passwords regularly as discussed in Chapter 9 of the *Microsoft Windows Server 2003 Administrator's Pocket Consultant* (Microsoft Press, 2003). These policies only apply when users log on to the domain. If a user is on vacation or otherwise unavailable, the last time the password changed could exceed the limit (but normally the user would have to change his password on the next login). Most disabled accounts will also show up on your stale password list.

Finally, you might also want to search for computer or user accounts that have been inactive for at least the number of weeks specified. An inactive account is one that hasn't logged on to the domain within the specified time period. For example, if you wanted to find out which user accounts haven't logged on to the domain for at least two weeks, you could type **dsquery user –inactive 2**.

Generally, users don't log on to the domain because they are out of the office, which means they could be on vacation, sick, or working off-site. With computer accounts, being inactive means the computers have been shut down or disconnected from the network. For example, if a user goes on vacation and takes her laptop with her but doesn't connect to the office remotely while away, the related computer account would be inactive for that period of time.

Renaming and Moving Objects

Renaming and moving objects within a domain is handled with the DSMOVE command. Why one command instead of two? Because when you rename an object, you actually move it from its current DN to a new DN. Remember, a DN has two parts: a common name or RDN, and a location.

The syntax for DSMOVE is as follows:

```
dsmove ObjectDN [-newname NewName] [-newparent ParentDN]
    [{-s Server | -d Domain}] [-u UserName] [-p {Password | *}] [-q]
    [{-uc | -uco | -uci}]
```

To rename a user, computer, group, or other Active Directory object, you must specify the object's DN and then use the –Newname parameter to specify the new relative name. You could rename a user object from William Stanek to William R. Stanek, by typing **dsmove "CN=William Stanek,OU=Tech, DC=cpandl,DC=Com" –newname "William R. Stanek"**.

To move a user, computer, group, or other Active Directory object within a domain, you must specify the object's current DN and then use the –Newparent parameter to specify the new location or parent DN of the object. Suppose, for instance, that you wanted to move a user account from the Tech OU to the Engineering OU. Here, you would specify the object's DN, such as **"CN=William Stanek,OU=Tech,DC=cpandl,DC=com"**, and provide the DN for the new location, such as **"OU=Engineering,DC=cpandl,DC=com"**. The related command would look like this:

```
dsmove "CN=William Stanek,OU=Tech,DC=cpandl,DC=com" -newparent
OU=Engineering,DC=cpandl,DC=com
```

To rename an object while moving it, you simply add the –Newname parameter to give the object a new name. Consider the following example:

```
dsmove "CN=William Stanek,OU=Tech,DC=cpandl,DC=com" -newparent
OU=Engineering,DC=cpandl,DC=com -newname "William R. Stanek"
```

Here, you move the William Stanek user account to the Engineering OU and rename it William R. Stanek.

In any of these examples, we could have obtained the object DN by means of the DSQUERY command. To do this, you simply pipe the output of DSQUERY to DSMOVE, as shown in this example:

```
dsquery user -name "William Stanek" | dsmove -newname "William R.
Stanek"
```

Here, the object DN, "CN=William Stanek,OU=Tech,DC=cpandl,DC=Com", is obtained from DSQUERY USER and used as input to DSMOVE, which results in the renaming of the User object.

Tip Want to move objects between domains? Use the MOVETREE command in the Windows Support Tools. Similar to DSMOVE, this command requires source and destination DNs for objects you are moving. You must also connect to a specific domain controller in the source and destination domains.

Removing Objects from Active Directory

If you no longer want an object to be in Active Directory, you can delete it permanently using the DSRM command. The syntax for DSRM is

```
dsrm ObjectDN ... [-subtree [-exclude]] [-noprompt] [{-s Server | -d
Domain}] [-u UserName] [-p {Password | *}] [-c] [-q] [{-uc | -uco |
-uci}]
```

Caution Don't use DSRM unless you've experimented first on an isolated test domain. This command is powerful. It will delete any object you pass to it, including object containers.

The best way to use DSRM is to pass it a specific object to remove. In this example, you delete the engcomp18 computer account from the Eng OU in the cpandl.com domain:

```
dsrm "CN=engcomp18,OU=Eng,DC=cpandl,DC=com"
```

By default, DSRM prompts you to confirm the deletion:

```
Are you sure you wish to delete CN=engcomp18,OU=Eng,DC=cpandl,DC=com
(Y/N)?
```

You can disable the prompt using the *–noprompt* switch, such as in the following example:

```
dsrm "CN=engcomp18,OU=Eng,DC=cpandl,DC=com" -noprompt
```

However, you should only do this when you are absolutely certain that DSRM will delete only the object you expect it to.

DSRM can be used to delete objects in containers or OUs as well as the containers and OUs themselves. If the container or OU is empty, you would delete it by its DN, such as

```
dsrm "OU=Eng,DC=cpand1,DC=com"
```

If the container or OU is not empty, it cannot be deleted in this way, however, and DSRM will report:

```
Failed: The operation cannot be performed because child objects exist.
This operation can only be performed on a leaf object.
```

To delete the container and all the objects it contains, you can use the –Subtree parameter. Consider the following example:

```
dsrm "OU=Eng,DC=cpand1,DC=com" -subtree
```

Here, you use –Subtree to delete all the objects (regardless of type) from the Eng OU as well as the container itself. To delete all the objects in the container but not the container itself, you can use the –Subtree and –Exclude parameters. Consider the following example:

```
dsrm "OU=Eng,DC=cpand1,DC=com" -subtree -exclude
```

Here, you use –Subtree to delete all the objects (regardless of type) from the Eng OU and use the –Exclude parameter to exclude the Eng OU as one of the objects to delete.

Chapter 12
Managing Computer Accounts and Domain Controllers

The focus of this chapter is on managing domain computer accounts, which control access to the network and its resources. Like user accounts, domain computer accounts have attributes that you can manage, including names and group memberships. You can add computer accounts to any container or OU in the Active Directory directory service. However, the best containers to use are Computers, Domain Controllers, and any OUs that you've created. The standard Microsoft Windows tool for working with computer accounts is Active Directory Users And Computers. At the command line, you have many commands; each with a specific use. Whether you are logged on to a Windows XP Professional or Windows Server 2003 system, you can use the techniques discussed in this chapter to manage computer accounts and domain controllers.

Overview of Managing Computer Accounts from the Command Line

Two sets of command-line utilities are available for managing domain computer accounts. The first set can be used with any type of computer account, including workstations, member servers, and domain controllers. The second set of commands is used only with domain controllers and designed to help you manage their additional features and properties.

In addition to DSQUERY computer discussed in the previous chapter, the general computer account commands include

- **DSADD computer**   Creates a computer account in Active Directory.

```
dsadd computer ComputerDN [-samid SAMName] [-desc Description]
[-loc Location] [-memberof GroupDN ...] [{-s Server | -d
Domain}] [-u UserName] [-p {Password | *}] [-q] [{-uc | -uco |
-uci}]
```

- **DSGET computer** Displays the properties of a computer account using one of two syntaxes. The syntax for viewing the properties of multiple computers is

```
dsget computer ComputerDN ... [-dn] [-samid] [-sid] [-desc] [-loc]
[-disabled] [{-s Server | -d Domain}] [-u UserName] [-p {Password
| *}] [-c] [-q] [-l] [{-uc | -uco | -uci}] [-part PartitionDN
[-qlimit] [-qused]]
```

The syntax for viewing the membership information of a single computer is

```
dsget computer ComputerDN [-memberof [-expand]] [{-s Server | -d
Domain}] [-u UserName] [-p {Password | *}] [-c] [-q] [-l] [{-uc
| -uco | -uci}]
```

- **DSMOD computer** Modifies attributes of one or more computer accounts in the directory.

```
dsmod computer ComputerDN ... [-desc Description] [-loc Location]
[-disabled {yes | no}] [-reset] [{-s Server | -d Domain}] [-u
UserName] [-p {Password | *}] [-c] [-q] [{-uc | -uco | -uci}]
```

 Tip For any of the computer and server commands, you can use input from DSQUERY to specify the object or objects you want to work with. If you want to type the distinguished names (DNs) for each object you want to work with, you can do this as well. Simply separate each DN with a space.

In addition to DSQUERY server, discussed in the previous chapter, the utilities for managing the additional features of domain controllers include

- **DSGET server** Displays the various properties of domain controllers using one of three syntaxes. The syntax for displaying the general properties of a specified domain controller is

```
dsget server ServerDN ... [-dn] [-desc] [-dnsname] [-site] [-isgc]
[{-s Server | -d Domain}] [-u UserName] [-p {Password | *}] [-c]
[-q] [-l] [{-uc | -uco | -uci}]
```

The syntax for displaying a list of the security principals who own the largest number of directory objects on the specified domain controller is

```
dsget server ServerDN ... [{-s Server | -d Domain}] [-u User
Name] [-p {Password | *}] [-c] [-q] [-l] [{-uc | -uco | -uci}]
[-topobjowner NumbertoDisplay]
```

The syntax for displaying the DNs of the directory partitions on the specified server is

```
dsget server ServerDN ... [{-s Server | -d Domain}] [-u User
Name] [-p {Password | *}] [-c] [-q] [-l] [{-uc | -uco | -uci}]
[-part]
```

- **DSMOD server**   Modifies properties of a domain controller.

```
dsmod server ServerDN ... [-desc Description] [-isgc {yes | no}]
[{-s Server | -d Domain}] [-u UserName] [-p {Password | *}] [-c]
[-q] [{-uc | -uco | -uci}]
```

Note   Another useful command for working with domain controllers and Active Directory is NTDSUTIL. NTDSUtil is a text-mode command interpreter that you invoke so that you can manage directory services using a separate command prompt and internal commands. You invoke the NTDSUtil interpreter by typing **ntdsutil** in a command window and pressing Enter.

Creating Computer Accounts in Active Directory Domains

You can create a computer account for a workstation or server that you want to add to the domain using DSADD computer. When you do this, you create the computer account in advance so that it is available when the computer joins the domain. To create computer accounts, you must have the appropriate permissions. Most users can create a computer account in their logon domain. Group Policy and other permissions can change this.

Creating a Computer Account

When creating a computer account, the only required information is the account's DN. As you may recall from the previous chapter, a DN specifies the full name of an object in Active Directory and includes the path to the object's location. Because of this, when you provide a DN for a computer account, you specify the computer account name and the container in which the account should be created. Consider the following example:

```
dsadd computer "CN=CORPSERVER05,OU=Domain Controllers,DC=cpandl,
DC=com"
```

Tip The DN specifies where, within the domain hierarchy, the computer account is created. You can create computer accounts in any domain in the forest for which you have appropriate access permissions. In some cases, you might need to log on directly to a domain controller in the domain you want to work with. Use –S *Server* to connect to a specific domain controller in any domain in the forest. Use –D *Domain* to connect to any available domain controller in the specified domain.

Here you create the CORPSERVER05 computer account in the Domain Controllers container within Active Directory. If the account creation is successful, DSADD computer reports:

```
dsadd succeeded:CN=CORPSERVER05,OU=Domain Controllers,DC=cpandl,
DC=com
```

Use –U *UserName* and –P *Password* to set the Run As permissions.

Account creation isn't always successful, however. The most common reason is because you specified an incorrect DN. For example, if you were to use the command

```
dsadd computer "CN=CORPSERVER05,CN=Domain Controllers,DC=cpandl,
DC=com"
```

DSADD computer would report

```
dsadd failed:CN=CORPSERVER05,CN=Domain Controllers,DC=cpandl,
DC=com:Directory object not found.
```

The reason for this error is because Domain Controllers is created as an organizational unit (OU), not as a generic container. That is, we improperly used CN=Domain Controllers instead of correctly using OU=Domain Controllers.

Another common reason for failure is the instance when an account already exists with the name you attempt to use. In this case, select a different computer account name.

Customizing Computer Account Attributes and Group Memberships

When you provide only a DN, several parameters are set for you automatically. Group membership is set so that the computer is a member of Domain Computers. The SAM account name is derived from the common name attribute used in the computer's DN. Basically, the DSADD computer command adds a dollar sign as a suffix to this name. In the previous example, the common name is CORPSERVER05, so the SAM account name is CORPSERVER05$.

If you want to customize the computer account attributes when you create a computer account, you can do this using these additional parameters:

- **–Samid**   Use –Samid to set the SAM account name, which must end in a dollar sign, such as **–samid CORPSERVER05$**.

- **–Desc**   Use –Desc to set the description of the computer you want to add, such as **–desc "CNMember Server"**.

- **–Loc**   Use –Loc to provide a text description of the physical location of the computer you want to add. Typically, this is the office and building in which the computer is located. For example if the computer is located in office 110 of building E you could type **–loc "E/110"**.

You set group memberships for a new computer account by using the –Memberof parameter. This parameter accepts a space-separated list of DNs representing the groups in which you want the computer as a member. For example, if you wanted a new computer account to be a member of the Engineering group and the DN for this group was CN=Engineering,OU=Eng,DC=cpandl,DC=com, you could use a command line similar to the following:

```
dsadd computer "CN=CORPSERVER05,OU=Domain
Controllers,DC=cpandl,DC=com" -memberof
"CN=Engineering,OU=Eng,DC=cpandl,DC=com"
```

If you wanted a new computer account to be a member of the Engineering and Tech groups and the DNs for these groups were CN=Engineering,OU=Eng, DC=cpandl,DC=com and CN=Tech,CN=Users,DC=cpandl,DC=com respectively, you could use a command line similar to the following:

```
dsadd computer "CN=CORPSERVER05,OU=Domain
Controllers,DC=cpandl,DC=com" -memberof
"CN=Engineering,OU=Eng,DC=cpandl,DC=com"
"CN=Tech,CN=Users,DC=cpandl,DC=com"
```

Note   You don't have to specify Domain Computers as a group membership. New computer accounts are automatically members of Domain Computers as well as any other groups you specify.

Managing Computer Account Properties

Managing computer accounts from the command line is slightly different from managing them in Active Directory Users And Computers, chiefly because you have more options, especially when it comes to working with multiple computer accounts at the same time.

Viewing and Finding Computer Accounts

As discussed in Chapter 11, "Core Active Directory Services Administration," you can use the DSQUERY computer command to search for computers. Not only can you search by Active Directory account name, SAM account name, and description, but you can also use wildcards in any of these fields to facilitate matches. The output of DSQUERY computer contains the DN of computers that match the search criteria and can be piped as input to other commands, including DSGET computer, which you can use in turn to display computer account properties.

DSGET computer is best used with DSQUERY computer. Here, you use DSQUERY computer to obtain the DNs for one or more computers and then use DSGET computer to display the properties for the related accounts. Properties you can display are set with the search parameters:

- **–Dn**   Displays the DN of matching computer accounts in the output.
- **–Samid**   Displays the SAM account name of matching computer accounts in the output.
- **–Sid**   Displays the security identifier for matching computer accounts in the output.
- **–Desc**   Displays the description of matching computer accounts in the output.
- **–Loc**   Displays the location attribute of matching computer accounts in the output.
- **–Disabled**   Displays a Yes/No value indicating whether the computer account is disabled.

DSGET computer displays output in table format. Generally speaking, you will always want to use –Dn, –Samid, or –Sid as a parameter to help you make sense of and identify the computers in the output. For example, if you wanted to search for all engineering computers that were disabled, you could use the command line

```
dsquery computer -name engcomp* | dsget computer -dn -disabled
```

Here, the results display the DN and the disabled status:

```
dn                                       disabled
CN=engcomp18,OU=Eng,DC=cpand1,DC=com     yes
CN=engcomp19,OU=Eng,DC=cpand1,DC=com     yes
CN=engcomp20,OU=Eng,DC=cpand1,DC=com     no
CN=engcomp21,OU=Eng,DC=cpand1,DC=com     no
CN=engcomp22,OU=Eng,DC=cpand1,DC=com     no
dsget succeeded
```

You could also display the SAM account name as shown in this example:

```
dsquery computer -name engcomp* | dsget computer -samid -disabled
samid                  disabled
ENGCOMP18$             yes
ENGCOMP19$             yes
ENGCOMP20$             no
ENGCOMP21$             no
ENGCOMP22$             no
dsget succeeded
```

Or the security identifier:

```
dsquery computer -name engcomp* | dsget computer -sid -disabled
sid                                                    disabled
S-1-5-21-4087030303-3274042965-2323426166-1119         yes
S-1-5-21-4087030303-3274042965-2323426166-1120         yes
S-1-5-21-4087030303-3274042965-2323426166-1122         no
S-1-5-21-4087030303-3274042965-2323426166-1123         no
S-1-5-21-4087030303-3274042965-2323426166-1124         no
dsget succeeded
```

Either way, you have an identifier that makes it easier to differentiate the computer account entries. You can use the second syntax for DSGET computer to obtain the group membership of computers. For example, if you want to see what groups ENGCOMP18 is a member of, you could type the command

```
dsquery computer -name engcomp18 | dsget computer -memberof
```

or

```
dsget computer "CN=engcomp18,OU=Eng,DC=cpandl,DC=com" -memberof
```

Both commands work the same. In the first example, you use DSQUERY computer to obtain the DN of the computer account. In the second example, you specify the DN directly. Either way, the output would show the group memberships, such as

```
"CN=Tech,CN=Users,DC=cpandl,DC=com"
"CN=Engineering,OU=Eng,DC=cpandl,DC=com"
"CN=Domain Computers,CN=Users,DC=cpandl,DC=com"
```

Here, the computer is a member of the Tech, Engineering, and Domain Computers groups.

While this technique could be used to display the membership of multiple computers, there is no way to display a DN or SAM account name for the associated computers. Thus, you get a list of group memberships and the only indicator that the memberships are for different computers are the blank lines separating the responses. For example, if you used the query

```
dsquery computer -name engcomp* | dsget computer -memberof
```

the output might look like this:

```
"CN=Domain Computers,CN=Users,DC=cpandl,DC=com"

"CN=Engineering,OU=Eng,DC=cpandl,DC=com"
"CN=Domain Computers,CN=Users,DC=cpandl,DC=com"

"CN=Domain Computers,CN=Users,DC=cpandl,DC=com"

"CN=Domain Computers,CN=Users,DC=cpandl,DC=com"

"CN=Tech,CN=Users,DC=cpandl,DC=com"
"CN=Engineering,OU=Eng,DC=cpandl,DC=com"
"CN=Domain Computers,CN=Users,DC=cpandl,DC=com"
```

Here, you have output for five computer accounts (you can tell this because of the blank links separating each group membership listing), but you have no indication to which computer accounts the entries specifically relate.

 Real World Don't overlook the importance of being able to use DSQUERY computer to document the current computer account configuration. A sample command line for documenting computer accounts follows:

```
dsquery computer "DC=cpandl,DC=com" | dsget computer -dn
-samid -sid -desc -loc -disabled > domaincomputers.txt
```

Here, the command is used to list all the computer accounts in the cpandl.com domain as well as their properties and to save this information to a file.

Setting or Changing a Computer's Location or Description Attribute

From the command line, it is fast and easy to set or change computer account locations and descriptions using the DSMOD computer command. You can, in fact, set the location or description for 1, 10, 100, or more computers at the same time. Suppose that you want all 500 computers in the Engineering OU to have their description say "Engineering Computer" and their location say "Engineering Dept." You could do this with a single command line, as follows:

```
dsquery computer "OU=Engineering,DC=cpandl,DC=com" | dsmod computer
-loc "Engineering Dept." -desc "Engineering Computer"
```

The DSMOD computer command would then report the individual success or failure of each change:

```
dsmod succeeded:CN=Engineeringcomp01,OU=Engineering,DC=cpandl,DC=com
dsmod succeeded:CN=Engineeringcomp02,OU=Engineering,DC=cpandl,DC=com
dsmod succeeded:CN=Engineeringcomp03,OU=Engineering,DC=cpandl,DC=com
...
dsmod succeeded:CN=Engineeringcomp499,OU=Engineering,DC=cpandl,DC=com
dsmod succeeded:CN=Engineeringcomp500,OU=Engineering,DC=cpandl,DC=com
```

Although changing these values in the GUI could take you hours, the entire process from the command takes only a few minutes. You simply type the command line and let DSMOD computer do the work for you.

Disabling and Enabling Computer Accounts

You can enable or disable computer accounts from the command line using the DSMOD computer command and the –Disabled parameter. Type **–disabled yes** to disable the computer account and type **–disabled no** to enable the computer account.

In the following example, you disable all computers in the TestLab OU:

```
dsquery computer "OU=TestLab,DC=cpandl,DC=com" | dsmod computer
-disabled yes
```

The DSMOD computer command would then report the individual success or failure of each change:

```
dsmod succeeded:CN=TestLabcomp01,OU=TestLab,DC=cpandl,DC=com
dsmod succeeded:CN=TestLabcomp02,OU=TestLab,DC=cpandl,DC=com
dsmod succeeded:CN=TestLabcomp03,OU=TestLab,DC=cpandl,DC=com
```

Resetting Locked Computer Accounts

Just like user accounts, computer accounts have passwords. Unlike user accounts, however, computer-account passwords are managed and maintained automatically. Computer accounts use two passwords: a standard password, which by default is changed every 30 days; and a private-key password for establishing secure communications with domain controllers, which is also changed by default every 30 days.

Both passwords must be synchronized. If synchronization of the private-key password and the computer-account password lapses, the computer won't be allowed to log on to the domain and a domain authentication error message will be logged for the Netlogon service with an event ID of 3210 or 5722. If this happens, the computer-account password is said to be "stale" and you'll need to reset the account to get the passwords back in sync.

To reset a password that is out of sync, use DSMOD computer and the –Reset parameter. Consider the following example:

```
dsmod computer "CN=Engineeringcomp01,OU=Engineering,DC=cpandl,DC=com"
-reset
```

Here, you reset the password for the Engineeringcomp01 computer in the Engineering organization unit of the cpandl.com domain.

You could just as easily reset all computer accounts in the Engineering OU. To do this, you would use DSQUERY computer to obtain a list of all computers in the domain and DSMOD computer to reset their passwords, such as

```
dsquery computer "OU=Engineering,DC=cpandl,DC=com" | dsmod computer
-reset
```

Real World   One way to determine that a computer account has a stale password is to use the DSQUERY computer command with the –Stalepwd parameter. If you are using the default value, 30 days, for computer-account passwords, you would find stale passwords by using a value of -Stalepwd 30. Here is an example:

```
dsquery computer -stalepwd 30
```

The resulting output shows a list of computers with passwords older than 30 days, which could mean the passwords are stale or simply that the computers have been inactive.

Moving Computer Accounts

Computer accounts are normally placed in the Computers, Domain Controllers, or customized OU containers. You can move a computer account to a different container or OU within its current domain using DSMOVE. Specify the computer account's current DN and then use the –Newparent parameter to specify the new location or parent DN of the computer accounts. If you wanted to move the CORPSVR03 computer account from the Tech OU to the Engineering OU, you would specify the computer account's DN, such as "CN=CORPSVR03,OU=Tech, DC=cpandl,DC=com," and provide the parent DN for the new location, such as "OU=Engineering,DC=cpandl,DC=com." The related command would look like this:

```
dsmove "CN=CORPSVR03,OU=Tech,DC=cpandl,DC=com" -newparent
"OU=Engineering,DC=cpandl,DC=com"
```

We could have also obtained the computer account DN using the DSQUERY computer command. To do this, you simply pipe the output of DSQUERY computer to DSMOVE, as shown in this example:

```
dsquery computer -name "CORPSVR03" | dsmove -newparent
"OU=Engineering,DC=cpandl,DC=com"
```

Here, the computer account DN, "CN=CORPSVR03,OU=Tech,DC=cpandl, DC=com," is obtained from DSQUERY computer and used as input to DSMOVE. This example works regardless of whether the computer account is for a workstation, member server, or domain controller.

Deleting Computer Accounts

If you no longer need a computer account, you can delete it permanently from Active Directory using the DSRM command. In most cases, you'll want to delete only a specific computer account, such as Corpserver03. If this is the case, you remove the account by passing DSRM the DN of the computer account, such as

```
dsrm "CN=corpserver03,OU=Eng,DC=cpandl,DC=com"
```

By default, DSRM prompts you to confirm the deletion. If you don't want to see the prompt use the –Noprompt parameter, such as

```
dsrm "CN=corpserver03,OU=Eng,DC=cpandl,DC=com" -noprompt
```

Working with Domain Controllers

Computers running Windows Server 2003 can act as member servers or domain controllers. Although everything discussed in the previous sections of this chapter applies to any type of computer account, the discussion in this section applies only to domain controllers.

Installing and Demoting Domain Controllers

Domain controllers perform many important tasks in Active Directory domains. You make a member server a domain controller by running the DCPROMO command, which installs directory services and promotes the member server to be a domain controller. If you run DCPROMO a second time on the server, you will demote the domain controller so that it acts once again as a member server only.

Real World The DCPROMO command starts a graphical utility. It does, however, accept several command-line parameters, including /Answer:*FileName* and /Adv. With the /Answer parameter, you can provide the name of an answer file that scripts the directory services installation. If you are automating the installation of an entire server, you would add a GUIRunOnce entry in the Unattend.txt file to automatically start DCPROMO at the end of the Unattended Setup. With the /Adv parameter, you tell DCPROMO to run in advanced mode, which gives you the option to create the domain controller from restored backup files. To be able to copy domain information from restored backup files, you will first need to back up the System State for a domain controller running Windows Server 2003 in the same domain as the member server you want to promote, and then you will need to restore the System State files to a drive on the member server.

Finding Domain Controllers in Active Directory

When you want to work strictly with domain controllers rather than all computer accounts, you can use the DSQUERY server and DSGET server commands. By default when you use DSQUERY server, you search your logon domain. In fact, if you type **dsquery server** on a line by itself and press Enter, you'll get a list of all domain controllers in your logon domain. As necessary, you can specify the domain to search using the –Domain parameter. Consider the following example:

```
dsquery server -domain tech.cpandl.com
```

Here, you obtain a list of all the domain controllers in the tech.cpandl.com domain. If you want a list of all domain controllers in the entire forest, you can do this as well. Simply type **dsquery server –forest**.

In all these examples, the resulting output is a list of DNs for domain controllers. Unlike previous DNs that we've worked with, these DNs include site configuration information, such as:

```
"CN=CORPSVR02,CN=Servers,CN=Default-First-Site-
Name,CN=Sites,CN=Configuration,DC=cpandl,DC=com"
```

This additional information is provided by DSQUERY server to specify the site associated with the server. Remember, domains can span more than one physical location and the way you tell Active Directory about these physical locations is to use sites and subnets. In this example, the associated site is Default-First-Site-Name in the Sites configuration container.

Note DSQUERY server has additional parameters that help you search for global catalogs and operations masters. These parameters are discussed in the sections of this chapter titled "Finding Global Catalogs" and "Finding Operations Masters."

As with the computer-related commands, DSQUERY server and DSGET server are best used together. Here, you use DSQUERY server to obtain the DNs for one or more domain controllers and then use DSGET server to display the properties for the related accounts. Properties you can display are specified with the following parameters:

- **–Dn** Displays the DN of matching domain controllers in the output.
- **–Desc** Displays the description of matching domain controllers in the output.
- **–Dnsname** Displays the fully qualified domain name of the domain controller.
- **–Isgc** Displays a Yes/No value indicating whether the domain controller is a global catalog server as well.

For example, if you wanted a detailed summary of all domain controllers in the forest, you could type the command

```
dsquery server -forest | dsget server -desc -dnsname -isgc
```

To save this information, direct the output to a file, such as

```
dsquery server -forest | dsget server -desc -dnsname -isgc > forest-dcs.txt
```

Designating Global Catalog Servers

A domain controller designated as a global catalog stores a full replica of all objects in Active Directory for its host domain and a partial replica for all other domains in the domain forest. Global catalogs are used during logon and for information searches. In fact, if the global catalog is unavailable, normal users can't log on to the domain. The only way to change this behavior is to cache universal group membership on local domain controllers. By default, the first domain controller installed in a domain is designated as the global catalog. You can also add global catalogs to a domain to help improve response time for logon and search requests. The recommended technique is to have one global catalog per site within a domain.

Any domain controller hosting a global catalog should be well connected to the network and to domain controllers acting as infrastructure masters. Infrastructure master is one of the five operations master roles that you can assign to a domain controller and it is responsible for updating object references. The infrastructure master does this by comparing its data with that of a global catalog. If the infrastructure master finds outdated data, it requests the updated data from a global catalog. The infrastructure master then replicates the changes to the other domain controllers in the domain.

Tip When there's only one domain controller in a domain, you can assign the infrastructure master role and the global catalog to the same domain controller. When there are two or more domain controllers in the domain, however, the global catalog and the infrastructure master shouldn't be on the same domain controller as this can affect the infrastructure master's ability to determine that directory data is out of date.

Finding Global Catalog Servers

Want to determine where the global catalogs are? For your current (logon) domain, just type **dsquery server –isgc**. The resulting output is a list of DNs for global catalogs, such as

```
"CN=CORPSVR02,CN=Servers,CN=Default-First-Site-
Name,CN=Sites,CN=Configuration,DC=cpandl,DC=com"
```

DSQUERY server can also be used to locate global catalogs in a specific domain. To do this, use the –Domain parameter, and type

```
dsquery server -domain tech.cpandl.com -isgc
```

Here, you search for global catalog servers in the tech.cpandl.com domain. If you wanted to search the entire forest, you can do this as well. Just type

```
dsquery server -forest -isgc
```

You can also search for global catalog servers by site, but to do this, you must know the full site name, and cannot use wildcards. For example, if you wanted to find all the global catalog servers for Default-First-Site-Name, you would have to type **dsquery server –site Default-First-Site-Name**.

Note Being able to search site by site is important because you typically want at least one global catalog server per site. If you search a site and don't find a global catalog, you should consider adding one.

Adding or Removing a Global Catalog

You can designate a domain controller as a global catalog using DSMOD server. Specify the DN of the server you want to work with and type **–isgc yes** to make it a global catalog server, such as

```
dsmod server "CN=corpdc05,OU=Eng,DC=cpandl,DC=com" -isgc yes
```

Another way to perform this task would be to use DSQUERY server to obtain a list of servers that you want to work with. Let's say there are three domain controllers in the tech.cpandl.com domain and you want them all to be global catalogs. You could do this using the following command line:

```
dsquery server -domain tech.cpandl.com | dsmod server -isgc yes
```

Here, you use DSQUERY server to obtain the DNs for all domain controllers in the tech.cpandl.com domain and pass this information as input to DSMOD server, which in turn sets each domain controller as a global catalog.

If you later want a server to stop acting as a global catalog, type **–isgc no**. In this example, you no longer want the corpdc04 server in the tech.cpandl.com domain to host the global catalog:

```
dsmod server "CN=corpdc04,OU=Tech,DC=cpandl,DC=com" -isgc no
```

Checking Caching Settings and Global Catalog Preferences

Different levels of domain and forest functionality are available depending on the network configuration. If all domain controllers in your domain or forest are running at least Windows 2000 Server and the functional level is set to Windows 2000 Native mode, your organization can take advantage of the many additional features of Active Directory but can no longer use Windows NT primary domain controllers (PDC) and backup domain controllers (BDC). One of the features enabled in this mode is the caching of universal group membership.

In the event that no global catalog is available when the user tries to log on, caching of universal group membership makes it possible for normal users to log on. Caching is enabled or disabled on a per-site basis and you can determine if caching is enabled using DSGET site. To do this, provide the DN of the site you want to work with and pass the –Cachegroups parameter as shown in the following example:

```
dsget site "CN=Default-First-Site-
Name,CN=Sites,CN=Configuration,DC=cpandl,DC=com" -cachegroups
```

If universal group membership caching is enabled, the output is:

```
cachegroups
yes
dsget succeeded
```

Otherwise, the output is:

```
cachegroups
no
dsget succeeded
```

Another way to perform this search would be to use the DSQUERY site command. If you type **dsquery site** on a line by itself, the command will return a list of all sites in the forest. To limit the result set, you can use the –Name parameter and either specify the common name of the site or use wildcards to specify a part of the name, such as:

```
dsquery site -name *First*
```

Here, you are looking for any site with the letters "First" in the common name.

To put this together, you could use the following command to determine the caching setting for all sites in the forest:

```
dsquery site | dsget site -cachegroups
```

What you'll get is a list of "yes" and "no" answers similar to the following:

```
cachegroups
yes
yes
no
no
yes
dsget succeeded
```

To make the output more meaningful, you would add the –Dn parameter to display the DNs of the related sites, such as

```
dn                                                          cachegroups
CN=Seattle-Site-Name,CN=Sites,CN=Configuration,DC=cpandl,DC=com     yes
CN=LA-Site-Name,CN=Sites,CN=Configuration,DC=cpandl,DC=com          yes
CN=NY-Site-Name,CN=Sites,CN=Configuration,DC=cpandl,DC=com          yes
CN=Chicago-Site-Name,CN=Sites,CN=Configuration,DC=cpandl,DC=com     yes
CN=Detroit-Site-Name,CN=Sites,CN=Configuration,DC=cpandl,DC=com     yes
dsget succeeded
```

If universal group membership caching has been enabled, a domain with multiple global catalogs per site can have a preferred global catalog. This preferred global catalog is the one specifically used to refresh universal group membership caching for the site's domain controllers. You can determine the preferred global catalog using the –Prefgcsite parameter. For example, you could type **dsquery site | dsget site –cachegroups –prefgcsite** to return the complete caching configuration for all global catalogs in the forest. You'll see a "yes" or "no" value if preferred global catalogs are configured. If preferred global catalogs aren't configured, you'll see a value of "Not Configured."

Designating Operations Masters

In Active Directory, five distinct operations master roles are defined, each of which has a critical part in ensuring network operations. Although certain roles can be assigned only once in a domain forest, others must be defined once in each domain.

The forestwide roles that must be assigned are schema master and domain naming master. The schema master controls updates and modifications to directory schema. The domain naming master controls the addition or removal of domains in the forest. As these forestwide roles must be unique in the forest, you can assign only one schema master and domain naming master in a forest.

The domain roles that must be assigned are relative ID master, PDC emulator master, and infrastructure master. As the name implies, the relative ID master allocates relative IDs to domain controllers. Whenever you create a user, group, or computer object, domain controllers assign a unique security ID to the related object. The security ID consists of the domain's security ID prefix and a unique relative ID, which was allocated by the relative ID master. The PDC emulator master acts as a Windows NT PDC when the network is using mixed or interim mode operations. Its job is to authenticate Windows NT logons, process password changes, and replicate updates to the BDCs. The infrastructure master updates object references by comparing its directory data with that of a global catalog. If the data is outdated, the infrastructure master requests the updated data from a global catalog and then replicates the changes to the other domain controllers in the domain. These domainwide roles must be unique in each domain. This means you can assign only one relative ID master, PDC emulator master, and infrastructure master in each domain.

Finding Operations Masters

When you install a new network, the first domain controller in the first domain is assigned all the operations master roles. If you later create a new child domain or a root domain in a new tree, the first domain controller in the new domain is assigned operations master roles automatically as well. In a new domain forest, the domain controller is assigned all operations master roles. If the new domain is in the same forest, the assigned roles are relative ID master, PDC emulator master, and infrastructure master. The schema master and domain naming master roles remain in the first domain in the forest. Operations master roles can be transferred by administrators if necessary.

You can determine which domain controllers in a forest or domain have a designated operation's master role using the –Hasfsmo parameter of the DSQUERY server command. Use the following values with this parameter:

- **schema** Returns the DN for the schema master of the forest.
- **name** Returns the DN for the domain naming master of the forest.
- **infr** Returns the DN for the infrastructure master of the domain. If no domain is specified with the –Domain parameter, the current domain is used.
- **pdc** Returns the DN for the PDC emulator master of the domain. If no domain is specified with the –Domain parameter, the current domain is used.
- **rid** Returns the DN for the relative ID master of the domain. If no domain is specified with the –Domain parameter, the current domain is used.

Schema master and domain naming master are forestwide roles. When you type **dsquery server –hasfsmo schema** or **dsquery server –hasfsmo name**, you always obtain the DN for the related operations master in the Active Directory forest.

Infrastructure master, PDC emulator master, and relative ID master are domain-wide roles. When you type **dsquery server –hasfsmo infr**, **dsquery server –hasfsmo pdc**, or **dsquery server –hasfsmo rid**, you always obtain the DN for the related operations master in your logon domain. If you want the DN for an operations master in another domain, you must use the –Domain parameter. Consider the following example:

```
dsquery server -hasfsmo rid -domain tech.cpandl.com
```

Here, you obtain the DN for the relative ID master in the tech.cpandl.com domain. If there are multiple domains in the forest, you might also want a list of all the domain controllers that have a particular role on a per domain basis. To do this, use the –Forest parameter, such as

```
dsquery server -hasfsmo rid -forest
```

Configuring Operations Master Roles Using the Command Line

Although you can use the directory services commands to check where the operations masters are located, you cannot use them to configure operations master roles. To configure operations master roles, you must use NTDSUtil. NTDSUtil is a text-mode command interpreter that you invoke so that you can manage directory services using a separate command prompt and internal commands. You invoke the NTDSUtil interpreter by typing **ntdsutil** in a command window and pressing Enter.

Using NTDSUtil, you can transfer operations master roles from one domain controller to another and seize roles when a role cannot be transferred gracefully. For example, a domain controller acting as the infrastructure master might have a drive failure that takes down the entire server. If you're unable to get the server back online, you might need to seize the infrastructure role and assign this role to another domain controller. You should never seize a role on a domain controller you plan to bring back online eventually. Once you seize a role, the old server is permanently out of service and the only way to bring the original server master back online is to format the boot disk and reinstall Windows Server 2003.

You can transfer roles at the command line by following these steps:

1. Log on to the server you want to assign as the new operations master, then start a command prompt.

2. At the command prompt, type **ntdsutil** to invoke the text-mode command interpreter for NTDSUtil.

3. At the *ntdsutil* prompt, type **roles**. This puts the utility in Operations Master Maintenance mode and the prompt changes to

```
fsmo maintenance:
```

4. At the *fsmo maintenance* prompt, type **connections** to get to the *server connections* prompt. Then type **connect to server** followed by the fully qualified domain name of the current schema master for the role, such as

   `connect to server corpdc01.eng.cpandl.com`

5. Once a successful connection is established, type **quit** to exit the *server connections* prompt, and then at the *fsmo maintenance* prompt, type **transfer** and then type the identifier for the role to transfer. The identifiers are

   - *pdc*—For the PDC emulator master role
   - *rid master*—For the relative ID master role
   - *infrastructure master*—For the infrastructure master role
   - *schema master*—For the schema master role
   - *domain naming master*—For the domain naming master role

6. The role is transferred. Type **quit** at the *fsmo maintenance* prompt and type **quit** at the *ntdsutil* prompt.

If you can't transfer the role gracefully because the current server holding the role is offline or otherwise unavailable, you can seize the role by following these steps:

1. Ensure that the current domain controller with the role you want to seize is permanently offline. If the server can be brought back online, don't perform this procedure unless you intend to completely reinstall this server.

2. Log on to the server you want to assign as the new operations master, then start a command prompt.

3. At the command prompt, type **ntdsutil** to invoke the text-mode command interpreter for NTDSUtil.

4. At the *ntdsutil* prompt, type **roles**. This puts the utility in Operations Master Maintenance mode and the prompt changes to:

   `fsmo maintenance:`

5. At the *fsmo maintenance* prompt, type **connections** and then, at the *server connections* prompt, type **connect to server** followed by the fully qualified domain name of the current schema master for the role, such as

   `connect to server corpdc01.eng.cpandl.com`

6. Once a successful connection is established, type **quit** to exit the *server connections* prompt and then, at the *fsmo maintenance* prompt, type **seize** and then type the identifier for the role to seize. The identifiers are

   - *pdc*—For the PDC emulator master role
   - *rid master*—For the relative ID master role
   - *infrastructure master*—For the infrastructure master role
   - *schema master*—For the schema master role
   - *domain naming master*—For the domain naming master role

7. The role is seized. Type **quit** at the *fsmo maintenance* prompt and type **quit** at the *ntdsutil* prompt.

Chapter 13

Managing Active Directory Users and Groups

The heart of an administrator's job is creating and managing user and group accounts. In this chapter, you'll first learn how to create and manager user accounts from the command line. You'll then see how to create and manage groups from the command line. The focus of this chapter is on working with Active Directory directory service users and groups.

Overview of Managing User Accounts from the Command Line

In Microsoft Windows Server 2003, two types of user accounts are defined:

- **Domain user accounts** User accounts are defined in Active Directory and can access resources throughout the domain. You create and manage domain user accounts using the directory services commands.

- **Local user accounts** User accounts are defined on a local computer and must authenticate themselves before they can access network resources. You create and manage local user accounts with the network services commands.

Note Local machine accounts are used primarily in workgroup configurations rather than in Windows domains. Still, every computer on the network has one or more local machine accounts. The only exceptions are domain controllers, which do not have local machine accounts. When you want to work with local machine accounts, you use the network services commands.

The directory services commands that are used to manage domain user accounts include:

- **DSADD USER** Creates a user account in Active Directory. The syntax is

  ```
  dsadd user UserDN [-samid SAMName] [-upn UPN] [-fn FirstName] [-mi
  Initial] [-ln LastName] [-display DisplayName] [-empid EmployeeID]
  [-pwd {Password | *}] [-desc Description] [-memberof Group ...]
  ```

```
[-office Office] [-tel PhoneNumber] [-email EmailAddress]
[-hometel HomePhoneNumber] [-pager PagerNumber] [-mobile
CellPhoneNumber] [-fax FaxNumber] [-iptel IPPhoneNumber]
[-webpg WebPage] [-title Title] [-dept Department] [-company
Company] [-mgr Manager] [-hmdir HomeDirectory] [-hmdrv
DriveLetter:] [-profile ProfilePath] [-loscr ScriptPath]
[-mustchpwd {yes | no}] [-canchpwd {yes | no}] [-reversiblepwd
{yes | no}] [-pwdneverexpires {yes | no}] [-acctexpires
NumberOfDays] [-disabled {yes | no}] [{-s Server | -d Domain}]
[-u UserName] [-p {Password | *}] [-q] [{-uc | -uco | -uci}]
```

- **DSGET USER** Displays the properties of user accounts using one of two syntaxes. The syntax for viewing the properties of multiple users is

```
dsget user UserDN ... [-dn] [-samid] [-sid] [-upn] [-fn] [-mi]
[-ln] [-display] [-empid] [-desc] [-office] [-tel] [-email]
[-hometel] [-pager] [-mobile] [-fax] [-iptel] [-webpg] [-title]
[-dept] [-company] [-mgr] [-hmdir] [-hmdrv] [-profile] [-loscr]
[-mustchpwd] [-canchpwd] [-pwdneverexpires] [-disabled]
[-acctexpires] [-reversiblepwd] [{-uc | -uco | -uci}]
[-part PartitionDN [-qlimit] [-qused]] [{-s Server | -d Domain}]
[-u UserName] [-p {Password | *}] [-c] [-q] [-l]
```

The syntax for viewing the group membership for users is:

```
dsget user UserDN [-memberof [-expand]] [{-s Server | -d Domain}]
[-u UserName] [-p {Password | *}] [-c] [-q] [-l] [{-uc | -uco |
-uci}]
```

- **DSMOD USER** Modifies attributes of one or more user accounts in the directory.

```
dsmod user UserDN ... [-upn UPN] [-fn FirstName] [-mi Initial] [-ln
LastName] [-display DisplayName] [-empid EmployeeID] [-pwd {Password
| *}] [-desc Description] [-office Office] [-tel PhoneNumber]
[-email EmailAddress] [-hometel HomePhoneNumber] [-pager
PagerNumber] [-mobile CellPhoneNumber] [-fax FaxNumber] [-iptel
IPPhoneNumber] [-webpg WebPage] [-title Title] [-dept Department]
[-company Company] [-mgr Manager] [-hmdir HomeDirectory] [-hmdrv
DriveLetter:] [-profile ProfilePath] [-loscr ScriptPath]
[-mustchpwd {yes | no}] [-canchpwd {yes | no}] [-reversiblepwd
{yes | no}] [-pwdneverexpires {yes | no}] [-acctexpires
NumberOfDays] [-disabled {yes | no}] [{-s Server | -d Domain}]
[-u UserName] [-p {Password | *}] [-c] [-q] [{-uc | -uco | -uci}]
```

 Tip These user commands accept input from DSQUERY USER to set the distinguished name (DN) for the user or users you want to work with. You can also type the DNs for each user you want to work with. When you do this, make sure to separate each DN with a space.

At first glance, the user commands seem extraordinarily complex. Actually, the user commands aren't complex so much as they are versatile. They allow you to add, view, or modify user accounts and include an extensive set of user account properties that you can work with. The parameter for working with a particular property is the same whether you are adding, viewing, or modifying an account. For example, when you create an account, you can set the user's office telephone number with the –Tel parameter. To determine a user's telephone number, use the –Tel parameter of DSGET USER and if you need to modify a user's telephone number, you use the –Tel parameter of DSMOD USER.

To manage local machine user accounts, use the NET USER command, which is one of several network services commands. NET USER has several syntaxes, and the syntax you use depends on what you want to do, as follows:

Display local user accounts:

```
net user [UserName [Password | *] [/active:{no | yes}] [/comment:
"DescriptionText"] [/countrycode: NNN] [/expires:{{MM/DD/YYYY |
DD/MM/YYYY | mmm,dd,YYYY} | never}] [/fullname:"Name"]
[/homedir:Path] [/passwordchg:{yes | no}] [/passwordreq:{yes |
no}] [/profilepath:[Path]] [/scriptpath:Path] [/times:{Day[-Day]
[,Day[-Day]] ,Time[-Time] [,Time[-Time]] [;...] | all}]
[/usercomment:"Text"] [/workstations:{ComputerName[,...] | *}]]
```

Create or modify local user accounts:

```
net user [UserName {Password | *} /add [/active:{no | yes}]
[/comment:"DescriptionText"] [/countrycode:NNN] [/expires:
{{MM/DD/YYYY | DD/MM/YYYY | mmm,dd,YYYY} | never}] [/fullname:"Name"]
[/homedir:Path] [/passwordchg:{yes | no}] [/passwordreq:{yes | no}]
[/profilepath:[Path]] [/scriptpath:Path] [/times:{Day[-Day]
[,Day[-Day]] ,Time[-Time] [,Time[-Time]] [;...] | all}]
[/usercomment:"Text"] [/workstations:{ComputerName[,...] | *}]]]
```

Delete local user accounts:

```
net user UserName /delete
```

As you can see, NET USER lets you work with a fairly narrow set of user account properties. These account properties are best suited for working with local user accounts.

Note NET USER can also be used to work with domain accounts in your logon domain. Beyond the current (logon) domain, you have no access, however, in contrast to the directory services commands, which let you create and manage domain user accounts in any domain in the Active Directory forest.

Adding User Accounts

Each user that wants to access resources on the network must have a user account. The type of account needed depends on your network configuration. With Active Directory domains, you use domain user accounts. With workgroups, you use local user accounts that pertain only to specific machines.

Creating Domain User Accounts

When you create a domain user account, you pass the user's DN to DSADD USER. The common name component of the DN sets the user's name. The rest of the DN specifies where in Active Directory the user account is to be located, which includes the container in which the user account is to be created and the related domain. For example, you could create a user account for Mary Baker in the Sales organizational unit of the cpandl.com domain by typing: **dsadd user "CN=Mary Baker,OU=Sales,DC=cpandl,DC=com"**. The account would be created with Mary Baker as the user logon name, but because no other properties would be set, the account would be disabled automatically for security reasons.

User names aren't case-sensitive and can be as long as 64 characters. Typically, in addition to the user account's DN, you'll want to specify the following:

- First name as set with the –Fn parameter
- Middle initial as set with the –Mi parameter
- Last name as set with the –Ln parameter
- Display name as set with the –Display parameter

 Note In most cases, the display name should be set to the same value as the common name of the user account. This ensures that the account is easier to manage, because if you know the user's display name, you also know the common name component of the distinguished name.

- SAM account name (also referred to as the *logon name*) as set with the –Samid parameter
- Password as set with the –Pwd parameter. The password must follow the complexity requirements enforced through Group Policy (if any).

The first 20 characters of the common name are used to set the SAM account name of the user account, which is also referred to as the pre–Windows 2000 user logon name. The SAM account name must be unique in the domain and if there is overlap you might want the group's SAM account name to be different from its display name. In this case, you would need to set the SAM account name using the –Samid parameter.

Unlike accounts created in The Active Directory Users And Computers administrative tool, the user's first name, middle initial, and last name values are not used to set the user's display name. You must set this value using the –Display parameter. The display name is the name Windows displays in dialogs. The common name component of the user account name and the domain name component of the distinguished name are used to set the user's fully qualified logon name. The fully qualified logon name is used for logon and authentication. For example, if the user's logon domain is cpandl and the logon name is marybaker, the fully qualified logon name is cpandl\marybaker.

To create an account for Mary A. Baker that uses these parameters, you can use the following command:

```
dsadd user "CN=Mary Baker,OU=Sales,DC=cpandl,DC=com" -fn Mary -mi A
-ln Baker -samid "marybaker" -display "Mary Baker" -pwd dg56$2#
```

Note Note the use of double quotation marks in this example. Whenever a parameter value contains a space, you must enclose it in double quotation marks. I recommend always using double quotation marks with the user DN, samid, and display name values. That way you get used to using double quotation marks and if any of those values contains a space, the command will execute successfully. Otherwise, you might forget to use double quotation marks and, in such a case, account creation will fail.

If there are problems creating the account, you'll see a warning and you'll need to check your syntax, ensuring that all the values are set appropriately and that the DN values are valid. Otherwise, DSADD USER should report DSADD SUCCEEDED.

Real World The most confusing thing about creating accounts at the command line, whether for users or for groups, is that the accounts have so many different name values. To be clear, the common name of the account, also referred to as the *relative distinguished name*, is the name component you assign using the first CN= component of the DN, such as CN=Mary Baker. User accounts also have a display name. The user display name is the value used in Windows dialog boxes. Typically, the display name is the user's full name and you may see references to a user's full name rather than his or her display name. Both user and group accounts also have a pre-Windows 2000 name. For users, this name is used for domain logon and authentication so it is also referred to as the pre–Windows 2000 logon name.

Customizing Domain User Account Attributes and Group Memberships

All new domain users are members of the group Domain Users, and their primary group is specified as Domain Users. You can add group memberships using the –Memberof parameter. Follow the parameter name with the group DNs. If a group DN contains a space, it should be enclosed in quotation marks, such as

```
dsadd user "CN=Mary Baker,OU=Sales,DC=cpand1,DC=com" -memberof
"CN=Backup Operators,CN=Builtin,DC=cpand1,DC=com" "CN=DHCP
Administrators,CN=Builtin,DC=cpand1,DC=com"
```

 Note Pay particular attention to the space used between the group DNs. If you don't use a space, group membership will not be properly configured and an error will occur.

Here, the user account is created and then added as a member of the Backup Operators and DHCP Administrators groups. This is a two-stage process: account creation happens first and then group memberships are configured. If an error occurs when adding group membership, DSADD USER will specify that the object was created successfully but there was an error after creation occurred. Check the syntax you used when specifying the group DNs, then use DSMOD USER to configure the user's group membership correctly.

For security reasons, you might want to consider setting these parameters as well when creating user accounts:

- **–mustchpwd {yes | no}**   By default, the user doesn't have to change his or her password upon first logon, which means **–mustchpwd no** is assumed. If you set **–mustchpwd yes** the user must change his or her password upon first logon.

- **–canchpwd {yes | no}**   By default, the user can change his or her password, which means **–canchpwd yes** is assumed. If you set **–canchpwd no**, the user can't change the password.

- **–pwdneverexpires {yes | no}**   By default, **–pwdneverexpires no** is assumed and the user password expires according to the group policy settings. If you set **–pwdneverexpires yes**, the password for this account never expires.

 Note Using –pwdneverexpires yes overrides the domain account policy. Generally it isn't a good idea to set a password so that it doesn't expire. This defeats the purpose of having passwords in the first place.

- **–disabled {yes | no}** By default, so long as you create an account with a password, the account is created and enabled for use (meaning **–disabled no** is assumed). If you set **–disabled yes**, the account is disabled and can't be used. This temporarily prevents anyone from using the account.

Consider the following examples to learn more about DSADD USER:

Create an account for Scott L. Bishop in the Users container of the cpandl.com domain. Set the password so that it must be changed upon first logon.

```
dsadd user "CN=Scott L. Bishop,CN=Users,DC=cpandl,DC=com" -fn Scott
-mi L -ln Bishop -samid "scottb" -display "Scott L. Bishop" -pwd
acornTree -mustchpwd yes
```

Create an account for Bob Gage in the Engineering OU of the ny.cpandl.com domain. Set the password so that it never expires but disable the account.

```
dsadd user "CN=Bob Gage,OU=Engingeering,DC=ny,DC=cpandl,DC=com" -fn
Bob -ln Gage -samid "bgage" -display "Bob Gage" -pwd dazedOne
-pwdneverexpires yes
-disabled
```

Create an account for Eric F. Lang in the Marketing OU of the cpandl.com domain. Set the password so that it can't be changed.

```
dsadd user "CN=Eric F. Lang,OU=Marketing,DC=cpandl,DC=com" -fn Eric
-mi F -ln Lang -samid "eflang" -display "Eric F. Lang" -pwd albErt
-canchpwd no
```

Tip You can create accounts in any domain in the forest for which you have appropriate access permissions. In some cases, you might need to logon directly to a domain controller in the domain you want to work with. Use –S *Server* to connect to a specific domain controller in any domain in the forest. Use –D *Domain* to connect to any available domain controller in the specified domain.

Most of the time, the parameters discussed in this section will be the only ones you'll use when creating accounts. As you've seen, based on the DSADD USER syntax, there are many other user account parameters. You can set these properties for user accounts as discussed later in the chapter.

Real World Users who access Windows Server 2003 through services for Macintosh use primary groups. When a Macintosh user creates files or directories on a Windows Server 2003 system, the primary group is assigned to these files or directories. By default, all user accounts have their primary group set to Domain Users. In The Active Directory Users And Computers administrative tool, you can change the primary group. You cannot change the primary group through the command line, however.

Creating Local User Accounts

Local machine accounts are created on individual computers. If you want to create a local machine account for a particular computer, you must log on locally or use a remote logon to access a local command prompt. Once you are logged on to the computer you want to work with, you can create the required account using NET USER. In some cases, local computer policy might allow you to create an account using only the name of the account to create and the /Add parameter, such as

```
net user wrstanek /add
```

 Note You can't create local user accounts on domain controllers. Domain controllers do not have local machine accounts.

Here, you create a local account with the logon name **wrstanek** and use a blank password. Although you might be able to use a blank password, you risk the computer's and possibly the network's security by doing so. Therefore, at a minimum, I recommend you provide a user name and password for new local user accounts. The password follows the account name as shown in the following example:

```
net user wrstanek dg56$2# /add
```

Here, you create the local machine account for **wrstanek** and set the password to **dg56$2#**.

If the account creation is successful, NET USER will state "Command Completed Successfully." However, if there are problems creating the account, NET USER won't display an error message per se. Instead, it will display the command syntax. In this case, check your syntax and ensure that all the values are set appropriately.

Other values and parameters you might want to use with local user accounts include

- **/comment:"*DescriptionText*"** Sets a description of the user account. Normally, you would type the user's job title or department.
- **/fullname:"*Name*"** Sets the full name of the user account. The full name is also referred to as the display name.

- **/passwordchg {yes | no}** By default, users can change their passwords, which means **/password yes** is assumed. If you set **/passwordchg no**, users won't be able to change their passwords.

- **/passwordreq {yes | no}** By default, users are required to have a password for their accounts. This means **/passwordreq yes** is assumed, so a user's account must have a password and that password cannot be blank.

- **/active {yes | no}** By default, user accounts are enabled when they are created, which means **/active yes** is assumed. If you set **/active no** the account is disabled and can't be used. Use this parameter to temporarily prevent anyone from using an account.

Consider the following examples to learn more about using NET USER:

Create a local machine account for the Desktop Support team with a full name and description.

```
net user dsupport squ5 /fullname:"Desktop Support" /comment:"Desktop
Support Account" /add
```

Create a local machine account for Phil Spencer, include a full name and description, and require a password.

```
net user pspencer magma2 /fullname:"Phil Spencer" /comment:"Offsite
Sales Manager" /passwordreq yes /add
```

Create a local machine account for Chris Preston, include a full name and description. Set a password but don't let the user change it.

```
net user chrisp apples /fullname:"Chris Preston" /comment:"PR
Manager" /passwordchg no /add
```

Managing User Accounts

Managing user accounts from the command line is different from managing them in the Active Directory Users And Computers administrative tool, chiefly because you have more options and it is easier to work with multiple user accounts at the same time.

Viewing and Finding User Accounts

You can use the DSQUERY USER command to search for users. Not only can you search by common name, SAM account name, and description, but you can also use wildcards in any of these fields to facilitate matches. The output of DSQUERY USER contains the DNs of users that match the search criteria and can be piped as input to other commands, including DSGET USER, which you can use in turn to display user account properties.

DSQUERY USER and DSGET USER are best used together. Here, you use DSQUERY USER to obtain the DNs for one or more users, and then use DSGET USER to display the properties for the related accounts. Using DSGET USER, properties you can display are specified by using parameters, including

- **–display**   Displays the full name attribute of matching user accounts in the output
- **–desc**   Displays the description of matching user accounts in the output
- **–dn**   Displays the distinguished name of matching user accounts in the output
- **–empid**   Displays the employee ID attribute of matching user accounts in the output
- **–fn**   Displays the first name attribute of matching user accounts in the output
- **–mi**   Displays the middle initial attribute of matching user accounts in the output
- **–samid**   Displays the SAM account name of matching user accounts in the output
- **–sid**   Displays the security identifier for matching user accounts in the output
- **–disabled**   Displays a Yes/No value indicating whether the user account is disabled

DSGET USER displays output in table format. Generally speaking, you will always want to use –Dn, –Samid or –Display as a parameter to help you make sense of and identify the users in the output. For example, if you wanted to search for all engineering users that were disabled, you can use the command line

```
dsquery user "OU=Eng,DC=cpandl,DC=com" | dsget user -dn -disabled
```

Here, you list the disabled status of each user in the Engineering OU of the cpandl.com domain, such as

```
dn                                      disabled
CN=edwardh,OU=Eng,DC=cpandl,DC=com      yes
CN=jacobl,OU=Eng,DC=cpandl,DC=com       yes
CN=maryk,OU=Eng,DC=cpandl,DC=com        yes
CN=ellene,OU=Eng,DC=cpandl,DC=com       yes
CN=williams,OU=Eng,DC=cpandl,DC=com     yes
dsget succeeded
```

You could also display the SAM account name as shown in this example:

```
dsquery user -name william* | dsget user -samid -disabled
  samid                              disabled
  williamb                           yes
  williamd                           yes
  williams                           no
dsget succeeded
```

Here, you search for all user accounts whose common name begins with William, then display the SAM account name and disabled status of each.

Determining Group Membership for Individual User Accounts

You can use the second syntax for DSGET USER to obtain the group membership of individual user accounts. For example, if you wanted to see what groups WilliamS is a member of, you could type the command

```
dsquery user -name williams | dsget user -memberof
```

or

```
dsget user "CN=William Stanek,OU=Eng,DC=cpand1,DC=com" -memberof
```

Both commands work the same. In the first example, you use DSQUERY USER to obtain the DN of the user account. In the second example, you specify the DN directly. Either way, the output would show the group memberships, such as

```
"CN=Tech,CN=Users,DC=cpand1,DC=com"
"CN=Engineering,OU=Eng,DC=cpand1,DC=com"
"CN=Domain Users,CN=Users,DC=cpand1,DC=com"
```

Here, the user is a member of the Tech, Engineering, and Domain Users groups.

While this technique could be used to display the membership of multiple users, there is no way to display a DN or SAM account name for the associated users. Thus, you get a list of group memberships and the only indicator that the memberships are for different users are the blank lines in the listing. For example, if you used the query

```
dsquery user -name bill* | dsget user -memberof
```

the output might look like this:

```
"CN=Tech,CN=Users,DC=cpand1,DC=com"
"CN=Engineering,OU=Eng,DC=cpand1,DC=com"
"CN=Domain Users,CN=Users,DC=cpand1,DC=com"

"CN=Domain Users,CN=Users,DC=cpand1,DC=com"
```

```
"CN=Tech,CN=Users,DC=cpand1,DC=com"
"CN=Engineering,OU=Eng,DC=cpand1,DC=com"
"CN=Domain Users,CN=Users,DC=cpand1,DC=com"

"CN=Engineering,OU=Eng,DC=cpand1,DC=com"
"CN=Domain Users,CN=Users,DC=cpand1,DC=com"

"CN=Tech,CN=Users,DC=cpand1,DC=com"
"CN=Engineering,OU=Eng,DC=cpand1,DC=com"
"CN=Domain Users,CN=Users,DC=cpand1,DC=com"

"CN=Domain Users,CN=Users,DC=cpand1,DC=com"

"CN=Domain Users,CN=Users,DC=cpand1,DC=com"
```

Here, you have output for seven user accounts. You can tell this because of the blank lines separating each group membership listing. But you have no indication of which user accounts the entries specifically relate.

Setting or Changing User Account Attributes

From the command line, it is a swift and easy matter to set or change user account attributes using the DSMOD USER command. You can, in fact, set attributes for one or many users at the same time. Suppose that you want all 150 users in the Sales OU to have their department attribute set as "Sales & Marketing," their company attribute set as "City Power and Light," and their title set to "Customer Sales." You can do this with a single command-line entry:

```
dsquery user "OU=Sales,DC=cpand1,DC=com" | dsmod user -dept "Sales &
Marketing" -company "City Power and Light" -title "Customer Sales"
```

The DSMOD USER command would then report the individual success or failure of each change:

```
dsmod succeeded:CN=edwardh,OU=Sales,DC=cpand1,DC=com    no
dsmod succeeded:CN=erinp,OU=Sales,DC=cpand1,DC=com      no
dsmod succeeded:CN=jayo,OU=Sales,DC=cpand1,DC=com       no
dsmod succeeded:CN=johng,OU=Sales,DC=cpand1,DC=com      yes
...
dsmod succeeded:CN=williams,OU=Sales,DC=cpand1,DC=com   yes
```

Although changing these values in the GUI could take you hours, the entire process from the command line takes only a few minutes. You simply type the command-line entry and let DSMOD USER do the work for you.

Other parameters that you'll work with frequently include

- **–webpg**   Sets an intranet or Internet address that will appear in the directory listing for the associated user, such as \\Intranet\Sales.

- **–profile**   Sets the path to the user's profile, which provides the environment settings for user accounts, such as \\Gamma\Profiles\wrstanek.

- **–hmdrv**   Sets the drive letter of the user's home directory, such as X:. The user's home directory will be mapped to this drive letter.
- **–hmdir**   Sets the home directory for the user, such as \\Gamma\Users \wrstanek.

Caution   Generally, you don't want to change user profile paths, home drives, or home directories when users are logged on, because this might cause problems. So you might want to update this information after hours or ask the user to log off for a few minutes and then log back on.

Tip   By default, if an error occurs when processing changes, DSMOD USER will halt execution and report the error. Generally, this is the behavior you want, because you don't want to make improper changes. You can, however, use the –C parameter to tell DSMOD USER to report the error but continue.

These parameters accept the special value *$username$*. This value lets you assign paths and filenames that are based on individual user names. For example, if you assign the home directory path as \\Gamma\Users\\$username$\ or C:\Home\\$username$, Windows replaces the *$username$* value with the actual user name—and it does so for each user you're managing. This would mean if you are working with the accounts for erinb, sandyr, miked and kyler, they would all be assigned unique home directories—either \\Gama\Users\erinb, \\Gama\Users\sandyr, \\Gama\Users\miked and \\Gama\Users\kyler or C:\Home\erinb, C:\Home\sandyr, C:\Home\miked and C:\Home\kyler. In these examples, \\Gama\Users is a path to a network share and C:\Home represents a directory on the user's computer.

Following this, you could set the Web page, profile, home drive, and home directory for all users in the Sales OU by typing

```
dsquery user "OU=Sales,DC=cpandl,DC=com" | dsmod user -webpg
\\Intranet\Sales\$username$ -profile "\\corpdc02\sales\$username$"
-hmdrv "X:" -hmdir "\\corpserver01\users\$username$"
```

Real World   With The Active Directory Users And Computers administrative tool, you enter the value *%username%* to get paths and filename based on individual user names. Don't use this value with the special parameters discussed here. *%username%* is an environment variable and the GUI knows to replace the environment variable on a per-user basis. The command line interprets this and other environment variables based on the current logged on user, however. So in this case the value of *%username%* is the SAM account name of the user account under which you run the command.

Disabling and Enabling User Accounts

You can enable or disable users accounts from the command line using the DSMOD USER command and the –Disabled parameter. Use **–disabled yes** to disable the user account and **–disabled no** to enable the user account.

In the following example, you disable all users in the OffsiteUsers OU:

```
dsquery user "OU=OffsiteUsers,DC=cpand1,DC=com" | dsmod user -disabled
yes
```

The DSMOD USER command would then report the individual success or failure of each change.

Resetting Expired User Accounts

Domain user accounts can be set with a specific expiration date. You can check the account expiration date using DSGET USER with the –Acctexpires parameter. For example, if you wanted to check the expiration date of all user accounts in the Sales OU, you can type

```
dsquery user "OU=Sales,DC=cpand1,DC=com" | dsget user -dn -acctexpires
```

The resulting output would show you the account expiration dates of each account in the Sales OU according to the distinguished name of the account, such as

```
dn                                            acctexpires
CN=Mary Baker,OU=Sales,DC=cpand1,DC=com       never
CN=Bradley Beck,OU=Sales,DC=cpand1,DC=com     11/15/2006
CN=Ann Bebbe,OU=Sales,DC=cpand1,DC=com        never
CN=Max Benson,OU=Sales,DC=cpand1,DC=com       12/31/2006
dsget succeeded
```

Here, accounts without expiration dates have an account expires value of "never" and other accounts have a specific expiration date, such as 11/15/2006.

If you need to extend or change the account expiration date to allow a user to log on to the domain, you can do this with DSMOD USER. Set the –Acctexpires parameter to the number of days for which the account should be valid. For example, if an account should be valid for the next 60 days, you would type **–acctexpires 60**, such as

```
dsquery user -name johnw | dsmod user -acctexpires 60
```

or

```
dsmod user "CN=John Wood,OU=Sales,DC=cpand1,DC=com" -acctexpires 60
```

In these examples you change the account expiration for John Wood.

If you want to remove an account expiration date, use a value of 0 to specify that the account never expires, such as

```
dsquery user -name johnw | dsmod user -acctexpires 0
```

Note To set an account so that it is past the expiration date, you can type a negative value, such as **–acctexpires -1**.

Controlling and Resetting User Passwords

Using DSGET USER, you can check the password settings on user accounts. Typically, you'll want to know if a user can change their password, whether the password expires and whether the password uses reversible encryption. You can check for these settings using the –Canchpwd, –Pwdneverexpires, and –Reversiblepwd parameters respectively. You might also want to know if the account is set so the user must change his or her password on next logon. To do this, you can use the –Mustchpwd parameter. For example, if you wanted to check these values all user accounts in the Users container, you can type

```
dsquery user "CN=Users,DC=cpandl,DC=com" | dsget user -samid -canchpwd
-pwdneverexpires -reversiblepwd -mustchpwd
```

The resulting output would show you the related password settings of each account in the Users container according to the SAM account name, such as

samid	mustchpwd	canchpwd	reversiblepwd	pwdneverexpires
andya	no	yes	no	no
billg	no	yes	no	no
bobh	yes	yes	no	no
brianw	no	yes	no	no
conniej	no	yes	yes	yes

dsget succeeded

DSMOD USER provides several parameters for controlling these and other password settings. You can use the –Pwd parameter to set the password for a particular user account. You can then configure how the password is used as follows:

- Use **–mustchpwd yes** to force users to change the password after their next logon.

- Use **–canchpwd no** to set the account so users can't change the password for their account.

- Use **–pwdneverexpires no** to set the account so that the password never expires, which overrides Group Policy settings.

The wonderful thing about the command line is that you can control passwords for many user accounts as easily as for one user. Say you wanted to change the password for every user in the TempEmployee OU to Time2ChangeMe and force these users to change their passwords on next logon, you can do this by typing the command

```
dsquery user "OU=TempEmployee,DC=cpandl,DC=com" | dsmod user -pwd
Time2ChangeMe -mustchpwd yes
```

Moving User Accounts

User accounts are normally placed in the Users container or in OUs. You can move a user account to a different container or OU within its current domain using DSMOVE. Specify the user account's current DN and then use the –Newparent parameter to specify the new location or parent DN of the user account. For instance if you wanted to move the William Stanek user account from the Tech OU to the Engineering OU, you would specify the user account's DN, such as **"CN=William Stanek,OU=Tech,DC=cpandl,DC=com"**, and provide the parent DN for the new location, such as **"OU=Engineering,DC=cpandl, DC=com"**. The related command would look like this:

```
dsmove "CN=William Stanek,OU=Tech,DC=cpandl,DC=com" -newparent
"OU=Engineering,DC=cpandl,DC=com"
```

You could have also obtained the user account DN using the DSQUERY USER command. To do this, you simply pipe the output of DSQUERY USER to DSMOVE, as shown in this example:

```
dsquery user -name "William Stanek" | dsmove -newparent
"OU=Engineering,DC=cpandl,DC=com"
```

Here, the user account DN, "CN=William Stanek,OU=Tech,DC=cpandl, DC=com", is obtained from DSQUERY USER and used as input to DSMOVE.

Renaming User Accounts

Although moving user accounts is fairly straightforward, you don't want to rename user accounts without some planning. When you rename a user account, you give the account a new common name. You'll find that you might have to rename accounts in cases of marriage, divorce, or adoption. For example, if Nancy Anderson (nancya) gets married, she might want her user name to be changed to Nancy Buchanan (nancyb). When you rename her account, all associated privileges and permissions will reflect the name change. Thus, if you view the permissions on a file that nancya had access to, nancyb will now have access (and nancya will no longer be listed).

You rename user accounts using the DSMOVE command. Specify the user's DN and then use the –Newname parameter to specify the new common name. You can rename a user object from Nancy Anderson to Nancy Buchanan by typing

```
dsmove "CN=Nancy Anderson,OU=Marketing,DC=cpandl,DC=com" -newname
"Nancy Buchanan"
```

You could obtain the user DN by means of DSQUERY USER as well. Consider the following example:

```
dsquery user -name N*Anderson | dsmove -newname "Nancy Buchanan"
```

Here you use DSQUERY USER to find an account that begins with the letters "N" and ends with "Anderson." You then use DSMOVE to rename this account.

Renaming the user account doesn't change any of the other account properties. Because some properties may reflect the old last name, you will need to update these properties to reflect the name change using DSMOD USER. The parameters you might want to modify include

- **–Ln**   Used to change the last name for the user account.
- **–Display**   Used to change the user account's Display Name.
- **–Samid**   Used to change the SAM account name.
- **–Profile**   Used to change the profile path for the account. Afterward, you'll need to rename the corresponding directory on disk.
- **–Loscr**   If you use individual logon scripts for each user, you can use –Loscr to change the logon script name property. Afterward, you'll need to rename the logon script on disk.
- **–Hmdir**   Used to change the home directory path. Afterward, you'll need to rename the corresponding directory on disk.

Note   In most cases, you won't want to modify this information while a user is logged on because this might cause problems. Instead, update this information after hours or ask the user to log off for a few minutes and then log back on.

Consider the following example:

```
dsquery user -name N*Buchanan | dsmod -samid nancyb -ln Buchanan
-display Nancy Buchanan
```

Here, you change the SAM account name, last name and display name to match the previous name change for the user Nancy Buchanan.

Real World   User names are used to make managing and using accounts easier. Behind the scenes, Windows Server 2003 actually uses the account's security identifier (SID) to identify, track, and handle the account independently from the user name. SIDs are unique identifiers that are generated when accounts are created. Because SIDs are mapped to account names internally, you don't need to change the privileges or permissions on renamed accounts. Windows Server 2003 simply maps the SID to the new account name as necessary.

Deleting User Accounts

If you no longer need a user account, you can delete it permanently from Active Directory using the DSRM command. In most cases, you'll want to delete only a specific user account, such as the account for Mary Baker. If this is the case, you remove the account by passing DSRM the DN of the user account, such as

```
dsrm "CN=Mary Baker,OU=Sales,DC=cpandl,DC=com"
```

By default, DSRM prompts you to confirm the deletion. If you don't want to see the prompt use the –Noprompt parameter, such as

```
dsrm "CN=Mary Baker,OU=Sales,DC=cpandl,DC=com" -noprompt
```

 Note Even though you delete a user's account, Windows Server 2003 won't delete the user's profile, personal files, or home directory. If you want to delete these files and directories, you'll have to do it manually. If this is a task you perform routinely, you might want to create a script that performs the necessary tasks for you. Keep in mind you should back up files or data that might be needed before you do this.

Overview of Managing Group Accounts from the Command Line

Group accounts help you manage privileges for multiple users. In Windows Server 2003, there are three types of groups:

- **Security groups** Groups that have security descriptors associated with them and are used to help manage access permissions. You create and manage security groups with the directory services commands.

- **Distribution groups** Groups used as e-mail distribution lists, which don't have security descriptors associated with them. You create and manage distribution groups with the directory services commands.

- **Local groups** Groups used on the local computer only. You create and manage local groups with the network services commands.

Security and distribution groups are used with domains. This makes them available throughout the directory. Local groups, however, are available only on the computer on which they are created. The general domain group account command-line utilities include

- **DSADD GROUP** Creates a group account in Active Directory. The syntax is

```
dsadd group GroupDN [-secgrp {yes | no}] [-scope {l | g | u}]
[-samid SAMName] [-desc Description] [-memberof Group ...]
[-members Member ...] [{-s Server | -d Domain}] [-u UserName] [-p
{Password | *}] [-q] [{-uc | -uco | -uci}]
```

- **DSGET GROUP** Displays the properties of group accounts using one of two syntaxes. The syntax for viewing the properties of multiple groups is

```
dsget group GroupDN ... [-dn] [-samid] [-sid] [-desc] [-secgrp]
[-scope] [{-s Server | -d Domain}] [-u UserName] [-p {Password |
*}] [-c] [-q] [-l] [{-uc | -uco | -uci}] [-part PartitionDN
[-qlimit] [-qused]]
```

The syntax for viewing the group membership information for an individual group is

```
dsget group GroupDN [{-memberof | -members} [-expand]] [{-s Server
| -d Domain}] [-u UserName] [-p {Password | *}] [-c] [-q] [-1]
[{-uc | -uco | -uci}]
```

- **DSMOD GROUP** Modifies attributes of one or more group accounts in the directory. The syntax is

```
dsmod group GroupDN ... [-samid SAMName] [-desc Description]
[-secgrp {yes | no}] [-scope {l | g | u}] [{-addmbr | -rmmbr |
-chmbr} MemberDN ...] [{-s Server | -d Domain}] [-u UserName]
[-p {Password | *}] [-c] [-q] [{-uc | -uco | -uci}]
```

Tip You can use input from DSQUERY GROUP to set the DN for the security group or groups you want to work with. You can also type the DNs for each group you want to work with. When you do this, make sure to separate each DN with a space.

To manage local group accounts, you use the NET LOCALGROUP command. This command has several different syntaxes. The syntax you use depends on what you want to do, as follows:

- **Create local group accounts** net localgroup [*GroupName* {/add [/comment:"*Text*"]}
- **Modify local group accounts** net localgroup [*GroupName Name* [...] {/add | /delete}]
- **Delete local group accounts** net localgroup [*GroupName* {/delete [/comment:"*Text*"]}

Note NET LOCALGROUP can be used to add a local group to a group in the current (logon) domain. In some limited situations you might want to consider doing this but ordinarily you wouldn't use this technique to grant access permissions for regular users. For example, if you created a local group called DevTesters you can add this group to the Developers domain group. This would give local machine users who are members of the DevTesters group the same domain permissions as other members of the Developers domain group. Here, developers who are testing local system configurations need access to the domain.

Adding Group Accounts

The type of group you need depends on your network configuration. In domains, you'll typically work with security and distribution groups. In workgroups, you'll typically work with local groups that pertain only to specific machines.

Creating Security and Distribution Groups

As discussed previously, security groups are used to manage access permissions for groups of users, and distribution groups are used for mail distribution lists. Regardless of which type of group you create, the way the group is used depends on the scope. Scope controls the areas in which the groups are valid and the defined scopes are

- **Domain local groups**   Groups used to grant permissions within a single domain. Its members can include only accounts (both user and computer accounts) and groups from the domain in which they're defined.

- **Global groups**   Groups used to grant permissions to objects in any domain in the domain tree or forest. Its members can include only accounts and groups from the domain in which they're defined.

- **Universal groups**   Groups used to grant permissions on a wide scale throughout a domain tree or forest. Its members can include accounts, global groups, and other universal groups from any domain in the domain tree or forest.

 Note   Universal security groups are available only when Active Directory is running at the Windows 2000 native functional level or at the Windows Server 2003 functional level, and are more useful on larger networks than on smaller ones. Primarily this is because they add another level of group hierarchy for administrators to manage; therefore, their benefits are clearer in large installations where you need more control over groups.

Table 13-1 summarizes the capabilities of groups based on the scope and the operations mode. As the table shows, both affect what you can and can't do with groups.

Table 13-1.   Group Capabilities With Regard to Functional Level and Scope

Group Capability	Domain Local Scope	Global Scope	Universal Scope
Windows Server 2003/ Windows 2000 Native functional level	Members can include user accounts, global groups, and universal groups from any domain; domain local groups from the same domain only.	Members can include only user accounts from the same domain and global groups from the same domain.	Members can include user accounts from any domain, as well as groups from any domain regardless of scope.

Table 13-1.   **Group Capabilities With Regard to Functional Level and Scope**

Group Capability	Domain Local Scope	Global Scope	Universal Scope
Windows 2000 Mixed functional level	Members can include user accounts and global groups from any domain.	Members can include only user and group accounts from the same domain.	Universal security groups can't be created in mixed-mode domains.
Member Of	Can be put into other domain local groups and assigned permissions only in the same domain.	Can be put into other groups and assigned permissions in any domain.	Can be put into other groups and assigned permissions in any domain.

When you create groups, you pass DSADD GROUP the group's DN. The common name component of the DN sets the group's display name. The rest of the DN specifies where in Active Directory the group is to be located, which includes the container in which the group is to be created and the related domain. By default, if you provide no other parameters, a global security group is created. For example, you could create a global security group called Sales in the Sales organizational unit of the cpandl.com domain by typing **dsadd group "CN=Sales,OU=Sales,DC=cpandl,DC=com"**. The group would be created with Sales as the group's display name and the same value as the SAM account name. No other properties would be set, however.

Group names aren't case-sensitive and can be as long as 64 characters. In most cases, you'll want to specify the group type and scope directly. You use the –Secgrp parameter to specify whether the group is a security group, as follows:

- Type **–secgrp yes** to specify that you are creating a security group.
- Type **–secgrp no** to specify that you are creating a distribution group.

To set the group scope, use the –Scope parameter, as follows:

- Type **–scope l** to create a local domain group
- Type **–scope g** to create a global group
- Type **–scope u** to create a universal group. For security groups, valid only when running at the Windows Server 2003 functional level.

Note   By default, groups are created as security groups with a global scope. Therefore, even if you create a security group with a different scope, you don't have to specify **–secgrp yes** because this is the default.

The first 20 characters of the group name are used to set the SAM account name of the group, which is also referred to as the pre–Windows 2000 group name. The SAM account name must be unique in the domain and if there is overlap you might want the group's SAM account name to be different from its display name. In this case, you would need to set the SAM account name using the –Samid parameter.

You can also specify the group membership when you create the group. If the group you are creating should be a member of an existing group, you can use the –Memberof parameter to specify the DNs for these groups. If the group should have users or other groups as its members, you can specify the DNs for these members using the –Members parameter. However, it is much easier to use DSMOD GROUP to configure group membership. Why? You can pass DSMOD GROUP a list of DNs as input from DSQUERY USER. This saves you from having to type several dozen and sometimes hundreds of DNs.

Consider the following examples to see how groups can be created:

Create a domain local security group called Engineering. Add the group to the Engineering OU in the tech.cpandl.com domain.

```
dsadd group "CN=Engineering,OU=Engineering,DC=tech,DC=cpandl,
DC=com" -scope l
```

Create a global security group called Engineering Global in the Users container of the cpandl.com domain. Set the SAM account name to gEngineering.

```
dsadd group "CN=Engineering Global,CN=Users,DC=cpandl,DC=com"
-samid "gEngineering"
```

Create a universal distribution group called Engineering All in the Engineering OU of the cpandl.com domain. Set the SAM account name to allEngineering.

```
dsadd group "CN=Engineering All,OU=Engineering,DC=cpandl,DC=com"
-samid "allEngineering" -secgrp no -scope u
```

If there are problems creating the group, you'll see a warning and you'll need to check your syntax, ensuring that all the values are set appropriately and that the DN values are valid. Otherwise, DSADD GROUP should report DSADD SUCCEEDED. Once the group is created, you can add members and set additional properties, as discussed later in this chapter.

Creating a Local Group and Assigning Members

Local groups are created on individual computers to help manage permissions for users that log on locally instead of logging on to the domain. To create a local group, you'll need to log on to the computer you want to work with or use a remote logon to access a local command prompt. Once you are logged on to the computer, you can create the required local group account using NET LOCALGROUP.

You can create the local group simply by following the command name with the name of the group and then using the /Add parameter. Consider the following example:

```
net localgroup localDevs /add
```

Note You can't create local group accounts on domain controllers. Domain controllers do not have local machine accounts.

Here, you create a group called localDevs on the local computer. If you wanted, you could also use the /Comment parameter to add a description of the group, such as

```
net localgroup localDevs /comment:"Local Developers and Testers" /add
```

If the account creation is successful, NET LOCALGROUP will state "Command Completed Successfully." However, if there are problems creating the account, NET LOCALGROUP won't display an error message per se. Instead, it will display the command syntax. In this case, check your syntax and ensure that all the values are set appropriately.

When you create a local group, you can also specify a list of local user accounts which should be members of the group. This list of names follows the group name as shown in this example:

```
net localgroup localDevs williams johng edwardh /add
```

Here, you create a group called localDevs and add WilliamS, JohnG, and EdwardH as members.

If you want to add members to a local group later rather than when you create the group, you can do this as well. The syntax is the same as for creating the group. For example if you create a group called custSupport by typing

```
net localgroup custSupport /add
```

You could later add members to this group by typing

```
net localgroup custSupport williams johng edwardh /add
```

Here, you add WilliamS, JohnG, and EdwardH as members to the custSupport group.

Managing Group Accounts

Managing group accounts from the command line is different from managing them in Active Directory Groups and Computers, chiefly because the command line offers more options and it is easier to work with multiple group accounts at the same time.

Viewing and Finding Group Accounts

When you want to obtain information about group accounts, you can use the DSQUERY GROUP command. This command lets you search by common name, SAM account name, and description. It also accepts wildcards in any of these fields. The output of DSQUERY GROUP contains the distinguished name of groups that match the search criteria and can be piped as input to other commands, including DSGET GROUP.

Typically, you'll use DSQUERY GROUP and DSGET GROUP together. You start by using DSQUERY GROUP to obtain the distinguished names of one or more groups and then use DSGET GROUP to display the properties for the related accounts. DSGET GROUP parameters that you might find useful include

- **–Desc**   Displays the description of matching group accounts in the output
- **–Dn**   Displays the distinguished name of matching group accounts in the output
- **–Samid**   Displays the SAM account name of matching group accounts in the output
- **–Scope**   Displays the scope of matching groups as domain local, global or universal
- **–Secgrp**   Displays yes if a group is a security group and no if a group is a distribution group
- **–Sid**   Displays the security identifier for matching group accounts in the output

As with the other DSGET commands, DSGET GROUP displays output in table format and you will usually want to include –Dn or –Samid as a parameter to help you make sense of and identify the groups in the output. For example, if you wanted to search for all marketing groups that were available, you could use the command line

```
dsquery group -name marketing* | dsget group -dn -scope -secgrp
```

Here, the results display the DN, the scope, and security group information:

```
dn                                               scope          secgrp
CN=MarketingAll,OU=Sales,DC=cpandl,DC=com        universal      no
CN=Marketing Global,OU=Sales,DC=cpandl,DC=com    global         no
CN=Marketing Local,OU=Sales,DC=cpandl,DC=com     domain local   no
dsget succeeded
```

Determining Group Membership

When you want to determine group membership, you use the second syntax for DSGET GROUP, which includes two special parameters: –Members and –Memberof. You use the –Members parameter to determine which users and groups belong to a specific group. You use the –Memberof parameter to determine the groups to which the specified group belongs. How do these parameters work? Let's suppose that you wanted to see the current members of a group called AllUsers. You could do this by typing

```
dsquery group -name AllUsers | dsget group -members
```

Or you could type the group DN directly, such as

```
dsget group "CN=AllUsers,CN=Users,DC=cpandl,DC=com" -members
```

Here the group is in the Users container of the cpandl.com domain. Either way, the output would show the DNs for members of this group, such as

```
"CN=Tech,OU=Tech,DC=cpandl,DC=com"
"CN=Engineering,OU=Eng,DC=cpandl,DC=com"
"CN=Sales,OU=Sales,DC=cpandl,DC=com"
"CN=Domain Users,CN=Users,DC=cpandl,DC=com"
```

As the listing shows, the AllUsers group has as its members the Tech, Engineering, Sales, and Domain Users groups. The AllUsers group could have also had user accounts as its members.

If you want to determine to which groups a group belongs, you can use the –Memberof parameter. For example, the group DevUsers could be a member of the Domain Administrators group and the Developers group, and you could display this membership information by typing

```
dsquery group -name devusers | dsget group -memberof
```

or

```
dsget group "CN=devusers,OU=Dev,DC=cpandl,DC=com" -memberof
```

Both commands work the same. In the first example, you use DSQUERY GROUP to obtain the DN of the group account. In the second example, you specify the DN directly. Either way the output would be a list of groups in which DevUsers is a member.

Note Both techniques could be used to display the membership information of multiple groups. However, there is no way to display a DN or SAM account name for the associated groups because the second syntax for DSGET GROUP doesn't allow this.

Changing Group Type or Scope

Sometimes after you create a group you'll want to change the group type or scope. This isn't as easy as you might think, because there are a number of controls in place to prevent arbitrary changes that can affect access throughout the organization. First of all, group type or scope cannot be changed in

Windows 2000 Mixed or Windows Server 2003 Interim functional levels. In Windows 2000 Native or Windows Server 2003 functional level, the following is true:

- **Domain Local Groups** Can be converted to universal scope, provided it doesn't have as its member another group having domain local scope
- **Global Groups** Can be converted to universal scope, provided it's not a member of any other group having global scope
- **Universal Groups** Can be converted to any other group scope. Keep in mind a global group cannot have a universal group as a member and that local groups can only be members of other local groups

With these restrictions in mind, you can use DSMOD GROUP and its –Secgrp parameter to change the group type as follows:

- Change a distribution group to a security group by including **–secgrp yes**
- Change a security group to a distribution group by including **–secgrp no**

Consider the following examples:

Convert the Engineering security group to a distribution group:

```
dsquery group -name Engineering | dsmod group =secgrp no
```

Convert the AllMarketing distribution group to a security group:

```
dsmod group "CN=AllMarketing,OU=Marketing,DC=cpandl,DC=com" =secgrp yes
```

You change the group scope using the –Scope parameter of DSMOD GROUP as follows:

- Set the scope as domain local by including **–scope l**
- Set the scope as global by including **–scope g**
- Set the scope as universal by including **–scope u**

Consider the following examples:

Set the scope of the Marketing group to domain local:

```
dsquery group -name Marketing | dsmod group -scope l
```

Set the scope of the Sales group to global:

```
dsmod group "CN=Sales,CN=Users,DC=cpandl,DC=com" -scope g
```

Adding, Removing, or Replacing Group Members

Using the command line, it is easy to change the membership of any group. As with the GUI, you can easily add or remove users, groups, or computers as members of a group. But the command-line utilities take this a step further in making it easy to add or remove multiple members. You can also replace the existing membership list entirely.

Adding Members to a Group

You can, for example, use a single command line to add all 100 users in the Sales organizational unit to the AllSales group. To do this, you would use DSQUERY USER to obtain a list of user accounts that you want to work with and then pass this list as input to DSMOD GROUP. The parameter for adding group members is –Addmbr so the command would look like this:

```
dsquery user "OU=Sales,DC=ny,DC=cpandl,DC=com" | dsmod group
"CN=AllSales,OU=Sales,DC=ny,DC=cpandl,DC=com" -addmbr
```

Here, you obtain a list of all user accounts in the Sales OU of the ny.cpandl.com domain and pass this as input to DSMOD GROUP. DSMOD GROUP then adds these users as members to the AllSales group, which is located in the Sales container of the ny.cpandl.com domain.

Another way to use –Addmbr is to specify the DNs of the objects you want to add. So for example, if you wanted to add the SalesLocal and SalesGlobal groups to the AllSales group, you could do this with the following command-line entry:

```
dsquery group -name AllSales | dsmod group -addmbr
"CN=SalesLocal,OU=Sales,DC=ny,DC=cpandl,DC=com"
"CN=SalesGlobal,OU=Sales,DC=ny,DC=cpandl,DC=com"
```

Note   Remember, the object DNs could include user and group accounts as well as computer accounts.

Removing Members from a Group

The counterpart to –Addmbr is –Rmmbr, which is used to remove members from groups. As with –Addmbr, –rmmbr accepts object DNs from input or in a space-separated list. So if you wanted to remove all marketing and customer support users from the AllSales group, one way to do this is to use the following commands:

```
dsquery user "OU=Marketing,DC=ny,DC=cpandl,DC=com" | dsmod group
"CN=AllSales,OU=Sales,DC=ny,DC=cpandl,DC=com" -rmmbr
```

```
dsquery user "OU=CustSupport,DC=ny,DC=cpandl,DC=com" | dsmod group
"CN=AllSales,OU=Sales,DC=ny,DC=cpandl,DC=com" -rmmbr
```

Here, the first command obtains a list of all users in the Marketing OU and then passes this as input to DSMOD GROUP so that these users can be removed from the AllSales group. The second command obtains a list of all users in the Cust-Support OU and then passes this as input to DSMOD GROUP so that these users can be removed from the AllSales group.

 Tip A problem is introduced if the two lists of users don't match exactly to the current membership for the AllSales group. For example, if new marketing users have started working and they've been added to the Marketing OU but not been granted access to Sales information, they wouldn't be in the AllSales group. In this case, when the DSMOD GROUP command finds the first mismatch, it will exit and report an error. But you don't want that to happen because of a slight mismatch, so, to prevent this, add the –C parameter. This parameter says to report errors but continue processing changes.

As with –Addmbr, you can also specify the DNs of the objects you want to remove directly. Say you wanted to remove the SalesLocal and SalesGlobal groups from the AllSales group, you could do this with the following command-line entry:

```
dsquery group -name AllSales | dsmod group -rmmbr
"CN=SalesLocal,OU=Sales,DC=ny,DC=cpandl,DC=com"
"CN=SalesGlobal,OU=Sales,DC=ny,DC=cpandl,DC=com"
```

 Note With the formatting of the page, you might not notice it but there is a space between each of the group DNs. The space is necessary so that each group DN is interpreted correctly.

Replacing All Members in a Group

The command line takes the notion of adding and removing group members a step further than the GUI by allowing you to replace the entire membership list of a group. For example, if the group membership for the AllUsers group wasn't up to date and it would be hard to add and remove members manually, you might want to replace the existing membership and start over.

You replace the existing group members with a list of your choosing with the –Chmbr parameter of the DSMOD GROUP command. This parameter accepts input that is passed from DSQUERY USER or a space-separated list of DNs. So one way to replace the existing membership list and add all users in the organization to the AllUsers group is to type the following command:

```
dsquery user -name * | dsmod group
"CN=AllUsers,CN=Users,DC=seattle,DC=cpandl,DC=com" -chmbr
```

Here, DSMOD GROUP first removes all the existing objects that are members and then adds the objects passed as input. If any error occurs in either part of the processing the command will fail and no changes will occur.

Note   Although you can use the –C parameter to ensure the operation continues even if there are errors, this can result in the group having an empty membership. What happens is that the DSMOD GROUP command removes the current members without any problems but fails when trying to add members. The removal of members requires only the proper administrative permissions. The addition of members, however, depends on the input you provide.

Moving Group Accounts

As with user accounts, you can easily move a group account to a different container or OU within its current domain. To do this, you use the DSMOVE command to specify the group account's current DN and then use the –Newparent parameter to specify the new location or parent DN of the group account. For instance, if you wanted to move the ProdDev group from the Users container to the Developers organizational unit, you would specify the group account's DN, such as **"CN=ProdDev,CN=Users,DC=cpandl,DC=com"**, and provide the parent DN for the new location, such as **"OU=Developers,DC=cpandl,DC=com"**. The related command would look like this:

```
dsmove "CN=ProdDev,CN=Users,DC=cpandl,DC=com" -newparent
"OU=Developers,DC=cpandl,DC=com"
```

DSQUERY GROUP can also save you some typing by sending the group DN to DSMOVE as input, as shown in this example:

```
dsquery group -name "ProdDev" | dsmove -newparent
"OU=Developers,DC=cpandl,DC=com"
```

Here, the group account DN, "CN=ProdDev,CN=Users,DC=cpandl,DC=com", is obtained from DSQUERY GROUP and used as input to DSMOVE.

Renaming Group Accounts

As with users, groups have security identifiers. This allows you to change a group name without having to change the access permissions later on individual resources, such as files and folders. When you rename a group, you change its common name.

You rename groups using the DSMOVE command. Specify the group's DN and then use the –Newname parameter to specify the new common name. You can rename a group object from ProdDevs to TechDevs by typing

```
dsmove "CN=ProdDevs,OU=Developers,DC=cpandl,DC=com" -newname
"TechDevs"
```

As when moving groups, you can also obtain the group DN from DSQUERY GROUP. Consider the following example:

```
dsquery group -name ProdDevs | dsmove -newname "TechDevs"
```

Here you use DSQUERY GROUP to obtain the DN for the ProdDevs group, and then use DSMOVE to rename the group.

As renaming a group doesn't change the pre–Windows 2000 group name or description associated with the group, you'll need to change these properties next. To do this, use the DSMOD GROUP command. The –Samid parameter sets the pre–Windows 2000 group name and the –Desc parameter sets the description. Consider the following example:

```
dsquery group -name TechDevs | dsmod -samid techdevs -desc "Technical
Developers Group"
```

Here, you change the pre–Windows 2000 group name to **techdevs** and the description to "Technical Developers Group."

Deleting Group Accounts

To delete a group permanently from Active Directory, you can use the DSRM command. In most cases, you'll want to delete only a named group rather than say all groups whose names start with "M." If this is the case, you remove the group by passing DSRM the DN of the group account, such as:

```
dsrm "CN=AllSales,OU=Sales,DC=chicago,DC=cpand1,DC=com"
```

By default, DSRM prompts you to confirm the deletion. If you don't want to see the prompt, use the -Noprompt parameter, such as

```
dsrm "CN=AllSales,OU=Sales,DC=chicago,DC=cpand1,DC=com" -noprompt
```

In some limited situations, you might want to remove several groups at once. For example, if there is a companywide reorganization and the marketing department is outsourced as a result of this, you might find that you no longer need marketing-related groups. If the group names begin with the keyword *Marketing*, you could delete them by typing

```
dsquery group -name Marketing* | dsrm -c
```

Here, you pass as input to DSRM the group DNs for all groups that begin with the keyword *Marketing*. The –C parameter is added to allow the operation to continue if an error occurs.

Caution Even though input is passed to the command from DSQUERY GROUP, you can't use DSRM by itself. For example, you couldn't type **dsquery group –name Marketing* | dsrm**. The reason for this is that the command line still expects the DN of the object or a parameter to follow the DSRM command. Because of this you would have to use some parameter and –C is the safest as it only tells DSRM to continue in the event of an error. –Noprompt, on the other hand, tells DSRM go ahead and delete everything without prompting the user, which could lead to many more groups than expected being deleted and no way to cancel the operation.

Chapter 14

Administering Network Printers and Print Services

Most organizations have a mix of high-volume and low-volume low-cost printers. Typically, the high-volume printers handle the heavy, daily loads of multiple users and the low-volume, low-cost printers handle the print loads of small groups or individual users. Regardless of usage, the print server needs sufficient memory and processing power to handle the print services. In a high-volume environment or an environment in which very large or complex documents are routinely printed, the server may need to be specially configured or dedicated to print services only. Otherwise, print servers typically aren't expensive or dedicated machines. In fact, many print servers are standard desktop systems that handle other network jobs as well. Just keep in mind that Microsoft Windows Server 2003 and Windows XP Professional give higher priority to file sharing than to print sharing, so if a system handles both services, printing might be slowed to accommodate file services and prevent any file access performance problems.

Print servers must have sufficient disk space to handle print jobs as well. The amount of disk space required depends on the size of the print jobs and how long the print queue gets. For best performance, the printer's spool folder should be on a dedicated drive that isn't used for any other purpose. A key part of print services administration is maintenance. To maintain and support print services properly, you should keep track of print spooler information and usage statistics. This information helps you determine how print services are performing. Although you are focused on performance issues, you'll find that there are several useful command-line utilities that help you maintain print servers and troubleshoot printer issues. These utilities are discussed in this chapter.

Obtaining Support and Troubleshooting Information for Printers

Printers are often purchased and deployed without much thought given to how the printers will be used. Someone sees that a printer is needed in an area and a printer is ordered and installed. Sometimes it's not even an administrator that does the printer ordering and installation, so when you try to manage and maintain it, you may be flying blind. Regardless of how printers were obtained, the administration or support teams should maintain information about the printer's configuration, including what drivers are available and which drivers are used. You need to check periodically how busy the printer is and if it is handling the workload. You'll also want to track the printer status, the number of jobs queued and other important information that can help you determine if there are problems. In many cases, this information is also useful for capacity planning.

Tracking Print Drivers and Printer Information

When you want to track detailed information about the printers installed on a system, you can use the PRINTDRIVERINFO command. This command is included in the Windows Server 2003 Resource Kit and is designed to work with local and remote systems.

Getting Driver Details for Support and Troubleshooting

By default, PRINTDRIVERINFO returns the driver information for all printer drivers configured on the local system. This means you could type **printdriverinfo** at a command prompt and get a complete list of printer drivers for the local computer. As Listing 14-1 shows, the driver information is very detailed:

Listing 14-1 Output from PRINTDRIVERINFO

```
--------------Report by driver name--------------
Driver Name: hp business inkjet 1100 series
Environment: Windows NT x86
Kernel Mode Driver: FALSE
Using inf : C:\WINDOWS\inf\ntprint.inf
Inbox Driver: FALSE
Driver Technology: Monolithic
Driver Stack File: hpz2ku08.dll , Date:
27/06/2003 , Version: 2.224
Driver Stack File: hpf0uk08.dat , Date: 27/06/2003 , Version: 2.224
Driver Stack File: hpzpm308.dll , Date: 27/06/2003 , Version: 2.224
Driver Stack File: hpfmom08.hlp , Date: 27/06/2003 , Version: 2.224
Driver Stack File: hpzrer08.dll , Date: 27/06/2003 , Version: 2.224
Driver Stack File: hpzl3208.dll , Date: 27/06/2003 , Version: 2.224
Driver Stack File: hpzcfg08.exe , Date: 27/06/2003 , Version: 2.224
Driver Stack File: hpzeng08.exe , Date: 27/06/2003 , Version: 2.224
Driver Stack File: hpzflt08.dll , Date: 27/06/2003 , Version: 2.224
Driver Stack File: hpzime08.dll , Date: 27/06/2003 , Version: 3.02
Driver Stack File: hpzjui08.dll , Date: 27/06/2003 , Version: 2.224
Driver Stack File: hpzpre08.exe , Date: 27/06/2003 , Version: 2.224
Driver Stack File: hpzres08.dll , Date: 27/06/2003 , Version: 0.00
Driver Stack File: hpzvip08.dll , Date: 27/06/2003 , Version: 2.224
Driver Stack File: hpzrm308.dll , Date: 27/06/2003 , Version: 2.224
Driver Stack File: hpwhlmn.dll , Date: 27/06/2003 , Version: 2.213
Driver Stack File: hpwhsvb.dll , Date: 27/06/2003 , Version: 2.213
```

```
-=Misc Driver Info=-
DriverPath: C:\WINDOWS\System32\spool\DRIVERS\W32X86\3\hpz2ku08.dll
Data File: C:\WINDOWS\System32\spool\DRIVERS\W32X86\3\hpf0uk08.dat
Config File: C:\WINDOWS\System32\spool\DRIVERS\W32X86\3\hpzpm308.dll
Help file: C:\WINDOWS\System32\spool\DRIVERS\W32X86\3\hpfmom08.hlp
Monitor Name: HPWHLMN
Default Data Type: RAW
```

If you examine the detailed driver information, you'll see the following information is included:

- **The printer driver name, such as hp business inkjet 1100 series**   The printer driver name is the name used by Windows to track the printer driver. The driver used for a printer should match the actual type of printer being used. In this case, the printer is a Hewlett-Packard (HP) Business InkJet 1100 series printer. When you print a document, the application from which you are printing uses the printer driver to translate the document into a file format understandable by the physical print device. If you were having problems with a printer and suspected the wrong driver was loaded, this would be one of the best indicators.

- **The printer driver mode**   Printer drivers either operate in kernel mode or user mode. In kernel mode, the driver operates like other programs run directly by the operating system. In user mode, the driver runs like programs run by users. Stop errors from kernel mode printer drivers are typically more detailed than those from user mode printer drivers. However, printer drivers operating in kernel mode are more likely to cause system instability if they have problems. Group policy controls whether you are permitted to install kernel-mode printer drivers. In Windows Server 2003, installation of kernel-mode printer drives is blocked by default. In Windows XP Professional, installation of kernel-mode printer drives is not blocked by default. The Disallow Installation Of Printers Using Kernel-Mode Drivers policy is under Local Computer Policy\Computer Configuration\Administrative Templates \Printers.

- **The INF file the printer driver is using**   Every driver installed on a system has an associated INF file. The INF file is used to configure the printer driver.

- **The print spooler DLL and related data files**   The specific DLL for the print spooler is specified by the driver path. The spooler has associated data, config and help files. The print spooler is what passes documents that users want printed to the print processor. The print processor in turn creates the raw print data necessary for printing on the print device. This data is in turn passed back to the print spooler so that it can be routed.

- **The printer driver stack files** The printer driver stack details all the stack files associated with a particular printer driver. Each file is listed according to creation date and version. Documents are routed (using the print router) from the print spooler to the printer stack, which is also called the print queue. Once in the print queue, documents are referred to as print jobs, which essentially means the documents are tasks for the print spooler to handle.

- **The print monitor being used** Each print device has an associated print monitor. Printers that support bi-directional printing have a language monitor that handles two-way communications between the printer and the print spooler as well as a port monitor that controls the I/O port to the printer. These collectively are referred to as the *print monitor for a print device*. If a printer has an associated language monitor, the name of this monitor is specified and that name is the same as its file name without the .dll extension. If a printer doesn't have an associated language monitor, the value (Null) is specified. When a document reaches the top of the printer stack, the print monitor is responsible for sending it to the print device. The print device is the physical hardware on which the document is actually printed. Most print devices have their own print monitors, which were created by the manufacturer of the device. A print monitor is required to print to a print device. If the print monitor is corrupted or missing, you might need to reinstall it.

- **The default data type** The default type of data used by the printer. Commonly used printer data types include: enhanced metafile (EMF) and RAW. EMF uses the printer control language (PCL) page description language. EMF documents are sent to the print server with minimal preliminary processing and are then processed, which requires more processing on the print server. RAW is commonly used with PostScript printers. RAW documents are fully processed on the client before they are sent to the print server and aren't modified by the print server.

Checking Specific Printers, Drivers, and Systems

To use PRINTDRIVERINFO to return driver information for remote print servers and network printers, use the /S: parameter followed by the domain name of the server, such as

```
printdriverinfo /s:corpserver01
```

Here, you are examining printer driver information on CorpServer01.

PRINTDRIVERINFO also lets you search for a specific driver by name. To do this, you use the /D: parameter followed by the driver name, such as

```
printdriverinfo /d:"hp business inkjet 1100 series"
```

Here, you are looking for the HP Business InkJet 1100 series driver information.

Note   Unfortunately, you cannot use a wildcard when specifying the driver name. You must type the full driver name.

If you know the printer name, based on the entry in the Printer And Faxes folder of Control Panel, you can also search for a specific printer by name. Here, you use the /P: parameter followed by the printer name, such as

```
printdriverinfo /p:"magicolor 2300 dl"
```

The result is a report from PRINTDRIVERINFO by printer name. This report contains additional information, including the printer name and a printer info section that looks like this:

```
-=Misc Printer Info=-
Share Name: centralprinter
Port Name: IP_192.168.1.100
Print Processor Name: MIMFPR_B
Data type Name: IMF
```

The additional information tells you the following:

- **The print share name**   If the printer is shared over the network, the name is given. By default, the print share name is the first eight characters of the printer name with any spaces omitted.

- **The printer port**   The port used by the printer. Printers directly connected to a print server use LPT, COM or USB ports. Network-attached printers usually have TCP/IP ports. The default TCP/IP port name shows the IP address of the port. More typically, however, the TCP/IP port name is based on the printer name. This is generally the case for HP printers that are attached to a network.

- **The print processor**   Each print device has an associated print processor. The print processor is responsible for creating the RAW print data necessary for printing on the print device.

Tracking Print Spooler Information and Usage Statistics

Tracking print spooler information and usage statistics can help you answer these important questions about the print services in your organization:

- How busy is the print server on average?
- What is the average size of print jobs?
- How many print jobs are queued and waiting?
- What is the current printer status?
- How long has the print spooler been running?
- How long has the printer been up?
- How long has the print server been up?

Why are the answers to these questions important? They're important because, if you know the answers, you can proactively manage and maintain your organization's print services. You can also plan for future needs. Thus, rather than being a firefighter who responds only to problems, you'll be able to stay a step ahead of any major issues, thereby providing a better experience for users throughout your organization.

Getting Spooling Information for Capacity Planning and Troubleshooting

The key tool you'll use to track print spool information and usage statistics is the SPLINFO command from the Windows Server 2003 Resource Kit. This command has two display modes: summary and verbose. The summary display mode is the default and it shows you the overall statistics for a particular print server. The verbose mode, displayed when you use the /V parameter, adds individual printer details to the summary information.

To see summary information for a print server to which you are logged on, type **splinfo** at the command prompt. For a remote print server, add the UNC name of the server. If, for instance, you wanted to see the summary statistics for CorpServer03, you would type

```
splinfo \\corpserver03
```

Whether you are working with a local or a remote print server, the summary details are similar to Listing 14-2.

Listing 14-2 Standard Output from SPLINFO

```
Number Local Printers        3
Windows Version              5.1 Build 2600 (Service Pack 1)
Number of Processors         1 PROCESSOR_INTEL Level 15
Total Jobs Spooled           258
Total Bytes Printed          14,512,067,850
Average Bytes/Job            56,248,325
Browse List Requested        0
Browse Printer Added         0
Spooler Up Time              04:17:18
Server Up Time               04:17:52
```

 Note If there aren't any printers installed on the system you are checking, SPLINFO will report "No local printers installed."

Here, three printers are configured on a single-processor system running Windows XP Professional. Although these are referred to as local printers, they aren't necessarily attached to the computer physically. They could also

be network-attached, as is the case for printers that have their own network cards. If you examine the usage statistics, you find that

- On average, the server prints about one job per minute. That is 258 total print jobs on a print spooler that's been up for four hours and 17 minutes (257 minutes).

- The average print job is about 50 megabytes (MB) in size. You can calculate this by dividing the average number of bytes by 1,024 to get the kilobyte (KB) size and then dividing again by 1,024 to get the MB size.

- In total, about 12 gigabytes (GB) of print data has been spooled over the four hours and 17 minutes.

Here, you have a busy print server that is taking a heavy load, especially considering print services are running on Windows XP Professional (and this is likely a desktop-class system). If you examined the printer statistics over several intervals and after several restarts of the printer/spooler and found the same usage, you would have several causes for concern, because the printer is very busy and the average print job is fairly large at 50 MB. With this level of usage, you would want to monitor the server's usage and performance closely as discussed in Chapter 7, "Monitoring Processes and Performance." You would want to dig deeper into the usage statistics, looking at details for each printer configured. You might also want to consider whether print services would perform better on Windows Server 2003 or whether there are additional services being performed that should be moved to another system on the network. After monitoring the system's performance and usage over a sufficient interval, you might find that

- Additional memory is required because of the large average size of print jobs.

- Additional processing power is required because of the number of jobs handled on average.

- Additional disk space is required or that a dedicated disk drive for the spooler folder is needed.

You might also find that this system is simply one that you should routinely monitor to help ensure smooth print services operations. Here, you could easily automate the monitoring by creating a script that writes the usage statistics to a log file and then scheduling the script to run on a periodic basis as discussed in Chapter 4, "Scheduling Tasks to Run Automatically."

Getting Detailed Spooler Information for Capacity Planning and Troubleshooting

When you use the /V parameter for the SPLINFO command, you get detailed information on each configured printer. To see how this information is displayed, consider Listing 14-3. Keep in mind that you usually want to monitor printer usage over several days to evaluate any upgrades or changes that might be required. During that time, you might want to stop and then start the spooling to reset the statistics.

Listing 14-3 Verbose Output from SPLINFO

```
Number Local Printers      3
Windows Version            5.1 Build 2600 (Service Pack 1)
Number of Processors       1 PROCESSOR_INTEL Level 15
Total Jobs Spooled         258
Total Bytes Printed        14,512,067,850
Average Bytes/Job          56,248,325
Browse List Requested      0
Browse Printer Added       0
Spooler Up Time            04:17:18
Server Up Time             04:17:52


Printer Name               magicolor 2300 DL
Total Printer Jobs:        96
Total Printed Bytes:       8,451,245,024
Printer Up Time            04:17:21
Number of Jobs in Queue    3
cRef                       2
cRefIC                     0
Max cRef                   5
Number spooling            2
Max Number spooling        3
Printer Started            11/15/2004  16:57 (UTC)
Average Bytes/Job          88,033,802
Printer Change Count ID    28633
Printer Status             0


Printer Name               hp businessjet 1100 series
Total Printer Jobs:        162
Total Printed Bytes:       6,060,822,826
Printer Up Time            04:17:21
Number of Jobs in Queue    24
cRef                       0
cRefIC                     0
Max cRef                   1
Number spooling            1
Max Number spooling        2
Printer Started            11/15/2004  16:57 (UTC)
Average Bytes/Job          37,412,486
Printer Change Count ID    43c3c1
Printer Status             0
```

```
Printer Name                   hp officejet 5500 series
Total Printer Jobs:            0
Total Printed Bytes:           0
Printer Up Time                04:17:21
Number of Jobs in Queue        0
cRef                           8
cRefIC                         0
Max cRef                       10
Number spooling                0
Max Number spooling            0
Printer Started                11/15/2004  16:57 (UTC)
Average Bytes/Job              0
Printer Change Count ID        54619b
Printer Status                 0
```

For each printer, you'll want to examine the following statistics:

- **Total printer jobs** Shows how many printer jobs have been processed since the printer was started. Compare the total number of printer jobs to the printer's "up" time to get a good indicator of how busy the printer really is. The Minolta QMS magicolor color laser printer in the listing handles about 22 print jobs per hour, so it is fairly busy.

- **Total printed bytes** Shows the total number of bytes printed since the printer was started. This gives you a good idea of how much data the printer is handling. Compare the total printed bytes to the printer "up" time to get a good indicator of how much data the printer is handling on an hourly or daily basis. The Minolta QMS magicolor color laser printer in the listing handles about 1.84 GB of data per hour.

Note In some printer configurations, print jobs are saved after they've been queued. This allows a user to resubmit a document to the printer from the print queue instead of from an application. If you've configured a printer to keep print jobs, you'd want to keep close tabs on how much data is being printed on average per hour. This would help you determine how much disk space will be required to maintain print services and give you a good indicator of how frequently you might need to clear old jobs from the print queue.

- **Number of jobs in queue** Shows the number of printer jobs queued and waiting to print. Busy printers will typically have several jobs queued and waiting, especially at peak usage times. If you frequently see many jobs waiting to print, however, the printer may be overloaded. In the listing, three printers are configured but only two are being used: a Minolta QMS magicolor color laser printer and an HP Business InkJet printer. Of the two printers, the Business InkJet is used more often and, with 24 print jobs queued, the printer might be overloaded. Here, you could help improve the situation by letting users know about the faster magicolor printer available or perhaps setting the magicolor as the default for some of these users. You might also want to let a select number of users know about the HP OfficeJet printer. However, this printer is more likely someone's personal printer and it's just not being used at this time.

- **Average bytes per print job** Shows the average size of jobs that are being printed. Most printers have internal memory and ideally you want that memory to be large enough so that entire print jobs can be handed off to the print device. In the listing, the average size of jobs printed to the Minolta QMS magicolor color laser printer is about 84 MB and as the printer has only 32 MB of memory this is a cause for concern. Here, you would probably want to add memory to the print device. Note that you would need to refer to the printer's config page (which can be printed on the printer itself) to determine its installed RAM.

- **Printer up time** Shows how long the printer has been up, meaning the spool and the print queue. This statistic doesn't show how long the physical print device has been up.

Managing Printers

From the command line, you can install and manage printers using the Prnmngr utility. Prnmngr is configured as a Windows script so if this is your first time working with Windows scripts from the system's command line or you've configured WScript as the primary script host, you will need to set CScript as the default script host. You do this by typing **cscript //h:cscript //s** at the command prompt. You will then work with the command-line script host rather than the graphical script host. Keep in mind that the script host is set on a per-user basis. Thus, if you are running a script as a specific user, that user might not have CScript configured as the default script host and you might want to type **cscript //h:cscript //s** as a line in your script.

Understanding Printer Management

With Prnmngr, you can work with print devices that are physically attached to a computer and employed only by the user who logs on to that computer, called *local print devices*, and print devices that are set up for remote access over the network, called *network print devices*. The key difference between a local printer and a network printer is that local printers aren't shared. When you share printers over the network, you use a computer to host the necessary print services. This computer is called a *print server*.

The primary job of a print server is to share the print device out to the network and to handle print spooling. Using a printer server gives you a central print queue that you can manage easily and makes it so that you don't have to install printer drivers on client systems. You don't have to use a print server, however. Users can connect directly to a network-attached printer and in this case, the network-attached printer is handled much like a local printer attached directly to the user's computer. Here, users connect to the printer and each user has a different print queue that must be managed separately.

When you install a printer on a computer, you are actually configuring a print queue so that it can be used to route print jobs to the physical print device. So when we talk about installing a printer or configuring a printer, we are really talking about installing and configuring a print queue so that it can be used to route jobs to the physical print device.

If you want to install or configure printers, you'll need the appropriate administrator privileges. In a domain, this means you must be a member of the Administrators, Print Operators, or Server Operators group. To connect to and use a printer, you don't have to be an administrator. You only need the appropriate access permissions.

Installing Physically Attached Print Devices

Physically attached print devices are connected to a computer directly and can be configured as local print devices or as network print devices. Although a local print device is only available to users logged on to the computer, a network device is accessible to any network users as a shared print device. To get started, connect the print device to the server using the appropriate serial, parallel, or USB cable and then turn on the printer. If you are configuring a network printer, this computer will act as the print server. With Plug-and-Play printers, simply plugging in the printer will start the automatic installation and configuration process if someone is logged on to the computer.

You can install a local printer manually using Prnmngr and the following parameters:

- **–A AddPrinter** Specifies that you want to add or install a local printer.

- **–P PrinterName** Assigns a name to the printer. This is the name you'll see whether working with Printers And Faxes or with the command line.

- **–M PrinterModel** Specifies the model of the printer. This must be the exact model as specified by the manufacturer. The model name determines the printer driver used.

- **–R PrinterPort** Sets the port to which the printer is connected. This can be a parallel port, such as LPT1:, LPT2:, or LPT3:, a serial port, such as COM1:, COM2:, or COM3:, or a USB port, such as USB001.

Note The case you use when setting the printer name and model is the case that is displayed at the command prompt and in dialog boxes. However, although these names are case-aware, they aren't case-sensitive. This means that, so far as Windows is concerned, centralcolorlaser is the same as CentralColorLaser.

To configure physically attached printers, you don't have to be logged on to the computer locally. You can also remotely install this type of printer. To do this, use the –S parameter to specify the name of the remote computer to which you want to add a local printer. If necessary, use the –U and –W parameters to specify the user name and password to use when connecting to a remote computer.

 Note You cannot specify a username and password when working at a local command prompt whether physically logged on or remotely connected. If you try to do this, you will get an error. On Windows Server 2003, this error is misleading because it states, "User credentials cannot be used for connections." Windows XP Professional more correctly states, "User credentials cannot be used for local connections."

To see how Prnmngr is used, consider the following examples:

Configure an HP 5500 Series InkJet printer on USB001:

```
prnmngr -a -p "OfficeJetPrinter" -m "hp officejet 5500 series" -r
USB001
```

Configure an HP 1100 DN Series InkJet printer on LPT1:

```
prnmngr -a -p "BusinessJetPrinter" -m "hp businessjet 1100 series
DN" -r LPT1
```

Configure an Epson Stylus Photo printer on cdesign09 using USB001:

```
prnmngr -a -p "PhotoPrinter" -m "epson stylus photo 1270 esc/p 2"
-r USB001 -s cdesign09
```

Configure an Epson Stylus Color printer on mteam06 using LPT1:

```
prnmngr -a -p "ColorPrinter" -m "epson stylus color esc/p 2" -r LPT1:
-s mteam06 -u wrstanek -w goldfish
```

If a printer is installed successfully, Prnmngr will report "Added printer". Otherwise, it will report "Unable to add printer" and describe the error that occurred. The most common error is due to a misentered or unknown device model, which causes Prnmngr to report that the printer driver is unknown. Ensure that you are using the correct model name.

Note If this is the first printer installed on a computer, it will be set at the default printer. The printer will not be shared, however. If you want to share the printer so that others can use it, see the section of this chapter titled "Sharing Printers."

Tip You can create additional printers for the same print device. The only requirements are that the printer name and the share name be unique. Having additional printers for the same print device allows you to set different properties to serve different needs. You can, for example, have one configuration for low priority print jobs and another for high-priority print jobs.

Installing Network-Attached Print Devices

Network-attached print devices are attached directly to the network through a network adapter card and are typically configured as network print devices so that they are accessible to network users as shared print devices. To get started, connect the printer to the network and configure it to use an appropriate IP address or obtain an IP address from a DHCP server. Follow the steps as discussed in the printer manual from the manufacturer.

After you configure TCP/IP on the printer, you will need to create a TCP/IP port on the computer which will act as the print server for the printer. The port is used to make a connection over the network to the printer. You can then install the printer as you would a physically attached print device. The only difference is that you use –R to specify the TCP/IP port you created rather than an LPT, COM or USB port. For example, if you created a TCP/IP port called IP_192.168.10.15, you can add a printer that uses the port using the following command line

```
prnmngr -a -p "CentralColorLaser" -m "magicolor 2300 dl" -r
IP_192.168.10.15 -s corpsvr03
```

Here, you install a Minolta QMS magicolor color laser printer so that it uses a TCP/IP port. Because the printer is configured on CorpSvr03, that computer will act as the printer server for this device. The printer will not be set as the default printer for any users, nor will it be shared. If you want to share the printer so that others can use it, see the section of this chapter titled "Sharing Printers."

Listing Printers Configured on a Computer

You can list all the printers that are configured on the local computer by typing **prnmngr –l**. If you want to view this information for a remote computer, add the –S parameter followed by the computer name, such as: **prnmngr –l –s corpsvr03**. As necessary, you can use the –U and –W parameters to set the user name and password of the logon account to use as well.

The output shows the name of the print server (or blank if you are working on a local computer) as well as other important information about each printer that is configured. Here is an example:

```
Server name corpsvr03
Printer name magicolor 2300 DL
Share name magicolo
Driver name magicolor 2300 DL
Port name hpbusinessinkjet1100
Comment Main printer for the fifth floor.
Location 5/ne
Print processor MIMFPR_B
Data type IMF
Parameters
Attributes 2633
Priority 1
Default priority 0
Status Idle
Average pages per minute 0

Number of printers enumerated 1
```

The printer, driver, and port names were set when the printer was installed. The printer is shared as well, making it available to users in the domain for printing. If you wanted to move the printer to a new print server, the only information you really need to note is the driver name, which in most cases is the same as the printer's model.

Viewing and Setting the Default Printer

You can display the default printer for the current logged on user by typing **prnmngr –g** at the command prompt. If you want the user to have a different default printer, you can type **prnmngr –t –p** followed by the name of the printer that should be the default, such as

```
prnmngr -t -p "magicolor 2300 DL"
```

If successful, Prnmngr will report that the printer is now set as the default. Otherwise, Prnmngr will report an error. Typically, a "Not Found" error means that you entered an invalid printer name.

Renaming Printers

Renaming printers is one printer task that you can't perform with Prnmngr. The command utility that you use for this task is Prncnfg, which is available in the Windows Server 2003 Resource Kit. The syntax for renaming printers is

```
prncnfg -x -p CurrentPrinterName -z NewPrinterName
```

Here, you use Prncnfg with the –X parameter to indicate that you want to rename a printer. Then specify the current printer name with the –P parameter and set the new printer name with the –Z parameter, such as

```
prncnfg -x -p "CentralColorLaser" -z "EngineeringPrinter"
```

If the printer exists, Prncnfg will report that it has renamed the printer and set the new printer name.

You can also rename printers that are on remote computers. To do this, use the –S parameter to specify the name of the remote computer, such as

```
prncnfg -x -s corpsvr03 -p "CentralColorLaser" -z "EngineeringPrinter"
```

Here, you are renaming a printer on CorpSvr03. This command doesn't let you set the account for logon, however.

Deleting Printers

Prnmngr provides two ways to delete printers that you no longer want to be available on a particular computer. You can delete individual printers using the command

```
prnmngr -d -p PrinterName
```

such as

```
prnmngr -d -p "magicolor 2300 DL"
```

If you enter an invalid printer name, Prnmngr will report that it is unable to delete the printer because the printer wasn't found. If you do not have permission to delete the printer, Prnmngr will report that it is unable to enumerate printers due to the user credentials. You'll need to log on with an account that has the appropriate administrator privileges. Note that this isn't the case when you work with remote computers. When you work with remote computers, you can specify the logon account using the –U and –W parameters, such as

```
prnmngr -d -p "magicolor 2300 DL" -s corpsvr03 -u wrstanek -p goldfish
```

You can delete all printers from a computer using

```
prnmngr -x
```

Prnmngr won't prompt you to confirm this action, but it will tell you about each printer deleted, such as

```
Deleted printer OfficeJet
Deleted printer CentralPrinter

Number of local printers and connections enumerated 2
Number of local printers and connections deleted 2
```

Managing TCP/IP Ports for Network-Attached Printers

TCP/IP ports are used to make connections to network-attached printers. You create and manage TCP/IP ports using Prnport. Like Prnmngr, Prnport is a Windows script that must be run using the command-line script host.

Creating and Changing TCP/IP Ports for Printers

You tell Prnport that you want to add a TCP/IP port by using the –A parameter. Then you specify the port name using the –R parameter and specify the printer's IP address using the –H parameter. It is common to base the port name on the IP address for the printer to which you are connecting. For example, if you are configuring a port for a printer on IP address 192.168.10.15, you might use a port name of IP_192.168.10.15.

You must also specify the output protocol that the port should use. The output protocol is set with the –O parameter and is either **raw** or **lpr**. Most printers use the Raw protocol. With Raw, data is sent unmodified over the port to the printer using a designated port number. In most cases, this is port 9100, which is why this is used as the default value. You can set the port number to a different value using the –N parameter. With LPR, the port is used in conjunction with a LPD (line printer daemon) print queue. You set the print queue name using the –Q parameter.

As with most printer configuration commands, you don't have to be logged on to the computer locally to configure ports. If you want to configure ports on a remote computer, use the –S parameter to specify the name of the remote computer to work with. As necessary, use the –U and –W parameters to specify the user name and password to use when connecting to the remote computer. The user name can be specified as domain\username if the logon domain is different from the current domain.

Consider the following examples:

Configure a port to use TCP Raw and connect to 192.168.10.15 over port 9100:

```
prnport -a -r IP_192.168.10.15 -h 192.168.10.15 -o raw
```

Configure a port to use Raw output and connect to 10.10.1.50 over port 9500:

```
prnport -a -r IP_192.168.10.15 -h 10.10.1.50 -o raw -n 9500
```

Configure a port to use LPR output and connect to 172.20.18.2. Set the queue name to LPRQUEUE:

```
prnport -a -r IP_192.168.10.15 -h 172.20.18.2 -o lpr -q lprqueue
```

Configure a port on CORPSVR03 to use TCP Raw and connect to 192.168.10.15 over port 9100:

```
prnport -a -r IP_192.168.10.15 -h 192.168.10.15 -o raw -s corpsvr03
```

If a port is created successfully, Prnport will report "Created/updated port." Otherwise, it will report "Unable to create/update port" and describe the error that occurred.

Most network-attached printers also support the Simple Network Management Protocol (SNMP). To allow the printer to use this protocol, you must enable SNMP using the –Me parameter then set an SNMP community name using the –Y parameter and SNMP device index using the –I parameter. Typically, the community name is set to *public*, which indicates the print device is available for use and management by anyone on the network. The device index is used to designate a particular device in an SNMP community. The first device has an index of 1, the second an index of 2, and so on.

Consider the following example:

prnport –a –r IP_192.168.10.15 –h 192.168.10.15 –o raw –me –y public –i 1

Note You can specifically disable SNMP using the –Md parameter.

Here you configure a port to use TCP Raw and connect to 192.168.10.15 over Port 9100. You also enable SNMP and configure the SNMP community name as public and the device index as 1.

If you want to change the TCP/IP port configuration later, you can do this using Prnport with the –T parameter. Here, you use the –R parameter to specify the port you want to work with, and any other parameters to set the related property values. Consider the following example:

prnport –a –r MainPrinter –h 10.10.12.50 –o raw –md

Here, you specify that you want to change the MainPrinter TCP/IP port. You set 10.10.12.50 as the IP address, the output protocol as Raw and disable SNMP.

Listing Information About TCP/IP Ports Used by Printers

You can list all the printer TCP/IP ports that are configured on the local computer by typing **prnport –l**. If you want to view this information for a remote computer, add the –S parameter followed by the computer name, such as: **prnport –l –s corpsvr03**. As necessary, you can use the –U and –W parameters to set the user name and password of the logon account to use as well.

The output shows the name of the print server (or blank if you are working a local computer) as well as other important information about each port that is configured. Here is an example of the information provided for a RAW port:

```
Server name
Port name IP_192.168.1.101
Host address 192.168.1.101
Protocol RAW
Port number 9100
SNMP Enabled
Community public
Device index 1
```

Here is an example of the information provided for an LPR port:

```
Server name
Port name IP_192.168.1.101
Host address 192.168.1.101
Protocol LPR
Queue crownnet
Byte Count Enabled
SNMP Enabled
Community public
Device index 1
```

Note The LPR port information may show incorrectly that byte counting is enabled. When enabled, the computer counts the number of bytes in a document before sending it to the printer. Most printers do not require byte counting and it can slow performance because it is very time-consuming to count each byte in documents when printing.

Deleting TCP/IP Ports Used by Printers

You can delete individual ports used by printers with the following syntax:

```
prnport -d -r PortName
```

such as

```
prnport -d -r IP_192.168.1.101
```

If you enter an invalid printer name, Prnport will report that it is unable to delete the port because it wasn't found. If you do not have permission to delete the printer, Prnport will report that it is unable to enumerate printers due to the user credentials. You'll need to log on with an account that has the appropriate administrator privileges. Note that this isn't the case when you work with remote computers. When you work with remote computers, you can specify the logon account using the –U and –W parameters, such as

```
prnport -d -r IP_192.168.1.101 -s corpsvr03 -u wrstanek -p goldfish
```

Configuring Printer Properties

You can view and configure printer properties using the Prncnfg Windows script with the –T parameter. Regardless of which property you are working with, Prncnfg expects you to use the –P parameter to specify the name of the printer you want to work with. As with most printer configuration commands, you don't have to be logged on to the computer locally to configure printer properties. If you want to change printer properties for remote computers (other than the printer name), you can use the –S parameter to specify the name of the remote computer. As necessary, use the –U and –W parameters to specify the user name and password to use when connecting to the remote computer. The user name can be specified as *domain\username* if the logon domain is different from the current domain.

Adding Comments and Location Information

You can make it easier for users to determine which printer to use when by adding comments and location information to printers. Comments provide general information about the printer, such as the type of print device and who is responsible for it. Location describes the actual physical location of the print device. Once these values are provided, they are displayed on the General tab in the printer's Properties dialog box.

The syntax for adding comments and location information to printers is

```
prncnfg -t -p PrinterName -m "Comment" -l "Location"
```

Here, you use Prncnfg with the –T parameter to indicate that you want to change printer properties. Then specify the comment text with the –M parameter and set the printer location information with the –L parameter, such as

```
prncnfg -t -s corpsrv03 -p "CentralColorLaser" -m "Main Engineering
Printer" -l "5th Floor SE"
```

Prncnfg should report that it configured the printer. If it doesn't, you probably forgot a double quotation mark or one of the parameter switches. You don't, of course, have to set both a comment and a location. You can set these values separately as well.

Sharing Printers

Printers you add at the command line aren't automatically shared for others to use. If you want to share such a printer, you must specifically configure this using Prncnfg. Use the –T parameter to specify that you are setting or changing a printer property and the –P parameter to specify the printer to work with. Then use the –H parameter to set the share name and the +Shared parameter to enable sharing. For compatibility with pre–Windows 2000 computers, the share name should be only eight characters in length and should not contain spaces.

In large organizations, you might want the printer share name to indicate where the printer is located to save users from having to examine the printer properties. For example, if a printer were located in the southeast corner of the fifth floor, you might want to name the printer share FifthSE. Consider the following example:

```
prncnfg -t -s corpsrv03 -p "CentralColorLaser" -h "FifthSE" +shared
```

Here you are configuring the CentralColorLaser printer on CorpSrv03 to be shared as FifthSE.

To remove printer sharing, you use the –Shared parameter. Here you are removing printer sharing from the printer configured in the previous example:

```
prncnfg -t -s corpsrv03 -p "CentralColorLaser" -shared
```

Publishing Printers in Active Directory

You can make it easier for users to find printers that are available by publishing their information in Active Directory. Once a printer is published, users can search for it based on its location and capabilities, such as whether it is on the fifth floor or whether it can print in color.

You configure printer publishing using Prncnfg. If you want to publish a printer in Active Directory, you use the –T parameter to specify that you are setting or changing a printer property and –P to specify the printer to work with. Then use the +Published parameter to specify that the printer should be published or the –Published parameter to specify that the printer should be removed from the directory.

Consider the following examples:

Publish the CentralColorLaser printer on CorpSrv03 in Active Directory:

```
Prncnfg -t -s corpsrv03 -p "CentralColorLaser" +published
```

Remove the local printer named OfficeJet from Active Directory:

```
Prncnfg -t-p "OfficeJet" -published
```

In either case, Prncnfg should report that it configured the printer. It won't report an error, however, if the printer was already published or removed.

Setting a Separator Page and Changing Print Device Mode

Separator pages can be used at the beginning of a print job to make it easier to find a document on a busy print device. They can be used to change the print device mode, such as whether the print device uses PostScript or Printer Control Language (PCL).

Separator pages are stored in the *%SystemRoot%*\System32 folder. Three default separator pages are defined on Windows systems:

- **pcl.sep**   Switches the print device to PCL mode and prints a separator page before each document

- **pscript.sep**   Switches the print device to PostScript mode but doesn't print a separator page

- **sysprint.sep**   Switches the print device to PostScript mode and prints a separator page before each document

You can specify that a printer should use one of these separator pages or any other separator page that is in the *%SystemRoot%*\System32 folder by using Prncnfg. Use the –T parameter to specify that you are setting or changing a printer property and the –P parameter to specify the printer to work with. Then use the –F parameter to specify the separator page to use.

Consider the following example:

```
Prncnfg -t -s corpsrv03 -p "CentralColorLaser" -f sysprint.sep
```

Here you configure the CentralColorLaser printer on CorpSrv03 to use sysprint.sep.

To stop using the separator page, use the –F parameter with the value " ", such as

```
Prncnfg -t -s corpsrv03 -p "CentralColorLaser" -f " "
```

Scheduling and Prioritizing Print Jobs

You can use Prncnfg to manage print job priorities and scheduling from the command line. Print jobs always print in order of priority, with 1 being the lowest priority and 99 being the highest priority. Jobs with higher priority print before jobs with lower priority. Thus if a physical print device has several printers (print queues), any print job with a higher priority will print before a print job with lower priority. Use the –T parameter to specify that you are setting or changing a printer property and the –P parameter to specify the printer to work with. Then use the –O parameter to set the priority, such as

```
prncnfg -t -p "EngineeringPrinter" -o 50
```

Here you specify that print jobs using the EngineeringPrinter to route print jobs to the related printer have a priority of 50. If for example a Marketing Printer was also configured to use the same physical print device but had a lower priority, engineering print jobs would always print first.

Printers are either always available or available only during the hours specified. You set printer availability using the –St parameter to specify the time of day after which the printer is available and the –Ut parameter to specify the time of day after which the printer is no longer available. Times are set using a 24-hour clock, such as

```
prncnfg -t -p "EngineeringPrinter" -st 0530 -ut 1930
```

Here you specify that the printer is available from 05:30 A.M. to 7:30 P.M. each day.

Configuring Spooling and Other Advanced Printer Options

For print devices attached to the network, you'll usually want the printer to spool files rather than print files directly. Print spooling makes it possible to use a printer (print queue) to manage print jobs. Spooling can be configured using the following Prncnfg options:

- **+Direct** With +Direct, you spool print documents so programs finish printing faster rather than printing directly. This is the default.

- **–Direct** With –Direct, you configure the printer to print directly rather than spool. Use –Direct if you cannot print using any of the spooling options.

- **+Queued** With +Queued, you start printing after last page is spooled. Select this option if you want the entire document to be spooled before printing begins. This option ensures that the entire document makes it into the print queue before printing. If for some reason printing is canceled or not completed, the job won't be printed.

- **–Queued** With –Queued, you start printing as soon as the document begins spooling. Select this option if you want printing to begin immediately when the print device isn't already in use. This option is preferable when you want print jobs to be completed faster or when you want to ensure that the application returns control to users as soon as possible. This is the default.

- **+Enabledevq** With +Enabledevq, the spooler checks the printer setup and matches it to the document setup before sending the document to the print device. If there's a mismatch, the spooler holds the print job but allows correctly matched documents to keep printing. Selecting this option is a good idea if you frequently have to change printer form or tray assignments.

- **–Enabledevq** With –Enabledevq, the spooler doesn't check the printer setup before sending documents to the print device. If there's a mismatch, the printer will usually stop printing and wait for a user to cancel the print job, change printer form or insert a paper tray with the necessary paper type. This is the default.

Other advanced Prncnfg options that you can configure include the following:

- **+Keepprintedjobs** With +Keepprintedjobs, jobs aren't deleted from the queue after they've printed. Use this option if you're printing files that can't easily be recreated. You can reprint the document without having to recreate it.

- **–Keepprintedjobs** With –Keepprintedjobs, jobs are deleted from the queue after they've printed. This frees the disk space being used by the print job but doesn't allow you to reprint the document from the print queue. This is the default.

- **+Docompletefirst** With +Docompletefirst, jobs that have completed spooling will print before jobs in the process of spooling—regardless of whether the spooling jobs have higher priority. This is the default.

- **–Docompletefirst** With –Docompletefirst, jobs with higher priority will preempt jobs with lower priority. Thus if a higher priority job comes into the queue, a lower priority job would stop printing and the higher priority job would start printing.

- **+Enablebidi** With +Enablebidi, you enable metafile spooling and turn on advanced printing features if they are supported, such as page order, booklet printing and pages per sheet. If you note compatibility problems when using +Enablebidi, you should disable this feature. This is the default.

- **–Enablebidi** With –Enablebidi, you disable metafile spooling and turn off advanced printing features. Use this option if you experience compatibility problems with the printer.

To see how these options can be used, consider the following examples:

Configure SalesPrinter on sales06 to print directly and keep printed jobs:

```
prncnfg -t -s sales06 -p "SalesPrinter" +direct +keepprintedjobs
```

Configure MainPrinter on the local computer to start printing after the last page is spooled:

```
prncnfg -t -p "MainPrinter" -queued
```

Configure HPLaserJet on corpsvr09 to hold mismatched documents and disabled metafile spooling:

```
prncnfg -t -s corpsvr09 -p "HPLaserJet" +enabledevq -enablebidi
```

Solving Spooling Problems

Windows uses the Print Spooler service to control the spooling of print jobs. If this service isn't running, print jobs can't be spooled.

Checking the Print Spooler Service

You can check the status of the Print Spooler service on a local computer by typing

```
sc query type= service | find /v "x0"
```

For a remote computer, you specify the UNC server name, such as

```
sc \\Engsvr04 query type= service | find /v "x0"
```

Either way the output should have a section for the spooler, which will look similar to this:

```
SERVICE_NAME: Spooler
DISPLAY_NAME: Print Spooler
TYPE                  : 110WIN32_OWN_PROCESS (interactive)
STATE                 : 4RUNNING
(STOPPABLE,NOT_PAUSABLE,ACCEPTS_SHUTDOWN)
```

This tells you that the Print Spooler service is running. If it was stopped, you might want to check the service configuration. You could do this by typing

```
sc qc spooler
```

or

```
sc \\Engsvr04 qc
```

Among other things, the output tells you the startup setting for the Print Spooler, as shown here:

```
[SC] QueryServiceConfig SUCCESS

SERVICE_NAME: spooler
        TYPE                  : 110WIN32_OWN_PROCESS (interactive)
        START_TYPE            : 2AUTO_START
        ERROR_CONTROL         : 1NORMAL
        BINARY_PATH_NAME      : C:\WINDOWS\system32\spoolsv.exe
        LOAD_ORDER_GROUP      : SpoolerGroup
        TAG                   : 0
        DISPLAY_NAME          : Print Spooler
        DEPENDENCIES          : RPCSS
        SERVICE_START_NAME    : LocalSystem
```

The start_type should be AUTO_START, which indicates Print Spooler is set to start automatically.

Fixing a Corrupted Spooler

Spoolers can also become corrupted. If this happens, you'll find that the printer freezes or doesn't send jobs to the print device. Sometimes the print device may print pages of garbled data. In most of these cases, stopping and starting the Print Spooler service will resolve the problem. You can stop Print Spooler by typing

```
sc stop spooler
```

After the spool stops, restart it by typing

```
sc start spooler
```

If you are working with a remote computer, you can enter the computer name you want to work with as well, such as

```
sc \\Engsvr04 stop spooler
```

```
sc \\Engsvr04 start spooler
```

Other Services to Check

If this doesn't resolve the problem, you may want to check other related services, including any of the following if they are installed:

- TCP/IP Print Server
- Print Server for Macintosh
- Print Server for Unix

Note Some spooling problems can be related to permissions. You'll also want to check the printer access permissions.

Managing Print Queues and Individual Print Jobs

Several Windows scripts are available for working with print queues and the print jobs they contain. You use the Prnqctl utility to start, stop, or pause the printing of all documents in a printer queue. You use the Prnjobs utility to work with print jobs.

Viewing Jobs in the Queue

You can view jobs in print queues using Prnjobs. If you want to view all jobs for all printers on the local computer, type **prnjobs –l**. To view the jobs for a particular printer use the –P parameter to specify the printer name. For a remote computer, you can use the –S parameter to specify the remote computer you want to work with and if necessary use the –U and –W parameters to provide the user name and password required for access to the remote computer.

Consider the following examples:

View all print jobs on CorpSrv03:

```
prnjobs -l -s corpsrv03
```

View all print jobs for MainPrinter on the local computer:

```
prnjobs -l -p MainPrinter
```

The output for an individual job tells you the following:

- **Job ID**   The job identification number, which is needed when you want to work with individual print jobs.
- **Printer**   The name of the printer.
- **Document**   The document file name, which can include the name of the application that printed it.
- **Data Type**   The printer data type.
- **Driver Name**   The name of the print driver, which indicates the model of the printer.
- **Description**   The description of the printer.
- **Elapsed Time**   The length of time the document has been printing.
- **Job Status**   The status of the print job. Entries you'll see include Printing, Spooling, Paused, Deleting, and Restarting.
- **Notify**   The person notified when the print job is complete (if notification is configured)
- **Owner**   The document's owner.
- **Pages Printed**   The number of pages printed so far (if any).
- **Size**   The document size in bytes.
- **Time Submitted**   The time and date the print job was submitted.
- **Total Pages**   The total number of pages in the document.

Pausing the Printer and Resuming Printing

From time to time, you might need to pause a printer so that you can work with the physical print device or troubleshoot a problem. When you pause printing, the printer completes the current job and then halts all other jobs. You pause printing using Prnqctl. On a local printer, type **prnqctl –z**, using the –P parameter to set the name of the printer you want to pause. For a remote computer, you can use the –S parameter to specify the remote computer you want to work with and if necessary use the –U and –W parameters to provide the user name and password required for access to the remote computer.

To resume printing, use the –M parameter instead of the –Z parameter. This should restart printing of all documents in the print queue.

Consider the following examples:

Pause printing for EngineeringPrinter on CorpSrv03:

```
prnqctl -z -s corpsrv03 -p EngineeringPrinter
```

Pause print jobs for 5thfloorPrinter on the local computer:

```
prnqctl -z -p 5thfloorPrinter
```

Resume printing for EngineeringPrinter on CorpSrv03:

```
prnqctl -m -s corpsrv03 -p EngineeringPrinter
```

Emptying the Print Queue

You can use Prnqctl to empty a print queue and delete all of its contents. On a local printer, type **prnqctl –x**, using the –P parameter to set the name of the printer whose print queue you wish to empty. For a remote computer, you can use the –S parameter to specify the remote computer you want to work with and if necessary use the –U and –W parameters to provide the user name and password required for access to the remote computer.

Consider the following examples:

Empty the print queue for SalesPrinter on salespc06:

```
prnqctl -x -s salespc06 -p SalesPrinter
```

Empty the print queue for TempPrinter on the local computer:

```
prnqctl -x -p TempPrinter
```

If successful, Prnqctl reports that it successfully purged documents from the print queue. It will do so even if there are no documents in the print queue initially.

Pausing, Resuming, and Restarting Individual Document Printing

You can pause or resume printing of individual jobs as well. When you pause a job, you halt the printing of that document and let other documents print. When you resume a job, you tell the printer to resume printing the document from the point at which it was halted.

To pause a print job, you use the following syntax:

```
prnjobs -z -p PrinterName -j JobID
```

where *PrinterName* is the name of the printer you want to work with and *JobID* is the ID number of the print job to pause.

To resume a print job, you use the following syntax:

```
prnjobs -m -p PrinterName -j JobID
```

where *PrinterName* is the name of the printer you want to work with and *JobID* is the ID number of the print job to resume.

In either case, you work with printers on the local computer by default. For print queues on remote computers, you can use the –S parameter to specify the remote computer you want to work with and if necessary use the –U and –W parameters to provide the user name and password required for access to the remote computer.

Consider the following examples:

Pause printing job number 6 for EngineeringPrinter on CorpSrv03:

```
prnjobs -z -s corpsrv03 -p EngineeringPrinter -j 6
```

Pause printing job number 17 for 5thfloorPrinter on the local computer:

```
prnjobs -z -p 5thfloorPrinter -j 17
```

Resume printing job number 6 for EngineeringPrinter on CorpSrv03:

```
prnjobs -m -s corpsrv03 -p EngineeringPrinter -j 6
```

Prnjobs should report that it successfully paused or resumed printing of that job ID. If you use an invalid job ID, Prnjobs will report "unable to set the print job".

Removing a Document and Canceling a Print Job

You can use Prnjobs to cancel an individual print job and delete it from a print queue. On a local printer, type **prnjobs –x**, using the –P parameter to set the name of the printer and **–j** to specify the ID number of the document to be deleted. For a remote computer, you can use the –S parameter to specify the remote computer you want to work with and if necessary use the –U and –W parameters to provide the user name and password required for access to the remote computer.

Cancel printing job number 12 for MainPrinter on the local computer:

```
prnjobs -x -p MainPrinter -j 12
```

Cancel printing job number 9 for EngineeringPrinter on CorpSrv03:

```
prnjobs -x -s corpsrv03 -p EngineeringPrinter -j 9
```

If successful, Prnjobs reports that it successfully cancelled the print job. If you use an invalid job ID, Prnjobs will report "unable to set the print job".

Note If a document is printing when you cancel it, the print device may continue to print part or all of the document. This is because most print devices cache documents in an internal buffer, and the print device may continue to print the contents of this cache.

Chapter 15

Configuring, Maintaining, and Troubleshooting TCP/IP Networking

Being able to configure, maintain, and troubleshoot Transmission Control Protocol/Internet Protocol (TCP/IP) networking is a vital part of every administrator's job. This chapter starts with a discussion of the command-line tools available for performing these tasks, then delves into each area separately giving you the knowledge and techniques you'll need for successfully managing and supporting TCP/IP networking on Windows XP Professional and Windows Server 2003 systems.

Using the Network Services Shell

The network services shell (Netsh) is a command-line scripting utility that allows you to manage the configuration of various network services on local and remote computers. Netsh provides a separate command prompt that you can use in either interactive or noninteractive mode.

Working with Netsh Contexts

In interactive mode, you enter the shell by typing **netsh** and then specifying the context name of the network service you want to work with. Context names and their meanings are as follows:

- **aaaa** Authentication, authorization, accounting, and auditing. The context used to view and work with the AAAA database. That database is used by the Internet Authentication Service (IAS) and the Routing And Remote Access service.

- **dhcp** Dynamic Host Configuration Protocol (DHCP). The context used for viewing and managing DHCP servers. You use the DHCP context to assign TCP/IP configuration information dynamically to network clients.

- **diag** Network diagnostics. The context for viewing and troubleshooting network service parameters.

- **interface ip** Interface IP. The context used to view and manage the TCP/ IP network configuration of a computer. With Windows XP Service Pack 2, can also be used to manage the IPv4 Internet Connection Firewall (ICF).

 Security Alert When the IPv4 ICF is enabled under Windows XP SP2 or later, boot-time security is also enabled. Boot-time security makes it so the computer can only perform basic networking tasks at bootup for DNS, DHCP, and communications with domain controllers. Once the ICF is running, it loads and applies the run-time ICF policy and then removes the boot-time filters. While you cannot control boot-time security policy, you can configure the way ICF is used; you use Netsh to do this.

- **interface ipv6** Interface IP version 6. The context used to view and manage the IPv6 network configuration of a computer. With Windows XP Advanced Networking Pack or Service Pack 2 or later, can also be used to manage the IPv6 Internet Connection Firewall.
- **interface portproxy** Interface Port Proxy. The context used to manage proxies between IPv4 and IPv6 networks.
- **ipsec** Internet Protocol Security (IPsec). The context used to view and configure IPsec.
- **bridge** Network Bridge. The context used to enable or disable transport layer (OSI model layer 3) compatibility mode for network bridges. Also used to view the configuration settings of network bridges.
- **ras** Remote access server (RAS). The context used to view and manage remote access server configurations.
- **routing** Routing. The context used to manage routing servers. Used with Routing And Remote Access server.
- **rpc** Remote procedure call (RPC) helper. The context used to view and manage IP address interface settings as well as IP subnet addresses that are configured on a computer.
- **wins** Windows Internet Name Service (WINS). The context used to view and manage WINS server settings. You use WINS to resolve NetBIOS computer names to Internet Protocol (IP) addresses for pre–Windows 2000 computers.

 Note Some contexts and subcontexts are only available when you use Netsh on a local computer. The key one you'll notice is RPC, which is only available when working locally. In addition, some Netsh contexts and subcommands require the Routing And Remote Access service to be configured even when you are working with a local computer at the command line. If this is the case, you must set the Connections To Other Access Servers remote access policy to grant remote access permission, and then ensure that the remote access service is running.

The context name tells Netsh which helper DLL to load. The helper DLL pro-vides context-specific commands that you can use. For example, if you typed **netsh** to work interactively with Netsh and then typed **rpc** you would enter the RPC context. You could then type **show interfaces** to see the IP address inter-faces configured on the computer. As a series of steps, this would look like this:

1. Type **netsh**. The command prompt changes to: **Netsh>**.

2. Type **rpc**. The command prompt changes to: **Netsh rpc>**.

3. Type **show interfaces**. The IP address interfaces configured on the com-puter are displayed, such as

```
Subnet        Interface      Status     Description

127.0.0.0     127.0.0.1      Enabled    MS TCP Loopback interface

192.168.1.0   192.168.1.56   Enabled    Intel(R) PRO/100 VE Network Connection
```

Each context has a different set of commands available and some of these com-mands lead to subcontexts that have their own commands as well. Keep in mind the related service for the context must be configured on the domain to allow you to do meaningful work within a particular context. Regardless of what con-text you are working with, you can view the list of available commands by typ-ing **help**. Similarly, regardless of what context you are in, typing **quit** will exit the network services shell, returning you to the Windows command prompt. Well, that's how Netsh works interactively; it's slow and plodding, but it's good for beginners or while digging around to find out what commands are available.

Once you grow accustomed to working with Netsh, you'll want to use this utility in noninteractive mode. Noninteractive mode allows you to type in complete command sequences at the command-line prompt or within batch scripts. For example, the previous procedure which took three steps can be performed with this one command line:

```
netsh rpc show interfaces
```

Whether you insert this line into a script or type it directly at a command-line prompt, the resulting output is the same: a list of interfaces on the computer you are working with. As you can see, typing commands directly is a lot faster.

Working with Remote Computers

Netsh can be used to work with remote computers. To work interactively with a remote computer, you start netsh with the –R parameter and then specify the IP address or domain name of the computer to which you want to connect, such as

```
netsh -r 192.168.10.15
```

or

```
netsh -r corpsvr02
```

While you work with the remote computer, Netsh will include the computer IP address or name in its command prompt, such as

```
[corpsvr02] netsh>
```

Here you use Netsh to work remotely with CorpSvr02.

If you want to work noninteractively with remote computers, you must use the following syntax:

```
netsh -c Context -r RemoteComputer Command
```

where *Context* is the identifier for the context you want to work with, *Remote-Computer* is the name or IP address of the remote computer, and *Command* is the command to execute. Consider the following example:

```
netsh -c "interface ip" -r corpsvr02 show ipaddress
```

In this example, you use the Interface IP context to obtain a list of IP addresses configured on CorpSvr02. Here, you cannot use the RPC context to perform this task, because this context is only available on a local computer.

 Real World   To use Netsh, the Routing And Remote Access service must be configured on the network. Specifically, you must set the Connections To Other Access Servers remote access policy to grant remote access permission. Then, ensure that the remote access service is running.

Working with Script Files

As discussed previously, you can type in complete Netsh command sequences at the command line or within batch scripts. The catch is that you must know the complete command line you want to use and cannot rely on Netsh for help. Some command lines can be very long and complex. For example, the following commands connect to a DHCP server, configure a DHCP scope, and then activate the scope:

```
netsh dhcp server \\corpsvr02 add scope 192.168.1.0 255.255.255.0
MainScope PrimaryScope

netsh dhcp server \\corpsvr02 scope 192.168.1.0 add iprange
192.168.1.1 192.168.1.254

netsh dhcp server \\corpsvr02 scope 192.168.1.0 add excluderange
192.168.1.1 192.168.1.25

netsh dhcp server \\corpsvr02 scope 192.168.1.0 set state 1
```

If you save these commands to a batch script, you can run the script just as you would any other batch script. For example, if you named the script dhcpconfig.bat, you would type **dhcpconfig** to run the script.

When working with remote computers, you can place the script on a network share accessible from the remote computer and then log on remotely to execute the script. Or you can copy the script directly to the remote computer and then log on to execute it remotely. Either way works, but both involve a couple of extra steps. Fortunately, there's a faster way to run a script on a remote computer. To do this, you must change the script a bit and use the following syntax:

```
netsh -c Context -r RemoteComputer -f Script
```

where *Context* is the identifier for the context you want to work with, *Remote-Computer* is the name or IP address of the remote computer, and *Script* is the file or network path to the script to execute. Consider the following example:

```
netsh -c "dhcp server" -r corpsvr02 -f dhcpconfig.bat
```

In this example, you run a Netsh script called dhcpconfig.bat on CorpSvr02 using the DHCP Server context. Note that Server is a subcontext of the DHCP context. The script contains the following commands:

```
add scope 192.168.1.0 255.255.255.0 MainScope PrimaryScope
scope 192.168.1.0 add iprange 192.168.1.1 192.168.1.254
scope 192.168.1.0 add excluderange 192.168.1.1 192.168.1.25
scope 192.168.1.0 set state 1
```

These commands create, configure, and then activate a DHCP scope on the designated DHCP Server, CorpSvr02. Because you are already using the DHCP Server context on CorpSvr02, you don't need to type **netsh dhcp server \\corpsvr02** at the beginning of each command.

Managing TCP/IP Settings

Computers use IP addresses to communicate over TCP/IP. IP addressing can be configured manually or dynamically at the command line. With a manual configuration, you assign the computer a static IP address. Static IP addresses are fixed and don't change unless you change them. With a dynamic configuration, you configure the computer to get its IP address assignment from a DHCP server on the network. This IP address is assigned when the computer starts and might change over time. In domains, Windows servers use static IP addresses and Windows workstations used dynamic IP addresses.

Setting a Static IP Address

When you set a static IP address, you tell the computer the IP address to use, the subnet mask for this IP address, and, if necessary, the default gateway to use for internetwork communications. After you configure these IP settings, you will also need to configure name-resolution settings for Domain Name System (DNS) and possibly WINS.

You assign a static IP address using the Netsh Interface IP context. The command is SET ADDRESS and its syntax is

```
set address [name=]InterfaceName source=static addr=IPAddress
mask=SubnetMask [gateway={none | DefaultGateway
[[gwmetric=]GatewayMetric]}
```

In most cases, the interface name you are working with is "Local Area Connection." You can check to see the available interfaces by typing **netsh interface ip show interface** at the command prompt or, if you are in the Netsh Interface IP context, by typing **show interface**. The IP address you assign to the computer must not be used anywhere else on the network. The subnet mask field ensures that the computer communicates over the network properly. If the network uses subnets, the value you use may be different on each network segment within the company. If the computer needs to access other TCP/IP networks, the Internet, or other subnets, you must specify a default gateway. Use the IP address of the network's default router.

The gateway metric indicates the relative cost of using a gateway. If multiple default routes are available for a particular IP address, the gateway with the lowest cost is used first. If the computer can't communicate with the initial gateway, Windows Server 2003 tries to use the gateway with the next lowest metric. Unlike the GUI, Windows Server 2003 doesn't automatically assign a metric to the gateway. You must assign the metric manually.

Consider the following example:

```
set address name="Local Area Connection" source=static
addr=192.168.1.50 mask=255.255.255.0 gateway=192.168.1.1 gwmetric=1
```

Here you specify that you are working with the "Local Area Connection" interface, setting a static IP address of 192.168.1.50 with a network mask of 255.255.255.0. The default gateway is 192.168.1.1 and the gateway metric is 1.

Tip You can confirm the settings you just made by typing **netsh interface ip show address** at the command prompt or, if you are in the Netsh Interface IP context, by typing **show address**.

Setting a Dynamic IP Address

You can assign a dynamic IP address to any of the network adapters on a computer, provided there is a DHCP server available on the network. Afterward, you rely on the DHCP server to supply the necessary IP addressing information. Because the dynamic IP address can change, you shouldn't use a dynamic IP address for servers running Windows Server 2003.

You assign a dynamic IP address using the Netsh Interface IP context. The command is SET ADDRESS and its syntax is

```
set address name=InterfaceName source=dhcp
```

Note   If the computer already had an IP address configuration, using SET ADDRESS replaces the existing values. To add to the existing settings instead of replacing them, use the ADD ADDRESS command.

Consider the following example:

```
set address name="Local Area Connection" source=dhcp
```

Here you are working in the Netsh Interface IP context and specify that you want to set a dynamic IP address for the "Local Area Connection" interface.

Adding IP Addresses and Gateways

Both Windows XP Professional and Windows Server 2003 systems can have multiple IP addresses, even if the computer only has a single network adapter. Multiple IP addresses are useful if you want a single computer to appear as several computers or your network is divided into subnets and the computer needs access to these subnets to route information or provide other internetworking services.

Note   Keep in mind that when you use a single network adapter, IP addresses must be assigned to the same network segment or segments that are part of a single logical network. If your network consists of multiple physical networks, you must use multiple network adapters, with each network adapter being assigned an IP address in a different physical network segment.

You assign multiple IP addresses and gateways to a single network adapter using the ADD ADDRESS command of the Netsh Interface IP context. The syntax for this command is similar to that of SET ADDRESS. It is

```
add address [name=]InterfaceName addr=IPAddress mask=SubnetMask
[[gateway=]DefaultGateway [gwmetric=]GatewayMetric]
```

Consider the following example:

```
add address name="Local Area Connection" addr=192.168.2.12
mask=255.255.255.0 gateway=192.168.2.1 gwmetric=1
```

Note   If you specify a gateway, you must also specify the gateway metric. As before, you can confirm the settings you just made by typing **show address**.

Here you specify that you are working with the "Local Area Connection" interface and adding the IP address of 192.168.2.12 with a network mask of 255.255.255.0. The default gateway for this IP address is 192.168.2.1 and the gateway metric is 1.

Setting DNS Servers to Use

Computers use DNS to determine a computer's IP address from its host name or its host name from an IP address. For computers using static IP addresses, you must tell them which DNS servers to use; you can do this using the Netsh Interface IP context. The syntax for setting a specific DNS server to use is

```
set dns name=InterfaceName source=static addr=DNSAddress
```

Consider the following example:

```
set dns name="Local Area Connection" source=static addr=192.168.1.56
```

Here you specify that you are working with the "Local Area Connection" interface and specifying the DNS server address as 192.168.1.56.

If a computer is using DHCP and you want DHCP to provide the DNS server address, you can provide the DNS server address as well or specify that the IP address should be obtained from DHCP. You tell the computer to get the DNS server settings from DHCP by typing

```
set dns name=InterfaceName source=dhcp
```

Consider the following example:

```
set dns name="Local Area Connection" source=dhcp
```

Here you specify that the "Local Area Connection" interface should get its DNS server address settings from DHCP.

 Note If the computer already had DNS server IP addresses set, using SET DNS replaces the existing values. To add DNS server IP addresses instead of replacing them, use the ADD DNS command. You can confirm the DNS server settings by typing **show dns**.

Other optional parameters:

- **ddns= enabled | disabled** By default, all IP addresses for interfaces are registered in DNS under the computer's fully qualified domain name. This automatic registration uses the DNS dynamic update protocol. If you want to disable this behavior, add the value by including **ddns=disabled**.

- **suffix= interface | primary** By default, the computer's full name is registered only in its primary domain. When using dynamic DNS, you can also specify that the connection-specific DNS name should be registered with DNS. Type the parameter **suffix=interface**. This allows for occasions when the computer has multiple network adapters that connect to multiple domains.

Specifying Additional DNS Servers to Use

Most networks have multiple DNS servers that are used for resolving domain names. This allows for name resolution if one DNS server isn't available. When you use DHCP to specify the DNS servers, it can automatically tell computers about other DNS servers that may be available. This isn't the case when you manually specify DNS servers to be used.

To tell a computer about other DNS servers that may be available in addition to the primary DNS server specified previously, you can use the Netsh Interface IP context and the ADD DNS command. The syntax is

```
add dns name=InterfaceName addr=DNSAddress
```

Consider the following example:

```
add dns name="Local Area Connection" addr=192.168.1.75
```

Here you specify that you are working with the "Local Area Connection" interface and designating an alternate DNS server with an IP address of 192.168.1.75.

By default, a DNS server is added to the end of the DNS server's list in the TCP/IP configuration. If you want the DNS server to be in a specific position in the list use the Index= parameter. For example, if you wanted an additional server to be listed first (making it the primary) you'd set an index of 1, such as:

```
add dns name="Local Area Connection" addr=192.168.1.75 index=1
```

Setting WINS Servers to Use

WINS is used to resolve NetBIOS computer names to IP addresses. You can use WINS to help computers on a network determine the address of pre–Windows 2000 computers on the network. Although WINS is supported in all versions of Windows, Windows Server 2003 primarily uses WINS for backward compatibility.

For computers using static IP addresses you must specify which WINS servers are to be used. Within the Netsh Interface IP context, the syntax for specifying the use of a specific WINS server is

```
set wins name=InterfaceName source=static addr=WINSAddress
```

Consider the following example:

```
set wins name="Local Area Connection" source=static addr=192.168.1.64
```

Here you specify that you are working with the "Local Area Connection" interface and specifying the WINS server address as 192.168.1.64.

If a computer is using DHCP and you want DHCP to provide the WINS server address, you can provide the WINS server address as well or specify that the IP address should be obtained from DHCP. You tell the computer to get the WINS server settings from DHCP by typing

```
set wins name=InterfaceName source=dhcp
```

Consider the following example:

```
set wins name="Local Area Connection" source=dhcp
```

Here you specify that the "Local Area Connection" interface should get its WINS server address settings from DHCP.

 Note If the WINS server IP addresses were already set, using SET WINS replaces the existing values. To add WINS server IP addresses instead of replacing them, use the ADD WINS command. You can confirm the WINS server settings by typing **show wins**.

Specifying Additional WINS Servers to Use

Most networks have a primary and a backup WINS server. This allows for name resolution if one WINS server isn't available. If you use DHCP to specify the WINS servers, DHCP can automatically tell computers about other WINS servers that may be available. This isn't the case when you manually specify which WINS servers to use.

To tell a computer about other WINS servers that may be available in addition to the primary WINS server specified previously, you can use the Netsh Interface IP context and the ADD WINS command. The syntax is

```
add wins name=InterfaceName addr=WINSAddress
```

Consider the following example:

```
add wins name="Local Area Connection" addr=192.168.1.155
```

Here you specify that you are working with the "Local Area Connection" interface and designating an alternate WINS server with an IP address of 192.168.1.155.

By default, a WINS server is added to the end of the WINS server's list in the TCP/IP configuration. If you want a WINS server to be in a specific position in the list use the Index= parameter. For example, if you wanted an additional server to be listed first (making it the primary) you'd set an index of 1, such as

```
add wins name="Local Area Connection" addr=192.168.1.155 index=1
```

Deleting Address Resolution Protocol Cache

When computers look up domain name information, the related information is stored in the Address Resolution Protocol (ARP) cache so that the next time the information is needed no name lookup is necessary. The address resolution information expires according to a time-to-live (TTL) value set when the information was received, after which time it must again be looked up to get current information and a new TTL. In general, this automated system of obtaining, clearing out, and renewing name information works well. Sometimes, however, old name-resolution information on a system will cause problems before the information is purged. For example, if a computer changes its name information and the TTL hasn't expired on a previous lookup, temporarily you won't be able to find the computer.

DNS administrators have several tricks they can use to reduce the impact of name changes, such as setting an increasingly shorter TTL just prior to a name change to ensure that old information is deleted more quickly and doesn't cause a problem. However, you may find that it's easier just to get rid of the old information and force a computer to make new DNS lookups. You can do this by typing **netsh interface ip delete arpcache** at the command prompt or, if you are in the Netsh Interface IP context, by typing **delete arpcache**. This deletes name information for all interfaces configured on the computer you are working with. When there are multiple interfaces and you only want name-resolution information purged for one interface, you can name the interface to work with by including **name=InterfaceName**, such as

```
delete arpcache name="Local Area Connection"
```

Deleting TCP/IP Settings

Using the Netsh Interface IP context, you can delete TCP/IP configuration settings as well. Table 15-1 summarizes the available commands according to the task to be performed.

Table 15-1.   Netsh Interface IP Commands for Deleting TCP/IP Settings

Task	Syntax	Example
Delete a designated IP address from the named interface.	delete address name=*InterfaceName* addr=*IPAddress*	delete address name="Local Area Network" address=192.168.1.56
Delete a static gateway IP address from the named interface.	delete address name=*InterfaceName* gateway=*GatewayAddress*	delete address name="Local Area Network" gateway=192.168.1.1
Delete all static gateway IP addresses from the named interface.	delete address name=*InterfaceName* gateway=all	delete address name="Local Area Network" gateway=all
Delete a DNS server from the named interface.	delete dns name=*InterfaceName* addr=*IPAddress*	delete dns name="Local Area Network" address=192.168.1.56
Delete all DNS servers from the named interface.	delete dns name=*InterfaceName* addr=all	delete dns name="Local Area Network" address=all

Table 15-1. Netsh Interface IP Commands for Deleting TCP/IP Settings

Task	Syntax	Example
Delete a WINS server from the named interface.	delete wins name=*InterfaceName* addr=*IPAddress*	delete wins name="Local Area Network" address=192.168.1.56
Delete all WINS servers from the named interface.	delete wins name=*InterfaceName* addr=all	delete wins name="Local Area Network" address=all

Supporting TCP/IP Networking

The Netsh shell provides two contexts for working with TCP/IP. You use the Interface IP context to view TCP/IP statistics and to change settings. You use the Diag context to diagnose TCP/IP problems. The use of these contexts assumes that the necessary TCP/IP network components are already installed on the computer you are working with. If TCP/IP network components aren't installed, install them as discussed in Chapter 16 of the *Microsoft Windows Server 2003 Administrator's Pocket Consultant* (Microsoft Press, 2003).

Obtaining and Saving the TCP/IP Configuration

If you've worked with Windows for a while, you probably know that you can type **ipconfig** at a command prompt to get basic Windows IP configuration information, such as

```
Windows IP Configuration

Ethernet adapter Local Area Connection:

    Connection-specific DNS Suffix:
    IP Address:                 192.168.1.50
    Subnet Mask:                255.255.255.0
    Default Gateway:            192.168.1.1
```

As you can see, this information shows the IP address, subnet mask, and default gateway being used for the Local Area Connection Ethernet adapter. When you want more details, you type **ipconfig /all** to display additional information including the physical (MAC) address of the adapter, DHCP status, DNS servers used, and host information, such as

```
Windows IP Configuration

    Host Name:                  salespc09
    Primary Dns Suffix:         cpandl.com
    Node Type:                  Unknown
    IP Routing Enabled:         No
    WINS Proxy Enabled:         No
```

```
Ethernet adapter Local Area Connection:

   Connection-specific DNS Suffix:
   Description:                      Linksys LNE100TX Fast Ethernet
   Physical Address:                 EA-BF-C2-D4-EF-12
   Dhcp Enabled:                     Yes
   Autoconfiguration Enabled:        Yes
   IP Address:                       192.168.1.35
   Subnet Mask:                      255.255.255.0
   Default Gateway:                  192.168.1.1
   DHCP Server:                      192.168.1.50
   Lease Obtained:                   Sunday, January 18, 2006 1:25 PM
   Lease Expires:                    Monday, January 26, 2006 1:25 PM
```

Here a computer with the fully qualified DNS name salespc09.cpandl.com is configured to use DHCP and has an IP address of 192.168.1.35 with subnet mask 255.255.255.0. Because the IP address was dynamically assigned, it has specific Lease Obtained and Lease Expiration date and time stamps.

If you type **netsh interface ip show config** at a command prompt, you can obtain similar, albeit abbreviated, configuration information, such as

```
Configuration for interface "Local Area Connection"
   DHCP enabled:                     No
   IP Address:                       192.168.1.50
   SubnetMask:                       255.255.255.0
   Default Gateway:                  192.168.1.50
   GatewayMetric:                    1
   InterfaceMetric:                  0
   Statically Configured DNS Servers: 192.168.1.56
   Statically Configured WINS Servers: None
   Register with which suffix:       Primary only
```

As you can see, these are all ways to obtain similar information about the TCP/IP configuration.

Netsh also gives you the means to save the IP configuration so that the settings can be recreated simply by running a Netsh script. If you want to save the IP settings to a file, type:

```
netsh interface ip dump > FileName
```

where *FileName* is the name of the file to which you want to write the IP configuration information. When you dump the IP configuration, the file contents will be similar to those in Listing 15-1.

Listing 15-1 IP Configuration Script
```
# ----------------------------------------
# Interface IP Configuration
# ----------------------------------------
pushd interface ip
```

```
# Interface IP Configuration for "Local Area Connection"

set address name="Local Area Connection" source=static
addr = 192.168.1.50 mask=255.255.255.0
set address name="Local Area Connection" gateway=192.168.1.1
gwmetric=1
set dns name="Local Area Connection" source=static addr=192.168.1.56
register = PRIMARY
set wins name ="Local Area Connection" source=static addr=none

popd
# End of interface IP configuration
```

Listing 15-1 is a Netsh script that you can run using the syntax

```
netsh -c "interface ip" -f FileName
```

Consider the following example:

```
netsh -c "interface ip" -f corpsvr02-ipconfig.txt
```

In this example, you run a Netsh script called corpsvr02-ipconfig.txt using the Interface IP context to apply the IP configuration defined in the script. One of the key reasons for creating a configuration dump is so that you have a backup of the IP configuration. If the configuration is altered incorrectly in the future, you could restore the original configuration from the script.

Examining IP Address and Interface Configurations

The Netsh Interface IP context provides several commands for viewing IP address and interface configurations. Here, an interface refers to a network adapter used by a computer to communicate over TCP/IP. Most computers have two interfaces: a local loopback interface and a Local Area Connection interface.

The local loopback interface is a pseudo interface that uses the IP address 127.0.0.1 and a network mask of 255.0.0.0. All IP messages sent over this interface are looped back to the computer and are not sent out over the network.

The Local Area Connection interface is created automatically when you install TCP/IP networking. There will be one such interface for each network adapter. By default the first interface is named Local Area Connection, the second is Local Area Connection 2 and so on.

At the Windows command line, you can view IP address configuration information by typing **netsh interface ip show ipaddress**. The output should be similar to the following:

```
MIB-II IP Address Entry
IP Address          Mask          BC Fmt   Reasm Sz   Interface
---------------     -------       ------   --------   ----------------
127.0.0.1           255.0.0.0        1       65535    Loopback
192.168.1.50        255.255.255.0    1       65535    Local Area Connection
```

Note Any interface that is disabled won't be listed, meaning the interface is not available and cannot be configured.

This information lists the IP address and mask for each interface configured on the computer. The reassembly size value, specified in the Reasm Sz column, indicates the reassembly size of IP datagrams is 65,535 bytes. This means IP datagrams sent or received using this interface are also 65,535 bytes in size. Blocks of data aren't usually sent as 65,535 byte chunks of data, however. Instead, they are separated into fragments, which are reassembled upon receipt into a complete IP datagram. We'll discuss IP datagram fragmentation in more detail in a moment.

To view more detailed information about interfaces, type **netsh interface ip show interface**. The output shows the detailed configuration of each interface, such as

```
MIB-II Interface Information
--------------------------------------------------------
Index:                          65539
User-friendly Name:             Local Area Connection
GUID Name:                      {BG333345-F234-4335-25FB-43D3456B4464}
Type:                           Ethernet
MTU:                            1500
Speed:                          100000000
Physical Address:               EA-BF-C2-D4-EF-12
Admin Status:                   Up
Operational Status:             Operational
Last Change:                    583112798
In Octets:                      396173
In Unicast Packets:             1323
In Non-unicast Packets:         377
In Packets Discarded:           0
In Erroneous Packets:           0
In Unknown Protocol Packets:    0
```

```
Out Octets:                    926667
Out Unicast Packets:           1351
Out Non-unicast Packets:       134
Out Packets Discarded:         0
Out Erroneous Packets:         0
Output Queue Length:           0
Description:                   Intel(R) PRO/100 VE Network Connection
```

 Note   As before, any interface that is disabled won't be listed as an interface available or configured on the computer.

 Tip   All Interface IP SHOW commands allow you to set the Rr= parameter to the number of seconds to use as a refresh interval. For example, if you wanted the interface statistics to be refreshed automatically every 30 seconds you would type **netsh interface ip show interface rr=30**. Once you set a refresh rate, you use Ctrl+C to exit the command so that no more updates are made.

Here, the Local Area Connection interface is configured for Ethernet networking. The Ethernet maximum transmission unit (MTU) is 1,500 bytes when using Ethernet II encapsulation. This means each block of data transmitted is 1,500 bytes in length, with 20 bytes of this data block used for the IP header. The remaining 1,480 bytes are used as the IP payload for the data block. Thus, an IP datagram of 65,535 bytes would need to be fragmented in many smaller data blocks for transmission. These fragments would then be reassembled on the destination node.

Several other important parameters are given as well, including the following:

- **Speed**   Speed refers to the transmission speed used by the interface. In this case it is 100,000,000 (100 megabits per second). You may also see a speed of 10,000,000 (10 megabits per second) and other speeds as well.

- **Physical Address**   Physical Address is the MAC address encoded on the network adapter. The MAC address is used to uniquely track every device transmitting data over IP networks.

- **Operational Status**   The status of the interface. Unfortunately, this usually reads as Operational even if there is a problem with the interface. For example, if the network cable is unplugged the interface won't report this as an error .

The interface details also provide useful information about the type of packets being received (*in packets*) and being sent (*out packets*). In general, packets are either unicast or nonunicast. Unicast packets are sent or received using a specific IP address. Nonunicast packets are sent or received to multiple IP addresses, and usually represent broadcast traffic. If a routing or delivery error occurs along the transmission path or at the destination, the computer discards the problem datagram and this action is recorded. *In packets* that were created using an unknown networking protocol are marked as Unknown Protocol Packets. Packets containing general errors are marked as erroneous.

Working with TCP Internet Control and Error Messages

Each packet sent over IP is a datagram, meaning that it is an unacknowledged and nonsequenced message forwarded by routers to a destination IP address. Each router receiving a datagram decides how best it should be forwarded. This means different datagrams can take different routes between the sending IP address (the source node) and the destination IP address (the destination node). It also means the return route for individual datagrams can be different as well.

Although IP provides end-to-end delivery capabilities for IP datagrams, it does not provide any facilities for reporting routing or delivery errors encountered. Errors and control messages are tracked by the Internet Control Message Protocol (ICMP). You can view ICMP statistics by typing **netsh interface ip show icmp**. The output from this command looks like this:

```
MIB-II ICMP Statistics
-----------------------------------------------------------

INPUT
Messages:                       20302
Errors:                         120
Destination Unreachable:        45
Time Exceeded:                  88
Parameter Problems:             0
Source Quench:                  4
Redirects:                      6
Echo Requests:                  966
Echo Replies:                   966
Time Stamp Requests:            0
Time Stamp Replies:             0
Address Mask Requests:          0
Address Mask Replies:           0

OUTPUT
Messages:                       20302
Errors:                         120
Destination Unreachable:        45
Time Exceeded:                  88
Parameter Problems:             0
Source Quench:                  4
Redirects:                      6
Echo Requests:                  966
Echo Replies:                   966
```

```
Time Stamp Requests:          0
Time Stamp Replies:           0
Address Mask Requests:        0
Address Mask Replies:         0
```

Tip These statistics can be refreshed automatically. Add the **Rr=RefreshRate** parameter, where *RefreshRate* is the number of seconds to use as the refresh interval.

Here, you see detailed statistics on IP datagram messages being received (input messages) and those being sent (output messages). Decoding these statistics is easy if you know what you are looking for. The most basic type of IP datagram message is *Echo*. It is used to send a simple message to an IP node and have an *Echo Reply* echoed back to the sender. Many TCP/IP network commands use Echo and Echo Reply to provide information about the reachability and the path taken to a destination IP node.

Any error that occurs during transfer of an IP datagram, in or out, is recorded as an error. IP attempts a best-effort delivery of datagrams to their destination IP nodes. If a routing or delivery error occurs along the transmission path or at the destination, a router or the destination node discards the problem datagram and tries to report the error by sending a "Destination Unreachable" message.

A time to live (TTL) value is set in an IP datagram before it is sent. This value represents the maximum number of hops to use between the source and the destination nodes. "Time exceeded" messages are sent back to the IP datagram originator when the TTL value of the datagram expires. Typically this means there are more links than expected between the source and the destination node. Here, you'd need to increase the TTL value to successfully send traffic between the source and destination node. An expired TTL could also be an indicator of a routing loop in the network. Routing loops occur when routers have incorrect routing information and forward IP datagrams in such a way that they never reach their destinations.

A router or destination node sends a "Parameter Problem" message when an error occurs while processing in the IP header within an IP datagram. The IP header error causes the IP datagram to be discarded and if there are no other ICMP messages that can be used to describe the error that occurred, the "Parameter Problem" message is sent back to the source node. Typically this indicates an incorrect formatting of the IP header or incorrect arguments in IP option fields.

When a router becomes congested whether due to a sudden increase of traffic, a slow or sporadic link, or inadequate resources, it will discard incoming IP datagrams. When it does this, the router might send a "Source Quench" message back to the originator of the IP datagram telling the originator that datagrams are arriving too quickly to be processed. The destination node can also send "Source Quench" messages back to the originator for similar reasons. This isn't done for each datagram discarded; rather, it is done for segments of messages or not all. The Internet Engineering Task Force's (IETF) RFC 1812 recommends that "Source Quench" messages not be sent at all because they create more traffic on an already crowded circuit. If received, however, the originator will resend the related TCP segment at a slower transmission rate to avoid the congestion.

When subnetting is used, the first part of the IP address cannot be used to determine the subnet mask. To discover its subnet mask, an IP node sends an "Address Request" message to a known router or uses either an all-subnets-directed broadcast or a limited broadcast IP address. A router responding to the message sends an "Address Reply" message, which contains the subnet mask for the network segment on which the "Address Request" message was received. If an IP node doesn't know its IP address it can also send an "Address Request" message with a source IP address of 0.0.0.0. The receiver of this message assumes the source IP node uses a class-based subnet mask and responds accordingly using a broadcast.

Before data is transmitted over TCP, the receiver advertises how much data it can receive at one time. This value is called the TCP window size. When transferring data, the TCP window size determines how much data can be transmitted before the sender has to wait for an acknowledgment from the receiver. The TCP window size is a 16-bit field, allowing for a maximum receive window size of 65,535 bytes. This means that a source node could send up to that amount of data in a single TCP window. Using the TCP window scale option, a receiver can advertise a larger window size of up to approximately 1 GB.

To calculate the retransmission time-out (RTO) value to use, TCP tracks the round-trip time (RTT) between TCP segments on an ongoing basis. Normally, the RTO is calculated once for every full window of data sent. In many network environments, this approach works well and prevents having to retransmit data. However, in a high-bandwidth environment or if there are long delays in any environment, this technique doesn't work so well. One sampling of data for each window cannot be used to determine the current RTO correctly and prevent unnecessary retransmission of data.

To allow for calculating the RTT and in turn the RTO on any TCP segment, a timestamp value based on the local clock is sent in a "Timestamp Request" message. The acknowledgement for the data on the TCP segment echoes back the timestamp, which allows the RTT to be calculated using the echoed timestamp and the time that the segment's acknowledgement arrived. These messages are recorded as Timestamp Requests and Timestamp Replies.

The final type of ICMP message of import in troubleshooting is the "Redirect" message. Redirect messages are used to tell the senders of IP datagrams about a more optimal route from the sender to the destination node. Because most hosts maintain minimal routing tables, this information is used to improve message routing while decreasing transfer times and errors. So when you see "Redirect" messages, you know traffic is being rerouted to a destination node.

Examining Fragmentation, Reassembly and Error Details

To dig deeper into IP datagram fragmenting and reassembly, you can type **netsh interface ip show ipstats**. The output should look similar to the following:

```
MIB-II IP Statistics
------------------------------------------------------

Forwarding is:              Enabled
Default TTL:                128
In Receives:                24219
In Header Errors:           0
In Address Errors:          250
Datagrams Forwarded:        0
In Unknown Protocol:        0
In Discarded:               0
In Delivered:               23969
Out Requests:               20738
Routing Discards:           0
Out Discards:               0
Out No Routes:              0
Reassembly Timeouts:        60
Reassembly Required         0
Reassembled Ok:             0
Reassembly Failures:        0
Fragments Ok:               0
Fragments Failed:           0
Fragments Created:          0
```

As you can see the IP statistics show the default TTL value for *out packets* created on this computer for transmission. Here, the TTL value is 128. This means that there can be up to 128 links between this computer and the destination computer. If packets use more hops than that, the packets would be discarded and a "Time Exceeded" message would be sent back to the computer.

The In Receives value specifies how many inbound packets have been received. The actual number of packets used is represented by the In Delivered value and the difference between these values is due to *in packets*:

- Received with errors, designated as either In Header Errors or In Address Errors.

- Forwarded to other IP nodes, designated as Datagrams Forwarded

- Using an unknown protocol, designated as In Unknown Protocol

- Discarded, such as when a packet's TTL is exceeded, designated as In Discarded

Here, there is a 250-datagram difference between the In Receives and In Delivered values, due to 250 inbound packets with addressing errors.

The number and disposition of outbound packets is also recorded. The number of packets being transmitted out is listed as Out Requests. Any errors coming back as a result of those transmissions are recorded according to type. If a router or other node sends back a "Destination Unreachable" message, this is usually recorded as a Routing Discard. Other types of error messages, such as "Parameter Problem" or "Source Quench" messages, might be recorded as Routing Discards or Out Discards. If there is no route out or if a "No Route" message is returned, they might be recorded as Out No Routes.

When data is transmitted outside the local network over routers, it is typically fragmented and reassembled as mentioned previously. Statistics for the reassembly of the original datagrams is recorded and so is the status of received fragments.

Examining Current TCP and UDP Connections

Firewalls and proxy servers can affect the ability to connect a system on the local network to systems on remote networks. Typically an administrator will have to open TCP or UDP ports to allow remote communications between a computer on the local network and the remote computer or network. Each type of application or utility that you use may require different ports to be opened. A complete list of TCP and UDP ports used by well-known services is stored in \%*SystemRoot*%\System32\Drivers\Etc\Services.

Sometimes, however, the tool you want to work with won't have a well-known service associated with it and you may need to experiment a bit to find out what TCP or UPD ports it works with. One way to do this is to start the tool and use a TCP or UPD listener to see what ports become active.

Working with TCP

TCP ports are made available using a passive open, which basically says the port is available to receive requests. When a client wants to use an available port, it must try to establish a connection. A TCP connection is a two-way connection between two clients using Application Layer protocols on an IP network. The TCP endpoints are identified by an IP address and TCP port pair. There is a local TCP endpoint and a remote TCP endpoint, which can be used to identify loopback connections from the local machine to the local machine as well as standard connections from the local machine to a remote machine somewhere on the network. TCP connections are established using a three-way handshake. Here's how that works:

1. A client wanting to use a port sends an active open request (SYN).

2. The local client acknowledges the request, sending a SYN-ACK.

3. To which the client wanting to use the port sends a final acknowledgement (ACK).

Data passed over a TCP connection is apportioned into segments. Segments are sent as IP datagrams that contain a TCP header and TCP data. When a connection is established, the maximum segment size (MSS) is also set. Typically, the maximum value for the MSS is 65,495 bytes, which is 65,535 bytes for the IP datagram minus the minimum IP header (20 bytes) and the minimum TCP header (20 bytes). Technically speaking SYN, SYN-ACK, and ACK messages are SYN, SYN-ACK, and ACK segments.

You can view current TCP connection statistics by typing **netsh interface ip show tcpconn**. Refresh the statistics automatically by adding the Rr=*RefreshRate* parameter. The output shows you which TCP ports are being listened on, which TCP ports have established connections, and which ports are in a wait state, as shown in this example:

```
MIB-II TCP Connection Entry
```

Local Address	Local Port	Remote Address	Remote Port	State
0.0.0.0	42	0.0.0.0	18520	Listen
0.0.0.0	53	0.0.0.0	16499	Listen
0.0.0.0	88	0.0.0.0	45165	Listen
0.0.0.0	135	0.0.0.0	2176	Listen
0.0.0.0	389	0.0.0.0	2256	Listen
0.0.0.0	1025	0.0.0.0	43054	Listen
0.0.0.0	1026	0.0.0.0	35016	Listen
0.0.0.0	1028	0.0.0.0	53398	Listen
0.0.0.0	3069	0.0.0.0	43189	Listen
0.0.0.0	3268	0.0.0.0	43230	Listen
0.0.0.0	3269	0.0.0.0	36957	Listen
127.0.0.1	389	127.0.0.1	1033	Established
127.0.0.1	389	127.0.0.1	1034	Established
127.0.0.1	389	127.0.0.1	1035	Established
127.0.0.1	389	127.0.0.1	1039	Established
127.0.0.1	1033	127.0.0.1	389	Established
127.0.0.1	1034	127.0.0.1	389	Established
127.0.0.1	1035	127.0.0.1	389	Established
127.0.0.1	1039	127.0.0.1	389	Established
127.0.0.1	3073	0.0.0.0	10251	Listen
192.168.1.50	135	192.168.1.56	1040	Listen
192.168.1.50	139	0.0.0.0	12369	Listen
192.168.1.50	389	192.168.1.50	3287	Established
192.168.1.50	3287	192.168.1.50	389	Established
192.168.1.50	3289	192.168.1.50	135	Wait
192.168.1.50	290	192.168.1.50	1025	Wait

Entries for 0.0.0.0 represent TCP broadcasts. Entries for 127.0.0.1 represent local loopback ports used by the local computer. You'll also see entries on the physical IP address used by the computer back to the computer. Here, these are shown with the local and remote IP address set to 192.168.1.50. The entries you are most interested in are those in which the remote IP address is different from the local IP address; these represent connections to other systems and networks.

The Local Port and Remote Port columns show you how local TCP ports are mapped to remote TCP ports. For example, in this output local port 135 on IP address 192.168.1.50 is mapped to the remote port 1040 on IP address 192.168.1.56. Each TCP connection also has a state. The most common state values are summarized in Table 15-2.

Table 15-2. TCP Connection States

State	Description
Closed	No TCP connection currently exists.
Listen	An Application Layer protocol has issued a passive open function call to permit incoming connection requests on the specified port. This doesn't create any TCP traffic.
Syn Sent	A client using an Application Layer protocol has issued an active open function call (SYN), which creates and sends the first segment of the TCP three-way handshake.
Syn Rcvd	A client using an Application Layer protocol has received the SYN and sent back an acknowledgement (SYN-ACK).
Established	The final ACK has been received and the TCP connection is established. Data can be transferred in both directions.
Wait	The TCP connection has been terminated and this has been acknowledged by both the local and remote client (FIN-ACK).

You can view additional TCP statistics by typing **netsh interface ip show tcpstats**. The output should be similar to the following:

```
MIB-II TCP Statistics
----------------------------------------------------------
Timeout Algorithm:              Van Jacobson's Algorithm
Minimum Timeout:                300
Maximum Timeout:                120000
Maximum Connections:            Dynamic
Active Opens:                   381
Passive Opens:                  443
Attempts Failed:                0
Established Resets:             26
Currently Established:          25
In Segments:                    27852
Out Segments:                   27518
Retransmitted Segments:         611
In Errors:                      0
Out Resets:                     4
```

The TCP statistics detail the following:

- Minimum and maximum timeout values in use

- Total number of active and passive opens since TCP/IP networking was started on the computer.

- Any connections that were attempted but failed
- Any connections that were established then reset
- The total number of connections currently established
- The number of TCP segments sent (in segments) and received (out segments)
- The number of segments that had to be retransmitted
- The number of segments with errors that were received (in errors)

Working with UDP

Unlike TCP which is connection-oriented, UDP is connectionless, meaning that UDP messages are sent without negotiating a connection. UDP ports are completely separate from TCP ports, even for the same port number. Because UDP messages are sent without sequencing or acknowledgement, they are unreliable, in stark contrast to TCP, which is very reliable. When you work with UPD, you have only a local address and local port pair, which represent the ports being listened on. You can view the related listener entries by typing **netsh interface ip show udpconn**. The output will be similar to the following:

```
MIB-II UDP Listener Entry
Local Address                                   LocalPort
------------------------------------------------------
        0.0.0.0                                      42
        0.0.0.0                                     445
        0.0.0.0                                     500
        0.0.0.0                                    1030
        0.0.0.0                                    1032
        0.0.0.0                                    1701
        0.0.0.0                                    3002
        0.0.0.0                                    3103
        0.0.0.0                                    3114
        0.0.0.0                                    4500
      127.0.0.1                                      53
      127.0.0.1                                     123
      127.0.0.1                                    1036
      127.0.0.1                                    3101
      127.0.0.1                                    3102
   192.168.1.50                                      53
   192.168.1.50                                      67
   192.168.1.50                                     137
   192.168.1.50                                     138
   192.168.1.50                                     389
   192.168.1.50                                     464
   192.168.1.50                                    2535
```

Entries for 0.0.0.0 represent UDP broadcast ports. Entries for 127.0.0.1 represent local loopback ports used by the local computer. Entries on the physical IP address for a network adapter are ports which are listening for connections.

UPD messages are sent as IP datagrams and consist of a UDP header and UDP message data. You can view additional UDP statistics by typing **netsh interface ip show udpstats**. The output should be similar to the following:

```
MIB-II UDP Statistics
-------------------------------------------
In Datagrams:                   42640
In Invalid Port:                732
In Erroneous Datagrams:         20
Out Datagrams:                  72217
```

The UDP statistics detail:

- The total number of datagrams received on UDP ports.
- The number of datagrams received on invalid ports and discarded.
- The number of erroneous datagrams that were received and discarded.
- The number of datagrams sent over UDP ports.

Troubleshooting TCP/IP Networking

Problems with TCP/IP networking can be difficult to track down, which is why there are so many tools to help you try to determine what's happening. As you start to troubleshoot, make sure you have a clear understanding of the concepts and procedures discussed in the "Supporting TCP/IP Networking" section of this chapter. The tools and techniques discussed there will help you uncover and diagnose some of the most complex TCP/IP networking problems. In addition to that discussion, you can use the discussion in this section to troubleshoot connectivity and configuration issues.

Viewing Diagnostic Information

Many TCP/IP networking problems relate to incorrect configuration of networking components and you'll find that the Netsh Diag context is really good at helping you discover what's going on. Start by viewing summary configuration information by typing **netsh diag show all**. Listing 15-2 shows the summary configuration information for CorpSvr02.

Note Don't overlook how useful Netsh can be to remotely trouble-shoot problems. With Netsh, you don't need to sit at the user's computer or logon remotely using Remote Desktop. You simply start netsh with the –R parameter to provide the name of the remote computer you want to work with and then go about diagnosing the problem at hand.

Listing 15-2 Netsh Diag Show All Output

```
Default Outlook Express Mail (pop3.cpandl.com / mail.cpandl.com)

Default Outlook Express News (Not Configured)

Internet Explorer Web Proxy (Internet Explorer is not using the
proxy)

Loopback (127.0.0.1)

Computer System (CORPSVR02)

Operating System (Microsoft(R) Windows(R) Server 2003, Standard
Edition)

Version (5.2.3790)

Modems

Network Adapters
    1. [00000001]  Intel(R) PRO/100 VE Network Connection
    2. [00000002]  1394 Net Adapter
    3. [00000003]  RAS Async Adapter
    4. [00000004]  WAN Miniport (L2TP)
    5. [00000005]  WAN Miniport (PPTP)
    6. [00000006]  WAN Miniport (PPPOE)
    7. [00000007]  Direct Parallel
    8. [00000008]  WAN Miniport (IP)
Network Clients
    1. Microsoft Terminal Services
    2. Microsoft Windows Network
    3. Web Client Network
```

You can also obtain detailed configuration information by typing **netsh diag show all /v**. However, this typically gives you too much information, so it is better to examine one potential problem area at a time. Typically, you'll next want to examine the network adapter configuration on the computer. Type **netsh diag show adapter** to view summary details for the network adapters configured on the computer. The output should confirm what adapters are available, such as

```
Network Adapters
    1. [00000001]  Intel(R) PRO/100 VE Network Connection
    2. [00000002]  1394 Net Adapter
    3. [00000003]  RAS Async Adapter
    4. [00000004]  WAN Miniport (L2TP)
    5. [00000005]  WAN Miniport (PPTP)
```

```
6. [00000006]  WAN Miniport (PPPOE)
7. [00000007]  Direct Parallel
8. [00000008]  WAN Miniport (IP)
```

Here, the computer is configured with

1. An Intel Ethernet 100-megabits-per-second (Mbps) network card
2. An IEEE 1394 (FireWire) adapter
3. An RAS asynchronous adapter, meaning RAS is installed on the computer
4. IPSec port for Layer Two Tunneling Protocol (L2TP)
5. IPSec port for Point-to-Point Tunneling Protocol
6. IPSec port for Point-to-Point Protocol over Ethernet
7. Parallel printer port
8. Internet Protocol (IP) port

Next, you'll probably want to get detailed information on the configuration of these adapters by adding the /V parameter. Typically, you'll want to limit this to a specific adapter by following the command text with the index number of the adapter to review, or a full or partial name of the adapter. Consider the following examples:

Display the detailed configuration information for the network adapter with an index of 1:

```
netsh diag show adapter 1 /v
```

Display the detailed configuration information for the network adapter whose name starts with the keyword Intel:

```
netsh diag show adapter intel* /v
```

Listing 15-3 shows an example detailed output for a network adapter. As you can see, the verbose adapter output shows the configuration of default gateways, dynamic IP addressing from DHCP, DNS, IP addressing and WINS.

Listing 15-3 Netsh Diag Show Adapter Verbose Output
```
Network Adapters
    1. [00000001] Intel(R) PRO/100 VE Network Connection
       ArpAlwaysSourceRoute = (empty)
       ArpUseEtherSNAP = (empty)
       Caption = [00000001] Intel(R) PRO/100 VE Network Connection
       DatabasePath = %SystemRoot%\System32\drivers\etc
       DeadGWDetectEnabled = (empty)
       DefaultIPGateway = 192.168.1.1 Same Subnet
                          192.168.1.2 Same Subnet
       DefaultTOS = (empty)
       DefaultTTL = (empty)
```

```
Description = Intel(R) PRO/100 VE Network Connection
DHCPEnabled = FALSE
DHCPLeaseExpires = (empty)
DHCPLeaseObtained = (empty)
DHCPServer = (empty)
DNSDomain = (empty)
DNSDomainSuffixSearchOrder=(empty)
DNSEnabledForWINSResolution=FALSE
DNSHostName = corpsvr02
DNSServerSearchOrder = 192.168.1.50
                       192.168.1.67
DomainDNSRegistrationEnabled = FALSE
ForwardBufferMemory = (empty)
FullDNSRegistrationEnabled = TRUE
GatewayCostMetric =1
                   2
IGMPLevel = (empty)
Index = 1
InterfaceIndex = 65539
IPAddress = 192.168.1.50
            192.168.2.12
IPConnectionMetric = 20
IPEnabled = TRUE
IPFilterSecurityEnabled = FALSE
IPPortSecurityEnabled = (empty)
IPSecPermitIPProtocols = 0
IPSecPermitTCPPorts = 0
IPSecPermitUDPPorts = 0
IPSubnet =  255.255.255.0
            255.255.255.0
IPUseZeroBroadcast = (empty)
IPXAddress = (empty)
IPXEnabled = FALSE
IPXFrameType = (empty)
IPXMediaType = (empty)
IPXNetworkNumber = (empty)
IPXVirtualNetNumber = (empty)
KeepAliveInterval = (empty)
KeepAliveTime = (empty)
MACAddress = 00:E0:B8:53:05:F1
MTU = (empty)
NumForwardPackets = (empty)
PMTUBHDetectEnabled = (empty)
PMTUDiscoveryEnabled = (empty)
```

```
ServiceName = E100B
SettingID = {A908BB00-F027-4E25-8EE8-47FD6E7DA507}
TcpipNetbiosOptions = 0
TcpMaxConnectRetransmissions = (empty)
TcpMaxDataRetransmissions = (empty)
TcpNumConnections = (empty)
TcpUseRFC1122UrgentPointer = (empty)
TcpWindowSize = (empty)
WINSEnableLMHostsLookup = TRUE
WINSHostLookupFile = (empty)
WINSPrimaryServer = 192.168.1.102
WINSScopeID = (empty)
WINSSecondaryServer = 192.168.1.108
```

Diagnosing Mail, News, Proxy Client Problems

In Listing 15-2, the first line of output shows that the default e-mail program is
Outlook Express and it is configured to use pop3.cpandl.com to receive mail
and mail.cpandl.com to send mail:

```
Default Outlook Express Mail (pop3.cpandl.com / mail.cpandl.com)
```

You can display this information by itself by typing **netsh diag show mail**. If
you suspect a problem with the e-mail configuration you would want to look at
the detailed configuration information by typing **netsh diag show mail /v**. The
output would look similar to the following:

```
Default Outlook Express Mail (pop3.cpandl.com / mail.cpandl.com)
    InBoundMailPort = 110
    InBoundMailServer = pop3.cpandl.com
    InBoundMailType = POP3
    OutBoundMailPort = 25
    OutBoundMailServer = mail.cpandl.com
    OutBoundMailType = SMTP
```

Here, inbound mail is configured to use POP3 on port 110 and pop3.cpandl.com
as the inbound mail server. Outbound mail is configured to use SMTP on port 25
and mail.cpandl.com as the outbound mail server. If any of this information
were incorrect, you would want to reconfigure mail.

In Listing 15-2, after providing the default mail information, the configuration of
the default Usenet news client and Internet Explorer web proxy are displayed. If
these clients aren't configured, the output shows this, as is the case in many
organizations. For an organization that uses these clients, you can type **netsh
diag show news /v** or **netsh diag show ieproxy /v** to get detailed configuration information, which should help identify any configuration issues.

Diagnosing General Computer Configuration Issues

The Netsh Diag context provides three commands for diagnosing general computer configuration issues:

- **Netsh diag show computer** Shows general computer configuration information

- **Netsh diag show os** Shows general operating system configuration information

- **Netsh diag show version** Shows the version number of the operating system, such as Version (5.1.2600) where 5.1 is the version number and 2600 is the build number.

The summary information for these commands shows only the computer name, operating system edition, and operating system version. The detailed output is much more useful in diagnosing problems. The detailed computer information, obtained by typing **netsh diag show computer /v**, is shown as Listing 15-4.

Listing 15-4 Verbose Computer Configuration Output

```
Computer System (CORPSVR02)
    AdminPasswordStatus = 3
    AutomaticResetBootOption = TRUE
    AutomaticResetCapability = TRUE
    BootOptionOnLimit = (empty)
    BootOptionOnWatchDog = (empty)
    BootROMSupported = TRUE
    BootupState = Normal boot
    Caption = CORPSVR02
    ChassisBootupState = 3
    CreationClassName = Win32_ComputerSystem
    CurrentTimeZone = 480
    DaylightInEffect = FALSE
    Description = AT/AT COMPATIBLE
    DNSHostName = corpsvr02
    Domain = cpandl.com
    DomainRole = 5
    EnableDaylightSavingsTime = TRUE
    FrontPanelResetStatus = 3
    InfraredSupported = FALSE
    InitialLoadInfo = (empty)
    InstallDate = (empty)
    KeyboardPasswordStatus = 3
    LastLoadInfo = (empty)
    Manufacturer = Gateway
```

```
Model = Gateway 800EA2
Name = CORPSVR02
NameFormat = (empty)
NetworkServerModeEnabled = TRUE
NumberOfProcessors = 1
OEMStringArray = SMBIOS 2.3
Customer Reference Platform
PartOfDomain = TRUE
PauseAfterReset = -1
PowerManagementCapabilities = (empty)
PowerManagementSupported = (empty)
PowerOnPasswordStatus = 3
PowerState = 0
PowerSupplyState = 3
PrimaryOwnerContact = (empty)
PrimaryOwnerName = wrs
ResetCapability = 1
ResetCount = -1
ResetLimit = -1
Roles =    LM_Workstation
           LM_Server
           Primary_Domain_Controller
           Timesource
           Print
           DialIn
           NT
           Master_Browser
           DFS
Status = OK
SupportContactDescription = (empty)
SystemStartupDelay = 30
SystemStartupOptions = "Windows Server 2003, Standard" /fastdetect
                       "Microsoft Windows XP Home Edition" /fastdetect
SystemStartupSetting = 0
SystemType = X86-based PC
ThermalState = 3
TotalPhysicalMemory = 535805952
UserName = CPANDL\administrator
WakeUpType = 6
Workgroup = (empty)
```

A summary of the computer configuration entries and their meaning is provided in Table 15-3.

Table 15-3.   Computer Configuration Entries and Their Meaning

Property	Description
AdminPasswordStatus	Status of the Administrator password. Values are: 1 = Disabled, 2 = Enabled, 3 = Not Implemented, 4 = Unknown.
AutomaticResetBootOption	Indicates whether the automatic reset boot option is enabled.
AutomaticResetCapability	Indicates whether the automatic reset is enabled.
BootOptionOnLimit	System action to be taken when the ResetLimit value is reached. Values are: 1 = Reserved, 2 = Operating system, 3 = System utilities, 4 = Do not reboot.
BootOptionOnWatchDog	Reboot action to be taken after the time on the watchdog timer has elapsed. Values are: 1 = Reserved, 2 = Operating system, 3 = System utilities, 4 = Do not reboot.
BootROMSupported	Indicates whether a boot ROM is supported.
BootupState	Indicates how the system was started. Values are: "Normal boot", "Fail-safe boot", and "Fail-safe with network boot".
Caption	System name.
ChassisBootupState	Bootup state of the system chassis. Values are: 1 = Other, 2 = Unknown, 3 = Safe, 4 = Warning, 5 = Critical, 6 = Non-recoverable.
CreationClassName	Name of class from which object is derived.
CurrentTimeZone	Number of minutes the computer is offset from Coordinated Universal Time.
DaylightInEffect	Indicates whether daylight savings mode is on.
Description	Description of the computer.
DNSHostName	Name of the server according to DNS.
Domain	Name of the domain to which the computer belongs.
DomainRole	Domain role of the computer. Values are: 0 = Standalone Workstation, 1 = Member Workstation, 2 = Standalone Server, 3 = Member Server, 4 = Backup Domain Controller, 5 = Primary Domain Controller.
EnableDaylightSavingsTime	Indicates whether Daylight Savings Time is enabled. If TRUE, the system changes to an hour ahead or behind when DST starts or ends. If FALSE, the system does not change to an hour ahead or behind when DST starts or ends.
FrontPanelResetStatus	Hardware security settings for the reset button on the computer. Values are: 0 = Disabled, 1 = Enabled, 2 = Not Implemented, 3 = Unknown.

Table 15-3.   Computer Configuration Entries and Their Meaning

Property	Description
InfraredSupported	Indicates whether an infrared (IR) port exists on the computer system.
InitialLoadInfo	Data needed to find either the initial load device (its key) or the boot service to request the operating system to start up.
InstallDate	When the computer was installed.
KeyboardPasswordStatus	Indicates the keyboard password status. Values are: 0 = Disabled, 1 = Enabled, 2 = Not Implemented, 3 = Unknown.
LastLoadInfo	Array entry of the InitialLoadInfo property, that holds the data corresponding to booting the currently loaded operating system.
Manufacturer	Computer manufacturer name.
Model	Product name given by the manufacturer.
Name	The computer name.
NameFormat	Identifies how the computer system name is generated.
NetworkServerModeEnabled	Indicates whether Network Server Mode is enabled.
NumberOfProcessors	Number of enabled processors on the computer.
OEMStringArray	List of descriptive strings set by the OEM.
PartOfDomain	Indicates whether the computer is part of a domain. If TRUE, the computer is a member of a domain. If FALSE, the computer is a member of a workgroup.
PauseAfterReset	Time delay in milliseconds before a reboot is initiated after a system power cycle or reset.
PowerManagementCapabilities	Power management capabilities of a logical device. Values are: 0 = Unknown, 1 = Not Supported, 2 = Disabled, 3 = Enabled, 4 = Power Saving Modes Entered Automatically, 5 = Power State Settable, 6 = Power Cycling Supported, 7 = Timed Power On Supported.
PowerManagementSupported	Indicates whether the device's power can be managed.
PowerOnPasswordStatus	Power on password status. Values are: 0 = Disabled, 1 = Enabled, 2 = Not Implemented, 3 = Unknown.
PowerState	Indicates the current power state of the computer. Values are: 0 = Unknown, 1 = Full Power, 2 = Power Save – Low Power Mode, 3 = Power Save – Standby, 4 = Power Save – Unknown, 5 = Power Cycle, 6 = Power Off, 7 = Power Save – Warning.

Table 15-3. Computer Configuration Entries and Their Meaning

Property	Description
PowerSupplyState	State of the enclosure's power supply when last booted. Values are: 1 = Other, 2 = Unknown, 3 = Safe, 4 = Warning, 5 = Critical, 6 = Non-recoverable.
PrimaryOwnerContact	Contact information for the computer's owner.
PrimaryOwnerName	Name of the system owner.
ResetCapability	Value indicates whether a computer can be reset using the power and reset buttons (or other hardware means). Values are: 1 = Other, 2 = Unknown, 3 = Disabled, 4 = Enabled, 5 = Nonrecoverable.
ResetCount	Number of automatic resets since the last intentional reset. A value of -1 indicates that the count is unknown.
ResetLimit	Number of consecutive times a system reset will be attempted. A value of -1 indicates that the limit is unknown.
Roles	System roles.
Status	Current status of the computer. Values are: "OK", "Error", "Degraded", "Unknown", "Pred Fail", "Starting", "Stopping", "Service".
SupportContactDescription	List of the support contact information for the computer.
SystemStartupDelay	The startup delay in seconds.
SystemStartupOptions	List of the startup options for the computer.
SystemStartupSetting	Index of the default start profile.
SystemType	System architecture type, such as "X86-based PC" or "64-bit Intel PC".
ThermalState	Thermal state of the system chassis when last booted. Values are: 1 = Other, 2 = Unknown, 3 = Safe, 4 = Warning, 5 = Critical, 6 = Non-recoverable.
TotalPhysicalMemory	Total byte size of physical memory.
UserName	Name of the currently logged-on user.
WakeUpType	Event that caused the system to power up. Values are: 0 = Reserved, 1 = Other, 2 = Unknown, 3 = APM Timer, 4 = Modem Ring, 5 = LAN Remote, 6 = Power Switch, 7 = PCI PME#, 8 = AC Power Restored.
Workgroup	When a computer is a member of a workgroup, the workgroup name is listed here.

As you can see, the detailed configuration information tells you a great deal about the computer's configuration. The same is true for the operating system

details, which can be obtained by typing **netsh diag show os /v**. Listing 15-5
provides an example.

Listing 15-5 Verbose Operating System Configuration Output

```
Operating System (Microsoft(R) Windows(R) Server 2003, Standard Edition)
    BootDevice = \Device\HarddiskVolume1
    BuildNumber = 3790
    BuildType = Uniprocessor Free
    Caption = Microsoft(R) Windows(R) Server 2003, Standard Edition
    CodeSet = 1252
    CountryCode = 1
    CreationClassName = Win32_OperatingSystem
    CSCreationClassName = Win32_ComputerSystem
    CSDVersion = (empty)
    CSName = CORPSVR02
    CurrentTimeZone = -480
    Debug = FALSE
    Description = (empty)
    Distributed = FALSE
    EncryptionLevel = 168
    ForegroundApplicationBoost = 2
    FreePhysicalMemory = 357176
    FreeSpaceInPagingFiles = 1114384
    FreeVirtualMemory = 1471560
    InstallDate = 3:53:12 PM 11/21/2004
    LargeSystemCache = 1
    LastBootUpTime = 10:37:11 AM 11/19/2005
    LocalDateTime = 10:42:00 AM 11/19/2005
    Locale = 0409
    Manufacturer = Microsoft Corporation
    MaxNumberOfProcesses = -1
    MaxProcessMemorySize = 2097024
    Name = Microsoft Windows Server 2003 Standard Edition|C:\WINDOWS|\
      Device\Harddisk0\Partition1
    NumberOfLicensedUsers = 500
    NumberOfProcesses = 33
    NumberOfUsers = 2
    Organization = wrs
    OSLanguage = 1033
    OSProductSuite = 272
    OSType = 18
    OtherTypeDescription = (empty)
    PAEEnabled = FALSE
    PlusProductID = (empty)
    PlusVersionNumber = (empty)
    Primary = TRUE
    ProductType = 2
    QuantumLength = 0
```

```
QuantumType = 0
RegisteredUser = wrs
SerialNumber = 38383-022-1234343-43434
ServicePackMajorVersion = 0
ServicePackMinorVersion = 0
SizeStoredInPagingFiles = 1280320
Status = OK
SuiteMask = 272
SystemDevice = \Device\HarddiskVolume1
SystemDirectory = C:\WINDOWS\system32
SystemDrive = C:
TotalSwapSpaceSize = (empty)
TotalVirtualMemorySize = 1803568
TotalVisibleMemorySize = 523248
Version = 5.2.3790
WindowsDirectory = C:\WINDOWS
```

A summary of the operating system entries and their meanings is provided in Table 15-4.

Table 15-4. Operating System Configuration Entries and Their Meanings

Property	Description
BootDevice	Disk drive from which the Win32 operating system boots.
BuildNumber	Build number of the operating system.
BuildType	Type of build used for the operating system, such as "retail build" or "checked build".
Caption	Operating system name.
CodeSet	Code page value used by the operating system.
CountryCode	Country code used by the operating system.
CreationClassName	Name of class from which the object is derived.
CSCreationClassName	Name of class from which computer system object is derived.
CSDVersion	Indicates the latest Service Pack installed on the computer. Value is NULL if no Service Pack is installed.
CSName	Name of the computer system associated with this object class.
CurrentTimeZone	Number of minutes the operating system is offset from Greenwich Mean Time. The value is positive, negative, or zero.
Debug	Indicates whether the operating system is a checked (debug) build. If TRUE, the debugging version of User.exe is installed.
Description	Description of the Windows operating system.

Table 15-4.   Operating System Configuration Entries and Their Meanings

Property	Description
Distributed	Indicates whether the operating system is distributed across multiple computer system nodes. If so, these nodes should be grouped as a cluster.
EncryptionLevel	The level of encryption for secure transactions as 40-bit, 128-bit, or n-bit.
ForegroundApplicationBoost	Sets the priority of the foreground application. On Windows NT 4 and Windows 2000, application boost is implemented by giving an application more processor time. Values are: 0 = None, 1 = Minimum, 2 = Maximum (Default).
FreePhysicalMemory	Physical memory in kilobytes currently unused and available.
FreeSpaceInPagingFiles	Amount of free space in kilobytes in the operating system's paging files. Swapping occurs when the free space fills up.
FreeVirtualMemory	Virtual memory in kilobytes unused and available.
InstallDate	When the operating system was installed.
LargeSystemCache	Indicates whether memory usage is optimized for program or the system cache. Values are: 0 = memory usage is optimized for programs, 1 = memory usage is optimized for the system cache.
LastBootUpTime	When the operating system was last booted.
LocalDateTime	Local date and time on the computer.
Locale	Language identifier used by the operating system.
Manufacturer	Operating system manufacturer. For Win32 systems, this value will be "Microsoft Corporation".
MaxNumberOfProcesses	Maximum number of process contexts the operating system can support. If there is no fixed maximum, the value is 0.
MaxProcessMemorySize	Maximum memory in kilobytes that can be allocated to a process. A value of zero indicates that there is no maximum.
Name	Name of the operating system instance.
NumberOfLicensedUsers	Number of user licenses for the operating system. A value of 0 = unlimited, a value of −1 = unknown.
NumberOfProcesses	Current number of process contexts on the system.
NumberOfUsers	Current number of user sessions.
Organization	Company name set for the registered user of the operating system.
OSLanguage	Language version of the operating system installed.

Table 15-4. **Operating System Configuration Entries and Their Meanings**

Property	Description
OSProductSuite	Operating system product suites installed. Values are: 1 = Small Business, 2 = Enterprise, 4 = BackOffice, 8 = Communication Server, 16 = Terminal Server, 32 = Small Business (Restricted), 64 = Embedded NT, and 128 = Data Center.
OSType	Type of operating system. Values include: 1 = Other, 18 = Windows NT or later.
OtherTypeDescription	Sets additional description; used when OSType = 1.
PlusProductID	Product number for Windows Plus! (if installed).
PlusVersionNumber	Version number of Windows Plus! (if installed).
Primary	Indicates whether this is the primary operating system.
ProductType	The operating system product type. Values are: 1 = workstation, 2 = domain controller, 3 = server.
QuantumLength	Number of clock ticks per unit of processor execution. Values are: 1 = Unknown, 2 = One tick, 3 = Two ticks.
QuantumType	Length type for units of processor execution. Values are: 1 = Unknown, 2 = Fixed, 3 = Variable. With variable length, foreground and background applications can have different values. With fixed length, the foreground and background values are the same.
RegisteredUser	Name set for the registered user of the operating system.
SerialNumber	Operating system product serial number.
ServicePackMajorVersion	Major version number of the service pack installed on the computer. If no service pack has been installed, the value is zero or NULL.
ServicePackMinorVersion	Minor version number of the service pack installed on the computer. If no service pack has been installed, the value is zero or NULL.
SizeStoredInPagingFiles	Total number of kilobytes that can be stored in the operating system's paging files. A value of zero indicates that there are no paging files.
Status	Current status of the object. Values include: "OK", "Error", "Unknown", "Degraded", "Pred Fail", "Starting", "Stopping", and "Service".
SuiteMask	Bit flags that identify the product suites available on the system. Values include: 1 = Small Business, 2 = Enterprise, 4 = Back Office, 8 = Communications, 16 = Terminal, 32 = Small Business Restricted, 64 = Embedded NT, 128 = Data Center.

Table 15-4. Operating System Configuration Entries and Their Meanings

Property	Description
SystemDevice	Physical disk partition on which the operating system is installed.
SystemDirectory	System directory of the operating system.
SystemDrive	The physical disk partition on which the operating system is installed.
TotalSwapSpaceSize	Total swap space in kilobytes. This value may be unspecified (NULL) if swap space is not distinguished from page files.
TotalVirtualMemorySize	Virtual memory size in kilobytes.
TotalVisibleMemorySize	Total amount of physical memory in kilobytes that is available to the operating system.
Version	Version number of the operating system.
WindowsDirectory	Windows directory of the operating system.

Diagnosing IP, DNS, WINS Configuration Issues

The Netsh Diag context provides commands for viewing the IP, DNS, and WINS configuration on a computer. These commands, with example output, are as follows:

- **Netsh diag show ip**   Shows the IP addresses used by network adapters on the computer. An example of the output follows:

```
IP Address
    1. [00000001] Intel(R) PRO/100 VE Network Connection
       IPAddress = 192.168.1.50
    2. [00000002] Intel(R) PRO/100 VE Network Connection
       IPAddress = 192.168.2.108
```

Each network adapter is listed in order. As this computer has two network adapters, there are two entries. Any network adapter that is disabled or otherwise unavailable won't be listed.

- **Netsh diag show gateway**   Shows the Internet gateways defined for network adapters on the computer. An example of the output follows:

```
Default Gateways
    1. [00000001] Intel(R) PRO/100 VE Network Connection
       DefaultIPGateway = 192.168.1.1 Same Subnet
                          192.168.1.2 Same Subnet
    2. [00000002] Intel(R) PRO/100 VE Network Connection
       DefaultIPGateway = 192.168.2.1 Same Subnet
```

Each gateway is listed on a per-adapter basis in the order it is used. If a computer has multiple network adapters, there should be an entry for each network adapter that is configured and used. There is a notation telling you that a gateway used is on the same subnet as the IP addresses used by the adapter. However, there is no notation for an incorrectly configured gateway (that is, one that isn't on the same subnet). In this case, there may be no default gateway entry for the adapter or, as is the case when there are multiple gateways configured for an adapter, the bad gateway may simply be omitted from the listing. If you suspect this is the case, compare the output of typing **netsh diag show gateway** to the output produced by typing **netsh interface ip show config**. Although the bad gateway address entry won't be shown in the *netsg diag show gateway* output, it will appear in the *netsh interface ip show config* output.

- **Netsh diag show dns**   Shows the DNS servers defined for network adapters on the computer. An example of the output follows:

```
DNS Servers
    1. [00000001] Intel(R) PRO/100 VE Network Connection
       DNSServerSearchOrder = 192.168.1.50
                             192.168.1.67
    2. [00000002] Intel(R) PRO/100 VE Network Connection
       DNSServerSearchOrder = 192.168.2.10
                             192.168.2.20
```

Each DNS server configured is shown in the search order used. Confirm that the correct IP addresses are used and that the search order is correct.

- **Netsh diag show wins**   Shows the WINS servers defined for network adapters on the computer. An example of the output follows:

```
WINS Servers
    1. [00000001] Intel(R) PRO/100 VE Network Connection
       WINSPrimaryServer = 192.168.1.102
       WINSSecondaryServer = 192.168.1.108
    2. [00000002] Intel(R) PRO/100 VE Network Connection
       WINSPrimaryServer = 192.168.2.205
       WINSSecondaryServer = 192.168.2.227
```

Each WINS server configured is shown in the search order used. Confirm that the correct IP addresses are used and that the search order is correct.

 Note   Although these commands accept a /V parameter, this doesn't provide any additional information.

Making TCP/IP Connections for Troubleshooting

The Netsh Diag context provides commands you can use to make TCP/IP connections for troubleshooting. There are specific commands for attempting to establish and then verify TCP/IP connections for mail, Usenet news, and Internet Explorer proxies as well as a general command to connect to a TCP host on a specified port.

To check mail connectivity using the default mail client, type **netsh diag connect mail**. If there's a connectivity problem, the output will confirm this. In this example, the computer is unable to connect to the inbound and outbound mail servers:

```
Default Outlook Express Mail (pop3.cpandl.com / mail.cpandl.com)
    InBoundMailPort = 110
    InBoundMailServer = pop3.cpandl.com
    Unable to connect to pop3.cpandl.com port 110
    OutBoundMailPort = 25
    OutBoundMailServer = mail.cpandl.com
    Unable to connect to mail.cpandl.com port 25
```

Here, the computer might not have connectivity to the network or the e-mail configuration may be incorrect.

To check news connectivity using the default news client, type **netsh diag connect news**. As with e-mail, if there's a news server connectivity problem, the output will confirm this. If no news client is configured, the output will state this, such as

```
Default Outlook Express News (Not Configured)
```

To check Internet Explorer proxy connectivity using the default Web proxy, type **netsh diag connect ieproxy**. The output will report the connection status, such as

```
Internet Explorer Proxy (cpandlproxy)
    IEProxyPort = 80
    IEProxy = cpandlproxy
    Server appears to be running on port(s) [80]
```

Here, Netsh was able to make a connection to the Web proxy. The proxy server, cpandlproxy, was running on port 80, which is the standard port used by Web servers.

You can also make connections to any IP host using a designated TCP port. The syntax for doing this is

```
netsh diag connect iphost HostName PortNumber
```

where *HostName* specifies the IP address, computer name, or fully qualified domain name of the host to which you want to connect and *PortNumber* specifies the TCP port through which you want to connect. Some of the common TCP ports and their related protocols are summarized in Table 15-5.

Table 15-5.   Common TCP Protocols and Ports

Protocol	Port
FTP	21
Telnet	23
SMTP	25
Time Server	37
Nameserver	42

Table 15-5. Common TCP Protocols and Ports

Protocol	Port
DNS	53
HTTP	80
Kerberos	88
POP3	110
NNTP	119
IMAP	143
HTTPS	443
Microsoft Directory Services	445
WINS	1512
PPTP	1723

To see how you can connect to specific hosts, consider the following examples:

Connect to 192.168.1.100 on Port 37:

```
netsh diag connect iphost 192.168.1.100 37
```

Connect to corpdc07 on Port 445:

```
netsh diag connect iphost corpdc07 445
```

Connect to services.cpandl.com on Port 443:

```
netsh diag connect iphost services.cpandl.com 443
```

Attempting to Verify Connectivity

Using the Netsh diag context, you can also attempt to verify connectivity to various remote hosts. The most basic of these commands test connectivity to a specific type of server. For instance, you can type **netsh diag ping mail**, **netsh diag ping news**, and **netsh diag ping ieproxy** to check mail, news, and IE Proxy server connectivity respectively. Consider the following example:

```
netsh diag ping mail
```

Here, you test connectivity using the default mail client. Output such as the following shows a connectivity or configuration problem:

```
Default Outlook Express Mail (pop3.cpandl.com / mail.cpandl.com)
    InBoundMailServer = pop3.cpandl.com
    Ping request could not find host pop3.cpandl.com. Please check the
name and try again.
```

```
OutBoundMailServer = mail.cpandl.com
Ping request could not find host mail.cpandl.com. Please check the
name and try again.
```

Other commands used to verify connectivity are a bit more complex. These commands include the following:

- **Netsh diag ping iphost**   Verifies connectivity with a remote host according to IP address, computer name, or fully qualified domain name. For example, if you wanted to test connectivity between the computer you are working with and 192.168.1.100, you would type

```
netsh diag ping iphost 192.168.1.100
```

- **Netsh diag ping adapter**   Verifies the TCP/IP configuration of network adapters. Typically, you'll want to limit this to a specific adapter by following the command text with the index number of the adapter to review or a full or partial name of the adapter. For example, if you want to test the configuration of the network adapter with an index of 1, you could type

```
netsh diag ping adapter 1
```

- **Netsh diag ping dhcp**   Verifies the DHCP server settings of network adapters. You can limit this to a specific adapter by following the command text with the index number of the adapter to review or a full or partial name of the adapter. For example, if you want to test the DHCP configuration of the network adapter whose name starts with 3com, you could type

```
netsh diag ping dhcp 3com*
```

- **Netsh diag ping dns**   Verifies the DNS server settings of network adapters. You can limit this to a specific adapter by following the command text with the index number of the adapter to review or a full or partial name of the adapter. For example, if you want to test the DNS configuration of the network adapter whose name starts with Intel, you could type

```
netsh diag ping dns Intel*
```

- **Netsh diag ping gateway**   Verifies the default gateways settings of network adapters. You can limit this to a specific adapter by following the command text with the index number of the adapter to review or a full or partial name of the adapter. For example, if you want to test the default gateway configuration of the network adapter whose name starts with 3com, you could type

```
netsh diag ping gateway 3com*
```

- **Netsh diag ping ip**   Verifies that the IP addresses assigned to network adapters are valid. You can limit this to a specific adapter by following the command text with the index number of the adapter to review or a full or partial name of the adapter, such as

```
netsh diag ping ip Intel*
```

- **Netsh diag ping wins** Verifies the WINS server settings of network adapters. You can limit this to a specific adapter by following the command text with the index number of the adapter to review or a full or partial name of the adapter. For example, if you want to test the WINS configuration of the network adapter with an index of 2, you could type

```
netsh diag ping wins 2
```

The most useful command here is **netsh diag ping adapter**. It tests the full TCP/IP configuration of adapters, which includes the IP, DHCP, DNS, WINS, and default gateway settings. Listing 15-6 shows a sample output from this command.

Listing 15-6 Output from Netsh Diag Ping Adapter

```
Network Adapters
     1. [00000001] Intel(R) PRO/100 VE Network Connection
        DefaultIPGateway = 192.168.1.1 Same Subnet
            Pinging 192.168.1.1 with 32 bytes of data:
            Reply from 192.168.1.1: bytes=32 time<1ms TTL=0
            Reply from 192.168.1.1: bytes=32 time<1ms TTL=0
            Reply from 192.168.1.1: bytes=32 time<1ms TTL=0
            Reply from 192.168.1.1: bytes=32 time<1ms TTL=0
            Ping statistics for 192.168.1.1:
                Packets: Sent = 4, Received = 4, Lost = 0 (0% loss)
            Approximate round trip times in milliseconds:
                Minimum = 0ms, Maximum = 0ms, Average = 0ms
            Pinging 192.168.1.2 with 32 bytes of data:
            Request timed out.
            Request timed out.
            Request timed out.
            Request timed out.
            Ping statistics for 192.168.1.2:
                Packets: Sent = 4, Received = 0, Lost = 4 (100% loss)
        DNSServerSearchOrder = 192.168.1.50
            Pinging 192.168.1.50 with 32 bytes of data:
            Reply from 192.168.1.50: bytes=32 time<1ms TTL=0
            Reply from 192.168.1.50: bytes=32 time<1ms TTL=0
            Reply from 192.168.1.50: bytes=32 time<1ms TTL=0
            Reply from 192.168.1.50: bytes=32 time<1ms TTL=0
            Ping statistics for 192.168.1.50:
                Packets: Sent = 4, Received = 4, Lost = 0 (0% loss)
            Approximate round trip times in milliseconds:
                Minimum = 0ms, Maximum = 0ms, Average = 0ms
                192.168.1.67
```

```
        Pinging 192.168.1.67 with 32 bytes of data:
        Request timed out.
        Request timed out.
        Request timed out.
        Request timed out.
        Ping statistics for 192.168.1.67:
            Packets: Sent = 4, Received = 0, Lost = 4 (100% loss)
IPAddress = 192.168.1.12
        Pinging 192.168.1.12 with 32 bytes of data:
        Reply from 192.168.1.12: bytes=32 time<1ms TTL=0
        Reply from 192.168.1.12: bytes=32 time<1ms TTL=0
        Reply from 192.168.1.12: bytes=32 time<1ms TTL=0
        Reply from 192.168.1.12: bytes=32 time<1ms TTL=0
        Ping statistics for 192.168.1.12:
            Packets: Sent = 4, Received = 4, Lost = 0 (0% loss)
        Approximate round trip times in milli-seconds:
            Minimum = 0ms, Maximum = 0ms, Average = 0ms
            192.168.2.12
        Pinging 192.168.2.12 with 32 bytes of data:
        Reply from 192.168.2.12: bytes=32 time<1ms TTL=0
        Reply from 192.168.2.12: bytes=32 time<1ms TTL=0
        Reply from 192.168.2.12: bytes=32 time<1ms TTL=0
        Reply from 192.168.2.12: bytes=32 time<1ms TTL=0
        Ping statistics for 192.168.2.12:
            Packets: Sent = 4, Received = 4, Lost = 0 (0% loss)
        Approximate round trip times in milliseconds:
            Minimum = 0ms, Maximum = 0ms, Average = 0ms
WINSPrimaryServer = 192.168.1.102
        Pinging 192.168.1.102 with 32 bytes of data:
        Request timed out.
        Request timed out.
        Request timed out.
        Request timed out.
        Ping statistics for 192.168.1.102:
            Packets: Sent = 4, Received = 0, Lost = 4 (100% loss)
WINSSecondaryServer = 192.168.1.108
        Pinging 192.168.1.108 with 32 bytes of data:
        Request timed out.
        Request timed out.
        Request timed out.
        Request timed out.
        Ping statistics for 192.168.1.108:
            Packets: Sent = 4, Received = 0, Lost = 4 (100% loss)
```

In examining this output, you can see there are myriad possible connectivity or configuration problems. Immediate questions to ask yourself and verify are as follows:

- **Is the computer connected to the network?** Seeing this many errors, the first thing I would do is to verify that the computer is in fact connected to the network. If the computer can connect to one of its default gateways (and that gateway isn't configured on the same IP address as one of the computer's IP addresses), the computer is able to connect to the network. If the computer can't connect to any of its gateways, its network cable may be disconnected or it may have a bad network adapter.

- **Does the computer have a bad network adapter?** If the computer can't connect to any of its gateways, it may have a bad network adapter. To check this, look for the entries for IPAddress. These entries show the results of the computer connecting to its own network adapters. If the connectivity tests for a particular IP address fail consistently or intermittently you probably have a bad network adapter.

Seeing problems connecting to DNS and WINS is also a concern. Problems connecting to a designated DHCP server would be similar. If the computer can connect to the default gateway but can't get to a DNS, DHCP, or WINS server, the server may be down, the IP address in the configuration may be incorrect or another interconnection between the computer you are working with and the target server may be down.

Another useful Netsh Diag command is SHOW TEST. Type **netsh diag show test /v** and you'll get a very complete connectivity test for the following:

- Default mail client
- Default news client
- Default Internet Explorer proxy
- Local loopback on 127.0.0.1
- All modems configured and enabled
- All network adapters configured and enabled

Appendix

Essential Command-Line Tools Reference

In this book, I've discussed many command-line tools and scripts. This appendix is intended to provide a quick reference to the syntax and usage of these tools as well as other commands and utilities that you may find helpful. These tools are listed alphabetically by tool name. Unless otherwise noted, these tools work the same on both Microsoft Windows Server 2003 and Windows XP Professional. In addition, if a tool is not included with the standard Windows installation, the source of the tool is listed, such as "Windows Server 2003 Resource Kit" for the tools available only through the Microsoft Windows Server 2003 Resource Kit.

ARP

Displays and modifies the IP-to-physical address translation tables used by the address resolution protocol (ARP).

```
arp -a [inet_addr] [-n if_addr]
arp -d inet_addr [if_addr]
arp -s inet_addr eth_addr [if_addr]
```

ASSOC

Displays and modifies file extension associations.

```
assoc [.ext[=[fileType]]]
```

ATTRIB

Displays and changes file attributes.

```
attrib [+r|-r] [+a|-a] [+s|-s] [+h|-h]
[[drive:] [path] filename] [/s] [/d]
```

CACLS
Displays and modifies a file's access control list (ACL).

```
cacls filename [/t] [/e] [/c] [/g user:perm]
[/r user [...]] [/p user:perm [...]]
[/d user [...]]
```

CALL
Calls a script or script label as a procedure.

```
call [drive:][path]filename [batch-parameters]
call :label [args]
```

CD
Displays the name of or changes the current directory.

```
chdir [/d] [drive:][path]
chdir [..]
cd [/d] [drive:][path]
cd [..]
```

CHDIR
See CD.

CHKDSK
Checks a disk for errors and displays a report.

```
chkdsk [drive:][[path]filename]
[/f][/v][/r][/x][/i][/c][/l[:size]]
```

CHKNTFS
Displays the status of volumes. Sets or excludes volumes from automatic system checking when the computer is started.

```
chkntfs [/x | /c] volume: [...]
chkntfs /t[:time]
chkntfs /d
```

CHOICE
Creates a selection list from which users can select a choice in batch scripts.

```
choice [/c choices] [/n] [/cs] [/t nnnn /d choice] [/m "text"]
```

CIPHER

Displays current encryption status or modifies folder and file encryption on NTFS volumes.

In Windows Server 2003, use

```
cipher [/e| /d] [/s:dir] [/a] [/i] [/f] [/q]
       [/h] [[path]filename [...]]
cipher [/k | /r:filename | w:dir]
cipher /u [/n]
cipher /x[:efsfile] [filename]
```

In Windows XP Professional, use

```
cipher [/e| /d] [/s:dir] [/a] [/i] [/f] [/q]
       [/h] [[path]filename [...]]
cipher [/k | /r:filename | w:dir]
cipher /u [/n]
```

CLIP

With piping, redirects output of command-line tools to the Windows clipboard.

```
[command |] clip
```

This command applies only to Windows Server 2003.

Note The symbol "|", in this instance, is the pipe symbol.

CLS

Clears the console window.

```
cls
```

CMD

Starts a new instance of the Windows command shell.

```
cmd [/a | /u] [/q] [/d] [/e:on | /e:off]
[/f:on | /f:off] [/v:on | /v:off]
[[/s] [/c | /k] string]
```

CMDKEY

Creates and manages stored user names and passwords.

```
cmdkey [{/add | /generic}:targetname
{/smartcard | /user:user@domain
{/pass{:pwd}}} | /delete{:targetname
| /ras} | /list{:targetname}]
```

This command applies only to Windows Server 2003.

COLOR
Sets the colors of the command-shell window.

```
color [bf]
```

COMP
Compares the contents of two files or sets of files.

```
comp [data1] [data2] [/d] [/a] [/l]
[/n=number] [/c] [/offline]
```

COMPACT
Displays or alters the compression of files on NTFS partitions.

```
compact [/c | /u] [/s[:dir]] [/a] [/i] [/f]
[/q] [filename [...]]
```

CONVERT
Converts FAT volumes to NTFS.

```
convert drive: /fs:NTFS [/v] [/x]
[/cvtarea:filename] [/nosecurity]
```

COPY
Copies or combines files.

```
copy [/d][/v][/n][/y|/-y][/z][/a|/b] source [/a | /b]
[+ source [/a | /b] [+ ...]][destination [/a|/b]]
```

DATE
Displays or sets the system date.

```
date [/T | mm-dd-yy]
```

DCGPOFIX
Restores default group policy objects.

```
dcgpofix [/ignoreschema]
[/target: {domain | dc | both}]
```

This command applies only to Windows Server 2003.

DEFRAG

Defragments hard drives.

```
defrag volume [/a] [/v]
defrag volume [/f]
```

DEL

Deletes one or more files.

```
del [/p] [/f] [/s] [/q] [/a[[:]attributes]]
[drive:][path]filename[...]
```

DIR

Displays a list of files and subdirectories within a directory.

```
dir [drive:][path][filename] [/p] [/w] [/d]
[/a[[:]attributes]] [/o[[:]sortorder]]
[/t[[:]timefield]] [/s] [/b] [/l] [/n]
[/x] [/c] [/q] [/4]
```

DISKCOMP

Compares the contents of two floppy disks.

```
diskcomp [drive1: [drive2:]]
```

DISKCOPY

Copies the contents of one floppy disk to another.

```
diskcopy [drive1: [drive2:]] [/v]
```

DISKPART

Invokes a text-mode command interpreter so that you can manage disks, partitions, and volumes using a separate command prompt and commands that are internal to DISKPART.

```
diskpart
```

More Info   Techniques for working with DISKPART are covered in Chapter 8, "Configuring and Maintaining Hard Disk Drives," Chapter 9, "Partitioning Basic Disks," and Chapter 10, "Managing Volumes and RAID on Dynamic Disks."

DOSKEY

Edits command lines, recalls Windows commands, and creates macros.

```
doskey [/reinstall] [/listsize=size]
[/macros[:all | :exename]]
[/history] [/insert | /overstrike]
[/exename=exename]
[/macrofile=fname] [macroname=[text]]
```

DRIVERQUERY

Displays a list of all installed device drivers and their properties.

```
driverquery [/s computer [/u [domain\]user [/p [pwd]]]]
[/fo {table|list|csv}] [/nh] [/v] [/si]
```

DSADD COMPUTER

Creates a computer account in the Active Directory directory service.

```
dsadd computer ComputerDN [-samid SAMName] [-desc Description]
[-loc Location] [-memberof GroupDN ...] [{-s Server | -d Domain}]
[-u UserName] [-p {Password | *}] [-q] [{-uc | -uco | -uci}]
```

This command is available in Windows XP Professional if Windows Server 2003 Administration Tools Pack has been installed.

DSADD GROUP

Creates a group account in Active Directory.

```
dsadd group GroupDN [-secgrp {yes | no}] [-scope {l | g | u}] [-samid
SAMName] [-desc Description] [-memberof Group ...] [-members Member
...] [{-s Server | -d Domain}] [-u UserName] [-p {Password | *}]
[-q] [{-uc | -uco | -uci}]
```

This command is available in Windows XP Professional if Windows Server 2003 Administration Tools Pack has been installed.

DSADD USER

Creates a user account in Active Directory.

```
dsadd user UserDN [-samid SAMName] [-upn UPN] [-fn FirstName] [-mi
Initial] [-ln LastName] [-display DisplayName] [-empid EmployeeID]
[-pwd {Password | *}] [-desc Description] [-memberof Group ...]
[-office Office] [-tel PhoneNumber] [-email EmailAddress] [-hometel
HomePhoneNumber] [-pager PagerNumber] [-mobile CellPhoneNumber]
[-fax FaxNumber] [-iptel IPPhoneNumber] [-webpg WebPage] [-title
Title] [-dept Department] [-company Company] [-mgr Manager] [-hmdir
```

```
HomeDirectory] [-hmdrv DriveLetter:] [-profile ProfilePath]
[-loscr ScriptPath] [-mustchpwd {yes | no}] [-canchpwd {yes | no}]
[-reversiblepwd {yes | no}] [-pwdneverexpires {yes | no}]
[-acctexpires NumberOfDays] [-disabled {yes | no}] [{-s Server | -d
Domain}] [-u UserName] [-p {Password | *}] [-q] [{-uc | -uco | -uci}]
```

This command is available in Windows XP Professional if Windows Server 2003 Administration Tools Pack has been installed.

DSGET COMPUTER

Displays the properties of a computer account using one of two syntaxes. The syntax for viewing the properties of multiple computers is

```
dsget computer ComputerDN ... [-dn] [-samid] [-sid] [-desc] [-loc]
[-disabled] [{-s Server | -d Domain}] [-u UserName] [-p {Password |
*}] [-c] [-q] [-l] [{-uc | -uco | -uci}] [-part PartitionDN
[-qlimit] [-qused]]
```

The syntax for viewing the membership information of a single computer is

```
dsget computer ComputerDN [-memberof [-expand]] [{-s Server | -d
Domain}] [-u UserName] [-p {Password | *}] [-c] [-q] [-l] [{-uc |
-uco | -uci}]
```

This command is available in Windows XP Professional if Windows Server 2003 Administration Tools Pack has been installed.

DSGET GROUP

Displays the properties of group accounts using one of two syntaxes. The syntax for viewing the properties of multiple groups is

```
dsget group GroupDN ... [-dn] [-samid] [-sid] [-desc] [-secgrp]
[-scope] [{-s Server | -d Domain}] [-u UserName] [-p {Password | *}]
[-c] [-q] [-l] [{-uc | -uco | -uci}] [-part PartitionDN [-qlimit]
[-qused]]
```

The syntax for viewing the group membership information for an individual group is

```
dsget group GroupDN [{-memberof | -members} [-expand]] [{-s Server
| -d Domain}] [-u UserName] [-p {Password | *}] [-c] [-q] [-l]
[{-uc | -uco | -uci}]
```

This command is available in Windows XP Professional if Windows Server 2003 Administration Tools Pack has been installed.

DSGET SERVER

Displays the various properties of domain controllers using any of three syntaxes. The syntax for displaying the general properties of a specified domain controller is:

```
dsget server ServerDN ... [-dn] [-desc] [-dnsname] [-site] [-isgc]
[{-s Server | -d Domain}] [-u UserName] [-p {Password | *}] [-c]
[-q] [-l] [{-uc | -uco | -uci}]
```

The syntax for displaying a list of the security principals who own the largest number of directory objects on the specified domain controller is

```
dsget server ServerDN [{-s Server | -d Domain}] [-u UserName]
[-p {Password | *}] [-c] [-q] [-l] [{-uc | -uco | -uci}]
[-topobjowner NumbertoDisplay]
```

The syntax for displaying the distinguished names of the directory partitions on the specified server is

```
dsget server ServerDN [{-s Server | -d Domain}] [-u UserName]
[-p {Password | *}] [-c] [-q] [-l] [{-uc | -uco | -uci}] [-part]
```

This command is available in Windows XP Professional if Windows Server 2003 Administration Tools Pack has been installed.

DSGET USER

Displays the properties of user accounts using one of two syntaxes. The syntax for viewing the properties of multiple users is

```
dsget user UserDN ... [-dn] [-samid] [-sid] [-upn] [-fn] [-mi] [-ln]
[-display] [-empid] [-desc] [-office] [-tel] [-email] [-hometel]
[-pager] [-mobile] [-fax] [-iptel] [-webpg] [-title] [-dept]
[-company] [-mgr] [-hmdir] [-hmdrv] [-profile] [-loscr] [-mustchpwd]
[-canchpwd] [-pwdneverexpires] [-disabled] [-acctexpires]
[-reversiblepwd] [{-uc | -uco | -uci}] [-part PartitionDN [-qlimit]
[-qused]] [{-s Server | -d Domain}] [-u UserName] [-p {Password |
*}] [-c] [-q] [-l]
```

The syntax for viewing the group membership for users is

```
dsget user UserDN [-memberof [-expand]] [{-uc | -uco | -uci}] [{-s
Server | -d Domain}] [-u UserName] [-p {Password | *}] [-c] [-q] [-l]
```

This command is available in Windows XP Professional if Windows Server 2003 Administration Tools Pack has been installed.

DSMOD COMPUTER

Modifies attributes of one or more computer accounts in the directory.

```
dsmod computer ComputerDN ... [-desc Description] [-loc Location]
[-disabled {yes | no}] [-reset] [{-s Server | -d Domain}] [-u
UserName] [-p {Password | *}] [-c] [-q] [{-uc | -uco | -uci}]
```

This command is available in Windows XP Professional if Windows Server 2003 Administration Tools Pack has been installed.

DSMOD GROUP

Modifies attributes of one or more group accounts in the directory.

```
dsmod group GroupDN ... [-samid SAMName] [-desc Description]
[-secgrp {yes | no}] [-scope {l | g | u}] [{-addmbr | -rmmbr |
-chmbr} MemberDN ...] [{-s Server | -d Domain}] [-u UserName]
[-p {Password | *}] [-c] [-q] [{-uc | -uco | -uci}]
```

This command is available in Windows XP Professional if Windows Server 2003 Administration Tools Pack has been installed.

DSMOD SERVER

Modifies properties of a domain controller.

```
dsmod server ServerDN ... [-desc Description] [-isgc {yes | no}]
[{-s Server | -d Domain}] [-u UserName] [-p {Password | *}] [-c]
[-q] [{-uc | -uco | -uci}]
```

This command is available in Windows XP Professional if Windows Server 2003 Administration Tools Pack has been installed.

DSMOD USER

Modifies attributes of one or more user accounts in the directory.

```
dsmod user UserDN ... [-upn UPN] [-fn FirstName] [-mi Initial]
[-ln LastName] [-display DisplayName] [-empid EmployeeID]
[-pwd {Password | *}] [-desc Description] [-office Office] [-tel
PhoneNumber] [-email EmailAddress] [-hometel HomePhoneNumber]
[-pager PagerNumber] [-mobile CellPhoneNumber] [-fax FaxNumber]
[-iptel IPPhoneNumber] [-webpg WebPage] [-title Title] [-dept
Department] [-company Company] [-mgr Manager] [-hmdir HomeDirectory]
[-hmdrv DriveLetter:] [-profile ProfilePath] [-loscr ScriptPath]
[-mustchpwd {yes | no}] [-canchpwd {yes | no}] [-reversiblepwd {yes
| no}] [-pwdneverexpires {yes | no}] [-acctexpires NumberOfDays]
[-disabled {yes | no}] [{-s Server | -d Domain}] [-u UserName]
[-p {Password | *}] [-c] [-q] [{-uc | -uco | -uci}]
```

This command is available in Windows XP Professional if Windows Server 2003 Administration Tools Pack has been installed.

DSMOVE

Moves or renames Active Directory objects.

```
dsmove objectdn [-newname newname] [-newparent parentdn]
[{-s server | -d domain}] [-u username] [-p {password | *}] [-q]
[{-uc | -uco | -uci}]
```

This command is available in Windows XP Professional if Windows Server 2003 Administration Tools Pack has been installed.

DSQUERY COMPUTER

Searches for computer accounts matching criteria.

```
dsquery computer [{startnode | forestroot | domainroot}] [-o {dn |
rdn | samid}] [-scope {subtree | onelevel | base}] [-name name]
[-desc description] [-samid samname] [-inactive numberofweeks]
[-stalepwd numberofdays] [-disabled] [{-s server | -d domain}]
[-u username] [-p {password | *}] [-q]    [-r] [-gc] [-limit
numberofobjects] [{-uc | -uco | -uci}]
```

This command is available in Windows XP Professional if Windows Server 2003 Administration Tools Pack has been installed.

DSQUERY CONTACT

Searches for contacts matching criteria.

```
dsquery contact [{startnode | forestroot | domainroot}] [-o {dn |
rdn}] [-scope {subtree | onelevel | base}] [-name name] [-desc
description] [{-s server | -d domain}] [-u username] [-p {password
| *}] [-q] [-r] [-gc] [-limit numberofobjects] [{-uc | -uco | -uci}]
```

This command is available in Windows XP Professional if Windows Server 2003 Administration Tools Pack has been installed.

DSQUERY GROUP

Searches for group accounts matching criteria.

```
dsquery group [{startnode | forestroot | domainroot}] [-o {dn |
rdn | samid}] [-scope {subtree | onelevel | base}] [-name name]
[-desc description] [-samid SAMName] [{-s server | -d domain}]
[-u username] [-p {password | *}] [-q] [-r] [-gc] [-limit
numberofobjects] [{-uc | -uco | -uci}]
```

This command is available in Windows XP Professional if Windows Server 2003 Administration Tools Pack has been installed.

DSQUERY PARTITION

Searches for Active Directory partitions matching criteria.

```
dsquery partition [-o {dn | rdn}] [-part filter] [{-s server |
-d domain}] [-u username] [-p {password | *}] [-q] [-r] [-limit
numberofobjects] [{-uc | -uco | -uci}]
```

This command is available in Windows XP Professional if Windows Server 2003
Administration Tools Pack has been installed.

DSQUERY QUOTA

Searches for disk quotas matching criteria.

```
dsquery quota {domainroot | objectdn} [-o {dn | rdn}] [-acct name]
[-qlimit filter] [-desc description] [{-s server | -d domain}]
[-u username] [-p {password | *}] [-q] [-r] [-limit numberofobjects]
[{-uc | -uco | -uci}]
```

This command is available in Windows XP Professional if Windows Server 2003
Administration Tools Pack has been installed.

DSQUERY SERVER

Searches for domain controllers matching criteria.

```
dsquery server [-o {dn | rdn}] [-forest] [-domain domainname] [-site
sitename] [-name name] [-desc description] [-hasfsmo {schema | name
| infr | pdc | rid}] [-isgc] [{-s server | -d domain}] [-u username]
[-p {password | *}] [-q] [-r] [-gc] [-limit numberofobjects] [{-uc
| -uco | -uci}]
```

This command is available in Windows XP Professional if Windows Server 2003
Administration Tools Pack has been installed.

DSQUERY SITE

Searches for Active Directory sites matching criteria.

```
dsquery site [-o {dn | rdn}] [-name name] [-desc description] [{-s
server | -d domain}] [-u username] [-p {password | *}] [-q] [-r]
[-gc] [-limit numberofobjects] [{-uc | -uco | -uci}]
```

This command is available in Windows XP Professional if Windows Server 2003
Administration Tools Pack has been installed.

DSQUERY USER

Searches for user accounts matching criteria.

```
dsquery user [{startnode | forestroot | domainroot}] [-o {dn | rdn
| upn | samid}] [-scope {subtree | onelevel | base}] [-name name]
[-desc description] [-upn upn] [-samid samname] [-inactive
numberofweeks] [-stalepwd numberofdays] [-disabled] [{-s server |
-d domain}] [-u username] [-p {password | *}] [-q] [-r] [-gc] [-limit
numberofobjects] [{-uc | -uco | -uci}]
```

This command is available in Windows XP Professional if Windows Server 2003 Administration Tools Pack has been installed.

DSQUERY *

Searches for any Active Directory objects matching criteria.

```
dsquery * [{startnode | forestroot | domainroot}] [-scope {subtree
| onelevel | base}] [-filter ldapfilter] [-attr {attributelist | *}]
[-attrsonly] [-l] [{-s server | -d domain}] [-u username] [-p
{password | *}] [-q] [-r] [-gc] [-limit numberofobjects] [{-uc |
-uco | -uci}]
```

This command is available in Windows XP Professional if Windows Server 2003 Administration Tools Pack has been installed.

DSRM

Deletes Active Directory objects.

```
dsrm objectdn ... [-subtree [-exclude]] [-noprompt] [{-s server |
-d domain}] [-u username] [-p {password | *}] [-c] [-q] [{-uc | -uco
| -uci}]
```

This command is available in Windows XP Professional if Windows Server 2003 Administration Tools Pack has been installed.

ECHO

Displays messages, or turns command echoing on or off.

```
echo [on | off]
echo [message]
```

ENDLOCAL

Ends localization of environment changes in a batch file.

```
endlocal
```

ERASE

See DEL.

EVENTCREATE

Creates custom events in the event logs.

In Windows Server 2003, use

```
eventcreate [/s computer [/u domain\user [/p password]]
{[/l {application | system}] | [/so srcname]}
/t {success | error | warning | information} /id eventid /d
description
```

In Windows XP Professional, use

```
eventcreate [/s computer [/u domain\user [/p password]]
{[/l {application | system}] | [/so srcname]}
/t {error | warning | information} /id eventid /d description
```

EVENTQUERY

Searches event logs and collects event entries.

```
eventquery [/s Computer [/u [Domain\]User [/p Password]]] [/fi
FilterName]
[/fo {table | list | csv}] [/r eventrange] [/nh] [/v]
[/l [application] [system] [security] ["dns server"]
[UserDefinedLog] [DirectoryLogName] [*]]
```

EVENTTRIGGERS /CREATE

Creates event triggers and sets the action to take.

```
eventtriggers /create [/s Computer [/u [Domain\]User [/p
[Password]]]] /tr Name [/l LogName] [/d Description] /tk Task {[/eid
id] | [/t type] | [[/so source]} [/ru username [/rp password}}
```

EVENTTRIGGERS /DELETE

Removes an event trigger when it is no longer needed.

```
eventtriggers /delete /tid {ID [...] | *} [/s Computer [/u [Domain\]
User [/p Password]]]
```

EVENTTRIGGERS /QUERY

Displays the event triggers currently configured on a specified system.

In Windows Server 2003, use

```
eventtriggers /query [/s Computer [/u [Domain\]User [/p Password]]]
[fo{table | list | csv}] [/nh] [/v] [/id]
```

In Windows XP Professional, use

```
eventtriggers /query [/s Computer [/u [Domain\]User [/p Password]]]
[fo{table | list | csv}] [/nh] [/v]
```

EXIT

Exits the command interpreter.

```
exit [/b] [exitcode]
```

EXPAND

Uncompresses files.

```
expand [-r] source destination
expand -r source [destination]
expand -d source.cab [-f:files]
expand source.cab -f:files destination
```

FC

Compares files and displays differences.

```
fc [/a] [/c] [/l] [/lbn] [/n] [/t] [/u] [/w]
   [/nnnn][/offline][drive1:][path1]filename1
   [drive2:][path2]filename2
fc /b [drive1:][path1]filename1
   [drive2:][path2]filename2
```

FIND

Searches for a text string in files.

```
find [/v] [/c] [/n] [/i] [/offline] "string"
[[drive:][path]filename[ ...]]
```

FINDSTR

Searches for strings in files using regular expressions.

```
findstr [/b] [/e] [/l] [/r] [/s] [/i] [/x] [/v] [/n]
[/m] [/o] [/p] [/f:file] [/a:attr] [/c:string]
[/d:dir] [/g:file] [/offline] [strings]
[[drive:][path]filename[ ...]]
```

FOR

Runs a specified command for each file in a set of files.

Command-line FOR looping:

```
for %variable in (set) do command [parameters]
for /d %variable in (set) do command [parameters]
for /r [[drive:]path] %variable in (set) do command [parameters]
for /l %variable in (start,step,end) do command [parameters]
for /f ["options"] %variable in (set) do command [parameters]
```

Script FOR looping:

```
for %%variable in (set) do command [parameters]
for /d %%variable in (set) do command [parameters]
for /r [[drive:]path] %%variable in (set) do command [parameters]
for /l %%variable in (start,step,end) do command [parameters]
for /f ["options"] %%variable in (set) do command [parameters]
```

FORCEDOS

Starts a program in MS-DOS (command.com) rather than in Windows command shell (cmd.exe).

```
forcedos [/d directory] filename [parameters]
```

FORFILES

Selects one or more files and executes a command on each file.

```
forfiles [/p pathname] [/m searchmask] [/s]  [/c command]
[/d [+ | -] {mm/dd/yyyy | dd}]
```

This command applies only to Windows Server 2003.

FORMAT

Formats a floppy disk or hard drive.

```
format drive: [/fs:file-system] [/v:label]
[/q] [/a:size] [/c] [/x]
format drive: [/v:label] [/q] [/f:size]
format drive: [/v:label] [/q] [/t:tracks
/n:sectors]
format drive: [/v:label] [/q]
```

FREEDISK

Checks a local or remote system to see if a necessary amount of free disk space is available on a particular drive.

```
freedisk [/s computer [/u [domain\]user [/p [pwd]]]] [/d drive]
[value]
```

This command applies only to Windows Server 2003.

FTP

Transfers files.

```
ftp [-v] [-d] [-i] [-n] [-g] [-s:filename]
[-a] [-w:windowsize] [host]
```

FTYPE

Displays or modifies file types used in file extension associations

```
ftype [fileType[=[command]]]
```

GETMAC

Displays network adapter information.

```
getmac [/s computer [/u [domain]\user [/p [pwd]]]]
[/fo {table|list|csv}] [/nh] [/v]
```

GETTYPE

Obtains basic configuration information from the operating system, including host name, operating system name, operating system version, role, and component information.

```
gettype [/s computer [/u [domain]\user [/p [pwd]]]] [/role | /sp |
/ver | /minv | /majv
 | /type | /build]
```

This command applies only to Windows Server 2003.

GOTO

Directs the Windows command interpreter to a labeled line in a script.

```
goto :label
goto :EOF
```

GPUPDATE

Forces a background refresh of group policy.

```
gpupdate [/target:{computer | user}] [/force] [/wait:<value>]
 [/logoff] [/boot] [/sync]
```

HOSTNAME

Prints the computer's name.

```
hostname
```

IF

Performs conditional processing in batch programs.

```
if [not] errorlevel number command
if [not] [/i] string1==string2 command
if [not] exist filename command
if [/i] string1 compare-op string2 command
if cmdextversion number command
if defined variable command
```

INUSE

schedules replacement of operating system files on reboot.

```
inuse new_path/file current_path/file [/y]
```

This command applies only to Windows Server 2003.

IPCONFIG

Displays TCP/IP configuration.

```
ipconfig [/all] | [/release [adapter] | /renew [adapter]]
ipconfig /flushdns | /displaydns | /registerdns
ipconfig /showclassid adapter
ipconfig /setclassid adapter [classidtoset]]
```

LABEL

Creates, changes, or deletes the volume label of a disk.

```
label [drive:][label]
label [/mp] [volume] [label]
```

MD

Creates a directory or subdirectory.

```
mkdir [drive:]path
md [drive:]path
```

MEMMONITOR

Tracks detailed memory usage for individual processes.

```
memmonitor {/p ProcessID | /pn Name | /ps Service} [/wait] [/nodbg]
[/assumedbg] [/int Seconds] [/ws Value] [/ppool Value]
[/nppool Value] [/vm Value]
```

Windows Server 2003 Resource Kit.

MEMTRIAGE

Helps pinpoint the source of suspected memory leaks.

```
memtriage {/m | /p | /mp | /h ProcID} [/t Retry /w Length]
LogFile.log
memtriage /s [/r RuleFile.ini /pid ProcID] LogFile.log
memtriage {/a [/pid ProcID] | /av} LogFile.log
```

Windows Server 2003 Resource Kit.

MKDIR

See MD.

MORE

Displays output one screen at a time.

```
more [/e [/c] [/p] [/s] [/tn] [+n]] <
 [drive:][path]filename
more /e [/c] [/p] [/s] [/tn] [+n] [files]
command-name | more [/e [/c] [/p] [/s]
[/tn] [+n]]
```

MOUNTVOL

Manages volume mount point.

```
mountvol [drive:]path volumeName
mountvol [drive:]path /d
mountvol [drive:]path /l
```

MOVE

Moves files from one directory to another directory on the same drive.

```
move [/y] [/-y] [source] [target]
```

NBTSTAT

Displays status of netbios.

```
nbtstat [-a remotename] [-A ipaddress] [-c]
[-n] [-r] [-R] [-RR] [-s] [-S]
[interval] ]
```

Note   This command uses case-sensitive switches.

NET ACCOUNTS

Manage user account and password policies.

```
net accounts [/forcelogoff:{minutes | no}]
  [/minpwlen:length]
  [/maxpwage:{days | unlimited}]
  [/minpwage:days]
  [/uniquepw:number] [/domain]
```

NET COMPUTER

Adds or remove computers from a domain.

```
net computer \\computername {/add | /del}
```

NET CONFIG SERVER

Displays or modifies configuration of server service.

```
net config server [/autodisconnect:time]
    [/srvcomment:"text"] [/hidden:{yes | no}]
```

NET CONFIG WORKSTATION

displays or modifies configuration of workstation service.

```
net config workstation [/charcount:bytes]
[/chartime:msec]
[/charwait:sec]
```

NET CONTINUE

Resumes a paused service.

```
net continue service
```

NET FILE

Displays or manages open files on a server.

```
net file [id [/close]]
```

NET GROUP

Displays or manages global groups.

```
net group [groupname [/comment:"text"]]
  [/domain]
net group groupname {/add [/comment:"text"]
  | /delete} [/domain]
net group groupname username [...]
  {/add | /delete} [/domain]
```

NET LOCALGROUP

Displays local group accounts.

```
net localgroup [GroupName [/comment:"Text"]] [/domain]
```

Creates a local group account.

```
net localgroup GroupName {/add [/comment:"Text"]} [/domain]
```

Modifies local group accounts.

```
net localgroup [GroupName Name [ ...] /add [/domain]
```

Deletes a local group account.

```
net localgroup GroupName /delete  [/domain]
```

NET NAME

Displays or modifies recipients for messenger service messages.

```
net name [name [/add | /delete]]
```

NET PAUSE

Suspends a service.

```
net pause service
```

NET PRINT

Displays or manages print jobs and shared queues.

```
net print \\computername\sharename
net print [\\computername] job#
  [/hold | /release | /delete]
```

NET SEND

Sends a messenger service message.

```
net send {name | * | /domain[:name] | /users}
  message
```

NET SESSION

Lists or disconnects sessions.

```
net session [\\computername] [/delete]
```

NET SHARE

Displays or manages shared printers and directories.

```
net share [sharename]
net share sharename[=drive:path]
  [/users:number | /unlimited]
  [/remark:"text"]
  [/cache:flag]
net share {sharename | devicename |
  drive:path} /delete
```

NET START

Lists or starts network services.

```
net start [service]
```

NET STATISTICS

Displays workstation and server statistics.

```
net statistics [workstation | server]
```

NET STOP

Stops services.

```
net stop service
```

NET TIME

Displays or synchronizes network time.

```
net time [\\computername |
 /domain[:domainname] |
 /rtsdomain[:domainname]] [/set]
net time [\\computername] /querysntp
net time [\\computername]
 /setsntp[:serverlist]
```

NET USE

Displays or manages remote connections.

```
net use [devicename | *] [\\computername\sharename[\volume]
[password | *]] [/user:[domainname\]username] [/user:
[username@domainname] [[/delete] | [/persistent:{yes | no}]]
[/smartcard] [/savecred] net use [devicename | *] [password | *]]
[/home] net use [/persistent:{yes | no}]
```

NET USER

Creates local user accounts.

```
net user UserName [Password | *] /add [/active:{no | yes}]
[/comment:"DescriptionText"] [/countrycode:NNN] [/expires:
{{MM/DD/YYYY / DD/MM/YYYY / mmm,dd,YYYY} | never}]
[/fullname:"Name"] [/homedir:Path] [/passwordchg:{yes | no}]
[/passwordreq:{yes | no}] [/profilepath:[Path]] [/scriptpath:Path]
[/times:{Day[-Day][,Day[-Day]] ,Time[-Time][,Time[-Time]] [;...] |
all}] [/usercomment:"Text"] [/workstations:{ComputerName[,...] |
*}] [/domain]
```

Modifies local user accounts.

```
net user [UserName [Password | *] [/active:{no | yes}]
[/comment:"DescriptionText"] [/countrycode:NNN] [/expires:
{{MM/DD/YYYY / DD/MM/YYYY | mmm,dd,YYYY} | never}]
[/fullname:"Name"] [/homedir:Path] [/passwordchg:{yes | no}]
[/passwordreq:{yes | no}] [/profilepath:[Path]] [/scriptpath:Path]
[/times:{Day[-Day][,Day[-Day]] ,Time[-Time][,Time[-Time]] [;...] |
all}] [/usercomment:"Text"] [/workstations:{ComputerName[,...] |
*}]] [/domain]
```

Deletes local user accounts.

```
net user UserName [/delete] [/domain]
```

NET VIEW

Displays network resources or computers.

```
net view [\\computername [/cache] |
 /domain[:domainname]]
net view /network:nw [\\computername]
```

NETSH

Invokes a separate command prompt that allows you to manage the configuration of various network services on local and remote computers.

```
netsh
```

More Info   Techniques for working with Netsh are discussed in Chapter 15, "Configuring, Maintaining, and Troubleshooting TCP/IP Networking."

NETSTAT

Displays status of network connections.

```
netstat [-a] [-e] [-n] [/o] [-s] [-p proto] [-r]
[interval]
```

NSLOOKUP

Shows the status of DNS.

```
nslookup [-option] [computer | server]
```

NTBACKUP

Backs up files.

```
ntbackup backup [systemstate] "@bksfilename"
/j {"jobname"}
[/p {"poolname"}]
[/t {"tapename"}]
[/n {"medianame"}]
[/f {"filename"}]
[/d {"setdescription"}]
[/ds {"servername"}]
[/is {"servername"}]
[/g {"guidname"}]
[/a] [/v:{yes|no}] [/r:{yes|no}]
[/l:{f|s|n}] [/m {backuptype}]
[/rs:{yes|no}] [/hc:{on|off}]
[/snap{on|off}]
```

PATH

Displays or sets a search path for executable files in the current command window.

```
path [[drive:]path[;...][;%PATH%]
path ;
```

PATHPING

Traces routes and provides packet loss information.

In Windows Server 2003, use

```
pathping [-n] [-h maxhops] [-g hostlist]
  [-i address] [-p period]
  [-q numqueries [-w timeout]
  targetname [-4] [-6]
```

In Windows XP Professional, use

```
pathping [-n] [-h maxhops] [-g hostlist]
  [-i address] [-p period] [-T] [-R] [-P]
  [-q numqueries [-w timeout]
  targetname [-4] [-6]
```

   Note   This command uses case-sensitive switches.

PAUSE

Suspends processing of a script and waits for keyboard input.

```
pause
```

PFMON

Displays detailed information on hard and soft page faults.

```
pfmon [/n | /l] [/c | /h] [/k | /K] [/p processid] [/d]
appcommandline
```

Windows Server 2003 Resource Kit.

   Note   This command uses case-sensitive switches.

PING
Determines if a network connection can be established.

```
ping [-t] [-a] [-n count] [-l size] [-f]
 [-i ttl] [-v tos] [-r count] [-s count]
 [[-j hostlist] | [-k hostlist]]
 [-w timeout] destinationlist
```

PMON
Displays a detailed snapshot of resource usage and running processes.

```
pmon
```

Windows Server 2003 Resource Kit.

POPD
Changes to the directory stored by PUSHD.

```
popd
```

PRINT
Prints a text file.

```
print [/d:device]
[[drive:][path]filename[...]]
```

PRINTDRIVERINFO
Displays driver information for all printer drivers configured on a local or remote system.

```
printdriverinfo [/s: ServerName] [/p: PrinterName] [/d: DriverName]
 [/f: FileName]
```

Windows Server 2003 Resource Kit.

PROMPT
Changes the Windows command prompt.

```
prompt [text]
```

PUSHD
Saves the current directory then changes to a new directory.

```
pushd [path | ..]
```

RD

Removes a directory.

```
rmdir [/s] [/q] [drive:]path
rd [/s] [/q] [drive:]path
```

RECOVER

Recovers readable information from a bad or defective disk.

```
recover [drive:][path]filename
```

REG ADD

Adds a new subkey or entry to the registry.

```
reg add keyname [/v valuename | /ve] [/t datatype] [/d data] [/f]
[/s separator]
```

REG COMPARE

Compares registry subkeys or entries.

```
reg compare keyname1 keyname2 [/v valuename | /ve] [/s]
[/outputoption]
```

REG COPY

Copies a registry entry to a specified key path on a local or remote system.

```
reg copy keyname1 keyname2 [/s] [/f]
```

REG DELETE

Deletes a subkey or entries from the registry.

```
reg delete keyname [/v valuename | /ve | /va] [/f]
```

REG QUERY

Lists the entries under a key and the names of subkeys (if any).

In Windows Server 2003, use

```
reg query keyname [/v valuename | /ve] [/s] [/d data] [/k] [/d]
[/c] [/e] [/t type] [/z] [/se separator]
```

In Windows XP Professional, use

```
reg query keyname [/v valuename | /ve] [/s]
```

REG RESTORE
Writes saved subkeys and entries back to the registry.

```
reg restore keyname "filename"
```

REG SAVE
Saves a copy of specified subkeys, entries and values to a file.

```
reg save keyname "filename"
```

REGSVR32
Register and unregister DLLs.

```
regsvr32 [/u] [/s] [/n] [/i[:cmdline]] dllname
```

REM
Adds comments to scripts.

```
rem [comment]
```

REN
Renames a file.

```
rename [drive:][path]filename1 filename2
ren [drive:][path]filename1 filename2
```

RMDIR
See RD.

ROUTE
Manages network routing tables.

```
route [-f] [-p] [command [destination]
[mask netmask] [gateway] [metric metric]] [if interface]
```

RUNAS
Run program with specific user permissions.

In Windows Server 2003, use

```
runas [/noprofile | /profile] [/env] [/netonly] [/savecred]
     /user:account program
runas [/noprofile | /profile] [/env] [/netonly] [/savecred]
/smartcard [/user:account] program
```

In Windows XP Professional, use

```
runas [/noprofile | /profile] [/env] [/netonly] /user:account
program
runas [/noprofile | /profile] [/env] [/netonly] /smartcard
    [/user:account] program
```

SC CONFIG

Configures service startup and logon accounts.

```
sc [\\ServerName] config ServiceName
  [type= {own|share|{interact type = {own | share}}|kernel|
filesys|rec|adapt}]
  [start= {boot|system|auto|demand|disabled}]
  [error= {normal|severe|critical|ignore}]
  [binPath= BinaryPathName]
  [group= LoadOrderGroup]
  [tag= {yes|no}]
  [depend= Dependencies]
  [obj= {AccountName|ObjectName}]
  [DisplayName= displayname]
  [password= password]
```

SC CONTINUE

Resumes a paused service.

```
sc [\\ServerName] continue ServiceName
```

SC FAILURE

Views the actions that will be taken if a service fails.

```
sc [\\ServerName] failure ServiceName [reset= ErrorFreePeriod]
  [reboot= BroadcastMessage] [command= CommandLine]
  [actions= FailureActionsAndDelayTime]
```

SC PAUSE

Pauses a service.

```
sc [\\ServerName] pause ServiceName
```

SC QC

Displays configuration information for a named service.

```
sc [\\ServerName] qc ServiceName [BufferSize]
```

SC QFAILURE

Sets the action to take upon failure of a service.

```
sc [\\ServerName] qfailure ServiceName [BufferSize]
```

SC QUERY

Displays the list of services configured on the computer.

```
sc [\\ServerName] query ServiceName
   [type= {driver | service | all}]
   [type= {own|share|interact|kernel|filesys|rec|adapt}]
   [state= {active | inactive | all}] [bufsize= BufferSize]
   [ri= ResumeIndex]
   [group= GroupName]
```

SC START

Starts a service.

```
sc [\\ServerName] start ServiceName [ServicesArgs]
```

SC STOP

Stops a service.

```
sc [\\ServerName] stop ServiceName
```

SCHTASKS /CHANGE

Changes the properties of existing tasks.

In Windows Server 2003, use

```
schtasks /change /tn taskname [/s system [/u [domain\] user
[/p [password]]]] parameterstochange {[/ru user[ ]/rp password]
[/tr tasktorun]} [/st starttime] [/ri runintrrval] [{/et endtime |
/du duration} [/k]] [/sd startdate] [/ed enddate] [enable | disable]
[/it] [/z]
```

In Windows XP Professional, use

```
schtasks /change /tn taskname [/s system [/u [domain\] user
[/p [password]]]] parameterstochange {[/ru user[ ]/rp password]
[/tr tasktorun]}
```

SCHTASKS /CREATE

Creates scheduled tasks.

In Windows Server 2003, use

```
schtasks /create [/s system [/u [domain\] user [/p [password]]]]
[/ru [domain\] username [rp password]]/tn taskname /tr tasktorun
/sc scheduletype [/mo modifier] [/d day] [/i idletime] [/st
starttime] [/m month [, month [...]]] [/sd startdate] [/ed enddate]
[/ri runintrrval] [{/et endtime | /du duration} [/k]] [/it] [/z] [/f]
```

In Windows XP Professional, use

```
schtasks /create [/s system [/u [domain\] user [/p [password]]]]
[/ru [domain\] username [rp password]]/tn taskname /tr tasktorun
/sc scheduletype [/mo modifier] [/d day] [/i idletime] [/st
starttime] [/m month [, month [...]]] [/sd startdate] [/ed enddate]
```

SCHTASKS /DELETE

Removes scheduled tasks that are no longer wanted.

```
schtasks /delete /tn {TaskName | *} [/f] [/s Computer [/u
[Domain\]User [/p [Password]]]]
```

SCHTASKS /END

Stops a running task.

```
schtasks /end /tn taskname [/s computer [/u [domain\]user [/p
[password]]]]
```

SCHTASKS /QUERY

Displays scheduled tasks on the local or named computer.

```
schtasks /query [/s computer [/u [domain\]user [/p [password]]]]
[/fo {table | list | csv}] [/nh/ [/v]
```

SCHTASKS /RUN

Starts a scheduled task.

```
schtasks /run /tn taskname [/s computer [/u [domain\]user [/p
[password]]]]
```

SET

Displays or modifies Windows environment variables. Also used to evaluate numeric expressions at the command line.

```
set [variable=[string]]
set /a expression
set /p variable=[promptstring]
```

SETLOCAL
Begins localization of environment changes in a batch file.

```
setlocal
setlocal {enableext | disableext}
```

SFC
Scans and verifies protected system files.

```
sfc [/scannow] [/scanonce] [/scanboot] [/revert] [/purgecache]
[/cachesize=n]
```

SHIFT
Shifts the position of replaceable parameters in scripts.

```
shift [/n]
```

SHUTDOWN
Shuts down or restarts a computer.

In Windows Server 2003, use

```
shutdown [{-i |-l|-s|-r|-a}] [-f] [-m [\\computerName]] [-t nn]
[-c "message"] [-d [p]:n1:n2] [-h] [-e] [-p]
```

In Windows XP Professional, use

```
shutdown [{-i |-l|-s|-r|-a}] [-f]
[-m [\\computerName]] [-t nn]
[-c "message"] [-d[u][p]:n1:n2]
```

SORT
Sorts input.

```
[command |] sort [/r] [/+n] [/m kb] [/l locale] [/rec recordbytes]
[drive1:][path1]filename1] [/t [drive2:][path2]]
[/o [drive3:][path3]filename3]
```

Note   The symbol "|", in this instance, is the pipe symbol.

SPLINFO
Displays print spooling information.

```
splinfo [/z] [/v] [/d] [\\UNC_ComputerName]
```

Windows Server 2003 Resource Kit.

START

Starts a new command-shell window to run a specified program or command.

```
start ["title"] [/d path] [/i] [/min] [/max] [/separate|/shared]
[/wait] [/b] [/low | /belownormal | /normal | /abovenormal
| /high | /realtime] [command/program] [parameters]
```

SUBST

Maps a path to a drive letter.

```
subst [drive1: [drive2:]path]
subst drive1: /d
```

SYSTEMINFO

Displays detailed configuration information.

```
systeminfo [/s computer [/u [domain\]user [/p [pwd]]]] [/fo
{table|list|csv}] [/nh]
```

TAKEOWN

Allows an administrator to take ownership of one or more files.

```
takeown [/s computer [/u [domain\]user [/p [pwd]]]] /f filename
[/a] [/r [/d prompt]]
```

This command applies only to Windows Server 2003.

TASKKILL

Stops running processes by name or process ID.

```
taskkill [/s computer] [/u [domain\]user [/p pwd]]] {[/fi "filter"
[/fi filter2 [ ... ]]] [/pid ID|/im imgName]} [/f][/t]
```

TASKLIST

Lists all running processes by name and process ID.

```
tasklist [/s computer [/u [domain\]user [/p [password]]]]
[{/m module | /svc | /v}] [/fo {table | list | csv}] [/nh]
[/fi filtername [/fi filtername2 [ ... ]]]
```

TIME

Displays or sets the system time.

```
time [time | /T]
```

TIMEOUT
Sets a timeout period or waits for key press in batch script.

```
TIMEOUT /t timeout [/nobreak]
```

TITLE
Sets the title for the command-shell window.

```
title [string]
```

TRACERT
Displays the path between computers.

```
tracert [-d] [-h maximumhops] [-j hostlist] [-w timeout] targetname
```

TYPE
Displays the contents of a text file.

```
type [drive:][path]filename
```

VER
Displays the Windows version.

```
ver
```

VERIFY
Tells Windows whether to verify that your files are written correctly to a disk.

```
verify [on | off]
```

VOL
Displays a disk volume label and serial number.

```
vol [drive:]
```

WAITFOR
Specifies that a computer should wait for a particular signal before continuing.

Send signal syntax:

```
waitfor [/s computer [/u [domain\]user [/p [pwd]]]] /si signal
```

Wait signal syntax:

```
waitfor [/t timeout] signal
```

This command applies only to Windows Server 2003.

WHERE

Displays a list of files that match a search pattern.

```
where [/r dir] [/q] [/f] [/t] pattern
where [/q] [/f] [/t] $env:pattern
where [/q] [/f] [/t] path:pattern
```

This command applies only to Windows Server 2003.

WHOAMI

Displays log on and security information for the current user.

In Windows Server 2003, use

```
whoami [/upn | /fqdn | /logonid]
whoami /all [/fo {table|list|csv}] [nh]
```

In Windows XP Professional, use

```
whoami [/all][/user [/sid] [/logonid [/sid] [/groups [/sid]
[/priv [/sid] [/noverbose]]
```

In Windows XP Professional, the command is available through Support Tools.

Index

About the Author

William R. Stanek has 20 years of hands-on experience with advanced programming and development. He is a leading technology expert and an award-winning author. Over the years, his practical advice has helped millions of programmers, developers, and network engineers all over the world. He has written more than two dozen computer books. Current and forthcoming books include *Microsoft Windows XP Professional Administrator's Pocket Consultant, Microsoft Windows 2000 Administrator's Pocket Consultant 2nd Edition, Microsoft Windows Server 2003 Administrator's Pocket Consultant,* and *IIS 6.0 Administrator's Pocket Consultant.*

Mr. Stanek has been involved in the commercial Internet community since 1991. His core business and technology experience comes from more than 11 years of military service. He has substantial experience in developing server technology, encryption, and Internet solutions. He has written many technical white papers and training courses on a wide variety of topics. In addition, he is widely sought after as a subject matter expert.

Mr. Stanek has an MS in Information Systems with distinction and a BS in Computer Science with highest honors. He is proud to have served in the Gulf War as a combat crew member on an electronic warfare aircraft. He flew on numerous combat missions into Iraq and was awarded nine medals for his wartime service, including the Air Force Distinguished Flying Cross, one of the highest flying honors in the United States. Currently, he resides in the Pacific Northwest with his wife and children.

The manuscript for this book was prepared and submitted to Microsoft Press in electronic form. Pages were composed by Microsoft Press using Adobe FrameMaker 7.0 for Windows, with text in Garamond and display type in ITC Franklin Gothic. Composed pages were delivered to the printer as electronic pre-press files.

Cover Designer:	Patricia Bradbury
Interior Graphic Designer:	James D. Kramer
Principal Compositors:	Mary Beth McDaniel, Donald Cowan
Project Manager:	Susan McClung
Technical Editor:	James Johnson
Copy Editor:	Peter Tietjen
Principal Proofreaders:	Katie O'Connell, Robert Saley, Jan Cocker
Indexer:	Jack Lewis